SAINT PATRICK'S WORLD

"Ros Dregnige, where Bron's chasuble is . . ."
Killaspugbrone, Co. Sligo

SAINT PATRICK'S WORLD

THE CHRISTIAN CULTURE OF
IRELAND'S APOSTOLIC AGE

Translations and Commentaries by
LIAM DE PAOR

FOUR COURTS PRESS

This book was set
in 10.5 on 11 pt Galliard
by Seton Music Graphics, Bantry, Co. Cork

First published in 1993 in Ireland by
FOUR COURTS PRESS LTD
Kill Lane, Blackrock, Co. Dublin

First paperback edition 1996

This edition is not for sale in North America,
where the book is published by
UNIVERSITY OF NOTRE DAME PRESS.

A catalogue record of this title
is available from the British Library.

ISBN 1-85182-144-9 pbk

ILLUSTRATIONS
All maps and illustrations in this book
are by the author.

Printed in Ireland
by Colour Books Ltd, Dublin

For Aoife

Preface

This book gathers together a number of ancient and medieval writings and offers them, in translation, to the reader who has an interest in the culture, history and religion of ancient Ireland. A few of the writers of these pieces bear contemporary witness: they describe either what they did themselves and saw with their own eyes, or, at least, what happened in their own time. Some of the writers, however, recount what happened generations earlier than the age they themselves lived in. What they offer, therefore, is not very good historical evidence for the subjects they write about. However, when there is no good historical evidence available for certain events, we must content ourselves with studying the words of those who pass on to us narratives which may contain, here or there, a faint reminiscence or shadow of the original occurrence. This is not very satisfactory; but at least a writer of the seventh or eighth century, describing the fifth century, will give us a picture of the mentality that was developed in the first age of Irish Christianity. Or, rather, of the mentalities; for there is no single tradition of thought. There is a wide intellectual and moral range. In this, of course, Early Christian Ireland is like other parts of Europe and the world.

   The principle of selection is to offer a picture of the conversion of Ireland to Christianity as it was seen through the eyes of contemporaries and through the eyes of those who lived in a somewhat later time when the church was firmly established and people were beginning to take an anti-quarian interest in its beginnings. Everything gathered here, or almost everything, has been translated before—but most commonly in the context of learned editions of the Latin texts—sometimes on pages facing the original and rendered word for word for the benefit of specialists whose concern is the close study of the text. Here, the translations are provided for the non-specialist reader who may have a general interest in the history of the beginning of Christianity in Ireland. An attempt is made in the Introduction and commentaries, to indicate the context of the various writings, and in the translations to provide, not quite word for word, but sense for sense.

All the translations have been newly made for this purpose, with one exception: the selection (of entries relating to ecclesiastical matters, with just a few others) from the Annals of the Four Masters has been left in John O'Donovan's words. This is partly because these Annals are themselves a modern (seventeenth-century) compilation and reinterpretation, and partly because O'Donovan's translation itself stands directly within the tradition of the earlier writings: it is a part of the canon and he is in the line of succession of the scholars who tried more than a thousand years ago to understand and explain the beginnings of Irish Christianity.

The book is not just about St Patrick. He was one of a number engaged in the long process of evangelization which transformed ancient Europe and Ireland. We are poorly informed about him; but we are still less well informed about his colleagues. But at least we know some of their names. Part of the book consists of little more than lists. Nor are they all Irish lists. Christianity came from outside the country. They can remind us that a whole world is all but lost to our knowledge; yet that world of fifteen centuries ago in some sense shaped us all.

Contents

PREFACE   vii

One: Introduction

1 Before the Monasteries   3
2 The Spread of Christianity to the West   8
3 The Church in Gaul and Britain   14
4 Ireland in the Fifth Century   23
5 Gaulish and British Bishops in Ireland   38
6 Women Founders of Churches   46

Two: Extracts from Writings of the Fourth and Fifth Centuries

7 The Council of Arles, 314   53
8 The Council of Orange, 441   57
9 The Council of Vaison, 442   59
10 The Synod of May 451   61
11 The Council of Tours, 18 November 461   64
12 The Council of Vannes   66
13 Prosper of Aquitaine on Pope Celestine and the Pelagians   70
14 The Chronicle of Prosper of Aquitaine   72
15 St Patrick's Writings   88
16 St Patrick's Declaration   96
17 St Patrick's Letter against the Soldiers of Coroticus   109

Three: Extracts from Later Writings

18	The Annals	117
19	From the Annals of Ulster	118
20	From the Annals of Inisfallen	123
21	From the Annals of the Four Masters	126
22	The "First Synod of St Patrick"	135
23	From Adomnán's Life of Columba	139
24	From St Columbanus's Letter to Pope Boniface IV	141
25	From Bede's Church History of the English People	144
26	From St Cummian's Letter on the Easter Question	151
27	Bishop Tírechán's Account of St Patrick	154
28	Muirchú's Life of St Patrick	175
29	A misplaced list from the Book of Armagh	198
30	From the notes to Tírechán's narrative in the Book of Armagh	200
31	"Sayings of Patrick"	202
32	From further fragments in the Book of Armagh	203
33	Cogitosus's Life of St Brigid the Virgin	207
34	The Three Orders of the Saints of Ireland	225
35	The Life of St Ailbe	227
36	The Life of St Declan of Ardmore	244
37	The Life of St Ciarán of Saigir	272
38	The Life of St Darerca, or Moninna, the Abbess	281
	TABLE OF DATES	295
	NOTES AND REFERENCES	299
	SELECT BIBLIOGRAPHY	311
	INDEX	315

PART ONE

Introduction

ONE

Before the Monasteries

Ireland is a Christian country. That is to say that most of the population, North and South, has a background in one or other version of Christian belief. The large majority of its people, indeed, consists of regularly practising Christians, who have their children baptized, go to church on Sunday, and mark the rites of passage in their lives—birth, marriage and death in particular—with Christian ceremonies. No matter how pluralistic Ireland may be or may become, and however much religious belief may wane or change in the future, the historical fact of fifteen centuries of Christianity remains. It is one of the most important facts of Irish history. The obvious should not be overlooked. Christianity in a thousand ways has shaped the history of Ireland.

This book deals with the time when the Christian religion was first established in the country. It is a difficult time to study, because, although the use of writing came to Ireland then, very little in writing has come down to us. And in terms of material remains—buildings, books, equipment—virtually nothing survives.

Almost everyone in Ireland is familiar with monuments of the early Irish Church. Throughout the country there are remains of Round Towers, ruinous stone churches and carved High Crosses. They stand on the sites of what were once monasteries, some of them very large. And almost everyone therefore has some sense that the early Irish Church was monastic; as indeed, for most of its history, it largely and predominantly was. But the Round Towers were built in the tenth, eleventh and twelfth centuries and the stone churches—with possibly a few rare exceptions—from the ninth century onwards. None of the High Crosses now surviving can be dated with any confidence earlier than the late seventh century.

The major monastic foundations, such as Clonmacnoise, Bangor and Durrow, were made in the sixth century, mainly from the 540s onwards. But a hundred years before that there was already an organized Christian Church in Ireland. Unfortunately, we can't go and visit its monuments. They have vanished off the face of the earth. The priests and bishops who founded the Church in Ireland built enduringly, but not in stone. Nor do we even have any of their manuscripts; although some few of their words have been preserved by later monastic copyists. With the singular and important exception of St Patrick they have been eclipsed by the great monastic founders who came after them.

That very early Church in Ireland was governed by bishops, not abbots, and at the beginning many of the bishops and their adjutants were people who came to Ireland from overseas—from Gaul or Britain, where the Church had been longer established. Again with the exception of the Briton, St Patrick, they have mostly been all but forgotten, and the sites of their churches—unlike those of the later great monasteries—receive little notice. This has been the case for so long that it is now impossible to find out much about most of them. The church organization they set up wasn't completely supplanted by the new monastic system, and, until the late seventh century, it retained an independent existence. But by then the strength of the monastic movement was so great that churches originally founded as bishops' sees—like Armagh—had themselves become monasteries. In the circumstances of Ireland of that time the change was probably not a very drastic one. By then the work of the early bishops' churches was done. Ireland was formally and legally a Christian country; and even if pagan beliefs and customs persisted widely among the people, Christianity had already transformed Irish society and institutions.

This book attempts to put together such information as we can glean to help us to some understanding of the men and women who established the Church in Ireland at the very beginning. The information comes in meagre and disconnected scraps and it is more than difficult to put it together. But it is worth the effort because of the crucial importance of the period in Ireland's history. The actual sources are supplied here for the reader—the writings that tell us about the beginnings of the early Irish Church. These are translations—mostly from Latin. In making the translations, I have given the meaning of the writers as accurately as possible, but have tried to convey it more readably in English by taking small liberties with the form—breaking up sentences into smaller sentences, for example, or putting in a person's name instead of a "he" or "she" here and there. They are not, therefore exact word-for-word translations. But wherever a meaningful change has been made in a word (because a scribal error is suspected), that change is indicated in a note.

For, of course, all these texts were written by hand, and were copied and recopied by generations of scribes, allowing errors to creep in. We have none of them in the original form. Many scholars have worked on the texts and have provided printed versions edited to show variations in the different manuscripts and have given other information necessary for understanding them. These editions are listed in the bibliography and have been used in making the translations.

Identifications of places mentioned in the texts have been inserted, so far as this was possible, into the translations, within square brackets and in italics. Where necessary, explanatory notes have also been supplied. Angle brackets < > indicate early interpolation in a text.

However, most of the explanatory matter has been gathered into the exposition in Part 1, which attempts to give the context of these early writings, and their historical background.

In Irish primary schools when I was a child, we learned about St Patrick in religious knowledge class, from the Maynooth "Penny Catechism"—as it was known then. We were taught that he was sent by Pope Celestine and came to Ireland as a missionary in the year 432. Teachers expanded on this, telling the story of how he had been carried off into slavery in heathen Ireland as a boy, how he had escaped, guided by God, and how he had been called back by "the Voice of the Irish" to the work of converting all Ireland to Christianity; which in due course he did.

Reliable information had been conflated with unreliable information to produce this account of Ireland's patron saint. The authors of the catechism had got the date 432 from the Irish annals, which say that Patrick arrived that year, the year in which Pope Celestine died. Early Irish writers had also worked out that it was this pope who sent Patrick.

The schoolteachers got the story of Patrick's captivity, escape and vocation from the saint's own account of himself, in his *Confessio* (Declaration). St Patrick, however, didn't claim to have converted all Ireland; but some hundreds of years after his death it became an established opinion in Ireland that he had converted *almost* all of the country.

When we try to deal with the fifth century in Ireland the difficulties are very great. No actual manuscript of any kind written in Ireland in that century now survives. There is virtually not a single Irish artefact in a museum or a single monument in the field of which an archaeologist could say with full confidence that it was made in the fifth century. Dr Binchy, in a famous article on the problem of St Patrick, declared with some feeling and a good deal of justification that, so far as Irish history is concerned, it is a lost century.

Yet the case isn't quite hopeless. Copies have survived of two writings of St Patrick. Are they genuine? The earliest copy dates from—that is to say the actual manuscript we now possess was written in—the ninth century, not the fifth. But certain tests can be applied. The documents are in Latin, and Latin changed very much in the period between Late Antiquity and the Early Middle Ages. What kind of Latin is in them? The expert opinion is that it is Latin of the fifth century. Is it the kind of Latin that would have been written by someone whose schooling had been in Britain or Gaul at that time? Yes. Were they both written by the same person? Yes; they have exactly the same idiosyncracies of style, and even repeat one or two distinctive phrases. Was that person St Patrick? Yes: he tells us his name, and a few things about himself. He was not, however, writing autobiography, so most of what he lets us know about himself concerns his character, his faith, his visions, his understanding of God, rather than his everyday circumstances—very little material for an entry in *Who's Who*.

Yet, at least we know that he existed (and roughly when); that he was a bishop in Ireland; that he came from Britain where his father had been of the Roman official class and well-to-do; that he baptized large numbers of Irish people and devoted much of his life to this evangelizing work. We know that his belief was (in the fifth-century sense) Catholic, or orthodox, and not, for example, Arian.

The date 432 comes from the annals. Now an annal is, in principle, an annual entry made in a chronicle to record outstanding events of the year just gone by, just as an entry in a diary records the events of the day. But the Irish annals we possess were not being compiled in this way in the fifth century. The custom began at least a hundred, perhaps two hundred years later. The people who began it then wanted to record not just contemporary history, but also the history of Ireland up to the point where they started. So they gathered together all the information they could, from stories, traditions, legends, some few documents too, and tried to arrange it in chronological order before they began their account of the times of which they had firsthand knowledge. They set it out in annalistic form, just as if there had been chroniclers in Ireland before them for centuries carefully noting the chief events of each year. But there hadn't.

Among the documents these scholars had available by the time they began to compile their annals were some chronicles that had been written outside Ireland. In fact, they drew extensively on these to provide a framework into which they could fit their reconstructed history of Ireland. One of the chronicles was that of Prosper of Aquitaine, who lived in the fifth century. He had an entry saying that in the year 431 Pope Celestine sent one Palladius to be "the first bishop of the Irish believers in Christ". This conflicted with what, by the later seventh century, had come to be widely believed in Ireland: that St Patrick had been the first and primary missionary, responsible for the conversion of the island. And he was a bishop.

What was to be done with the information about Palladius? The pseudo-annalists concluded that he must have been a failure. Several stories were developed to explain his failure. In one, he never reached Ireland at all. At any rate, they devised a chronological scheme that would save Patrick's reputation as far as was consistent with Prosper's information:

in 431 Pope Celestine sent Bishop Palladius to Ireland;
in 432 Bishop Patrick arrived in Ireland;
in 433 Patrick converted the Irish to Christianity.

7ᵗʰ century, Tírecháṉ

So the scheme appears in the Annals of Inisfallen and in a chronological summary given by the seventh-century bishop Tírechán in his account of St Patrick. The date 432 can be dismissed, in other words, as a pious fiction. It exemplifies the difficulties encountered by the student of the period, difficulties that explain the amount of scholarly controversy there has always been about St Patrick's life and career. An old argument was revived in 1941, when the late T.F. O'Rahilly, in a lecture sponsored by the Dublin Institute for Advanced Studies, resurrected the ancient idea that there had been "two Patricks". He suggested that Palladius, when he came to Ireland, was known as Patricius, and that all his deeds had in time come to be attributed to the other Patricius, or Patrick the Briton—first brought to Ireland as a slave—whose career began, however, a generation later.

It seems doubtful that Palladius was known in his own time in Ireland as "Patricius"; but O'Rahilly was almost certainly right in suggesting that some of the episodes in his life—and episodes in the lives of some others— came to be attributed to Patrick.

This is assumed here: it seems best to fit the confused and confusing historical information we have. But the matter remains controversial and there are other views.

St Patrick therefore doesn't occupy quite as central a position in this account of the conversion of Ireland as some readers might expect. Yet he deserves his preeminence because, as his own writings make abundantly clear, he is of great interest in himself. But part of the purpose of this collection is to introduce the general reader to some other labourers in the early Irish vineyard. Even if we will never know very much about them, at least some of their names have been preserved and we have a rough idea what parts of the country they evangelized.

TWO

The Spread of Christianity to the West

In the beginning, Christianity was disseminated through the Jewish communities of the Eastern Roman Empire. One of its first crises, recounted in the New Testament in the Acts of the Apostles, arose from an impassioned difference of opinion as to how much of Judaism the new teaching should retain—how much, for example, of the law of the Jews on diet, on circumcision and other matters. In this debate, the church of Jerusalem was conservative, but the movement led by St Paul opened up the new faith to the Gentiles and moved it away from Judaic practice and custom.

Yet, initially, to the Roman rulers, Christianity appeared as a sect of Judaism, and it was chiefly through the conversion of Jews that it spread at first. Outside Palestine, the scattered communities of Jews in exile mostly lived in cities, in highly distinct groups separated from their neighbours by strict laws and customs, dietary, marital and otherwise. They formed a sizeable part of the population of cities in the eastern part of the Empire.

So, although Jesus had preached in the Galilean countryside, the teaching was then spread through the cities. Christianity in its first two or three centuries was largely an urban religion, and it soon began to be shaped by the mould of Graeco-Roman civilization. By the end of the first century the Christian communities were, however, quite distinct from the Jewish, and indeed a hostility had already arisen between the two which was to persist for most of subsequent history.

In the Apostolic Age, it was along the excellent Roman roads and by the Roman seaways that the teaching of Jesus was propagated, from city to city in the eastern part of the Empire, by Paul, Barnabus, Philip and others. By the same means it may well have been brought at quite an early date to the West, not, however through conscious and systematic missions, but rather by early Christians travelling on other business, who proclaimed their faith to people whom they met.

There was a medieval tradition that Christianity had been preached in Britain as early as the time of the Apostles. This tradition is quite unreliable, but, even before the Roman invasion of Britain in AD 43, there was a considerable Roman trade with the island, and it may be that some time before the end of the first century, independently of the Roman conquest of large parts of Britain, Christianity could have arrived in the Celtic west, in the Glastonbury area where there was a flourishing aristocratic La Tène culture. And some people in or from Ireland could at least have heard the name of Christ by a very early date. But this is speculation.

Clearly the Christian faith was being spread in Gaul, almost from the beginning. The main trading route through that province led northwards from Marseille through Vienne and Lyon and in both of these cities there were early Christian communities.

In Celtic Gaul there had been something resembling a national assembly held annually on the day of the god Lug (the festival called *Lughnasa* in Ireland).[1] It was known as "the festival of the three Gauls" and the Romans took it over and associated it with the imperial cult. Sacrifice was offered to Rome and to the genius of the Emperor. Under Marcus Aurelius in AD 177, on the day of the festival (1 August) Christians were thrown to wild animals in the amphitheatre—evidence of a well established Christian community in the city. And by about 200, according to Eusebius, Christianity had penetrated Britain.

The advance of the faith, by that date, was considerable, throughout the Empire. It was still not propagated by systematic missionary activity but by personal contacts, word of mouth, and example.

The traders, soldiers, slaves, officials and other travellers who followed the main route northwards from Marseille are the most likely medium of transmission to Roman-dominated Britain, while those who followed the wine route from Bordeaux may have brought Christianity to the Celtic west and north. But the history of the Church in Britain before the fourth century is obscure.

The fourth century was a time of recurrent persecution of the Christians in one part of the Empire or another—sometimes throughout the Empire—and questions of hierarchy and jurisdiction were not the most urgent. From at least as early as the second century a primacy of honour was accorded to the church of Rome, reputedly the place of martyrdom of both Peter and Paul. But the bishop of Rome exercised influence rather than authority over other patriarchs.

The whole Empire was in considerable disarray throughout most of the middle decades of the third century. There were repeated barbarian incursions across the frontiers as well as formidable attacks from the sea on the coasts of Asia Minor and the Aegean. Certain Germanic nations made their appearance in history at this time: the Franks and the Alamanni threatened the Rhine frontier in 235 and overran it in the 250s. In 259 and 260 the Franks marched south through Gaul and Spain and crossed over to Mauretania in Roman North Africa. The Roman armies in Gaul, after a victory over the Franks in 259, proclaimed as emperor their general, Marcus Cassianus Latinius Postumus, and for a number of years there was a separate and independent Roman Empire of the Gauls, to which Spain and Britain adhered.

A restoration took place under the Emperor Aurelian, who drove Germanic invaders of Italy out of that country and beyond the Danube, reconquered the East, and finally returned Gaul and Britain to the Roman Empire by defeating the local Emperor (Tetricus) in 274. He described himself on his coins as "Restorer of the World", and he established the imperial cult of Sol Invictus, the "Invincible Sun", who now became the supreme deity of the state. The worship of the Sungod was to remain important for more than a hundred years. It appealed not only to the uneducated, but also to the educated who saw in the Sun a kind of metaphor, or expression of what educated agnostic people in eighteenth-century Europe were to refer to as "the supreme being". In an odd way, this decision to have a supreme god for the Empire as a whole, closely associated with the ruler, was to make easier the establishment of christianity as the state religion in the next century.

In those troubled years of the third century, however, Christianity was still mainly a religion of the lower and middle classes in the cities. Christians were becoming very numerous, and since they refused to take part in the state cults and also, in some communities, were opposed to military service, they were widely regarded as disloyal and unreliable. Commonly enough, the disasters of the time were blamed on them. The first comprehensive effort to wipe out Christianity throughout the Empire was made in 250, when the Emperor Decius issued an edict ordering all the citizens to take part in public ceremonies of worship of the state gods, under penalty of death.

Decius died in 251, but a few years later his successor Valerian renewed the edict and the persecution. Many christians conformed and saved their lives. Many refused and died bearing witness: martyrs.

A full reorganization of the Empire was carried out by Diocletian (285–305), who tried to reform the economy, the finances, the administration and the defensive system. He also issued edicts, at the end of his reign (in the years 303–305), against the Christians which led to what was in many ways the most severe of the persecutions.

Our first detailed information about Christianity in Britain probably relates to the persecutions of the third century. The English monk Bede, writing early in the eighth century and relying on such scraps of information as he could find, thought that the martyrdoms both of St Alban in Verulamium (*north of London: the modern St Albans*) and of Aaron and Julius in "the city of the legions" (*Urbs Legionum: Caerleon-on-Usk*) occurred

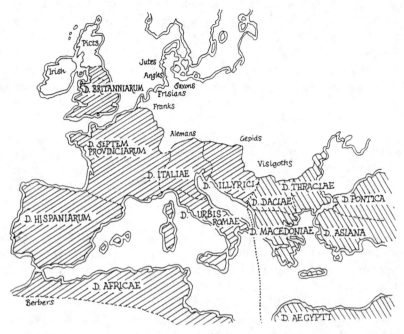

The Western Roman Empire, about AD *400*

in the persecution under Diocletian. Bede, however, took this information from the monk Gildas, who wrote about AD 540 and whose knowledge of events a century and a half before his own time was very imperfect. The memory of persecution was still vivid in Gildas's time, and it was known that the last great persecution had taken place under Diocletian. In fact, the persecution of christians under Diocletian (who was himself semi-retired at the time and not particularly interested in killing christians) was not severe in either Gaul or Britain. The local ruler, Caesar Constantius Chlorus, gave specific orders which kept it to a minimum. The numerous martyrdoms mentioned by Gildas may well have taken place somewhat earlier.

The position of the Christian Church throughout the empire was dramatically changed by imperial edicts of the early fourth century. Shortly before his death the senior Augustus, Galerius, in 311 gave Christians the right to rebuild their churches and practise their religion. And early in 313 the then joint rulers of the empire, Constantine (who had been born in Britain: the son of Constantius) and Licinius, met at Milan and issued an edict giving full freedom of worship to the Christians and restoring confiscated Christian property. After the edict of Milan it begins to be possible to give some sort of connected account of the Church in Gaul and Spain, and even in Britain. There were meetings, or councils, of bishops held in various cities of Gaul to regulate the affairs of the Church and make rulings on points of dispute —at

Arles in 314, Cologne in 346, Arles again in 353, Béziers in 356, Paris in 360 or 361, Valence in 374, Bordeaux in 384–385, Trier in 386, Nîmes in 394 or 396, Turin in 398. At the first of these, in Arles in August, 314, the bishops ruled that Easter should be observed on the same day everywhere (touching on a problem that was to persist for centuries), that bishops should stay in the sees to which they had been assigned, that it was wrong for Christians to bear arms in the arena, and that theatre and circus people should be excommunicated.

The evidence for an organised church in Britain in the fourth century is thinner, but is quite firm. Three British bishops—from London, York and Lincoln (or possibly Colchester—the name is corrupt in the text) attended the council of Arles in 314, and the bishop of London was accompanied by a priest and a deacon. This shows that in Britain, as elsewhere, metropolitan sees were functioning by this date and that the Church had modelled its territorial organization on that of the Empire. At a somewhat later date, bishops travelling to such councils were entitled, if they needed it, to draw an imperial *per diem* allowance equivalent to that of an officer or official travelling on State business. Three British bishops availed of this when they attended a council at Rimini in Italy in 359.

Meantime, the end of the persecutions had been followed immediately by serious disputes about doctrine: what exactly was the teaching of the Church on certain central matters? In particular there was dispute about the nature of God and the meaning of the Trinity—the Father, the Son and the Holy Spirit. In Egypt, a Libyan priest called Arius taught that the Son derives his being from the Father, was created by the Father and had a beginning, so that there was a time when he was not. This teaching was condemned by Arius's bishop on the grounds that it reduced the Son to the status of a demigod, but it gave rise to a controversy which threatened to divide deeply the whole Christian world.

The Emperor Constantine decided that the matter had to be settled, and he summoned a meeting that was intended to be a deliberative assembly of the whole Church—the First Ecumenical Council. It was he, on this occasion, who first made the public funds available for the travel costs of the bishops. The council met at Nicaea in Asia Minor and was opened by the Emperor himself on 20 May 325. The teachings of Arius were condemned and a creed was approved which acknowledged that the Son was coeternal and of one substance with the Father. The controversy, however, continued for another half century, particularly in the East; and for a long time to come orthodoxy was to be affirmed in terms of declarations concerning the relationship of the Father, Son and Holy Spirit in the Trinity. The Gaulish and British churches accepted the Nicene creed and were to affirm it at later local and provincial councils.

Although paganism was still widespread—and almost universal in the countryside—Christianity had continued to advance in the West throughout the fourth century, usually with the backing of the State. The Empire, however, still had its troubles, and Britain in particular was subject to both internal upheaval and external attack. Commanders of the troops there continued to try to seize imperial power. Magnus Maximus, a Spanish general governing Britain, who had some military success against barbarian attacks on the province, had himself acclaimed as Emperor by his troops in 383 and crossed over to Gaul to pursue his ambitions. After much fighting he was finally overthrown in 388.

Britain remained subject to attacks from the Irish in the west, the Picts in the north, and the Saxons in the east (across the North Sea). Its Roman garrison seemed to be unreliable and ineffective, and finally the Romano-British towns organized their own defences and the Roman legions left, in 410. By then the Rhine frontier had collapsed yet again (in 406) and large bodies of barbarians had once more marched through Gaul and Spain. This was, as it turned out, the beginning of the final disintegration of the Roman Empire in the West, although no one at the time could know that. What people knew was that it was a time of great trouble.

When the eternal city itself was taken by the Goths in 410, it seemed to very many people almost like a sign of the end of the world. And some pointed out that now the message of Christ had been preached throughout the whole world—even in the islands of the ocean at the world's end (Britain and Ireland): it was the fulness of time and these were the last days. This appears to have been the view, for example, of one who was instrumental in bringing the Gospel to those regions "beyond which there was no one": the fifth-century British bishop Patrick.

THREE

The Church in Gaul and Britain

The late antique world from which St Patrick and other fifth-century bishops came to Ireland was one to which they continued to belong, by language, by religion, by training, by attitude of mind. It was the world of the Roman Empire, encompassing all the lands around the Mediterranean Sea, from the Middle East through Egypt, all of North Africa, Spain, extensive territory north of the Alps (including a great part of Britain) roughly to the line of the Rhine, and south-eastern Europe roughly to the Danube. This world, this universal empire, was unified in theory and to a large extent in practice. But it was also divided. The emperor Diocletian had made the decision—fundamental to his reforms and to his attempt at restoration of the old order—to divide the Empire, for administrative purposes, into two. The system known as the Tetrarchy provided four rulers, a senior and a junior for the West and a senior and a junior for the East. The division was uneven. The inland sea continued to be the central—and unifying—feature of each division; but the West Mediterranean (from Italy to the Straits of Gibraltar) is much smaller and less topographically diversified than the East Mediterranean, from the heel of Italy to the Near East. An aspect of this division became increasingly important: the official, and dominant, language of the West was Latin; the official, and dominant, language of the East was Greek. When Constantine the Great transformed the old Greek city of Byzantium, on the Bosphorus, into the great imperial metropolis of Constantinople, a rival Rome was established. Its comparative importance was magnified when the fourth-century Western emperors for the most part no longer based themselves on the City of Rome, but lived in and functioned from other centres, such as Milan, and Cologne and Trier on the Rhine frontier.

The Western Empire included the region the Romans called "Africa"—that is, Africa north of the Sahara and west of the Libyan desert. "Egypt"—the eastern part of North Africa—belonged to the Eastern Empire. The Christian church, although it was, like the Empire, one, was also divided, East and West. To the patriarchal sees of Antioch, Alexandria and Rome, where the apostles had preached, came the new imperial see of Constantinople, to join them in prestige and rivalry; while Jerusalem enjoyed great prestige but not dominance in the government of the Church. Again there were two administrative languages—Latin in the West, Greek in the East—and this, among other differences, pointed a contrast and fostered a growing divergence.

The East was populous and highly urbanized by the measure of the time, with many ancient centres of civilization. In the West, Africa, then fertile and urbanized, was an active growth area of Christianity before the invasion of the Vandals. Italy, Spain, Gaul and Britain, north of the Mediterranean, were less urban and more slowly evangelized. Ireland lay outside the Empire; but the wine trade as well as other contacts connected it with Gaul and Britain throughout the imperial period; and from the third century onwards, Irish raids on the Empire reinforced these contacts violently. It is to Gaul and Britain that we must look for the background of the establishment of Christianity in Ireland, bearing in mind, however, that monastic impulses from Egypt were already affecting the West by the early fifth century, that the later Irish monastic movement was to be affected directly or indirectly by these influences and that contacts were to be maintained for many years—by way of the wine trade, for example—with the *east* Mediterranean.

Such church documents as survive from this time in the West show us a steady buildup of organization. It was normally based on the *civitas* (a city and its "canton" in the Roman administrative system), with the bishop's see in the *civitas*-capital. The Roman *civitas* in turn had proved, in the days of imperial expansion, to be a concept of great flexibility which could adapt the idea of a Mediterranean city-state readily to the looser and more amorphous northern tribe. It was to serve similarly now in the time of Christian expansion.

By the fifth century the Roman imperial system was breaking down piecemeal in the West. The British revolt of AD 409, which led to the final Roman military withdrawal from that province, was followed by further revolts in Gaul, even while Alans, Franks, Sueves and others were changing forever the social and political systems of the West. Salvian, writing around the middle of the fifth century, tells us that Trier, which had been the very centre of military government, has been four times invaded and laid waste, that Cologne is "filled with the enemy", and that Mainz has been ruined and destroyed.[1] The offices and machinery of government had been transferred by then from Trier to Arles in the south—and we find this reflected in the organization of the Church, which was called upon to be flexible and to adapt. In the West, the broad jurisdictional pattern of the Church conformed roughly to that of the Empire. There was a Gaulish church; there was a British church; there was a Spanish church; and they were all loosely connected on the model of the imperial dioceses and provinces. Provincial assemblies of bishops were customary. But a hierarchy of jurisdiction had not emerged as clearly as in the East, nor was the emperor as closely involved in church matters.

The system of relationships begins to emerge immediately after the Edict of Milan, and appears in the documents of the Council of Arles (314). At the council Gaul was represented in terms of the imperially recognized provinces. There were present bishops of five cities (as well as the port of Nice) from Vienne; bishops of five cities from *Gallia* (including the old *Lug-dunensis, Belgica* and part of Germany); bishops of four cities from *Aquitania* (but the bishop of Trier—in *Gallia*—is mistakenly included on this list). *Britannia* sent three bishops and *Hispania* six. (Diocletian's reorganization had established twelve dioceses in the whole empire—Spain, Gaul, Britain, Vienne, Italy and Pannonia in the West; Moesia, Thrace, Asia, Pontos, and the huge diocese of Oriens, which included Egypt and the Levant, in the East.)

By this stage the bishops of Rome had built up jurisdiction over the suburbicarian provinces of Italy and Sicily. Later, at the end of the fourth century, Pope Siricius (384–398) obtained control over Illyricum through a vicariate exercised by the bishop of Thessalonica. But the attempt of Pope Zozimus (417–418) to employ a similar vicariate of Arles to control Vienne and the two Narbonnes was not successful, and his successors for a time simply appointed personal vicars to act as intermediaries with local bishops. Arles itself, under its bishop Hilary, came into dispute with Leo the Great, who wished to curb its too great autonomy and was given an opportunity through its dispute with Vienne. But effectively, both in imperial and in ecclesiastical matters, Arles was the vicariate of the West throughout the fifth century. Popes exercised great authority in the West on doctrinal matters, although they were sometimes resisted, but less on jurisdiction: the Pope's decision on appeal was often contested.

The great ecumenical council of Nicaea in 325 recognized three primatial or metropolitan sees, on an equal level (although this point was not yielded by Rome): Rome, Alexandria and Antioch (Canon 6).[2] Canon 7 of the council held that special honour accompanied by metropolitan status should be accorded to the bishop of Jerusalem. This provision, ratified by later councils, came at some stage to be noted in Ireland. At the end of the sixth century, Columbanus, writing that the Irish accorded primacy to Rome, added the qualification "saving only the singular prerogative of the place of resurrection of the Lord".[3]

The developed pattern by this stage seems to have been that the bishops of a civil province normally formed a group under the presidency of the bishop of the metropolis, or provincial capital. But rivalries occurred when there was another large city in the province. In Gaul, for example, this led to conflict between Arles and Vienne. Pope Leo, on 5 May 450, in response to an emotional appeal from the bishops of the Arles province, against

Great Britain, about 400

Vienne, for the ancient privileges of their city—"mother of all the Gauls"—partitioned the province, allotting four cities to Vienne, the rest to Arles.[4]

Britain was, in the civil dispensation, a separate diocese, and it is likely that its church was organized accordingly, as a semi-autonomous body. But there is some evidence to suggest that its bishops may have looked, at least from time to time, to those of Gaul for support or guidance. The reports of a number of writers tell us that by the late fourth century the British churches were well established and organized. The archaeological evidence shows that there were some prosperous Christian communities. Apart from well-appointed Christian country houses, there are some objects of luxury. The silver hoard that was found in 1975 at Water Newton, near Peterborough, was buried near the Roman road from the north about 350, possibly on the occasion of a Pictish or Saxon raid. It suggests a reasonably rich church.[5]

It is likely that, following the general Western pattern, the Church in Britain was organized under five metropolitans, to correspond to the five civil provinces established by a reorganization of 369.[6] The most likely metropolitan sees would have been London, Lincoln, York, Verulamium (St Albans) and, in the small north-western rump-province, Carlisle.

By the late fourth century, the island, exposed to raids by *Scotti* (from Ireland), *Atecotti*, Picts and Saxons, had entered its time of troubles. The Roman armies were less and less able to cope and too many of their commanders were adventurers aiming murderously at the imperial purple. "Britain, the province fertile in producing tyrants" is how St Jerome described the country early in the fifth century.[7] After a Saxon attack of 408, the Romano-Britons severed themselves from the Empire and looked to the recovery of their cities and to their own defence.[8]

There must have been great disorganization, and some reorganization, of church government as territory began to pass from British, or partly Christian, control. Here Britain paralleled northern Gaul: the incomers from the east were unlike the Goths, Vandals and others who were crossing the Roman frontiers having already been converted to Arian Christianity. The early Anglo-Saxons in England, like the Franks on the northern Rhine frontier, were pagans.

Twenty years after the end of imperial rule, we have different reports of the British Church. The teachings on grace and on other matters which had brought controversy and dissension to Italy, Gaul, Africa and the East, had taken root in Britain. The teachings did not constitute a unified body of doctrine—indeed the chief purpose of the teachers, or preachers, seems to have been moral rather than doctrinal—but they have been lumped together under the general label, "Pelagianism", or, in respect of a modified later version, "semi-Pelagianism", after one of its leaders, Pelagius. He was British or Irish, but came to Rome in AD 400 and became well known in the City as a spiritual director and a popular preacher. He left Rome after the sack of 410 and went to Africa and then to Jerusalem. Although he visited Hippo, he did not meet its bishop, St Augustine, who was away at the time, but he left there his travelling companion, Celestius, a lawyer, who gave more extreme expression to the views that were to cause controversy. Pelagius had expressed concern at the shallow morality, as he saw it, of well-to-do Christians in Rome, and became alarmed at St Augustine's prayer to God in his *Confessions*: "Give what You command, and command what You will." St Augustine in turn became alarmed at the teachings of Pelagius and Celestius, and a prolonged controversy on Grace and Free Will ensued. The Pelagians were accused of denying Original Sin and of teaching that it was (at least theoretically) possible to achieve perfection and salvation without Divine Grace; that Adam had been created mortal and would have died even had he not sinned, and that his sin affected only himself; not the whole human race. Pelagianism was condemned by a number of councils but St Augustine's full teaching on grace was by no means universally accepted and the matter gave rise to continuing controversy.

Prosper of Aquitaine, a vigorous anti-Pelagian, tells us that Pope Celestine (423–432) rid Britain of this "disease" and that in the process he reached beyond Britain. "And, ordaining a bishop for the Irish, he made the barbarian island Christian while taking care to keep the Roman island Catholic."[9]

This is an important statement. It could be read to mean that, while Celestine was catering for Christians in Britain, he was directing the conversion of pagans in Ireland. However, Prosper's entry for 431 in his *Chronicle*[10] makes it clear that this cannot be what he meant. We must take it that he meant rather that, with the appointment of its first bishop, Ireland was brought fully within the comity of the organized Christian world.

For, in the *Chronicle*, he reports for the year 429 that one Agricola, a Pelagian and himself the son of a Pelagian bishop, had been spreading the teaching among the churches of Britain. But, through some sort of intermediation by the deacon Palladius, Pope Celestine sent Germanus, bishop of Auxerre, as his vicar to restore Catholic orthodoxy among the Britons. Two years later he tells us that the council meeting at Ephesus had condemned many Pelagians, along with their teaching; and then he adds that Palladius was ordained and sent by Pope Celestine to the Irish Christians to be their first bishop.

Deacons were important functionaries in the Church at the time, acting as emissaries, agents and counsellors for bishops—and often succeeding them in their sees. In the negotiations that led to the summoning of the Council of Ephesus, for example, an important part was played by the deacon Posidonius, sent by Cyril of Alexandria to Pope Celestine with communications concerning the teachings of Nestorius (which were to be condemned by the council).[11]

A recent translator and editor of the fifth-century Life of Germanus of Auxerre by Constantius of Lyon has expressed the opinion that Palladius must have been a deacon at Rome, because a deacon of the church of Auxerre would hardly have had enough influence on Pope Celestine to persuade him to send Germanus to Britain.[12] But, on the contrary, fifth-century practice would suggest that it is much more likely that Palladius was a deacon of Auxerre and a trusted emissary of Germanus to the pope.[13] Constantius was writing about two generations after the events he describes, and is an unreliable source, showing very imperfect knowledge of the time. However, in explaining the events of 429, he tells us that a delegation had arrived from Britain to let the Gaulish bishops know that Pelagianism was taking over the British churches (*in locis suis*)[14] and that the need to save the Catholic faith was urgent. A council was assembled in Gaul and it chose "two outstanding lights of religion", Germanus and Lupus (bishop of Troyes) to go to Britain.[15]

Putting together the two pieces of information, it seems possible that Germanus, in a delicate situation, took the precaution not only of obtaining the approval of Celestine, but of having the mission sent in his name.

If so, the procedure followed was regular and correct. The Gaulish bishops were intervening in the affairs of a neighbouring province, where plainly there was dissent among the local bishops. Conciliar legislation in the preceding years had tended to preserve provincial autonomy and to prevent interference by one province in the affairs of another. The council of Sardica, of 343, was important in its laying down of territorial rules. Its Canon 3, in the first section, states that a bishop may not pass from his own province to another "unless he be invited by his brethren".[16] Canon 5 of the council of Nicaea had ruled that a provincial council could act as a court of appeal from a disputed sentence pronounced against either a cleric or a lay person by an individual bishop. In other words, the provincial bishops as a body had authority to sit in judgment on acts of an individual bishop.[17] This was reinforced by Canons 14 and 15 of the council of Antioch, where it was provided that in the event of a disagreement among members of a provincial council over the case of an accused bishop, the metropolitan council should call in the bishops of a neighbouring province.[18] This may well have occurred in the case of the British Pelagian, Agricola (assuming him to have been, like his father, a bishop). Canon 3 of the Council of Sardica, however, in its third section, provided that if a bishop had been judged in some matter, but considered his cause to be just, and thought that the judgment should be reconsidered, those who judged him should write to the bishop of Rome. If the pope decided that the case required review, he should appoint judges from among the bishops of the neighbouring province, but if not, "the judgment once pronounced shall not be changed".[19]

The events meagrely sketched by Prosper and Constantius fit well into this context of current law on the inter-relationships of bishops. Prosper tells us that Germanus went to Britain in 429. How much earlier the first appeal from Britain came to the Gaulish bishops is unclear. But an exchange of messages with Rome in the interval is to be assumed. Even with the backing of conciliar councils, Celestine had to act prudently. The council of Sardica seemed to envisage in its "appeal clauses" a papal authority over the provinces; but this had not yet been fully established in practice. The primatial vicariate of Arles, established in 417 by Pope Zozimus, had lapsed in 419, and was not to be resumed again until 462, although Arles, from the early fifth century, was the leading church of Gaul. The pope, however, sent Germanus to Britain as his personal vicar,[20] not as judge, but to persuade. At a meeting of British bishops somewhere in southern Britain[21] he carried a debate against the Pelagians, according to Constantius. Shortly afterwards, as the same writer tells us, he rallied the Britons in battle, when they secured the so-called "Alleluia victory" over a force of Picts and Saxons.[22]

Palladius would have returned from Rome to Auxerre before Germanus departed for Britain. He would in fact have brought the pope's commission. This was a regular diaconal office. Did he himself then go to Britain? It is quite likely. He then went back to Rome again, it would seem, and there received his own, somewhat different, commission. It is obvious that either on his first or on his second visit to that see, he reported not only on Britain but on Ireland. In other words, some time before he was in Rome in 431—probably in 429–430—he was in touch, directly or indirectly, with "the Irish believers in Christ". He may even have visited Ireland. At any rate, we may take it as likely that some form of consent to his appointment as their bishop was secured from the Irish Christians, since this was the law of the time, strongly supported by Celestine.

Celestine had ruled, more than once, on the principles governing this. Popular election of bishops, a custom of the primitive Church, still survived vigorously and was supported by both councils and popes. Celestine puts it succinctly: "A bishop shall not be supplied without consent. Both the assent and the request of clergy, laity and people in authority are required."[23] And the numbers of Irish Christians must have been sufficient to warrant the appointment of a bishop. This too was required by canon law at the time.

How this Gallo-Roman initiative was followed through is most obscure. According to Constantius, Pelagianism or semi-Pelagianism revived in Britain, and another mission from Gaul was required; but there is no independent authority for this. The Christian church in Britain disappears into an obscurity little relieved by the sixth-century testimony of Gildas. The Britons, by the middle of the century, found themselves in mortal combat with the growing settlement, in eastern Britain, of the pagan Anglo-Saxons (whom they seem to have first summoned to their aid as auxiliary troops against the Irish and the Picts).

All over the West there was struggle. In the late fourth century, huge numbers of Goths, desperately migrating westwards after their homelands far beyond the Danube frontier had been invaded by the Huns, had crowded along the Roman borders, seeking permission to settle within the Empire. In 378, when the imperial army under the emperor Valens attacked them the Goths near Hadrianople, that army was defeated and the emperor was killed. His successor, Theodosius, finally reached an agreement with the Visigoths in 382, under which they kept their chiefs and culture but were allowed to settle within the frontiers. This became a precedent. After Theodosius the "masters of the soldiers", barbarian generals of barbarian armies, were the

Huns invaded the Goths

defence of the Western provinces, forming alliances with barbarians against barbarians. Roman life was to continue throughout the fifth century both in Gaul and in Britain, but in Britain only in diminished areas of the country, and without Roman government, and in Gaul subject to repeated incursions and destructive military campaigns.

FOUR

Ireland in the Fifth Century

We have no precise or detailed information about the Ireland to which Palladius and Patrick, Auxilius and Secundinus, came. Most of what we can read about the country as it then was comes from writings of later centuries, and these are unreliable in various ways. The writers themselves, in the seventh century and later, lacked adequate records and tended to project circumstances of their own day into the past. They did this either because they were unaware of the changes that had taken place in the interval, or because they were partisan and had an interest in maintaining fictions about the origins of the dynasties, churches, or property-relations they served. However, by putting together their accounts (treated with due caution) along with evidence of other kinds (for example, from archaeology), we may venture a tentative reconstruction.

It should begin with the basic facts of physical geography, since the island was in the same location then as now, was of more or less the same extent (give or take a little tideland here or there), and had a climate which was different but not much different. However, its superficial aspect was not at all the same as today. There were no towns or cities in the present-day, or even in the medieval, sense. Forests and bogs were extremely extensive, and the numerous undrained lake and river valleys and lowlands created many watery wildernesses in which the travelling stranger would be almost literally at sea. Settlement accordingly was discontinuous, and most inhabited tracts of country would have had something of the character of clearings, in a land where nature was—no doubt red in tooth and claw—but overwhelmingly green.

Yet the country had long been inhabited, and for the best part of three thousand years had been grazed and cultivated. It is possible to make a reasonable guess at the order of magnitude of the population: probably between a fifth of a million and half a million. The people were descended from immigrants who had arrived over many centuries from different parts of southern, western and northern Europe, and no doubt they had remote ancestors in North Africa too. There may well have been a number of different vernaculars spoken by small communities here and there in isolated glens, but we can be certain that by the fifth century one language was dominant throughout the island: Irish, a language of the Celtic group. This had by then virtually displaced all the other tongues that were spoken in more ancient times. The unity of speech was reflected in a unity (though not perhaps complete uniformity) of culture throughout the country.

It was a wholly rural society and then, as now, cattle were of the highest importance in the economy and in the estimation of the countryside. They were a primary measure of exchange value and of a man's (or a woman's) social worth. Sheep too were important, and the people of the time also hunted and trapped deer and other game. They planted wheat, oats, barley and flax, and to some extent they managed the bounty of the forest (sally copses for wattles, for example, to build the ubiquitous house type), and grazed pigs in the woods, to provide their most favoured meat. They used handmills to grind their grain, from which they made beer and porridge: this was heavy labour, the lot of slave women. Whether they had bread at this date is less certain. They consumed a variety of dairy foods, including milk, butter, cheese and curds. All this can be inferred from the attested customs of later centuries, together with such scanty archaeological evidence as there is; but even that simple economy was undergoing rapid and significant change in the fifth century. For example, a primitive type of plough was to be replaced, around this period, by the coulter plough, which allowed heavier and more fertile soils to be cultivated. A new type of handmill came into use, and water-mills were soon to appear. It is also probably the time when bee-keeping was introduced to Ireland. Most of these changes are due to the influence of the Roman Empire.

Roman influence, indeed, was to be the principal agent of change in the transformation of society. Neither Ireland nor any part of it was wholly self-sufficient, and from distant prehistoric times there had been some external as well as internal trade, as well as other forms of intercourse with the outside world. The imports from the Roman Empire had included wine, for which some at least of the tribal chiefs had acquired a taste (like their Celtic pre-decessors many centuries before in Central Europe). Irish exports probably included pelts and hides (for many of the later centuries this was to be a staple of the country's external commerce) and perhaps fish. Some quantities of materials not available in the country (such as tin, for making bronze) must have been included in the imports. Perhaps salt was one of them. There are indications that the Romans bought hunting dogs from Ireland, but these can hardly have been of great importance in trade. Yet overseas traffic was sufficient to provide business for enterprising seamen: St Patrick's account of his escape from slavery, and from Ireland, on board what would appear to have been a small merchant ship (seemingly Irish), is one of the several glimpses he gives us into the social history of the fifth century.

Another is his account of his own capture, along with "many thousands" of other Romano-Britons, by an Irish raiding party. "Many thousands" is almost certainly a rhetorical figure—arithmetic of this kind in Late Antique and medieval writing is decorative rather than factual—but Irish chiefs had been leading plundering expeditions for a long time into the Roman world before Patrick was carried from his home. The raids were mainly, if not wholly, on Britain. There may have been some as far as Gaul, but the evidence for this is slight. In the later historical traditions there are references to the deaths of Irish kings in "the Alps"—but this very likely results from a mistranscription of the old word for Britain—"Albu" (cf. "Albion"). The story is told of two different kings, but may refer to only one event, since it was not uncommon for the deeds or adventures of one person to be borrowed by the storytellers for embellishing the record of another.

The raids brought Irish leaders into close, if hostile, contact with the Roman Empire, and enriched them with booty which included large numbers of slaves. We know very little of the organization of Irish society before this date, except that it was obviously stratified. It may well have taken different forms in different parts of the country. The sagas such as *Táin Bó Cualgne* which depict the warfare of an "heroic age" are persuasively archaic in their character and in the society they depict, although in the forms in which they have come down to us they are works of the seventh century and later. They depict warrior kings, queens and nobles, quarreling over points of honour. These were lords of cattle and horses, impelled and often doomed by fate, extravagant in their prowess and in their boasting of it. The descriptions of Celtic society in Central Europe given by Posidonius and other ancient writers long before the Roman conquests, would fit very well the world depicted in the *Táin*. Caution is necessary, however. The archaeological evidence shows some similarities between the Irish material of the beginning of the Christian Era and material which is representative of the Continental Celts from about the fifth century BC to the Roman conquest of the first century; but there are many differences too; and the evidence in Ireland for the "La Tène" culture of the late Celtic world (an archaeological term, as "Celtic" is a linguistic one) is curiously aberrant and erratic. It is not impossible that the sagas, perhaps through several recompositions before they were first commited to writing, preserve stories and social details which came to Ireland from elsewhere. Oral literature—before the act of writing it down interferes with it—is notoriously conservative and tenacious of ancient forms.

Two focal areas in Ireland have produced a range of archaeological material which is reminiscent of pre-Roman Celtic Gaul and Britain. One area is in the north-east—in the country of the Ulaid of early historic (and, we can be certain, of late prehistoric) times. The other is around, but mainly west of, the upper Shannon, in the heartland of the "Connachta" of early

history. The name "Connachta" almost certainly originates sometime in
the fifth century or a little later, but this culture, dominated by a warlike
nobility, dates from much earlier. The warrior aristocracy, both in north-
east Ireland and in the upper Shannon area, can be inferred from the costly
objects of militaristic display—including elaborately decorated sword
scabbards and horse-bits for paired-draught (i.e., chariot) animals, among
other items, that have been found in the two regions. Elsewhere in Ireland,
particularly in the southern half of the island, the known La Tène material
is scarcer and humbler in its character. This includes the territory of the
Dési of the south coast, who not only raided but ultimately colonized parts
of western Britain—on the Welsh coasts and in Cornwall.

But it is in the two focal districts in the northern half that we find the
distinctive flashy equipment of an "heroic age" (a term developed by students
of literature to the benefit of students of early history). There are also
religious or cult monuments—bearing some resemblance to those known
from the territories of the Continental Celts—in a zone extending from
the Upper Shannon through the drumlin hills and winding lakes of the
Ulster borderlands. This zone is the setting for *Táin Bó Cualgne*, and also
for many other saga-tales of the Ulster heroes and their enemies—tales
which became for early historic Ireland a text like that of Homer for the
ancient Hellenes. They reinforced the cultural unity of the island through
an emphasis on the exploits of an atypical and localized élite of reavers,
whose deeds were presented as a *speculum regale* to the farmers and graziers
of early medieval Ireland—a reassurance of early "greatness", such as
national identity seems to have required even in those distant times.

In spite of the production of brilliantly wrought objects to proclaim the
glory of the leaders of some war-bands around the time of Christ, Ireland
entered a kind of "dark age" between the centuries in which Rome was
extending its dominion over southern and western Europe, and the
period, at the end of this Roman dominance, in which Christianity came
to the island. The Irish archaeological evidence for the first few centuries
of the Christian Era, and for the previous few ("BC") centuries, is thin. It
gives the impression, on the whole, of an isolated and regressive culture,
in which, quite possibly, population declined. There appears to have been
a deterioration of climate, which may have influenced this. It may be that
the localized brilliance in arts and crafts (catering for a barbarian aristocracy)
round about the time of Christ, is due to war-bands from Britain and
Gaul, who imposed themselves in those areas and came to dominance
over the local indigenous populations. At any rate, it is in the same zone
which produced brilliant La Tène metalworking and stone-carving that a
revival of such virtuosity begins—perhaps as early as the fourth century.

What gave rise to this revival? Probably a sudden access of wealth due
to the plunder and rapine of Roman Britain. The evidence for this is direct

(both in archaeological material and in the meagre Roman documentary references to Ireland), and indirect (in the numerous stories in the "historical" sagas which tell of Irish kings raiding overseas).

This is what constitutes an "heroic age": that a people subsisting stably on pasture and tillage, with a simple system of customary law and an already established social hierarchy, is provided with an opportunity to prey on a rich, highly organized and prestigious civilization. And in the heroic age of the fourth and fifth centuries in Ireland, chieftains who could organize well equipped raiding bands, arrange shipping, and conduct the necessary negotiations with other likeminded leaders (whether Irish or Pictish), were able to enrich themselves with loot and slaves.

In this kind of primitive enterprise, however, the leader of the war-bands is required to distribute the plunder lavishly among his followers, who are bound to him by an obligation of high honour founded on the expectation of rich reward. A rising expectation is created, of a continuous dole of booty—but the more successful the raiding enterprise, the more the source of supply is bound to diminish rapidly. The predatory energy and prowess are then likely to be turned on near neighbours. Heroic ages are destabilizing to the comparatively simple rural societies from which they spring. Our evidence for Ireland may be very skimpy, but there is somewhat more information available on the various combinations of tribes from Central and Eastern Europe (mostly Germans) who entered the Western Empire at this time. When tribes formed alliances and confederations for the purpose either of plunder or of land-winning, they tended, for practical reasons, to throw up supreme leaders who became "kings" over random conglomerations of peoples who had previously arranged their affairs through conferences of tribal elders in stable societies. War, and the perils of expeditions or migrations into hostile and unknown country, provided an impetus for the exaltation of the "one, true" leader of a heterogeneous alliance.

So, a feature of an "heroic age" is the emergence of "kings", who are primarily captains in war, leaders perhaps of whole migrating peoples winning new settlement land by the sword. When the migrations brought them across the frontiers of the Roman Empire, the leaders and their companions in arms commonly aspired to the prestige and trappings of high Roman office.

In Ireland another kind of kingship had probably existed for centuries. There are clear indications of a deep-rooted tradition in which the local "king" was a sacral person, controlled by grievous tabus, acting as a kind of lightning-conductor to protect a pastoral and agricultural people against the arbitrary forces of nature, such as drought, storm, famine, lightning and disease, imagined as malevolent interventions by divinities or otherworld beings. The king was bound to the land and territory of his people and, in a common pattern, was the mate of the goddess of place, who conferred sovranty on him. For example, the king of Tara—apparently since very early times a place of special sanctity and otherworldly force—seems to have been mate of the goddess Medb Lethderg, whose name Medb means something like "intoxication". Like her kind in general she "took a different lover every night" (i.e., the kings came and went; their kingdom, which was truly hers, went on forever). The inauguration of the king of Tara was a symbolic mating (*feis*) with the goddess. Exactly what form this took we don't know, but in prehistoric times the mating may have been something more than symbolic. At the end of the twelfth century, Gerald of Wales picked up a story in Ireland about the inauguration of the king of Cenél gConaill, in the north, which (on the analogy of other ancient Indo-European traditions) may embody a genuine tradition of a pre-Christian rite. He reports that at an assembly of the people a white mare was brought to the chosen man, who mated publicly with the animal, which was then killed, cut up and boiled. All ate the mare's flesh and the new king bathed in the broth and drank it. Prehistoric kingship, in other words, was intimately connected with pagan religious belief and custom and must in many respects have been extremely repugnant to the Christians whose numbers, plainly, were growing by about AD 400.

In the later writings, mostly penned by Christian clerics, we have little more than glimpses of this priestly kingship, with its rituals intimately associated with the propitiation of natural forces. We have reasonably abundant (although late) evidence for the presence in Ireland of special classes of sacral people corresponding to the bards, *vates* and druids described in Continental and British Celtic societies. The *filid*, or poets, were men of learning and long training and were possessed of supernatural powers. The *fáith*, corresponding to the *vates*, appears to have been a kind of soothsayer, while the *druí* (druid) had access to arcane knowledge and seems, in common belief, to have had some control over both natural and extra-natural powers. They formed a part of the retinue of the sacral king, and should probably be regarded as the repository of all tribal wisdom and knowledge. Their order was not exclusively male.

The correspondences to Gaulish and British institutions before the advent of the Romans are striking, but Irish society at this much later date had its own distinctive complexity, almost certainly including many pre-Celtic elements. There are numerous indications (not least in the Saints' Lives) of shamanistic practices and beliefs, which are not particularly Celtic. As to worship; there was a pantheon of gods and goddesses, but we have little evidence of formal worship and know nothing for certain of temples—although there were apparently holy places, perhaps including sacred groves. Caesar in his conquest of Gaul in the first century BC encountered druids. He also discusses the Gaulish pantheon, which he equates with the Roman, identifying Gaulish counterparts of the Roman divinities. The god most widely worshipped, he tells us, was "Mercury", by which he means Lug, whose shrine at the confluence of the Rhone and the Saone—"Lugdunum" (*Lyon*)—was the chief centre of religious assembly in Gaul. Lug was also the central male figure in the Irish pantheon; but it is fairly clear that, whatever about Gaulish gods, the Irish pantheon could not usefully be described in terms borrowed from the Roman. While there was some element of specialisation of function (war, fertility, etc.), most of the divinities, unlike the Roman gods, appear to have presided over a great many areas of life. Marie-Louise Sjoestedt, in her short but penetrating esssay on Celtic mythology, discerns a "male principle of society to which is opposed a female principle of nature, or rather . . . social forces of male character opposed by natural forces of female character".[1] Goddesses appear in every part of Ireland as spirits of place—whole territories, or hill-tops, rivers and springs—and as divinities of natural forces of motherhood, fertility, growth and destruction. They were often triple in character. War goddesses, in the form of crows or ravens, presided over the battlefield. The male divinities were warriors, craftsmen, magicians, seers, and nurturers, with, in crucial figures such as the Dagda (the "good god"), an emphasis on feasting and consumption generally. But there is little evidence for any central organizing principle in the complexities of the pantheon; it is rather as if the pagan Irish lived and breathed with one foot in this world and one foot in the otherworld: the two worlds interpenetrated. Most of what we can guess about pre-Christian Ireland suggests a tissue of magical practices and rituals, the observation of omens, the use of spells and incantatory formulas and the avoidance of unlucky actions. Christian teaching had to find a way through a labyrinth of fear, superstitious observance and worship (ultimately of the elements of nature)—which included some form of sun worship. The first preachers of the Gospel show a particular concern to emphasize God's power over the sun, the sky, the wind and all such elemental forces. It is not surprising that often in popular belief Christian teaching was overwhelmed by the pagan tradition, or that in the storytelling the very missionaries themselves disappear beneath a web of old anecdotes originally told about the local divinities who had preceded them.

It is probably the plundering expeditions to Roman Britain—which we know were in process from the middle of the fourth century onwards—that gave rise to the great movements of change which were to transform the old polity of late prehistoric Ireland in the course of the fifth century. In the older dispensation there appear to have been several large entities, which we might describe as tribal nations, recognized as having distinct identities and somewhat different ethnic histories. In the north was the territory of the Ulaid, with its southern boundary (according to later tradition) marked in the west by the river Drowes (separating the modern counties Leitrim and Donegal) and in the east by the river Boyne. This took its name from

Ireland in the early fifth century

its dominant people, the Ulaid (themselves seemingly a branch or derivative of an ancient people called Érainn or Iverni), whose central area in later times was in what is now Co. Down, where they became known as Dál Fiatach. Other important peoples in the north included the Cruthin (later Dál nAraide) in Co. Antrim, and the Reti (Dál Riata) in north Antrim. The name "Cruthin" was also given by the Irish to the Picts of Scotland and is a form of the ancient name "Pretani". West of the Shannon was the territory referred to in early writings as "the Fifth of Ól nÉcmacht", inhabited by peoples, such as the Domnainn (of north-west Mayo), of Laginian connections. South of the Shannon, and south of the zone of bogs and uplands that extends from Lough Derg to Waterford Harbour, was the Fifth of Muma, the territory particularly associated with the ancient Érainn. The eastern Fifth was that of the Lagin, whose territory included all the land east of the Barrow, the south midlands across to the Shannon, and a large part of the midland plains. The four major territories, corresponding to north, south, east and west, were long treated mythically and mystically, and assigned distinct properties and qualities—war in the north, music in the south, prosperity in the east, learning in the west, and so on—and, as Alwyn and Brinley Rees have persuasively argued, there was a fifth element, a centre, to complete this cosmic mandala.[2] The centre — *Mide*—included Uisnech (*Usnagh, Co. Westmeath*), the "navel of Ireland", where the four provinces were thought to meet.

In trying to reconstruct what was happening to this system round about AD 400, we walk on shifting sands, for the records made some centuries after the events (all we possess) are full of the justifications of later politics and of corresponding unhistorical revisionism. But it is possible to make a fairly confident guess that the fundamental changes which were to produce the secular polity of the early Christian centuries (from the sixth century AD to the eleventh) were set in train by wars of conquest which greatly modified the size, shape and character of the old tribal nations, and which were conducted by warlike groups whose own sagas and legendary histories boast of expeditions and exploits abroad—raids on the Roman world. The changes involved the shattering of the old "fifth" of the Ulaid; the drastic reduction of the territory of the Lagin, whose hostility and resistance to the new order were to be sustained for centuries and to be of some importance in the introduction of new external forces into Ireland in the eleventh and twelfth centuries; the reconstruction of the western fifth ("Connacht" from now on); and the firm establishment of the most successful (until the tenth century) of the new polities—a definitively Christian overlordship of Munster, whose priestly kings were free from the stigma of heathenism. In the process, two symbolic centres, one of ancient pagan sanctity and importance, one newly established under the aegis and with the prestige of Christianity —Tara and Cashel—came to be focal for the concept of a kingship of all Ireland.

There were different developments in the two corresponding halves of Ireland, north of the midlands and south of the midlands. The difference was of sufficient historical significance to give rise to the concept—very powerful and influential in Irish medieval political thought—of "Leth Moga" and "Leth Cuinn"—the "half of Mug" and the "half of Conn", or the "half of the slave" and the "half of the head (i.e. 'chief')", or, to add what was possibly an early medieval underlying meaning, the Christian half of the *Hibernii* and the pagan half of the *Scotti*.

The Conn in question here is Conn Cétchathach, "Conn of the Hundred Battles", the mythical ancestor of the various dynasties who ruled in early historic times, with their symbolic centres both at Tara and at Cruachu. The "Connachta" were "the descendants of Conn": the genealogists of later times devised the pedigree by which Eochu Mugmedón was the son of Muiredach Tírech, son of Fiachu Sraibtine, son of Cairbre Lifechair, son of Cormac, son of Art, son of Conn Cétchathach. Eochu Mugmedón in turn was said to have been the father of Fiachra, Brión, Ailill, Fergus and Niall Noígiallach. These five were all, by their ancestry, "Connachta"; but this name in later times was confined to the descendants of Fiachra, Brión and Ailill, who had conquered lands west of the Shannon, while the descendants of Niall Noígiallach, who conquered lands in Ulster and the midlands, were designated "Uí Néill". So, in historic times, "Connachta" became the name of the western province. However, David Sproule has pointed out that Conn Cétchathach was probably invented to explain the name "Connachta", which, he says, cannot "originally have meant 'the descendants of Conn': it may have meant 'headship' or 'supremacy' from *cond* or *conn* 'head'."[3]

For the northern half of Ireland the history of the fifth-century conquests which altered the socio-political pattern of the country has been deeply obscured by the politically inspired revisions of the period from which our earliest written accounts come. However, working backwards from the newly founded kingdoms and chiefdoms of that time, it is possible to establish roughly the centre from which the expansionist (or, by definition, centrifugal) conquering forces emanated. The centre is Cruachu, in north Co. Roscommon. T.F. O'Rahilly, in his book, *Early Irish History and Mythology*, argued that the *Táin*, which depicted warfare between the Connachta and the Ulaid before the dawn of history, had got the source of the attack on Ulster wrong, because, when the story came to be written down, "Connachta" was confined to the people west of the Shannon, whereas earlier, when the tale was first composed, the "descendants of Conn" included the rulers of Tara. The *Táin*, he held, really derived from warfare between the kings of Tara and the kings of Emain in Ulster. This insight may well be true of the basic myth underlying the *Táin*—a conflict between two divine bulls, connected with the Tara resident goddess Medb Lethderg— but it seems that the storytellers rightly represented it as a conflict between Cruachu and Emain.

The greatest of the conquests took over most of the northern Fifth of the Ulaid. According to the official version of the later dynasty of the Uí Néill, the "three Collas", three sons of Eochu Domlén, brother of Fiachu Sraibtine, king of Ireland, killed their uncle Fiachu but were pardoned by his son Muiredach Tírech who sent them to conquer the Ulaid. They enlisted the help of the men of Ól nÉcmacht, who won six battles at Carn Achaid Lethdeirg in Fernmag (*Co. Leitrim*); in a seventh battle the three Collas finally defeated the Ulaid. The Ulaid were driven beyond Glenn Rige (*the Newry river, in Co. Down*) and the territory they lost became the new overlordship of Airgialla, which was, in early historic times, tributary to the Uí Néill. The royal and sacral centre of the Ulaid, Emain, was destroyed, and the site was subsequently in Airgialla territory. Other accounts tell how two sons of Niall, Conall and Eógan, conquered the territory which is now Co. Donegal. Meanwhile, according to the tales, other sons of Eochu

Mugmedón (Niall's father) were conquering south-westward, westward, north-westward and eastward from Cruachu. Tara, at some time in this vague and legendary period, came into the hands of the same family. Niall held it, and according to the pseudo-history, after the late fifth century the Cruachu dynasties were cut out from it and from the midlands, and all the later kings of Tara were descendants of Niall—Uí Néill.

The record, as we have it from later centuries, is a mixture of legend and propaganda. The chronology shifts in different versions of the tales. The destruction of Emain floats between the late third century and the middle of the fifth, and the "three Collas" are contemporaries of Niall's grandfather or contemporaries of Niall himself. O'Rahilly argued that they were in fact Niall's three sons. That may be. At any rate their name, or description, "Collas", related again to the word *cond* ("head"), may well be another version of "Connachta". And perhaps this is another way of saying "Scotti", if that term represents the Irish word *scot*, meaning "point", "apex", "flower". "Heads rule OK": the jargon of modern street gangs may well serve to represent the message of ancient barbarian war-bands. What we are being told is that newly emerging warlike groups conquered large parts of the north, the west and the midlands, claimed close relationship with one another, and set up tribute-claiming dynastic chiefdoms which soon carved out separate spheres of influence among several lineages which asserted a common descent from the shadowy Eochu Mugmedón (Eochu, "master of slaves") and from the much more tenuous (fictitious rather than mythical) Conn of the Hundred Battles.

The expansion of the Uí Néill towards the midlands brought them into conflict with the Lagin, who largely controlled that territory, and the annals report a long series of battles with the Lagin until finally—in 516 according to the Annals of Ulster—the Lagin lost "the plain of Mide" (*chiefly in Co. Westmeath*) and ultimately were driven back beyond the Barrow. In the meantime that branch of the "Connachta" to whom the name had been restricted and who held Cruachu, had been excluded since the battle of Ocha (in 482, according to the Annals of Ulster) from the kingship of Tara, which thereafter was reserved for the Uí Néill—the dynastic groups who claimed descent from Niall Noígiallach. The Uí Néill held western Ulster as their own and branches of them were established in the midlands, from the Shannon to the sea, across the northern part of the modern province of Leinster. The warfare which established the rule of this lineage appears to have continued at intervals throughout the fifth century.

Meanwhile in the south another dynastic grouping overthrew the old order and emerged to power in circumstances which are even more obscure. The compilers of the pseudo-annals for the fifth century had virtually no interest in Munster, and the sagas and tales are too removed from reality to tell us what was happening. There is solid archaeological evidence that peoples of the far south were establishing colonies across the channel in western Britain. Theirs is the country with by far the greatest concentration of ogham stones—funerary or memorial monuments: standing stones with brief epigraphic inscriptions in a kind of cipher based on the Roman alphabet giving (in Irish) the name and ancestry (sometimes divine) of the man being commemorated. Ogham stones, with inscriptions in Irish (often with a Latin version as well) are also numerous in the colonies in Wales. The densest distribution of these monuments in Ireland is in east Cork and Co. Waterford, the territory of the people known (later) as "Dési". The Dési, according to the later historical expositions, were fighting people employed and granted settlement lands by the Eóganacht dynasties of Munster after they had been expelled from the country round Tara. The Tara origin may be rejected. That the Dési were warrior people serving the Eóganachta seems certain. Who the Eóganachta were is another matter. They seem to have been a widely dispersed group of dynastic families, whose relationship through a common descent may well be fictitious. They claimed as common ancestor one Eógan Már. But their group name, "Eóganachta", according to Sproule, is a copy of "Connachta", and Eógan, like Conn, is an invention to explain the name. Their takeover of Munster was aided by the warlike Dési, according to the legends, but they gained the province not by force but by marrying the daughters of the Érainn. What seems likely is that there is some truth in the persistent tradition of the migration of the Dési: that they were an alliance of war-bands who learned the trade of war and enriched themslves in Roman Britain; that they won rich land in Ireland, driving a wedge into the fat river valleys in the border country between ancient Munster and ancient Leinster. Their name means "vassals" and, along with the Múscraige (who like themselves were descended from tribes of the ancient Érainn), they seem to have played a part in the south of Ireland similar to that played by the Airgialla in the north in bringing about a drastic reshaping of the old tribal nation into a dynastically ruled province of chiefdoms hierarchically arranged in a pyramid of overlordships within which the process of state creation soon began. The warfare by which this was accomplished appears to have occurred chiefly in the late fifth and early sixth centuries.

In the east, the Lagin, while they ultimately lost such control as they had exercised over the midlands, yet held a large part of their "fifth"; but there was much warfare between rulers of the north and the south within Leinster, as well as warfare they conducted against the Uí Néill and the warfare against Munster. At the battle of Cenn Losnada (*Kellistown, Co. Carlow*) in 491, the northern Lagin defeated and killed Óengus son of Nad Froich, the Eóganacht king of Cashel who is consistently associated in all the tales with the organization of Christianity in Munster.

The model presented here suggests a radical transformation of Irish society in two phases in the course of the fifth century. In the first phase (extending back into the middle of the fourth century) some leaders organized tribal alliances for the purpose of plundering Roman provinces. In the process they acquired wealth, transformed tribal levies into formidable fighting forces, and brought large numbers of slaves—mostly British—back to Ireland. Many of these would have been Christians, so that Christian communities of some size must have existed by the beginning of the fifth century, especially in those areas from which the more sustained expeditions emanated. Those areas would include east Ulster, the country around Cruachu, parts of Leinster, and the south coast of Munster. The first Christian bishops came to minister to those communities, bringing with them the prestige of Rome (bishops at the time were largely drawn from the Roman aristocracy, gentry and official classes). In the second phase of warfare—which was probably mainly from about the middle of the fifth century to the early decades of the sixth—the war leaders, deprived of Roman plunder, carried out conquests in Ireland and replaced the tribal organization of society by a dynastic organization. A tribe may be defined for this purpose as a kind of greatly extended family, a primary and autonomous unit of society all of whose members, high and low, thought themselves to be derived from a common ancestry. This was now rapidly replaced by a system of chiefdoms, which in turn were to develop, in a few centuries, into a system of larger royal states. The transformation was in its most violent phase just as the Christian Church was being organized. And before that organization was complete, the church system itself underwent radical change with the triumph of monasticism.

The tribal chiefs brought much from Rome besides mere loot. They may originally have chopped up ornate Roman dinner services merely for the silver of which they were made, indifferent to the repoussé Cupids, Bacchae, vines and peacocks with which they were adorned; but soon, in their own way, they learned to emulate Roman fashions. They took over the gap-ring bronze pins with which Romans (or German soldiers of the Roman armies) of the military provinces fastened their cloaks, and their craftsmen transformed these into the penannular brooches which the Irish upper orders began to wear. They adapted, similarly without exact copying, the glittering heavy belt buckles, the straps and harness, the polychrome of semi-Roman, semi-barbarian, fashion. Craftsmen as well as scholars appear to have made their way to Ireland by the end of the fifth century, fleeing from the many disasters afflicting northern Gaul, and the ruling groups in Ireland were already beginning to develop a style and a confidence to which the Christian bishops and clerics contributed, besides their spiritual message (which possibly had its greatest appeal for the learned classes of pagan Ireland, who were—some of them—seeking truth), the intellectual order of a high civilization.

The new arrangements in Ireland, therefore, coming into being in the fifth century, might justifiably be described as "post-Roman". However, these arrangements, important and enduring though they were, were imposed on an ancient system, which was profoundly modified but by no means obliterated. For example, the new dynasts found it necessary to legitimize their rule by possessing the sacred hilltops which had long been the holy places of the prehistoric tribal nations, as well as the assembly places of the tribes where, at a great gathering—the *óenach*—immemorial rituals, including horse-races and games, were performed.

The hilltop sites vary, but most are marked by earthworks of different ages. Tara, a low ridge commanding remarkably extensive views across the midlands to the far mountain ranges of Leinster, Munster, Connacht and Ulster, is covered by a complex of earthworks two kilometres long, including Neolithic chambered tombs, Bronze Age burials and Iron Age raths. Its central feature is a large enclosure around the shallow summit which looks, at first glance, like the "hill-forts" or "oppida" which mark tribal centres in Britain, Gaul, parts of Celtic Germany, and elsewhere. An embankment combined with a fosse encircles a large area of the hilltop. But a second glance shows that this was not built to provide defence against any earthly power. The fosse is on the inside of the bank. It is a symbolic or ritual defensive work, protecting the outside world against the powerful mana within the enclosure. Its purpose is not military, but magical. (At the southern end of the ridge of Tara there is a "regular" hillfort.) We find similar magical enclosures on Emain Macha (*now Navan Fort, near Armagh*), the "capital" of the ancient Ulaid, and at Ailenn (*Knockaulin, near Kilcullen, Co. Kildare*), a royal site of the Lagin—in both cases enclosing other earthworks. Excavations at all three sites have revealed a great antiquity, going back everywhere at least to the Bronze Age, and evidence of (often extraordinary) ritual use. These were religious centres. They were also political centres. People lived at some of them some of them time, and sometimes built quite large enclosed homesteads; but they were not primarily dwelling places, and the many accounts of kingly forts and palaces in the sagas and tales derive more from literary models than from indigenous tradition about these places. Cruachu seems to lack the hillfort-like enclosure, but it has the most extensive of all the complexes of earthworks and—even without excavation—it can be seen to have been a very important place throughout a long prehistoric past. It is probable that there were one or two similar sacred centres in Munster (perhaps Carn Tigernaig in north Co. Cork was one of them), but Cashel, which the new "Eóganachta" of that province made their royal centre, appears to have been Christian from the beginning—and that beginning was probably in the late fifth century.

The Christian bishops who came into this world were not military conquerors. The Irish, already caught up in the most drastic internal change, accepted the new teaching on the whole without a sense of threat. When in due course the new Irish Christians sought to emulate the martyrs, they had to bear witness, not in blood, but in self-imposed deprivation, and they turned with enthusiasm to the ascetic renunciations of the monasticism of Egypt and Syria. At that point, however, they were no longer living in the fifth-century world of St Patrick in which all things bore the stamp of the civilization of ancient Rome.

FIVE

Gaulish and British Bishops in Ireland

Several passages in writings of the opening decades of the fifth centuy would suggest that the numbers of Christians in Ireland had increased in recent times—perhaps in the fourth century. Jerome, writing against Pelagianism, says that "even Britain, the province fertile in the breeding of tyrants, and the Irish peoples, and all the barbarian nations round to the very ocean, have come to know Moses and the prophets."[1] Augustine, in a work on the Psalms, says: "So it is that God's word has been preached not only on the Continent, but even in the islands which are set in the middle of the sea; even they are full of Christians, full of the servants of God."[2] And Augustine again, in a letter to Hesychius, in a longer passage, develops the theme of the preaching of the Gospel in the islands of the ocean, so that there are no lands, no islands, "where the Church is not".[3]

The passages date from the early fifth century. They are clearly founded on a prophetical topic, the theme of the fullness of time, when the word of God has finally reached the limits of the inhabited world. This is probably stimulated by the millenarian feelings aroused by the fall of Rome to the Goths in AD 410. But the rhetoric draws on the information that the Church is now founded on the oceanic islands, including Ireland. Patrick, in his Declaration many years later, shows an acute awareness of this prophetic theme.

That there were Christian communities in Ireland by the end of the fourth century is to be expected. Ireland had been in regular contact with the Roman Empire by way of trade, and, at least since the middle of the fourth century, Irish raiding bands had been repeatedly in the British provinces— probably sometimes for long periods. By the end of the century there were Irish settlements in western Britain (Pelagius may well have come from one of them). Christian cells, growing to Christian communities, are to be expected in the southern, eastern, and north-eastern coastal regions of Ireland—and probably along the upper Shannon where powerful warlords, raiding the Roman Empire, seem to have been established, as we have seen. There must have been many Christian slaves in the country, the booty of the numerous raids.[4]

What happened to Palladius after he came to Ireland is not known. The stories about him in the Irish documents are late and are best explained as speculations arising only after the Irish scholars came to learn of his mission through Prosper.[5] The absence of his name from the earliest sources is hard

Kileencormac, Co. Kildare
(probably Cell Fine, associated with Palladius)

to explain, even accepting the suggestions of O'Rahilly and Carney that, with the growth of the Patrick legend, episodes from the career of Palladius have been transferred to that saint. Such suggestions are particularly plausible with respect to those episodes in which Patrick is associated with St Germanus and Auxerre, since we know that, in fact, Palladius had those connections. That Palladius came to Leinster and founded churches there is a late but plausible legend.[6]

O'Rahilly discusses the interesting passage in the seventh-century Muirchú's Life of Patrick, in which Muirchú describes Patrick's activities previous to his coming to Ireland as a bishop, and he suggests that the passage "must go back ultimately to a written document obtained in Gaul, not later than the seventh century, by some Irish monk who had visited Auxerre and had had access to the church records there. The confusion which has already crept into Muirchú's account, such as the substitution of Amatorex for Amator, suggests that the document had been copied and re-copied before Muirchú's day." He suggests, most persuasively, that this document originally concerned, not Patrick, but Palladius.

The beginning of Muirchú's account of Patrick's life is based directly on the Declaration. But, after he recounts Patrick's escape from captivity in Ireland and his return to Britain, then, as O'Rahilly points out, "The remainder of Muirchú's account has a very different origin."[7] Muirchú tells us that Patrick left Britain to go to Rome before his Irish mission (a standard hagiographical motif). In Gaul, on the way, he met Germanus, and stayed thirty or forty years as his disciple. Then, after a vision in which Victoricus appeared to him with the Irish appeal for his return to Ireland (here Muirchú, as storyteller, has woven in another strand from the Declaration), he commenced his journey to Ireland, accompanied by a priest, Segitius, whom Germanus had sent with him as a witness. According to this story, Palladius had recently been sent by Pope Celestine to convert Ireland; but now news reached Patrick that Palladius had abandoned his mission and had died "in the lands of the Britons". Patrick now replaced Palladius. He visited a holy bishop, Amatorex, who lived not far away, and was consecrated bishop by him, inferior orders being conferred the same day on Auxilius and Iserninus.[8]

If we assume, with O'Rahilly and others, that we have here a synthesis produced by Muirchú (from the hypothetical and poorly transmitted Continental document; from Patrick's Declaration; from Irish stories attempting to explain away Palladius; and from traditions of other bishops working in Ireland) we can probably extract from it something of the original Continental document—which, however, concerned the Palladian rather than the Patrician mission.

Names and dates are garbled in Muirchú. "Amatorex" is almost certainly Amator, who was Germanus's predecessor as bishop of Auxerre and who was long dead at the date implied. Amator, however, could well have conferred diaconal orders on Palladius (perhaps on Auxilius and Iserninus too) and this—possibly through misreading—could provide the basis for the story that he consecrated Patrick/Palladius bishop.

Two of the personal names here mentioned by Muirchú occur in a south Gaulish context at an appropriate date. A priest, Segetius, attended with Bishop Constantius of Carpentras at the council of Orange in 441.[9] A deacon, Auxilius, attended that council, and also attended, with Bishop Claudius of Vienne, at the council of Vaison-la-Romaine in 442.[10] According to the Irish annals, Auxilius came to Ireland as a bishop in 439; but the dates in the fifth-century annals are artificial—constructs of a much later period when the annalistic synthesists were trying to stretch their evidence back to accommodate the spurious date of 432 for Patrick's arrival.

It is probable that the two attendants at the councils are the persons mentioned by Muirchú. The name Iserninus, however, is not found in the Continental records. Nor do we find any version of the names stated by Muirchú to be those of Palladius's disciples, who returned, according to him, after Palladius's death to Ebmoria—Augustine and Benedict. Bieler, following Grosjean, identifies Ebmoria as Eburobrica (Avrolles),[11] but the place was more probably Ebrodunesis (Edredunum, Erensis civitas)—Embrun.

As for Palladius, the name is common in the fourth and fifth centuries. Indeed, in the year 431, when Palladius was sent to the Irish as their first bishop, another bishop named Palladius (of Hellespontus) was attending the council of Ephesus.[12] However, twenty years later, a Palladius of no known diocese, was one of forty-three bishops who associated themselves with Ravennius, bishop of Arles, in exchanges of correspondence with Pope Leo the Great in 451–452.[13] It is within the bounds of possibility that this is the Palladius who was the first bishop in Ireland, assuming that for some reason he returned to Gaul.

Several other names of bishops occur plausibly in later accounts of this early period. Secundinus, Auxilius and Iserninus appear to have been bishops active in Ireland in the fifth century. Their churches were in the east midlands: Dunshaughlin (*Domnach Sechnaill*, Secundinus's church); Killassy or Killashee (*Cell Usailli*, Auxilius's church); Kilcullen (*Cell Chuilind*, attributed to Iserninus and also to one Mac Tail); Aghade (*Ath Fithboth*), also attributed to Iserninus. These occupy sites that command views of ancient (usually hilltop) places associated with pagan kingship. Dunshaughlin looks across at Tara, Killashee at Naas, Kilcullen at Dun Ailinne. Taken in conjunction with other such placings of churches, as, for example, at Armagh (which commands a view of the neighbouring hill of Emhain Macha) or Baslick (Sacellus's church of *Basilica Sanctorum*, which similarly looks across at Cruachu), this suggests deliberate policy. It also reinforces the tradition that makes Secundinus, Auxilius and Iserninus founders of the church in Ireland. The pagan hilltops were not primarily dwelling places: they were intimately associated with pagan ritual and pagan kingship. The Christian sitings must have been challenges.

The annals, confected long after the fifth century, portray Secundinus, Auxilius and Iserninus as a group—associated with St Patrick. So do other materials prepared (at least in the forms in which we now have them) equally long after the event.

St Secundinus has been discussed at length by James Carney.[14] The annals and other texts state that he died at an early date. He and Auxilius and Iserninus were sent, according to the annals, to "help Patrick", in 439. But the late texts drag Patrick's name into association with practically every fifth-century figure of note. The Annals of Inisfallen add to the 439 entry the revealing example of protesting too much and tell us that these bishops did not hold the Apostolate, but Patrick alone. The death of Secundinus is recorded for 447–448. In the late Life of St Declan a story tells how Declan, hastening to meet Patrick, was injured. Ailbe and Secundinus called Patrick, who cured him. In this passage Secundinus is described as a disciple of Patrick, a man of great wisdom and sanctity, who was the first bishop to be buried in Ireland.[15] There were efforts to associate his name very closely with that of Patrick. To him was attributed the hymn "*Audite omnes*", in praise of Patrick, said to have been sung by angels at Dunshaughlin when Patrick visited Secundinus. But this hymn has been shown to be of much later date.[16] The name of Secundinus may have appeared immediately after that of Patrick in the Armagh diptychs[17] (on which the names of those to be prayed for in church were recorded). And some of the decrees in the Book of the Angel copied into the Book of Armagh—an important statement of Armagh territorial and other claims— purported to have been enacted by Auxilius, Patrick, Secundinus and Benignus.

The episode from the Life of Declan already noted is interesting because it associates Secundinus with Declan and Ailbe, two figures belonging to the group which appears in the hagiographical literature as "pre-Patrician".[18] And pre-Patrician status is implied in an episode in the seventh-century Tírechán's narrative, in which the motif of the elder precursor seated under a tree of paradise occurs: Patrick went to the well of Mucno (*Mucnagh, Co. Longford*) and founded a church called *Senes*. "And Secund-inus was there under an elm with rich foliage . . .".[19]

Two stories link Patrick with Fiacc of Slebte (*Sleaty, Co. Laois*), a figure associated with the propagation of the Patrick and Armagh cult.[20] Another

Sleaty

legend makes Secundinus, Nachtan and Usaille (Auxilius) children of St Patrick's sister Lupait (otherwise Darerca, otherwise Liamhain) and of her husband, the Lombard Restitutus, from whom they are known as "moccu Baird".[21] This is a familiar hagiographical device to register a compact between churches.

Auxilus and Iserninus are more closely grouped together in the meagre references. Patrick, Auxilius and Iserninus are said to have issued the decrees that came to be known as those of the "First Synod of St Patrick".[22] Muirchú's Life tells us, as we have seen, that Patrick was consecrated by Bishop Amatorex in Gaul and that Auxilius and Iserninus were ordained to lower grades the same day—an obvious attempt to rank them below Patrick in the Irish apostolate. Tírechán tells us that Patrick went out to the plain of Liffe and established a church there, and ordained his pupil Auxilius as exorcist, with Esserninus and Mac Tail in Cell Cuilinn.[23] This is a re-telling, with different locality, of the conferring of orders of lower grade on Patrick's colleagues.

A more significant unfavourable contrast between Iserninus and Patrick is found in the additional notes in the Book of Armagh, in the story of how Iserninus at first refused to come to Ireland as commanded by Germanus, but then was forced there by the wind, and founded churches in Leinster which, however, were subordinate to Patrick.[24]

There is a certain consistency in these wisps and fragments. The propagators of the Patrick legend and supporters of the Armagh primacy in the seventh and eighth centuries are coping with unwelcome traces of other important fifth-century bishops in the record. They are concerned to introduce Patrick's primacy, retrospectively. But they have failed to erase the image of a church, apparently of Gaulish background, in the east midlands, whose bishops meet and function together from time to time. We can discern, very faintly, the outline of a fifth-century ecclesiastical province. The outline is obscured, not only by the pro-Patrician bias and intentions of the transmitters of the information, but also by their remoteness in time and mentality from the fifth century.

If we accept that in Secundinus, Auxilius and Iserninus we have representatives of an ecclesiastical province manned, in its early stages, from Gaul (presumably under the initial leadership of Palladius) we must ask whether, in the fifth-century concept, Ireland as a whole formed a single province, or whether there were provinces within Ireland. The question was discussed by James Carney, and he concluded that—although the papal letter of 640 appears to refer to Ireland as a province—the normal usage suggests that there were, ecclesiastically speaking, provinces within the country.[25] The matter is made more obscure by the changed circumstances and different usages of a century or so later, when most of our earliest accounts of these matters were written. At the beginning of the seventh century Pope Gregory gave Augustine (while he was still "the only bishop among the English") jurisdiction over the British bishops; then Gregory established two provinces in Britain (London and York, which became Canterbury and York because of the comparative failure of Augustine's mission). Augustine's successor Laurence attempted to exercise metropolitan jurisdiction in Ireland.[26] Within Ireland, by the seventh century, there may have been two provinces. The letter of the pope-elect John, of 640, addresses bishops, priests and abbots of the northern half of the country.[27] But the evidence is confusing. A careful reading of Cogitosus's Life of Brigid shows that in the text *provincia* is used with the sense of *tuath*—or, by extension, episcopal diocese—but a vague hegemony over "almost all" the Irish churches is claimed for Kildare. A generation later, Tírechán was to claim a similar vague hegemony for Armagh.

Since Ireland was outside the Roman Empire it provided no ready-made model for the framework of church organization, once that organization was extended to it by the consecration of Palladius. Nor are we very well informed about the internal, secular, territorial divisions. Mid-fifth-century Ireland may have presented a model for one, two, or four provinces for the territorial organization of the church. What we may well call "the Gaulish mission", on this model, was firmly located within the old country of the Lagin, but may well have extended westward across the Shannon into Mag Aí, around Cruachu.

We may note a few more names of supposed fifth-century bishops in the midlands and east that have come to us through the suspect medium of much later sources. Mel, founder of Ardagh in Longford (plausibly associated with St Patrick) is given an obit at 487 (Annals of Ulster). Mac Caille, probably a double of Mel, has his recorded two years later. Mac Caille is known only for giving the veil to Brigid at Croghan Hill on Offaly (or at Uisnech). The Brigidine stories are quite unhistorical: they belong less to hagiography than to mythology. But it should be noted that in some of the legendary material Brigid is associated with Ibar, who figures in the hagiographical tradition as one of the pre-Patrician saints. The death of Mac Cuilinn, bishop of Lusk, is recorded for 494/497. He is said to have been Cuinnidh, son of Cathmugh.[28] (Just possibly, there is a connection with Cell Chuilind, the church of Iserninus.)

The additional notes in the Book of Armagh show us another group of bishops on the borders of the Lagin.[29] They include Lommán of Trim on the Boyne (said in the Book of Armagh to have been founded twenty-five years earlier than Armagh itself); Munis of Forgnide among the Cuircni (*Forgney, Co. Longford*); Broccaid in Imbliuch Ech among the Ciarraige of Connacht (*Emlagh, Co. Roscommon*); Broccán in Brecmag among the Uí Doirthin (*Breaghy, Co. Longford*); Mugenóc in Cell Dumi Glinn in south Brega (*Kilglinn, Co. Meath*). These are said to have been Britons, not Gauls.[30]

We have several indications that the seventh-century compilers of these outlines had difficulty in asserting Patrick's primacy over the "bishops of Mag Aí"—that is, the bishops in the neighbourhood of the great Connacht centre of Cruachu. The text in the additions in the Book of Armagh telling how Patrick united this community under Armagh is a sweeping re-writing of history, and reminds us why so many of the fifth-century churches lapsed into obscurity—including for a while Armagh itself.[31] The political structures to which the fifth-century Church organization had initially accommodated were utterly transformed within a few generations, as the political map of Ireland was fundamentally redrawn. And the great organized European system from which Christianity had come to Ireland collapsed within the first generation or so of the effort.

Figure of an ecclesiastic,
Kileencormac, Co. Kildare
(Cell Fine, associated with Palladius)

SIX

Women Founders of Churches

St Patrick in his writings twice refers to "monks and virgins of Christ" among his converts. What does he mean by this? The circumstances of the fifth century in Ireland, when bishops were being appointed to Christian communities which must have been islands in a pagan sea, were hardly conducive to the establishment of such monasteries as we know of in later times. Patrick himself was clearly (at the time of which he wrote) an active and vigorous evangelist, converting whole pagan communities, and it may—just—have been possible for him to found small communities of monks or nuns. But we know of no monastic communities which go back to the fifth century. A possible exception is Kildare; but virtually all the famous monasteries we know of in early Ireland, either were founded later (usually considerably later) than AD 500, or were founded as bishops' churches and only became monastic establishments, governed by abbots, at some subsequent date. This applies, for example, to Armagh, to Emly, to Ardmore, to Sleaty.

But the monastic movement was already an active and powerful influence on the Western church as well as on the Eastern, by the early fifth century. St Ambrose had encouraged it. St Martin of Tours (whose Life had a wide circulation in Ireland) was a pioneer in the West both in monasticism and in evangelizing missions to the rural pagans. St Jerome not only greatly encouraged monasticism but devised rules of life for those who wished to withdraw from the world and live chaste lives dedicated to the salvation of their souls within Roman society. In particular he provided rules of life for well-to-do women who wished to withdraw within their own households. There are hints in St Patrick's writings of a somewhat similar approach to the spiritual direction of high-born women, in a barbarian society very different from the urban world of Ambrose, Jerome and Augustine. Yet he knew of that world, and thought of it as his own. It is plain from his words that he was conscious of, and valued, his Roman citizenship.

The Life of St Darerca printed here (there are other versions) would appear—if we prune away a comparatively small accrescence of folk miracle-tales and a few diplomatic insertions (such as the obligatory appearance of St Patrick in the story)—to give us a plausible outline of the career of a female founder of the period. She is represented as a pious woman directed by a (male) spiritual counsellor; first of all to lead a regulated life, under vows, in her own home; then to gather some kindred spirits around her; then to undergo a test, or trial, as an anchoress; then to become superior of a large community of nuns.

There are some parallels with the Life of St Brigid by Cogitosus (pp. 207–224.) This is the earliest Life of an Irish saint we possess, and it is possibly the first written—as Muirchú seems to tell us. The Life of Columba written by his successor Adomnán towards the end of the seventh century appears to quote from an earlier book on Columba written by Cumméne Ailbe, abbot of Iona from 657 to 669, which must have been close in date to Cogitosus's work. But it has not survived. Cogitosus, round the middle of the seventh century, tells us nothing that can give us reliable information about the founder of Kildare, whoever she was. What he has gathered together is a collection of folk tales, many of them not particularly Christian in form or content—probably retellings of old stories of pagan times. Aware of this to some extent, he links his little anecdotes with short commentaries, or "morals", in which what he is saying, each time, is that this or that extraordinary suspension of the laws of nature is due to the power of God working through St Brigid. Since many of the stories told about her are to be found in the Lives of the handful of other female saints who attracted the attention of the hagiographers, we are almost forced to conclude that these are stories told originally about the goddess, or goddesses, of whom the most widespread name is Brig[id], but who is known by different names in different localities.

"Brigid" the church foundress certainly existed. The nature and importance of Kildare for many centuries are indisputable testimony to the foundation (probably close to the year 500) of a major episcopal church under female governance. The Old Irish Life of St Brigid—which is not as old as that by Cogitosus and is not given here—retains a tradition that St Brigid, "by mistake", was herself consecrated a bishop. Cogitosus is careful to avoid this story, but his awareness of it is shown in his introductory section, where what he says, in effect, is that Brigid was bishop in all but name.

We know nothing for certain about her, therefore, although, along with Patrick and Columba, she was regarded as one of the three patrons of Ireland. Her foundation at Kildare, as is plain from Cogitosus's Life, was in later times a dual monastery (for men and women, who lived in separate but associated establishments) and was presided over by an abbess, who had a bishop as her coadjutor. Brigid is said to have lived in the late fifth and early sixth centuries. According to one tradition, she stemmed from a population group called *Fotharta*, apparently from a branch which occupied lands to the east of Brí

Fotharta
Faughart
Uí Eachach
Brí Éile?

Éile; that is, on the western edge of the Bog of Allen. Other legend has it that she was born in Faughart, Co. Louth, in the "Gap of the North", one of the chief strategic passes into Ulster. The similarity of the two names probably gave rise to a misreading at some time. Cogitosus (our earliest witness, for what that is worth—which is not much, in this kind of testimony) says that she was of the Uí Eachach, of whom there were several groups in the Louth, Armagh, Down area; that is, the country around Faughart.

In the stories she is associated with other saints, of whom, inevitably, St Patrick is one. But she is also connected with two of the so-called "pre-Patrician" saints of the south. One is Ibar, who founded a bishop's church on Becc Ériu in Wexford Harbour. The other is Ailbe of Emly. An Ibarus appears as the second name in the medieval lists of the bishops of Kildare. The name of Conláedh—said in the Life to have been her co-founder—does not appear first in the succession list, as might have been expected, but third.

She is said to have received the veil either at Uisnech (the navel of Ireland, a place with ancient mythological associations) or on Croghan Hill in Offaly (Brí Éile, another place of mythological significance) at the hands of the bishop Mac Caille or of bishop Mel of Ardagh. Mac Caille (whose name means "man of the veil") is a double of Mel.

The Life translated here was written in Latin, probably in Kildare, by a cleric of that place who calls himself Cogitosus. We get no sense from his work of the learning and discipline that are evident in the writings of Columbanus, about two generations earlier, or, for example, in the extant letter on the Easter question written by Cummian a generation or half a generation before Cogitosus's time. This is not unconnected with the genre in which Cogitosus wrote; for, by and large, Saints' Lives were popular writing and catered for the pilgrims to the monastic shrines: a form of promotional literature directed partly at early medieval tourists. They also served, however, and it was an important part of their function, as evidence for the rights, rents and dues of the churches and of the relationships in primacy and property between churches.

Cogitosus plainly had little or no real information on St Brigid, for whatever reason. His narrative consists of a string of little legendary anecdotes relating miracles performed by her during her life or after her death. Her true life was already forgotten when he wrote, but the wonder-tales (which had probably been in circulation long before her time) were remembered and re-told. And that is what we have in his account.

The Life of St Darerca from the Salamanca Codex, on the other hand—if we leave aside a few standard miracles of the type borrowed by the hagiographers from one Life to another—is a plausible account of the life of a monastic foundress of the beginning of the sixth century.

It may be reading too much into one name, but the statement that her father was called "Mocteus" suggests that in the original version of the

Life, or in whatever records, oral or written, the hagiographer drew upon, she was stated to be a convert, disciple, pupil or "fosterling" of St Mochta of Louth; and it is as certain as anything can be in this most obscure of periods that Mochta was a British disciple of Patrick. The introduction of St Patrick himself into Darerca's story may be discounted. Once the various churches founded throughout the country in the Apostolic age came to accept the primacy of Armagh (and, by the logic of hagiography, the consequent priority of Patrick) it became a standard assumption that the earliest Irish Christian founders of churches were Patrick's disciples.

St Ibar appears to have been in some sense St Patrick's main rival in posthumous claims to priority. (See the Life of Ailbe, pp. 227–243.) His connection with her must also be looked upon with some scepticism. But the other historical settings in the Life of Darerca are mutually consistent and plausible. And the account of how she came to govern a monastery of women is equally plausible: St Mochta (if it was he who was her spiritual guide) may well have been following—allowing for very different circumstances—the example of St Jerome. Of all the Saints' Lives, this is the one that seems to give the best—if very dim—glimpse of the Apostolic age, including in the comparison the work of Cogitosus, Muirchú and Tírechán.

There is an aspect of the early female foundations which is worth noticing. We have almost no good evidence of the existence of a male monastery before about 535–540. The early church organization was governed by bishops. This may be why there is the notion of a kind of ghost episcopacy of St Brigid (whose church at Kildare would seem to have been founded hardly much later than 500). But—even allowing for the remote possibility of an aberrant development at Kildare for a short period—female bishops could certainly not be accommodated by the Western church of that time. It may well be, then, that the great Irish monastic movement, which was to dominate the ecclesiastical history of the country from the seventh century through to the twelfth, was pioneered by communities of women from as early, perhaps, as the fifth century.

The records fail us here. The evidence for these female foundations in their earliest phase comes almost exclusively from hagiography—and this documentation, interesting in itself and for the light it sheds on the time and mind of its composers, is of very small value for understanding the period in which its heroes and heroines—the early church founders—lived. Irish hagiography is in the general pattern found in the early Church, with, of course, some local peculiarities arising from Irish culture of the early Middle Ages. The first accounts we have of Christian heroic virtue are the brief reports of the answers given by the martyrs to their interrogators during the persecutions of the Church, and of their bearing as they went to death. These are generally simple and convincing, and are often moving. Their most urgent function, probably, was to sustain the courage of those Christian communities to whom persecution had not yet come. This purpose—edification—was retained in the Saints' Lives which developed somewhat later as a form of Christian popular literature; but when the Irish began to create their own hagiography, other intentions governed the form to a large extent. So, the saint's Life became a kind of code, to exalt its hero or heroine in competition with others, to impress (and entertain) by marvels, to define the rights and claims of the church to which the saint (usually as founder) belonged and its relationship with other churches, and, sometimes, to extol the power and virtue of the saint's relics, held in the church shrines.

The collection of texts relating to St Patrick in the Book of Armagh is quite avowedly and explicitly intended to sustain the very extensive claims of the church of Armagh to jurisdiction and rents; and the widespread recognition of the primacy of Armagh by the eighth and ninth centuries required wholesale revision of the hagiographical tradition so that Patrick, Armagh's founder, could in some sense replace or supplant or be placed in a superior relationship to the various local founders of churches throughout the country. The accounts given by Muirchú and Tírechán— different as they are from each other in purpose, method and style—are somewhat distinct therefore from the later hagiography, not only because of their comparatively early date. The later work is represented here (apart from the Life of St Darerca) by Lives of three of the four tradionally "pre-Patrician" founders—all bishops. A Life of the fourth (St Ibar) does not survive, although there was one, and there are some extant fragments. St Patrick is introduced, as it were artificially, into all three, by formulas which allow the writers both to retain a claim to the independence of their saints from Patrick, and at the same time to acknowledge his precedence. In fact it is probably safe to assume that all the late accounts of St Patrick's activities in any part of the south are fictitious.

Yet this material contains some information, mostly in the background, about early centuries; although it is very difficult to tease out. The passing references to quite numerous female foundations in the early period are tantalizingly vague, but combine to indicate an aspect of the beginnings of Christianity in Ireland which has yet to receive adequate attention.

PART TWO

Extracts from Writings of the Fourth and Fifth Centuries

SEVEN

The Council of Arles, 314

Such records as survive of the meetings of bishops and other clerics in Gaul in the fourth and fifth centuries give us glimpses of the background from which at least some elements of the early Irish Church derived. Similar records do not survive from Britain, but Mansuetus,[1] "bishop of the Britons", attended the meeting of a comparatively small number of bishops from northern Gaul held at Tours in 461. This is a reminder of the troubled state of the times, for he was almost certainly the bishop of that large population from south-western Britain which had just conducted an organized mass migration to settle in north-western Gaul (since then named— from them—Brittany). The migration occurred because of the troubled state of Britain. Gaul was equally badly affected by the movements and depredations of barbarian peoples across and within the Roman frontiers, but both civil and ecclesiastical order seem to have been maintained fairly well in the south-east to the end of the century and records of a number of ecclesiastical meetings survive from that area. The selection provided below is intended to provide an outline of the organization of the Church in the region from which a full ecclesiastical system was first provided for the Irish.

The council of Arles was held, under the auspices of the Emperor Constantine, to deal with the dispute of Bishop Caecilianus of Carthage with the Donatists. The record as it has survived is defective. Some excerpts from what remains are given here. A smaller gathering of bishops had taken place in Rome in 313, but the Arles council is of special interest as having been the first fairly fully representative general meeting of the Church of the Latin Western part of the Empire to be held after the Edict of Milan. The meeting was convened to deal with a mainly African problem—the Donatist heresy—but the bishops used the occasion to regulate a number of other matters of concern—some of which continued to require legislation one or two centuries later, when the Church was being organized in Ireland. They also re-enacted, or confirmed, a number of resolutions passed at the council held in Elvira, in Spain, in the time of intermittent persecution, about AD 300. The list of clergy in attendance gives us a reasonable representation of the Western Church at the end of the persecutions. The names are given here showing the variant forms and spellings in the surviving copies of the records of the council.

[Letter to Silvester]

In the name of the eternal Lord, greetings to the most esteemed Pope Silvester . . .

Bound by mutual love, and by the unity of the Catholic Church, we have gathered in the city of Arles by the will of the most righteous Emperor; from where, most glorious Pope, we reverence and salute you as your merit well deserves . . .

We would have been overjoyed to have you, in your seniority, associated with our proceedings, passing judgment with us: and truly we believe the sentence would then have been more severe . . . .

Dearest brother, it seems that, besides the business for which we were summoned, we must deal with matters which came up for decision during our consultations. We have come together from a variety of provinces and the problems we think should be addressed are equally varied . . . .

[Canons sent to Sylvester]

1   Firstly, in the matter of observing the Lord's Easter: that you should write immediately to all, giving directions on this observance, so that it may be celebrated by us on the same day and at the same time throughout the whole world.

2   That ministers must remain in the places in which they have been ordained.

3   It was resolved that those who practise arms in peacetime [i.e., *gladiators*] should be excommunicated.

4   It was resolved that [*circus*] charioteers who are believers should be excommunicated so long as they continue to drive.

5   It was resolved that theatre people should be excommunicated, so long as they continue to perform . . .

9   Concerning the Africans—since they have their own special rule, and practise rebaptism—it was resolved that a person who renounces heresy to come to the Church, should be asked to show his creed by his sign. If they discover that he has been baptized in the Father, the Son and the Holy Spirit, then the imposition of hands will be sufficient for him to receive the Spirit; but if he does not answer with this Trinity, then he should be baptized . . . .

16   It was resolved that, as we know deacons to have offered [*the sacrifice of the Mass*] in many places, this must on no account happen . . . .

20   In the matter of those who undertake on their own the consecration of a bishop, it was resolved that no one should presume to do this. There should be seven other bishops taking part; or, if this is not possible, no number less than three should undertake to ordain . . . .

[Signatures]

The names of the bishops who gathered at the synod of Arles under Bishop Marinus.

The bishop Criscens [Chrispus, Cretus, Christus], the deacon Florus [Florentius], from the city of Syracuse in the province of Sicily.

The bishop Proterius [Protinus, Protenus], the deacons Agreppa [Agrepinus, Cyprianus, Agrippa] and Pinus [Agrepinus, Tutus], from the city of Capua in the province of Campania.

The bishop Pandus [Pardus], the deacon Criscens [Cressentius, Crescens, Criscens], from the city of Salapia in the province of Apulia.

The bishop Theodorus [Theudorus, Teudosus] and the deacon Agustun [Agathon, Agaton] from the city of Aquileia in the province of Dalmatia.

The priests Claudian [Claudius] and Thitus [Betus, Verus, Citus, Bitus], and the deacons Eugenius and Quiriacus [Chyriacus, Cyricus] from the City of Rome, sent by Bishop Sylvester.

The bishop Meroclis [Merocles] and the deacon Severus [Servus], from the city of Milan in the province of Italy.

The bishop Oresius [Horosius, Heresius] and the reader Nazareus [Nazoreus] from the city of Marseille in the province of Vienne.

The bishop Marinus [Marianus], the priest Salamas [Salmas, Silimas], and the deacons Nicasius {Nicacius, Niasius], Afer, Ursinus and Peter of the city of Arles, in the province of Vienne.

The bishop Verus and the exorcist Beflas [Beclus, Beclas] of the city of Vienne, of the province of the same name.

The bishop Dafenus [Dafinus, Danas, Damnas] and the exorcist Victor of the city of Vaison in the province of Vienne.

The priest Faustinus of the city of Orange in the above province.

The deacon Innocentius and the exorcist Agapitus [Agapius] of Nice.

The priest Romanus, the exorcist Victor, of the city of Apt.[2]

Also: Gaul.

The bishop Inbetausius [Imbitausius, Imptabiusius, Inbitausius] and the deacon Primigenius [Primogenius, Progenius, Nicetius] of the city of Reims.

The bishop Ausanius [Ibidanius, Avidianus, Avidanus, Avitanus] and the deacon Nicetius [Nicecius] of the city of Rouen.

The bishop Riticius [Reticius, Retius, Ruticius, Reticus], the priest Amandus [Amandinus], the deacon Felomasius [Flomatius, Flematius, Filomatius] of the city of Autun.

The bishop Vosius [Voceius, Vocitus, Voccius, Votius] and the exorcist Petulinus [Pytolinus, Pilatinus, Pitulinus, Bitulinus] of the city of Lyon.

The bishop Maternus and the deacon Macrinus [Magrinus] of the city of Cologne.

The deacon Genialis [Geniales] of the city of Gevaudan in the province of Aquitaine.

The bishop Orientalis [Orientales] and the deacon Flavius [Faustus, Flavus] of the city of Bordeaux.

The bishop Agrucius [Agraecius, Agricius, Agrecius] and the exorcist Felix of the city of Trier.

The bishop Mamertinus [Mamartinus] and the deacon Leontius [Leoncius] of the city of Eauze.

The bishop Eborius [Aeburius, Eburius, Euortius] of the city of York in the province of Britain.

The bishop Restitutus of the city of London in the above province.

The bishop Adelfius [Adelfus] of the city of Lincoln; also the priest Sacerdus [the bishop Sacerdos, the bishop Sacer] and the deacon Arminius [Menius].

The bishop Liberius and the deacon Florentius [Frominianus, Frondinus, Frontinus] of the city of Merida in the province of Spain.

The priest Sabinus [the bishop Sabinus, the priest Savinus] of the city of Beacia.

The priest Natalis [Natales] and the deacon Citerius [Ceterius, Citirius, Aetherius] of the city of Ossuna.

The priest Probatius [the bishop Probatius, the priest Provatius] and the deacon Castorius of the city of Tarragona.

The priest Clementius [Clemens, Lementius] and the exorcist Rufinus [Rofinus] of the city of Zaragoza.

The priest Getnesius [Termatius, Termasius, Cermasius] and the lector Victor of the city of Ecija.

The bishop Fortunatus and the deacon Deuterius [the bishop Deuterius, the deacon Theodorius] of the city of Cherchell in the province of Mauritania.

The bishop Quintasius [Quintatius, Quintinus, Quintas] and the priest Admonius [Ammomus, Ammonius] of the city of Cagliari in the province of Sardinia.

Also: the province of Africa.

The bishop Caecilianus [Cecilianus, Caeleanus, Cicilianus] of the city of Carthage, and with him the deacon Sperantius.

Lampadius of the city of Oudna.

The bishop Victor of the city of Bizerte.

The bishop Anastasius [Anestasius] of the city of Beniata.

The bishop Faustus [Faustinus] of the city of Tebourba.

Surgentius of the city of Pocofeltus [*Unknown*].

The bishop Victor of the city of Legis Volumni in the province of Numidia.

The bishop Vitalis of the city of Bordj-Bou-Djadi.

The bishop Gregory, of the Port of Rome.

The bishop Acpitetus [Epictatus, Epistitus] from Centocelli.

. . . The priests Leontius [the bishop Leontius] and Mercurius [Mamertinus] from Ostia . . .

Early Christian tomb in the Alyscamps at Arles

EIGHT

The Council of Orange, 441

The meeting at Orange in 441 is of interest here chiefly because of its attendance list, which includes the names of the deacon Auxilius, of Vienne, and the priest Segetius, of Carpentras in the province of Vienne. See the discussion, p. 40, of Muirchú's citing of the two names in connection with St Patrick. The council made a number of regulations of church matters. Some excerpts are given below.

5 . . . Those who take refuge in the church should not be handed over; but the precinct should be reverently guarded with legal sureties. However, should anyone think to seize church property in compensation for his slaves who have fled to the church let him be condemned most severely by all the churches . . .

16 [*The sacrifice of the Mass*] should be offered with pyx and chalice; and the consecration should be performed with the Eucharistic admixture.[1]

17 It was resolved that the Gospels should be read, in order, to the catechumens in the church throughout our provinces.

18 Catechumens should never be let in to the baptistery . . .

21 Furthermore, let it next be settled that married deacons should not be ordained unless they undertake beforehand to remain chaste for the future . . .

[List of those present at the Council of Orange, 8 November 441]

1 From the city of Arles in the province of Vienne, the bishop Hilary, the priest Ravennius and the deacon Petronius.
2 From the city of Vienne in the above mentioned province, the bishop Claudius and the deacons Auxilius[2] and Severus.
3 From Lyon, chief city of the province of Lyon, the bishop Eucherius, the priest Aper, the deacon Veranus.
4 From the city of Geneva in the province of Vienne, the bishop Salunius, the deacon Marius.

5   From the city of Carpentras in the province of Vienne, the bishop Constantianus, the priests Lycorius and Segetius.[3]

6   From the city and province of Die, the bishop Audentius.

7   From the city of Vaison in the above province, the bishop Auspicius, the priest Fontedius and the deacon Iulianus.

8   From the city of Apt in the second province of Narbonne, the bishop Iulius and the deacon Concordius.

9   From the city of Leon in the province of Galicia, the bishop Agrestius and the deacon Deudatus.

10   From the city of Avignon in the province of Vienne, the bishop Necterius and the deacon Fontedius.

11   From the city of Grenoble in the above province, the bishop Cheretius and the deacon Iocundus.

12   From the city of Frejus in the second province of Narbonne, the bishop Theudorus and the priest Chrispinus.

13   From the city of Riez in the above province, the bishop Maximus and the priest Magnentius.

14   From the city of Orange in the province of Vienne, the bishop Iustus and the priest Carentinus.

15   From the city of Embrun in the province of the Maritime Alps, the bishop Ingenuos.

16   From the church of Toulon in the province of Vienne, the bishop Agustalis.

17   From the city of Castellane in the province of the Maritime Alps, the priest Superuentur on behalf of the bishop Claudius.

Conclusion of the list of seventeen bishops at the council.

TEN

The Synod of May 451

This gathering of "many bishops of the provinces of Vienne, Narbonne and the Maritime Alps" was held at an unknown place (probably, however, Arles). It was the year of the great ecumenical council of Chalcedon, which reversed the findings of the council of Ephesus of 449. That council had found in favour of the Monophysite Eutyches, in his dispute with Flavian, bishop of Constantinople, who had condemned him and who appealed for help to Leo. Leo responded with a doctrinal statement, a "tome",[1] reasserting the dual nature of Christ (perfect God and perfect man), and joining in the condemnation of Eutyches. The Tome was drafted by Leo's secretary, Prosper of Aquitaine. He sent this Tome to the council at Chalcedon, and also conveyed his ruling to the bishops in Gaul. The meeting of the bishops of the southeastern provinces was held to respond to it. The reply was drafted by Ravennius, bishop of Arles. The meeting was clearly well attended and its composition must give a fairly comprehensive outline of the organization of the Church in that part of Gaul in the middle of the fifth century. Unfortunately the sees of a great many of the bishops are unknown. In view of the remote possibility that the bishop Palladius who attended was the same who had been appointed first bishop of the Irish twenty years before, it is of interest to note the attitude of this meeting to the Roman see, as expressed in Ravennius's letter, which all signed.

[Letter of the Gaulish Synod to Leo]

The letter from Your Holiness, which you had sent to the East in affirmation of the Catholic faith, was delivered to us. We would have wished straight away to return to your Apostolic Grace an indication of our gratitude for so immeasurable a boon. But the tempestuous season—which was worse than usual in our region—made it difficult for us to come together quickly—scattered far apart from one another as we were when both land and stormy weather came between us. May your Apostolic Grace therefore grant pardon for our tardiness, since it derives neither from sloth nor from indifference, but from sheer necessity. But if on the one hand this necessity prevented us from offering the courtesy of a speedy reply; yet, on the other hand, it cannot suppress our delight.

For we were exultant to read, by Christ's favour, Your Holiness's letter. Each one of us gained from your exposition, and we quickly brought joy also to all the others appointed in Gaul; while equally we sorrowed for those of your people who deserted the light of the Catholic faith and entered the darkness of error.

And anyone who does not neglect the sureties of redemption, will inscribe this writing of your Apostolic Grace on the tablets of his heart, as if it were the blazon of the faith, and will commit it firmly to memory so that he may be better prepared to confute the errors of the heretics. Accordingly, many people, both joyful and triumphant at this, reexamined their understanding of their faith, and rejoice that they always held to the law as your Apostolic Grace has expounded it, and as it was handed down by the fathers. Some were more moved, on receiving Your Holiness's exhortation, to reassurance at all the ways in which they were being taught; and they rejoiced in the chance given to them to speak out freely and confidently—each and every one to affirm his faith, supported by the authority of the Apostolic See itself.

Who indeed would reckon it possible to return fitting thanks to your Apostolic Grace for so great a boon, which, like the most precious of gems, has adorned not only Gaul but the whole world? The faithful believer owes it, after God, to your teaching to hold firmly to that which he believed; the very infidel owes it to you to acknowledge the truth and to abandon his perfidy and, filled with the light of Apostolic teaching, to leave the darkness of his error, to escape from charlatans, and to believe what Our Lord Jesus Christ teaches—through your voice—about the pledge of His Incarnation, rather than holding to what is instilled by the enemy of human salvation and of the truth—the devil.

We would also have wished to post a letter to the most glorious and faithful emperor, your son, concerning the same case, displaying both our admiration of his faith, and our own humble concern—in which we follow you in Christ—had not news been brought to us from the East leading us to think that there was no necessity to do this. Moreover, it was through the merits of your Apostolic Grace that the good Lord decided to reveal a heresy long nurtured in secret in your time. It is your praiseworthy solicitude that must be thanked for the fact that this error of wicked people was unable to remain concealed; it redounds to the glory of the faith that this warped persuasion either failed to gain adherents or, having gained them, lost them. We pray therefore that, protecting Your Apostolic Grace, the merciful Lord will look kindly on His Church, which has spread through the whole world: indeed that through your great watchfulness, and through those who serve His intentions, the disaffected will be brought back to the faith and those who are lax will be fired to zeal by this example. Let us never cease to give thanks and at the same time to pray to our Lord and God for that which we have always in view: let us praise Him for giving to the Apostolic See (from which the source and fountain of our religion poured out the blessing of Christ) a pontiff of such sanctity, such faith, such learning. We ask further that He maintain for the longest time the boon of your pontificate, which He has given and granted for the establishment of His churches. Moreover, although we are weak in merit, yet we are strong in faith. Should aggression be attempted against the Catholic Church (as we hope it will not), we are ready, with Your Holiness and with the Lord's help, to die for the truth of the faith and to yield this life to the Author of our salvation and the Giver of eternity.

[*Added by Ravennius*]: Pray for me, Lord Pope, most blessed in goodness and apostolic dignity.

[Signatories of the letter of May 451 to Leo the Great]

Ravennius [of Arles]
Rusticus [of Narbonne]
Venerius [of Marseille]
Constantianus [of Carpentras]
Maximus [of Riez]
Armentarius [of Antibes]
Florus [not known]
Sabinus [not known]
Valerianus [of Cimiez]
Constantius [of Uzes]
Nectarius [of Avignon]
Maximus [not known]
Asclepius [of Cavaillon];
Maximus [not known]
Ursus [not known]
Ingenuus [of Embrun]
Iustus [of Orange]
Valerius [not known]
Superventor [not known; but see pp. 58, 60]
Chrysaphius [not known]
Fonteius [of Vaison]
Petronius [of Digne]

Ydatius [not known]
Aetherius [not known]
Eulalius [not known]
Eustathius [not known]
Fraternus [of Langres?]
Victurus [not known]
Eugenius [not known]
Hilarus [not known]
Verus [not known]
Amandus [not known]
Gerontius [not known]
Proculeianus [not known]
Iulianus [not known; see p. 58]
Helladius [not known]
Armentarius [not known]
Honoratus [not known]
Eparchius [not known]
Anemius [not known]
Dynamius [not known]
Maximinus [not known]
Ynantius [not known]
Palladius [not known][1]

ELEVEN

The Council of Tours, 18 November 461

This meeting was held for the translation of the relics of St Martin, the bishop of Tours who died in AD 397 and whose Life, written by Sulpicius Severus *c*.403, became widely known later in Ireland and served as a model for Irish (as for other Western) hagiography. Although it was written so soon after Martin's death, the Life is largely a fanciful work of fiction, an extravagant hero-tale, full of extraordinary miracles. It was copied into the Book of Armagh, along with the New Testament and much Patrician material.

The bishops meeting at Tours decided that they should use the occasion for issuing, or re-issuing, ecclesiastical regulations. The prologue to these canons reads:

The Most Reverend Bishops whose names are signed below gathered in the city of Tours for a very sacred festival: the celebration of the reception of our lord Martin. Because the rule of church discipline had become decayed through long lack of attention to certain matters, they believed it was necessary for them to declare definitively (through the issue of the present document) what was in accordance with the authority of the fathers. Not to look back to wrongs of the past; but rather to look forward to the good of the future community as a whole, and maintain the statutes of the fathers according to the Gospel teachings and apostolic doctrine, so that the Church of the Lord may remain pure and unspotted.

The thirteen canons which followed dealt largely with clerical discipline, in particular matters of celibacy and chastity, and are omitted here. The list of the bishops present is short, but the names and their distribution are of interest. The list of signatures follows.

[Signatories of the Canons of Tours, 18 November 461]

I, Perpetuus, bishop of the city of Tours, was present and signed.

I, Victorius, bishop of the city of Le Mans, was present at this definition, and signed.

I, Leo, bishop of of the city of Bourges, was present and signed.

I, Eusebius, bishop of the city of Nantes, was present and signed.

I, Amandinus, bishop of the city of Chalons-sur-Marne, was present and signed.

I, Germanus, bishop of the city of Rouen, was present and signed.

I, Athenius, bishop of the city of Rennes, was present and signed.

I, Mansuetus, bishop of the Britons, was present and signed.

I, Iucundinus, priest, signed on the orders of my lord Venerandus, bishop, since he had not decided [*see unknown*].

I, Thalasius, a sinner, signed and consented to this document of my lords bishops, which they had forwarded to me and which I read over in my little city [*i.e., Angers, of which Thalasius was bishop*].

TWELVE

The Council of Vannes

The occasion of this gathering was the ordination of a bishop, Paternus, for Vannes. The precise date is unknown, but the bishop of Tours, Perpetuus, who presided, held his office from 461 to 491. It is of interest as an early record of a church on the Breton seacoast in an area which has always had a close connection by sea with southern Ireland, an area too which was to share with Ireland some of the distinctive institutions and customs of the "Celtic" churches. Some of the regulations promulgated deal with monasticism.

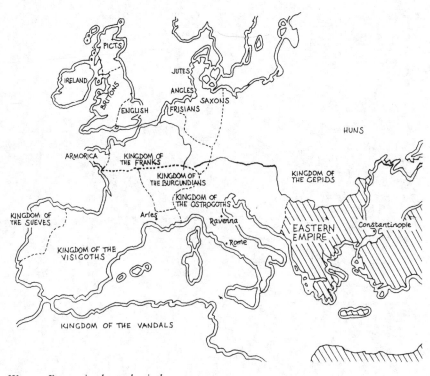

Western Europe in the early sixth century

To the most blessed lords bishops Victorius and Thalasius, our revered brothers in Christ, with every tribute of love, from the bishops Perpetuus, Paternus, Albinus, Athenius, Nonnechius and Liberalis.

Always when it has been our duty to tend to a matter of religion, it has been necessary to consider whether, at that particular time, the place in which we should convene should be determined by the occasion; or whether we might choose it freely, coming together in Christ to establish a common text out of a multitude of tracts and opinions.

Usually each of us must rely on his own judgment without consulation with his brothers. Since we have gathered together in the church of Vannes for the purpose of ordaining a bishop, now we have the opportunity by joint decision to establish regulations—which, reasonably enough, may not conform to any one person's opinion. We do this in order that statement of the law may not be perverted by the judgment of individuals, or by errors arising from inexperience, or by fits of arrogance or anger. We thought it right to take the opportunity to lay down laws that will be most beneficial in relation to the government of the Church (government granted and entrusted to us by the Lord) and in relation to those differences among us for which we must take responsibility; otherwise we would be at fault. It is in conference together that we have done this; to supply what seemed to us to have been omitted from previous statutes of the fathers and to correct what seemed to be neglectfully passed over as time went by and as observance became slack.

We believed this should be brought to the knowledge of your Holinesses, since circumstances deprived our meeting of your presence. We hope you may find it acceptable, so that by your authority you may strengthen it and disseminate it more widely.

1   And so: we decreed that those who commit homicide and those who bear false witness should be excluded from the communion of the Church until they confess their sins and wash them away with the reparation of penance.

2   And we ruled that those too *who put away their wives*, as the Gospel says, *saving for the cause of fornication*,[1] and marry others, without proof of adultery, should also be refused communion, lest by our leniency towards their sins, others might think themselves free to do wrong.

3   Further: penitents who, having undertaken to do public penance, fail to do so and turn back to the sinful ways of their former life, and to profane company, are to be removed not only from the communion of the sacraments of the Church, but also from the companionship of the faithful.

4   We decree that those women who have been dedicated, with the imposition of hands, to virginity and to the life of blessedness, and have vowed to be firm in following this commitment; if they have been found in adultery, they are to be excommunicated along with their adulterers.

5   Clerics may not have permission to wander without a letter of commendation from their own bishop; and in every place where they arrive without such a letter, they are to be refused communion.

6   And the same applies equally to monks; and we ruled that if words will not mend them, they should be punished by flogging.

7   This also will apply to monks: that they may not separate from the community and remove to a solitary cell except in cases where they have been tested through meritorious tasks, or where in case of illness the abbots remit the stricter rule.

8   Abbots are also forbidden each to have a separate cell; nor may they have more than one monastery; except insofar as they may organize refuges within the walls because of an enemy invasion.

9   Clerics are forbidden to attend the secular courts except by permission of their bishops; but if it should happen that anyone should begin to doubt the judgment of his bishop, or if he should start any dispute on his own behalf against his bishop, he should seek a hearing from other bishops and not approach the secular power. Otherwise he is to be excommunicated.

10   Furthermore, bishops are not to take it on themselves to raise to a higher order clerics ordained by other bishops without the permission of those who ordained them—so that they may not hurt fraternal harmony.

11   Priests, deacons and subdeacons, who, according to their orders, are not permitted to take wives, should avoid even the wedding feasts of others, lest they should join in gatherings where bawdy songs or obscene and shameful dances are performed—so that he who is dedicated to the sacred mysteries should not be soiled by witnessing and hearing shameful sights and words.

12   Further, all clerics are to avoid feasts of the Jews; nor should anyone admit Jews to a feast; because they do not eat in common with Christians and therefore it is demeaning and sacriligeous for them to accept a meal from Christians. When we eat food approved by the Apostle, they will judge it to be unclean; and so they would begin to think our clerics inferior to Jews; while if we accept what they serve, they would despise what we offer.

13   Above all, clerics are to avoid drunkenness which is the fuel and nourishment of all vice. No one can have free control of his own mind and body when as a slave of wine he is deprived of sense; when with addled mind he is led down the slope into vice, and when—often without even knowing what he is doing—he can commit sin or crime. But the penance due cannot be mitigated by ignorance which derives from a wilful dulling of the mind. Therefore we decreed that, according to the gravity of the matter, whoever is shown to have been drunk should either be excluded from communion for thirty days or be given corporal punishment.

14   The cleric who is bound to stay within the walls of his city and who is found, without reasonable excuse of illness, to be absent from the morning service, shall be excluded from communion for seven days; since he may not lawfully cease the devotion of salvation when there is no honourable necessity to relieve him of his duty in the sacred ministry.

15   We also deemed it right not to allow our worship to vary through different observances. As we hold one faith in the Trinity, so we should observe one rule in our services, in order that one single custom should be observed in the liturgy within our province.

16   And something which greatly impairs the faith of the Catholic religion should not even seem to be overlooked. Some clerics study auguries, and in the name of an invented religion—which they call the holy lottery—practise the art of divination, or foretell the future through conning all the scriptures. Whatever cleric is discovered either to have resorted to this or to have taught it, he is to be excluded from the church.

Lords and brothers, may God keep safe your enclave of his Church.

THIRTEEN

Prosper of Aquitaine on Pope Celestine and the Pelagians

[From Chapter 21 of Prosper of Aquitaine, *Against the Collator*]

Indeed there are teachers of this doctrine[1] who contaminate the purity of Catholic minds by slandering the defenders of grace. With rabid mouths they savage the chief ecclesiastical teacher of our time.[2] And they believe that, if they have broken down this mighty watch-tower of the shepherd with repeated blows of the Pelagian battering-ram, they can overthrow all the defences of authority. Yet, it follows naturally enough that they have had some success—although in fact: "the foundation of God standeth sure".[3] Of course, they mimic the insanity of those whose opinion they follow: that is fitting. And they have nothing to say except what has been spread about through the complaints of begrudgers and through the slanders of the most insolent Julian.[4] The sprouts of a single seed are small; and what is hidden in the root is revealed in the fruit. These people, therefore, should not be fought by inexperienced campaigners; nor should particular battles be engaged as if the enemy were unknown.

At that time their artifices were shattered. It was then that they and their allies and the leaders of their insolence were ruined: when Innocent,[4] of blessed memory, beheaded the abominable error with the apostolic sword; when a synod of Palestinian bishops constrained Pelagius to condemn himself and his people by revealing his ideas; when Pope Zozimus of blessed remembrance joined the strength of his own judgment to the decrees of the African councils and armed the right hands of all the bishops with the sword of Peter for the destruction of the wicked; when Pope Boniface of blessed memory could rejoice at the Catholic devotion of most pious emperors, and so use not only apostolic decrees against the enemies of grace, but princely ones too; and finally when the blessed bishop Augustine, who was the most learned of all, produced his answers to the books of the Pelagians.

Pelagius — heretical doctrine held by own enthusiast fuller

And so to the pontiff Celestine, of venerable memory. The Lord gave him many gifts of His grace for the defence of the Catholic Church. Celestine knew that as well as a judicial hearing the condemned must be offered the remedy of penance. But when Celestius[5] demanded a hearing—as if his case were not already utterly lost—he ordered him excluded from any part of Italy. He felt so strongly that the statutes and synodal decrees of his predecessors should be held inviolate, that he would on no account allow even what had once merited repeal to be modified in any way. And with no less active a concern, he freed Britain from the same disease; when he shut out from their remote Ocean retreat certain enemies of grace who were in possession of their ancestral land. And, ordaining a bishop [*Palladius*] for the Irish, he made the barbarian island Christian while taking care to keep the Roman island Catholic.

It is through this man that the churches in the East were rid of the double plague (when the Pelagians had joined up with other errors and renewed their mischief there). He offered the help of the apostolic sword to Cyril, Bishop of Alexandria (a most glorious defender of the Catholic faith), to cut away the Nestorian wickedness. It is through this man that those same people in Gaul who rejected the writings of Augustine of blessed memory were deprived of the liberty to speak evil. He took advice and approved the correctness of the books which had displeased those who were in error. He showed plainly in his holy discourse what should be made of their authority: he stated clearly how much he was displeased by the outlandishness of their presumption when some of them dared to rise up insolently against the ancient teachers and, with unrestrained calumny, to shout down the preaching of truth. He said [Celestine's *Letter to the Gaulish Bishops*]:

> Augustine was always in communion with us, a man of holy memory because of his life and merits. Not even the hint of unfavourable suspicion ever besmirched him. We think of him as a man of such learning in his time that he was always reckoned by my predecessors to be one of the greatest teachers. It would be well, therefore, if everyone would so regard him that he may have love and honour from all.[6]

FOURTEEN

The Chronicle of Prosper of Aquitaine

[The Chronicle is in two parts: this is Part Two.]

*From the death of the Emperor Valens to the death of Valentinian III
and the taking of Rome by the Vandals*

(. . . Therefore, Valens having been burnt to death in Thrace by the
Goths, Gratian reigned for six years with his brother Valentinian.)

[379] Gratian, after the death of his uncle, brought in Theodosius, the son
of Theodosius, as joint emperor and gave him the Eastern region.
Theodosius enjoyed supreme good fortune and in numerous great
battles defeated the Goths and drove them from Thrace.

The Lombards, from the remotest limits of Germany, from the
borders of the ocean shore and from the Scandinavian island,
migrated in huge numbers, under their leaders Iboreas and Aionis,
eager to find new places of settlement. They first defeated the Vandals.
Sempronius was acknowleged as a man of outstanding learning.

It was about this time that Priscillian, a bishop of Galicia[1] founded
the heresy named after him, on the basis of the teachings of the
Manichees and the Gnostics.

[380] Ambrose was producing many sublime writings on behalf of the
Catholic faith.

Theodosius fell ill in Thessalonica and received baptism from
Ascholius, bishop of that city.

A peace, arranged by Gratian, was made with the Goths because
Theodosius was ill.

A council of 153 fathers was held at Constantinople, opposing
Macedonius, who denied that the Holy Spirit was God.

[381] Martin, Bishop of the Gaulish city of Tours, was held in renown by many.

Gregory of Nanzianzus, the most eloquent man of his time and the teacher of Jerome, died.

[382] Athanaric, king of the Goths, was killed on the fifteenth day of his captivity at Constantinople.

[383] Arcadius, son of the Emperor Theodosius, was given the title Augustus.

Petronius, Bishop of Bonn, a man noted for his zeal and sanctity, died.

[384] Honorius, son of Theodosius, was born.

Succeeding Damasus, Siricius presided over the church of Rome (for twenty years).

Through a mutiny of the troops in Britain, Maximus was made emperor and quickly sailed to Gaul. At Paris, Gratian was overcome through the treachery of Merobaudis, Master of the Soldiers: he fled, was captured at Lyon, and was put to death. Maximus made his son, Victor, Caesar and joint ruler.

Valentinian ruled the Romans with Theodosius (for seven years).

[385] At this time, Jerome (who is now famous throughout the whole world) was living in Bethlehem, doing service to the universal Church with genius and diligence.

Priscillian learned that he had been condemned by the council of Bordeaux, and appealed to Maximus. On being examined at Trier by the praetorian prefect, Evodius, he was put to the sword by Maximus, along with Eucrocia, wife of the orator Delphidius, and Latronianus and other companions in error.

[386] A certain disciple of Priscillian's named Urbeia was stoned to death at Bordeaux, for her impious persistence in leading the common people astray.

[387] ——

[388] The despot Maximus was stripped of his regal trappings by the emperors Valentinian and Theodosius at the third milestone from Aquileia, and was tried and condemned to death. In the same year his son Victor was killed in Gaul by the Count Arbogast.

[389] Because of the killing of Priscillian, of whom they had been the accusers, the bishops Ithacius and Ursacius were deprived of the Church's communion.

The Lombards—their leaders being dead—chose as their first king Algelmund, son of Aionis, who reigned thirty-three years.

[390] A sign, like a burning dove suspended in the sky, appeared for thirty days.

Theodosius removed the venerable head of John the Baptist from the hamlet of Coslas (at the seventh milestone from Constantinople), and enshrined it in the splendid basilica which he had built in its honour.

[391] Eugenius, relying on the favour of Arbogast, took power for himself.

[392] Valentinian, led to contempt of life by the excessive stubbornness of Arbogast, Master of the Soldiers, died by strangling at Vienne.[2] Arbogast, Master of the Army, was discommoded by the death of Valentinian. He made Eugenius the ruler of Gaul. Theodosius, who had already ruled for fourteen years, reigned as forty-third head of the Romans with his sons Arcadius and Honorius (for three years).

[393] Honorius was constituted ruler by his father Theodosius in the same place where he had made his brother (Arcadius) Caesar, seventeen miles from the city, as darkness fell at the third hour.

[394] John, the eremitical monk—who had the gift of prophecy—was held in high renown. He foretold that Theodosius—who had sought advice on the outcome of the war he had begun against Eugenius—would be victorious.

[395] Theodosius defeated and killed the despot Eugenius.

Augustine, the disciple of blessed Ambrose, who excelled in eloquence and divine learning, was constituted bishop of the region of Hippo in Africa.

At this time the poet Claudian was held in high esteem.

The emperor Theodosius died at Milan. Arcadius, who had already been a ruler for twelve years, reigned as forty-fourth head of the Romans with his brother Honorius (for thirteen years).

[396] There was an earthquake for several days, and the sky appeared to be on fire.

The Spanish priest Orosius was famous for his eloquence and knowledge of history.

[397] A daughter, Flacilla, was born to Arcadius.

The monk Evagrius, a man of incredible self-denial who was also learned in Sacred Scripture, enjoyed fame in Egypt.

The council of Carthage, where the statutes of the council of Hippo were ratified and adopted.

[398] Anastasius held the position of thirty-seventh bishop of Rome (for three years and twenty-one days).

[399] Soon after the eunuch Eutropius entered on this consulate he was deprived of both that dignity and his life.

[400] The Goths, under their leaders Alaric and Rhadagaisus, invaded Italy.

[401] The bishops John of Constantinople and Theophilus of Alexandria were held to be as shining lights. But a mutual dissension arose, which dimmed each of them, and went so far that John was overthrown by Theophilus and was driven into exile in Pontus. Yet, nevertheless, the greater number of the bishops, following the example of the Roman pontiff, maintained communion with him.

[402] A fierce battle was fought against the Goths at Pollentia, with slaughter on both sides.
Innocent presided over the Roman church as its thirty-eighth head, (for fifteen years, two months and twenty-one days).

[403] A council was held in Carthage concerning the Donatists.
A statue of Eudoxia, wife of Arcadius, was erected on a porphyry column.

[404] Eudoxia, wife of Arcadius, came to the end of her days.

[405] Many Gothic warriors were cut to pieces in Thuscia [*Tuscany*] by Stilicho at the head of the army, and Radagaisus was defeated and captured.

[406] The Vandals and Alans crossed the Rhine on the last day of December and invaded Gaul.

[407] Constantine, pretending good fellowship, rose from the ranks of the military to despotism in Britain, and crossed over to Gaul.

[408] The Emperor Arcadius died in Constantinople. Honorius, with his brother's son Theodosius, reigned as the forty-fifth head of the Romans (for sixteen years).

[409] The Vandals took possession of Spain.
Attalus was given command in Rome. When he was quickly deprived of sovereignty he joined the Goths.

[410] Rome, once conqueror of the world, was taken by the Goths led by Alaric. Therefore there was only one consul—in the East—as may be noted for the following year also.

[411] Constantine was defeated and captured at the town of Arles by Honorius's generals Constantius and Ulphulas. Gerontius Cormes killed Constantine's son Constantius (who had begun to rule in Spain), handing over a measure of power to Maximus.

[412] Maximus, having won power in Spain, lost his life; because to his modesty and humility there was not added the envious drive of a man seeking empire.
The Goths invaded Gaul under their king Athaulph.
At this same time, Heros, a holy man and a disciple of blessed Martin, was expelled by the people of the town of Arles while he was presiding innocently as bishop of the city and was open to no accusation. In his place Patroclus was ordained, a friend and close connection of Constantius, Master of the Soldiers, whose favour he had cultivated. This matter between the bishops of that region was the cause of great discord.

[413] ([*The consul*] Heraclianus . . . was charged with sedition in Africa and was stripped of his office and put to death.)
The Burgundians obtained a part of Gaul along the Rhine.
The brothers Jovinus and Sebastian seized power in Gaul and were killed. At this time, with the aid and support of Celestius and Julian, the Briton Pelagius propagated the doctrine (named after him) denying the grace of Christ, and he led many into his error. He preached that each person was directed by his own will alone in arriving at justice and would receive grace according to his own merits—since Adam's sin harmed only himself and did not bind his posterity: therefore, by their own will, all could be free from sin; and that all infants were born as innocent as before the Fall and so should be baptized, not for the remission of sin but as a ceremony to signify their worthiness of adoption [into the Church].

[414] With the advice and support of the Goths Attalus resumed his despotic rule in Gaul.

[415] Attalus, deserted by the Goths (who migrated to Spain), and deprived of support, was captured and handed over alive to the patrician Constantine.
Athaulph was wounded by one of his own people, and died. Wallia seized his kingship, having destroyed those who had similar aims.

[416] Wallia seeking peace with Honorius, returned to him Placidia, daughter of the Emperor Theodosius, whom the Goths had captured in Rome and whom Athaulph had taken to wife. Now Constantius obtained her in marriage.

Zozimus became the thirty-ninth bishop of the church of Rome (for one year, nine months and nine days).

At this time vigorous resistance was offered to the Pelagians (now condemned by Pope Innocent) through the learning of the African bishops—most importantly Augustine.

[417] Honorius entered Rome in triumph with Attalus walking before his chariot. He condemned Attalus to live in exile in Lipara.

[418] At this time, Constantius, the servant of Christ, and a former offical of Rome, who was a most devoted opponent of the Pelagians on behalf of God's grace, had to endure much from a faction of those people—something he had in common with the holy confessors.

A council of 214 bishops was held at Carthage. Information about its decrees was brought to Pope Zozimus, who approved them. The Pelagian heresy was then condemned throughout the whole world.

A son, Valentinian, was born to Constantius and Placidia, on the second of July. Boniface succeeded as fortieth bishop of the Roman church (for three years, eight months and six days).

[419] At this time there was a third schism, when the antipope Eulalius was expelled by the Caesar Honorius—and it lasted for two years. The noble Constantius made peace with Wallia, having given him the second Aquitaine to settle in and certain cities of the adjoining provinces.

[420] Constantius was received by Honorius in joint rule.

The priest Jerome died in the ninety-first year of his age, on the last day of September.

[421] The Emperor Constantius died.

[422] At this time an army was sent to Spain against the Vandals, of which Castinus was general. Foolishly, and harmfully for the Empire, he refused to have in alliance with him on his expedition a man outstanding in the arts of war—Boniface. For he thought danger or shame might arise from bringing with him one whose quarrelsomeness and pride he knew from experience. So he took himself quickly to the seaport of the City, and from there on to Africa. This was the beginning of many difficulties for the State.

[423] Placidia Augusta, expelled by her brother Honorius, set out for the East with her sons Honorius and Valentinian.

Celestine presided as bishop and forty-first head of the church of Rome (for nine years).

Lamissus, the whore's son, reigned (for three years) as eleventh king of the Lombards.

Honorius died; and John took over his power, with the connivance, as it is thought, of Castinus, who was at the head of the army as Master of the Soldiers.

Theodosius took over as forty-sixth Roman Emperor (for thirty years).

[424] Theodosius made his aunt's son, Valentinian, Caesar, and sent him with his mother Augusta to restore government in the West; meanwhile so long as John attempted by force of arms to seize Africa, which Boniface held, he was weakened in the defence of his own territory.

[425] Placidia Augusta and the Caesar Valentinian with great good fortune overthrew the despot John; and restored government. This was by favour of Aëtius, since it was through his energy that the Huns (invited in by the same John) were driven back to their own lands. Castinus, however, was sent into exile, since it was perceived that without his connivance John would not have been able to seize power.

By decree of Theodosius, Valentian received the title Augustus.

The noble Gaulish town of Arles was forcefully assaulted by the Goths until they withdrew—not without casualties—on the arrival of Aëtius.

[426] Patroclus, Bishop of Arles, was murdered (mangled by many wounds) by a certain tribune, in barbarous fashion; this crime was said to have been done by the secret orders of Felix, Master of the Soldiers, at whose instigation also, it is believed, the deacon Titus, a holy man, was killed while he was distributing alms to the poor in Rome.

[427] By the decision of Felix war was waged in the name of the state, under the command of Mavortius, Galbio and Sinoces, on Boniface (whose power and fame had increased in Africa), because he had refused to come to Italy. Mavortius and Galbio, when they besieged Boniface, lost their lives through the treachery of Sinoces; but soon he too was killed, when Boniface found him treacherous.

Next, tribes who had no knowledge of the use of ships, were none-theless called in by the combatants for help, and succeeded in the sea-passage; and the Count Sigisvult was given the task of making war against Boniface.

The Vandal people crossed from Spain to Africa.

[428] Nestorius, Bishop of Constantinople, busied himself promoting a new error in the churches, preaching that Christ was born of Mary

as man only—not God—and that divinity was conferred on Him for His merits. The special diligence of Cyril, Bishop of Alexandria, and the authority of Pope Celestine confounded this impious person. The Count Aëtius, by force of arms, recovered that part of Gaul along the Rhine which had been occupied by the Franks for settlement.

[429] Felix was raised to the patrician dignity, and Aëtius was made Master of the Soldiers.

The Pelagian Agricola, son of the Pelagian Bishop Severianus, insidiously corrupted the churches of Britain with his teachings. But, through the negotiation of the deacon Palladius, Pope Celestine sent Germanus Bishop of Auxerre to act on his behalf, and he routed the heretics and directed the Britons to the Catholic faith.

[430] Aëtius put to death Felix, with his wife Padusia, and the deacon Grunnitus, when he suspected them of plotting against him.

Augustine, that bishop who was most excellent in all matters, died on 28 August, at the height of the Vandal sieges, still replying to the books of Julian[3] at this, the end of his days, and gloriously persistent in the affirmation of Christ's grace.

[431] Nestorius was condemned, along with the heresy that bears his name, and with many Pelagians who supported a dogma related to his, by a council of more than two hundred bishops assembled at Ephesus.

Palladius was ordained by Pope Celestine and sent to the Irish believers in Christ as their first bishop.

[432] Xistus was appointed forty-second head of the Roman church, with the assent of the whole City, and with marvellous accord (for eight years and nineteen days).

Boniface, appointed Master of the Soldiers, came from Africa to the City and to Italy. He defeated in battle Aëtius, who opposed him, but died of illness a few days later. Aëtius, deprived of his power, went to live on his estate, where a certain enemy of his, appearing suddenly, tried to seize him; he fled to the City and from there to Dalmatia; finally, making his way through Pannonia, he reached the Huns, and through their friendship and help, he made peace with the rulers, and had his authority renewed.

[433] Most of the northern part of the capital City was destroyed in three days of continuous conflagration, in the month of August.

The monk John, surnamed Cassian, of Massilia [*Marseilles*] was held to be an eminent and eloquent writer.

Theodosius's years as consul are reckoned at fourteen up to his
consulate with Maximus.
From the fifteenth year of Tiberius and the Lord's Passion, 406
years are reckoned.
From the renewal of the Temple under Darius 954 years.
From the first Olympiad and the prophet Isaiah, 1,210 years.
From Solomon and the first building of the Temple 1,466 years.
From Moses and Cecrops king of Attica, 1,990 years.
From Abraham and the reign of Ninis and Semiramis, 2,450 years.
Further; from the Flood to Abraham, 1,071 years.
From Adam, indeed, until the Flood 2,242 years.
That adds up, from Adam to the time of the above named consuls,
to 5,742 years.

[434] ——

[435] Peace was made with the Vandals and they were given a part of
Africa by Trigetius, at Hippo on the eleventh of February.
At the same time, by force of arms Aëtius captured Gundicar, king
of the Burgundians living in Gaul, and granted him peace at his
supplication. He did not enjoy it long. The Huns destroyed him, his
tribe and his people.

[436] The Goths broke the terms of the peace and seized many towns
near their settlements, greatly endangering the town of Narbonne,
which suffered a grievous siege and famine and was relieved of both
perils by the Count Littorius. For through his horsemen, who each
carried a double measure of wheat, he vigorously drove off the
enemy and at the same time restored the city's food supply.

[437] War was waged against the Goths with Hunnish auxiliaries.
In Africa, Geiseric king of the Vandals, impiously wishing to
pervert the Catholic faith to that of the Arians within the limits of
his settlements, went so far in persecuting some of our bishops
(among whom Possidus, Novatus and Severianus were the best
known) as to drive them by law out of their basilicas, and even out
of their cities; since in their constancy they yielded to none of the
terrorizings of this most arrogant king.
Valentinian Augustus travelled to Constantinople to the ruler
Theodosius and received his daughter in marriage.
In the same year, deserters from the barbarian federate troops
engaged in piracy.
At this time four Spanish men, Arcadius, Probus, Paschasius and
Eutychius, in their wise submission to the faith had long been held
in high regard by Geiseric. In order to bind them to himself he

commanded them to convert to the Arian sect. And when they firmly and repeatedly rejected this evil and so roused the barbarian's raging anger, they were first proscribed, then condemned to exile, then tormented with appalling tortures; finally put to death in various ways; until in the end these illustrious men were laid to rest in a marvellous martyrdom. However, a boy by the name of Paulillus, brother of Paschasius and Eutychius, was adopted by the king because of his beauty and intelligence. But, when he could not be moved from his profession and love of the Catholic faith, he was beaten with rods and then condemned to the vilest servitude. Yet, it seems he was not put to death—lest someone so young might gain glory through resisting to the end the impious king's ferocity.

[438] In this year too the same pirates ravaged many islands, but especially Sicily.

[439] Littorius, who was second to the patrician Aëtius in command of the Hunnish auxiliaries, joined battle with the Goths recklessly because he wished to outshine Aëtius, and because he relied on auguries and on the conjurings of demons. When he did so, he showed that the company which perished with him could have done great service had he chosen to follow better counsels than his own foolhardiness; since it did such slaughter among the enemy that, had he not fallen into captivity through his fecklessness in battle, it would have been doubtful which side might have claimed victory.

At this time Julian of Eclanum [*a town in Campania*] was a most officious champion of the Pelagian error, he who had long been driven by an immoderate desire to recover the office of bishop, of which he had been deprived. He advanced his ambition by using every art to conceal his error and he worked diligently to insinuate himself into the communion of the church. But Pope Xistus, urged on by the deacon Leo,[4] was vigilant to check his schemes and would allow no opening for his baleful endeavours, so causing all Catholics to rejoice at the rejection of this deceitful beast, as if then, for the first time, the apostolic sword beheaded this most arrogant heresy.

At the same time, Victricius, who had given many warlike evidences of his fidelity to our state, was held in high renown.

Peace was made with the Goths, when they pleaded for it more humbly than ever before, after their mournful experience of the uncertainties of battle.

While Aëtius was fully occupied with the settling of matters in Gaul, Geiseric, whose friendship had not been in question, treacherously broke the peace and seized Carthage on 19 October.

Torturing the citizens with various kinds of torments, he brought all the city's riches into his own possession. Nor did he refrain from spoiling the churches: they were plundered of the sacred vessels and were deprived of the service of their priests, and he ordered that they should no longer be places of divine worship, but dwellings for his people. He was savage in his treatment of the whole captive populace, and particularly hostile to the nobility and to religion, as if he could not sufficiently distinguish himself from the mass of men unless he made war on God. Carthage underwent this captivity in the 585th year since the beginning of Rome.

[440] On the death of Bishop Xistus, the Roman church was for more than forty days without a head, but waited—with marvellous peace and patience—for the deacon Leo, who was delayed in Gaul restoring amity between Aëtius and Albinus. This gave an opportunity—as if he had been intentionally taken aside for a long time—for both the merits of the elected and the judgment of the electors to be fully tested. Leo the deacon was then summoned by a public delegation, presented to his rejoicing native city, and ordained forty-third bishop of the Roman church.

Geiseric, while he was grievously harassing Sicily, received word that Sebastian had crossed from Spain to Africa. He hastened back to Carthage, certain that he and his would be in danger should that man, skilled in war, retake Carthage and occupy it. Sebastian, who wished to offer himself as a true friend rather than an enemy, found out that in every way the barbarian mind was different from what he expected. His hope was to be the major cause of calamity for him and of a miserable death.

[441] The Emperor Theodosius prepared war, through the generals Areobinda, Anaxilla and Germanus, who were provided with a great fleet to attack the Vandals. But they made long delays, put off their business and were more concerned with Sicily than with the defence of Africa.

[442] Since the Huns were savagely laying waste and plundering Thrace and Illyricum, the army which was delaying in Sicily, turned back to defend the East.

Peace was made, however, by Valentinian Augustus with Geiseric, and Africa was divided between them into agreed portions.

But certain magnates of Geiseric's conspired against him and his household because of his arrogance in his successes. The plot was detected and they were tortured, much interrogated by him, and put to death. The questioning suggested that others might attempt the same. The king in his fear now put many to death; so that he lost more men through this suspicion than he would by defeat in war.

[443] At this time Pope Leo's diligence uncovered many Manichees lurking in the City. He had all their secrets revealed, and all the shame of their doctrines condemned and exposed. Their books—of which great heaps were discovered—were burnt. The holy man seemed divinely inspired in this dutiful action, which was of very great benefit not only to the city of Rome, but to the whole world. For the confessions of those arrested in the City made abundantly clear which teachers, bishops and priests of theirs were active, and in what provinces or cities. And many clerical authorities in the East followed the example of the diligence of the apostolic ruler.

[444] In this year the Lord's Easter was celebrated on 23 April: this was correct. For the day of the Passion was 21 April. Out of reverence, the commemoration of the birth of the city of Rome was passed over without the circus.
Attila, king of the Huns killed Bledas, his brother and colleague in kingship, and compelled his peoples to submit.

[445] ——

[446] ——

[447] Eutyches, a heresiarch priest of Constantinople, relying on the friendship of Theodosius Augustus, began to assert that Christ was not perfectly human. Against him the bishop of the city, Flavian, undertook . . .⁵ . . . [Flavian], with his bishops, was condemned by the authority of Dioscorus, bishop of the city of Alexandria. To oppose Eutyches the pope of the City, Leo, sent a bishop, a priest and a deacon. They reported that Flavian had had suffered great wrong for his defence of the Catholic faith, but had been outrageously overcome.

[448] The Emperor Theodosius, supporting Eutyches, summoned Leo, pope of the City. He, when he wished to go, was prevented by the people, but he sent priests and deacons.

[449] A second time the Catholics were called to hear.
At this time the Eutychian heresy arose, initiated by a priest, Eutyches, who directed a celebrated monastery near Constantinople. He preached that Jesus Christ, Our Lord, Son of the Blessed Virgin Mary, did not possess anything of the maternal substance, but in the form of a man had His nature only in the Word of God. For this impiety, since he was unwilling to be corrected, he was condemned

by Flavian, bishop of that city. But he trusted in princely friendsip and courtly favour, and petitioned to be heard by a universal council. He received the assent of the Emperor Theodosius, who ordered all the bishops to convene at Ephesus for a re-trial of his case.

At this council, Dioscorus, bishop of Alexandria, claiming primacy for himself, issued a condemnation of Flavian, bishop of Constantinople: this was opposed by Hilary, deacon of the Roman church, who had been appointed, along with Julius, bishop of Puteolanum [*Pitgliano, near Orvieto, Italy*], to attend from the Apostolic See in place of the holy Pope Leo. Then, when all the bishops had assembled in conclave, they were compelled by force and by fear of the allies—or warriors—the emperor had assigned to support Dioscorus, bishop of the city of Alexandria, to give assent to this heresy. The already mentioned deacon determined, in spite of the great danger to his life, to raise a dissenting voice. When he was threatened with death for this, he abandoned all his possessions and went into hiding so that he could send his adverse report (preferably to the Pope, alternatively to other bishops of Italy) on how the Catholic faith had been violated.

And the holy Flavian, who was in their hands, was sent by them into exile, and gloriously passed over to Christ.

[450] Pope Leo showed his strength of character by sending priests and deacons a second time to the East to refute the heresy. And Theodosius Augustus died in the same year. The Emperor Theodosius having finished his days, Chrysaphius was placed in charge but was killed because of the wrong use he had made of the prince's friendship. Marcianus, a most serious man, and one urgently needed not only by the state but by the Church, took power with the consent of the whole army. His edicts, accepting the authority of the Apostolic See, condemned the Council of Ephesus and ordered a council of bishops to assemble at Chalcedon, to deal kindly with those who accepted correction and to expel those who persisted in heresy.

Placidia died on 27 November.

[451] After the killing of his brother, Attila's riches were augmented by the addition of the murdered man's wealth. He summoned many thousand tribesmen of his blood to war, and had them fall upon the Goths with a force so great that the guarantor of Roman friendship[6] gave warning. When many Gaulish cities experienced his ferocious onslaughts across the Rhine, we and the Goths quickly agreed to resist the frenzy of these arrogant enemies by an alliance

of armies. Such was the foresight of the patrician Aëtius that he suffered no delay in assembling warriors from all quarters and he attacked the enemy multitude with a not unequal force. The conflict was evenly balanced and an incalculable mutual slaughter occurred. Nevertheless it was the Huns who were the defeated, since they lost their stomach for war and those of them who survived returned to their own country.

[452] Having replaced the men he lost in Gaul, Attila advanced to invade Italy through Pannonia. After what had happened in the former war our leader Aëtius had failed to anticipate this; to the extent that he did not even block the Alpine passes to prevent the enemy's passage. Now the only hope for survival, in his view, was, along with the emperor, to abandon all of Italy. But this was decided to be both disgraceful and dangerous in the extreme. Shame was joined to fear: it was the ferocity and greed of the enemy, it was believed, that had caused the widespread destruction of so many excellent provinces. In all the consultations it seemed to the magnates and the Senate, and the Roman people, that there was nothing to be done but to send delegates ask this savage king for peace.

Confident in the help of God, Who would, he knew, not fail the pious in their endeavours, the most blessed Pope Leo undertook this business along with the former consul Avienus and the former prefect Trigetius. And what happened was exactly what faith would have foretold. Indeed, the whole delegation was received worthily, the king being so pleased at the presence of the supreme bishop, that he both ordered an end to the war, and, having given assurances of peace, withdrew beyond the Danube.

[453] When the council of Chalcedon concluded, Eutyches and Dioscorus were condemned; however, all those who had abandoned them were received into communion. The universal belief in the Incarnation of the Word, according to the evangelical and apostolic teaching, was confirmed and affirmed through Pope Leo.

On the death of Attila in his homeland, a great conflict immediately arose among his sons concerning the takeover of power. In the end some tribes which had been subordinate to the Huns, taking advantage of this weakness, stirred up wars in which these savage peoples in mutual attacks wrought terror on one another.

Among the Goths settled in Gaul a quarrel arose between the sons of King Theodoric, of whom Thorismodus most inherited his father's quality. And when as king he worked to forward the Roman peace and the neutrality of the Goths, he was killed by his kin because he was insisting on harmful and irrevocable plans.

[454] An evil enmity developed between Valentinian Augustus and Aëtius the patrician, after the marriage pact of their children, and although they had given each other pledges of mutual faith. Love, happily, had been growing; afterwards hatred flared, fanned, it is believed, by the eunuch Heraclius, who so bound the emperor's soul to himself in a corrupt servitude, that he could easily persuade him to do whatever he wanted. So, when Heraclius had convinced the emperor of all things bad about Aëtius, that prince was persuaded that the only way to secure his safety was to anticipate his enemy's machinations by his own action. So it came about that when Aëtius, in the emperor's presence became heated in arguing his son's case, he was killed by the emperor's own hand and by the swords of those around him. The praetorian prefect Boethius, a close friend, was killed at the same time.

[455] The death of Valentinian followed shortly on that of Aëtius. Instead of taking precautions against it, he carelessly mixed with the friends and soldiers of Aëtius. They watched for an occasion to put into effect a plan they had conceived; and when he had left the City on his way to a performance of the games, they stabbed him unexpectedly. At the same time Heraclius, who was nearby, was killed. And no one of the large number of the ruler's followers was impelled to avenge so great a crime.

When this treason was committed, Maximus, a man both of consular and of patrician rank, took over the Empire. Charged with the responsibility of the welfare of a state in danger, he soon gave evidence of what his intentions were. In fact, not only did he not punish the murderers of Valentinian, but he made friends of them, and having deprived Valentinian's wife Augusta of the liberty to mourn her husband, he shortly forced her into marriage with himself.

But such outrageous behaviour could not continue long. Indeed a month later, news came of Geiseric's arrival from Africa; and crowds of nobles and commoners were fleeing from the City. Maximus too, having given permission to all to leave, was anxious to get away. On the seventy-seventh day after he took over the Empire, he was torn to shreds by the royal servants and thrown piece by piece into the Tiber, so that he had no burial place.

After this death of Maximus there followed immediately—and fittingly—the fall of Rome, with much lamentation. Geiseric found the City bare of all defences. Outside the gates he met the holy bishop Leo, whose pleading, with the intervention of God, so softened him that on the surrender of the city he undertook, so far as was in his power, to refrain from fire, slaughter and rapine.

Then—open and unresisting—for fourteen days, without let or hindrance Rome was stripped of all its wealth. And many thousands of captives, chosen according to whether they were satisfactory in age or accomplishment, including the queen and her daughters, were carried off to Carthage.

In the same year the Lord's Easter was celebrated on 24 April, as a result of the persistent insistence of the bishop of Alexandria, with whom all the East found itself in agreement, in spite of Pope Leo's having affirmed that the feast should rather be celebrated on 17 April. There exist letters from the Pope, addressed to "the most clement Prince Marcian", in which the case that the truth has been tampered with is convincingly expounded, and in which Catholic zeal teaches that if his opinion were adopted it would be more effective for unity and peace than the view which had been approved. That view should not immediately be followed; since the offence it gave is damaging and will ruin authority in perpetuity.

FIFTEEN

St Patrick's Writings

Virtually all that we know for certain about St Patrick is derived from the two documents here printed in translation from his Latin texts. They are both open letters, addressed to particular groups of people on particular occasions: the *Confessio*, or "Declaration", and the "Letter against the soldiers of Coroticus". The reader will very quickly discover that they give us little factual information about the details of his career. Where they do allude to particular episodes or events it is by no means clear what exactly these events were. On the other hand, in a remarkable way, they allow us to know what kind of a person St Patrick was—they give us, not his exterior, but his interior, history.

Even our understanding of the exterior history, however, is helped by the two documents, since we have some information (although not very much) about the context in which they were produced.

Patrick was born in Roman Britain, at or near the place which appears in the manuscripts as "Bannavem Taberniae". The earliest manuscript we now possess of either of the letters was copied by the scribe Feardomhnach into the Book of Armagh early in the ninth century—more than three hundred years after the death of Patrick. The *Confessio* had obviously gone through a number of copyings and re-copyings by then, since there are omissions and blunders in the text. The placename "Bannavem Taberniae" is almost certainly one of these, and in the translation I follow Professor Charles Thomas's emendation to "Banna Venta Berniae".[1]

This would locate Patrick's father's estate at Birdoswald, a short distance west of Luguvalium (Carlisle), on the northern frontier of Roman Britain. There is no certainty about it, however, although the high probability is that Patrick's home was somewhere in the western parts of Britain, open to Irish raids. Patrick's grandfather was a priest. This was long before clerical celibacy became a general rule. His father was a deacon, but possibly (since he was also a decurion) he had taken the order for secular reasons—to evade tax.

As for the date of Patrick's birth, we can only make educated guesses. The Irish annals state that he commenced his mission in Ireland in AD

432, and much of the guesswork has centred on this information. However, the information is not only unreliable but almost certainly quite wrong. That annal was not written in 432, but at least a century later—probably more like two and a half centuries. It is an attempt by seventh-century writers to establish Patrick's mission as early as possible after the advent of Palladius, who was sent by Pope Celestine in 431 to be the first bishop of the Irish Christians (as those writers knew from Prosper).

The date is almost certainly much too early for Patrick, and its acceptance was to cause much confusion when the writers of two or three hundred years after his time tried to reconstruct a plausible biography for him. His career was stretched over the whole of the fifth century, so that in some versions he lived for 120 years. He is reported to have died in 461 but he is also reported to have died in 492/3. Some concluded that there were two Patricks, an older and a younger. Although it is perfectly clear from Patrick's own writings (the only good evidence) that he came from Britain and that the base of his mission was in Britain, the later legends bring him to Ireland from Gaul—probably, as T.F. O'Rahilly suggested, because he became confused to some extent with his Gaulish predecessor Palladius.

Since educated guesswork is all we have to go on, both the chronology and the details of Patrick's career will probably always be matters for debate. No one doubts that he lived and worked in the fifth century. But there are alternative chronologies for his mission: 432–461; or something more like 461(?)–493. As between these, the balance of the evidence, on which much detailed study has now been done, has been tilting towards the later.

Taking the later chronology, then, we may attempt a speculative outline of his biography. He was born, probably on the northern frontier of Roman Britain, about 415. His father was a decurion, a member of the provincial-Roman governing class, and was landlord of a small estate. He was also a deacon of the Church. Patrick himself (as he tells us) was neglectful of religion as a boy, and he suggests to us that this accorded with the general atmosphere surrounding him. When he was fourteen or fifteen, Patrick committed some sin for which his conscience was to trouble him long after. When he was sixteen—that is, by this reckoning, about 430–31—raiders descended on the district around his father's farm and he, along with many others, was carried off into slavery in Ireland.

Before he was born (assuming these dates to be more or less correct) the Roman Britons had already been organizing their own affairs and their own defence. The British revolt in 409 was followed by the final withdrawal of the legions from the province, apparently at the urging of the Romano-British, who had had enough of military plots and coups among their defenders.

When Rome fell to the Goths in AD 410, Britain, although not wholly Christian had, as we have seen, a well established and organized Christian

Church. If the chronology here adopted is correct, the anti-Pelagian mission of St Germanus to the British church and the sending of Palladius to Ireland would have happened at about the same time as the Irish raid on Britain which took Patrick captive.

Patrick, as he tells us, escaped from his servitude after six years—say, about 437. Where his escape took him to is not clear, but it would appear from his own account that some years were to pass before he returned to Britain. It is likely that he spent a period in northern Gaul.[2] But he returned to his home, perhaps some time in the early 440s. Here he had a dream calling him back to the people among whom he had served as a slave, and it was probably at this time that he took clerical orders and set out on the course that would lead him as a bishop to Ireland. It would have been about this time too that he confided in his closest friend, telling him of the sin of his youth that troubled his conscience. He may have been a deacon by 445, a priest by 450, a bishop by about 460. This is to assume, as we probably should, a normal progress in holy orders. The *Didiscalia* directed that candidates for the episcopate be fifty years old.[3] Canon II of the Council of Neocaesaria (314–319) directed that a presbyter should be not less than thirty years old at ordination.[4] Pope Siricius (384–399) directed that those chosen of the Lord, after being readers until puberty, should remain acolytes or subdeacons until the age of thirty, and be deacons and presbyters for at least five years in each order before being allowed to advance to the episcopate.[5] Deacons nonetheless often at this time rose directly to become bishops. Patrick throughout the *Confessio* shows that he is conscious of his shortcomings in respect of the earlier part of this programme. But it was as a bishop that he came to Ireland. This, by the reckoning above, would have been about 460–61. (The earlier date of his death given in the annals is 461.) Leo the Great died in 461. The Irish annals, noting Leo's accession to the Roman see in 440 (although they misplace the note under the year 441) add the information that this was the pope who "approved" Patrick. Where the annalists obtained this information is unknown (again, they were writing centuries after the event, reconstructing a chronology), but they may have had available to them some document, an original or a copy, certifying that Patrick's mission had been cleared by Leo.

For Patrick had come to his Irish episcopate not from Gaul but from Britain, perhaps from Carlisle. As Roman order broke down farther south, it seems that bishops in the north of Britain may have been attempting a new organization of the church in the border areas—among the Picts, the Manx and the Irish as well as the Britons—Celtic-speaking peoples all, mostly living outside the fortified frontier line. There were extensive Irish ("Scottic") settlements in Scotland by now. Ireland itself, never invaded by the Roman legions, was a wholly alien world to the inhabitants of the Empire.

Patrick probably came directly to north-eastern Ireland, but, as E.A.

Thompson has rightly emphasized,[6] *not* on a mission to pagans; rather, initially, to minister as bishop to a Christian community there. This was the regular and prescribed practice for bishops in the fifth century: they went to established and organized Christian communities, not as evangelists to gatherings of unbelievers. He was probably the first bishop among the Ulaid, as Palladius had been the first bishop of the Irish; and it is possible that Ulaid formed a separate ecclesiastical province.

At some stage, charges against Patrick were made before a gathering of his British "seniors," and he was condemned. As he tells us, he was not present himself at the meeting, and apparently he was later vindicated (perhaps on appeal to Rome). He informs us that the meeting took place about thirty years after he had confessed his boyhood sin to his friend "before he was a deacon". On the chronology here assumed, therefore, it occurred in the early 470s.

Some scholars have taken it that the purpose of the meeting was to prevent Patrick from being consecrated bishop to go to Ireland, and that the opponents of his mission succeeded for a time. This, however, is to strain the plain meaning of Patrick's words, which indicate that he was already involved in his "laborious episcopate" at the time. But Patrick's words are not always unambiguous.

His *Confessio*, in any event, is a response to the accusations made against him at the British meeting. In it he reiterates three points in particular. He repeatedly defends what he has done in going to the ends of the earth among the heathen, to preach to them and to baptize them. He insists that God has guided him directly, by inspiration received in dreams. He affirms that he is telling the truth when he says that he has not profited materially from his mission. The Declaration appears to be addressed in the main to people among whom he had lived and worked and it is consistent with a defence against a charge that he had left the Christian community to which he had been appointed as bishop, to go on a private mission to the pagans in the remote west, a mission to which he was convinced God had called him.

We can reasonably infer from what he says that he is responding to three principal accusations: (1) that his activity of converting the heathen was wrong or out of order; (2) that he lacked authority for what he was doing; (3) that he was acting for profit. His argument is directed at his accusers, and it was not necessary for him to spell out the accusations, since those whom he addressed were obviously already in possession of that information.

In the opening sentence of the second surviving writing of his—the Letter, an instrument of excommunication—he is at pains to state his authority for issuing such a document and carefully claims to have been duly appointed (*constitutus*) to Ireland and to be a bishop. He does not describe himself, according to the normal pattern of such statements of authority at this time, as bishop of Armagh, or of any see, or bishop of the

Irish. "*Constitutus*" here is a technical term meaning that he has been properly established and approved in, or just possibly to, Ireland. The word is found in this strict and formal sense in, for example, the correspondence of Pope Leo the Great. Patrick, for purpose of exercising authority, is saying that he is regularly appointed in Ireland and that he is a bishop. This suggests that his position has been approved but that he is in some way operating outside a regular jurisdiction.

It would fit the picture if Patrick, having been appointed bishop of a Christian community, or communities, in Ulster, had decided after some years to follow his lifelong ambition, or divinely inspired destiny, and return to the far west, to the heathen among whom he had spent six years as a slave, handing over his diocese or province to the clerical organization he had built up. The inquisitorial meeting in Britain, at which he was not present, could well have issued a reprimand for such dereliction—as the "seniors" saw it—since there were standing prohibitions of such action in the regulations of the Church.

The departure of clerics from their appointed place of ministry had been a cause of concern within the Church and can be seen to have been a problem even before the ending of the persecutions.[7] The reasons for objecting to the practice, revealed in the regulations made by fourth- and fifth-century church councils, fall broadly under three headings. H. Hess describes one of them as follows:

> The theological objection seems to be derived from the early view of the relationaship between the bishop and his church. His election by an almost independent Christian community and his essential fatherhood among his people, as standing in the place of Christ himself, appear to have given rise to the concept of a mystical union existing between the bishop and his see which was expressed as being akin to the marriage bond.[8]

A moral objection was that clerics might make their move in the interests of their own betterment, either because they wished for a superior appointment (as when a bishop moved in hope of finding himself in a richer or more prestigious see) or because they wished to conduct business in other provinces—which seems to have been not uncommon.

There was a third objection on administrative grounds. By moving from their appointed place into a place to which others had been assigned, clerics could cause confusion and dissension and could tend to undermine authority; as when a bishop moved into and attempted to exercise authority in the territory of another bishop.

The prohibitions of such dereliction, already cited, include clauses and sections which assume that the wandering of a bishop was frequently occasioned by the desire for personal advancement or gain. Now, Patrick's mission—whatever exactly its character may have been—was at least partly financed by himself, through the sale of his patrimony in Britain.[9] This, far from indicating his disinterestedness to his detractors, may have suggested an investment of some kind in the opening up of new territories. The legislation was available for covering this. Canon 19 of the council of Elvira in Spain (*c*.AD 300), for example (whose enactments were re-affirmed at the council of Arles and passed into the legislation of the Gaulish church) stated that:

> Bishops, priests and deacons must not leave their churches to engage in business, and must not go about the provinces in search of profitable markets; indeed, to restrict their activities, let them send son, or freedman, or merchant, or friend, or whomsoever, about their affairs; and, if they want to do business, let them do it in their own province.[10]

Patrick's activities must have been complex as well as perilous and—however unimpeachable they were—must have involved transactions in cattle and other stock, jewellery, perhaps ingots of silver or bronze. As he tells us himself, he had to make various payments for safe-conduct and legal protection. And no doubt the difficulties arising for his Christian converts within a pagan society must also have involved him in business transactions. In one shape or another, bishops and bingo go together. It would have been all too easy for Patrick's accusers, assuming them to have been affronted at his scandalous behaviour in abandoning his worthy Christian charges for a life among the wild barbarians of the west coast, to go beyond the dry technicalities of administrative and jurisdictional misdemeanour and introduce the juicier topic of peculation.

Patrick is driven by this second charge to the frustrated anger of a man at whom dirt has been unjustifiably thrown, who knows that, no matter what, dirt clings. It is in defending himself against this charge that he gives us a few tantalizing glimpses of his missionary work—especially in so far as it relates to the ruling classes.

His vocabulary is consistent and precise in this respect. Both in the Declaration and in the Letter he uses two different words whose distinction is masked when we follow the common and necessary practice of translating them both with the word 'Irish'. For him, the country in which he laboured is *Hiberione*. The name doesn't once occur in his narrative in the nominative. He never calls the country *Scottia*, the name by which it was most commonly known for some centuries before and after his time. For the ordinary people of Ireland his word was, apparently, *Hiberionaces*. He applies the word *Scotti* to Irish raiders and to the class ruling the chiefdoms. He avoids using the word directly of his own converts of that class, preferring to describe them as "sons" or "daughters" of *Scotti* or "of the race of the *Scotti*". It is as if to be a *Scottus* or a *Scotta* was to be a reprobate and was not consistent with being one of the baptized elect. In this his usage is similar to St Jerome's.

It is clear that he was in danger at times, that part of his work was with slaves and that he was concerned with their lot. The duty of finding the means for the manumission of Christian slaves is implied. More than once he emphasises his conviction that he has fulfilled prophecy by going to the remote and pagan west, preaching the Gospel to the far ends of the earth. And he indicates that, for him, to abandon his civilized home and live in barbarism was a great sacrifice of love.

He tells us that he delayed a long time before issuing his Statement. Following the suggested chronology, we may tentatively date his *Confessio* to the 470s, perhaps the late '70s. By this reckoning he would have been about sixty in 475, and could appropriately refer to himself as being in his old age.

Patrick's second surviving writing is a letter of excommunication directed against the soldiers of a petty British ruler called by him "Coroticus", who had carried off some of Patrick's newly baptized converts into slavery. Most scholars think this was written before the *Confessio*. The two documents, however, must be quite close together in time—phrases and passages recur. The matter is of comparatively little moment but I think it more likely that the letter against Coroticus is the later of the two.

It has several passages so close in wording to passages and phrases in the Declaration as to suggest that they are close in time. It sheds a little more light on Patrick's mission and his attitudes. For example, references to the *Scotti*, written in heat in the Letter, appear to be more hostile than references in the Declaration. The Letter, unlike the Declaration, does not appear to be the product of long rumination: it is hasty, angry, and indeed anguished.

Professor Thompson has put forward substantial arguments in favour of his view that Coroticus was a British tyrant established, not in Britain, but in Ireland, presumably in east Ulster.[11] In this view Coroticus is not to be identified with the shadowy Ceredic of Dumbarton, or the other shadowy Ceredic who is said to have founded the principality of Cardigan, or with any other half-known figure of that obscure age.

The Patrick of the Letter is unmistakeably the Patrick of the *Confessio*. That is to say that not only are they the work of the same man, but they are close in time. Not only turns of phrase but the same preoccupations occur, and Patrick was clearly in much the same circumstances when he wrote both. Bieler, the greatest authority on the texts, believed the Letter to be the earlier, and Professor Thomas and others agree. Certainty is impossible; but in the Letter Patrick appears to me to use words and phrases which he had recently composed for the Declaration, into whose argument they fit more naturally.

Just possibly the date 493, the second given in the annals for Patrick's death, may be based on a contemporary record and may be approximately correct. If so, on the proposed chronology, he would have been in his late seventies when he died. In the two letters we are given glimpses—little more—of Patrick's work in Ireland. Both were written when he was a travelling evangelist among pagans, winning large numbers of converts.

He gives us only one Irish placename, that of the wood of Foclut. He implies that it was the place of his captivity. The weight of the evidence is that this was a wood in the west of Ireland, in what is now County Mayo, on the western shore of Killala Bay. The medieval legend that Patrick tended his flocks as a slave on Slemish, in what is now County Antrim, in east Ulster, is already found in seventh-century writings, but these are too remote from the event to be wholly persuasive. Patrick, however, had associations with east Ulster, most notably his connection with Armagh, the church which claimed him as its founder and which became the primatial church and see in Ireland, largely with the backing of his name. But he was not buried in Armagh, nor was his burial place known, although in due course legends were created to offer locations.

He believed, as we have seen, that he represented the fulfilment of prophecy. He had brought the Christian faith to the remotest edge of the Ocean. The Gospel had now been preached throughout the inhabited earth, and the end of the world accordingly was near. His remarkable achievement was to found a new kind of church, one which broke the Roman imperial mould and was both catholic and barbarian. And he broke the Roman church mould by going among the pagans. His memory faded after his death but was revived, almost certainly through the accident of the survival of these two writings. That accident was a fitting one, for he was a singular man.

From the seventh century onward he was regarded as pre-eminent among Ireland's early saints. His feast-day, as a kind of national day, was already being celebrated by the Irish in Europe in the ninth and tenth centuries. In later times he became more and more widely known as the patron of Ireland. The crowds who march down Fifth Avenue in New York on 17 March each year, and down a thousand other avenues around the world, may not know a great deal about him, but in honouring his memory they follow a very ancient tradition.

Patrick's, it should be realised, is a lone voice from the silence of the fifth century in Britain and Ireland. His writings are the earliest sustained works, written in Ireland, that we can still read. And they show us the mind of a Christian Roman of the twilight of the Empire, a mind difficult for us to understand, but plainly that of a remarkable man.

SIXTEEN

St Patrick's Declaration

[Patrick introduces himself and states his creed]

I, Patrick, a sinner, am a most uncultivated man, and the least of all the faithful, and I am greatly despised by many.

My father was the deacon Calpornius, son of the late Potitus, a priest of the town of Banna Venta Berniae [*probably near Carlisle*]. He had a small estate nearby, where I was taken captive.

I was then barely sixteen. I had neglected the true God, and when I was carried off into captivity in Ireland, along with a great number of people, it was well deserved. For we cut ourselves off from God and did not keep His commandments, and we disobeyed our bishops who were reminding us of our salvation. God revealed His being to us through His wrath: He scattered us among foreign peoples, even to the end of the earth, where, appropriately, I have my own small existence among strangers.

Then the Lord made me aware of my unbelief, so that—however late—I might recollect my offences and turn with all my heart to the Lord my God. It was He Who took heed of my insignificance, Who pitied my youth and ignorance, Who watched over me before I knew Him and before I came to understand the difference between good and evil, and Who protected and comforted me as a father would his son. That is why I cannot remain silent (further, it would be inappropriate to do so) about the great favours and graces which the Lord deigned to grant me in the land of my captivity. For the way to make repayment for that revelation of God through capture and enslavement is to declare and make known His wonders to every race under heaven.

Because there is no other God, nor has there been, nor will there be in the future, other than God the Father, begotten without beginning, from Whom all things begin, Who governs all things, as we have been taught; and His Son Jesus Christ. Whom we testify to have been manifestly with the Father always, to have been spiritually with the Father since before the beginning of time, to have been born of the Father before the beginning in a way that cannot be described. And by Him were made things visible and invisible. He was made man. Having vanquished death He was taken back into heaven to the Father, Who gave him the full power to govern all things in heaven and earth and hell, so that every tongue should confess to Him that Jesus Christ is Lord and God. We believe in Him and expect His coming in the near future as Judge of the living and the dead, Who will make return to all according to what they have done. He poured out abundantly on us the Holy Spirit, the gift and pledge of immortality, Who makes of obedient believers sons of God and co-heirs of Christ. We confess and adore Him as one God in the Trinity of the Holy Name.

It was He Who said through His prophet: "Call on Me in the day of your trouble and I will free you and you will glorify Me."[1] And again He says: "It is an honourable thing to make known and proclaim the works of God."[2]

Although I am imperfect in many ways, nevertheless I wish my brethren and kin to know what sort of person I am, so that they may understand my motives. I am not unaware of what my Lord has taught, since He has made it clear in the psalm: "You shall destroy the speakers of lies."[3] And again He says: "The lying mouth kills the soul."[4] And the Lord also says in the Gospel: "The idle word that people speak, they shall account for it on the day of judgement."[5]

So, I realise I must be in the greatest dread—in fear and trembling—of incurring this sentence on that day when no one can hide himself or sneak away but we shall all, every one of us, have to account even for our smallest sins at the tribunal of the Lord Christ.

[Patrick explains his deficiencies]

Therefore, while I have had it in mind for a long time to write, up to now I have hesitated. I was afraid of being exposed to criticism, because I have not the education of others, who have absorbed to the full both law and sacred scripture alike and who have never, from infancy onward, had to change to another language; but rather could continually perfect the language they had. Whereas, with me, our words and our language have been translated into a foreign tongue, so that it is easy to ascertain—from the flavour of my writing—the manner of my education and of my training in expression. Because it is said: "The wise man will be distinguished by his language,"[6] as will judgment and knowledge and true teaching. But excuses, however true, are pointless, especially if we take them in conjunction with my presumption in attempting only now, in my old age, to achieve more than I could in my youth. For my sins prevented me from continuing to build on my early education. But who believes me, even if I repeat what I have already said? As a youth, indeed not much more than a beardless boy, I was taken captive; before I knew what to aim at, what to avoid. So, because of this, today I am ashamed, and agitated with fear, at exposing my lack of education; because I lack the fluency to express myself concisely, as my spirit longs to do and as I try with heart and soul.

But, even if I had been given what was given to others, nevertheless, out of gratitude, I would not be silent. And if perhaps I seem to many people to be pushing myself forward, with my lack of knowledge and my lame language, yet it is indeed written: "The stammering tongues will quickly learn to speak peace."[7]

How much more ought we not to aim at that, since, as it is written, we ourselves are "the letter of Christ for salvation, even to the end of the earth",[8] and, even if the language does not flow but is blocked and turgid "it is written on your hearts not with ink but with the Spirit of the living God."[9] And again the Spirit affirms that rustic backwardness, too, was created by the Most High.

So, in the first place I am a rustic person and an exile, plainly ignorant, and I do not know how to provide for the future. But this I know for certain: that before I was abased, I was like a stone that had fallen into a deep mire. And He Who is mighty came and in His mercy picked me up and indeed lifted me high to place me on top of the wall.

Because of this I ought also to shout aloud, giving some thanks to the Lord for His blessings, both here and in eternity, which are so great that the human mind cannot comprehend them.

So, therefore, be astonished, all you, both great and little, who fear God. And you, reverend professors, listen and pay close attention. Who was it that lifted up me—stupid me—from the middle of those who seemed to be wise and skilled in the law and powerful in rhetoric and in all matters? And Who was it that inspired me—me!—above others to be such a person (if only I were!) as could do good faithfully—in fear and reverence and without complaint—to that people to whom Christ's love transported me and gave me; if I should prove worthy in short to be of service to them in humility and truth?

Consequently, I take this to be a measure of my faith in the Trinity that, without regard to danger, I make known God's gift and the eternal comfort He provides: that I spread God's name everywhere dutifully and without fear, so that after my death I may leave a legacy to so many thousands of people—my brothers and sons whom I have baptized in the Lord.

[Patrick tells how God has singled him out]

And I was not a worthy or a fit person for what the Lord granted me, His minor servant: that after such calamities and such great burdens, after captivity, after many years, He should bestow on me, in relation to that people, so much that I had never hoped for or thought of in my youth.

But after I had arrived in Ireland, I found myself pasturing flocks daily, and I prayed a number of times each day. More and more the love and fear of God came to me, and faith grew and my spirit was exercised, until I was praying up to a hundred times every day—and in the night nearly as often. So that I would even remain in the woods and on the mountain in snow, frost and rain, waking to pray before first light. And I felt no ill effect, nor was I in any way sluggish—because, as I now realise, the Spirit was seething within me. *I was full of enthusiasm*

And it was there in fact that one night, in my sleep, I heard a voice saying to me: "It is good that you fast, who will go soon to your home-land." And again, after a short space of time I heard this pronouncement: "Look! Your ship is ready."

And it was not nearby, but was, as it happened, two hundred miles away. I had never been there, and I knew not a person there. And shortly afterwards I fled from that place, leaving the man with whom I had been for six years. I travelled with the aid of God's power, Who guided me successfully on my way, and I had nothing to fear, until I arrived at that ship.

On the day I arrived the ship had weighed anchor. I explained that I had the wherewithal to sail with them. And that day, furthermore, I refused, for fear of God, to suck their nipples.[10] Nevertheless I hoped that some of them would come to faith in Jesus Christ (for they were heathen). This displeased the captain, who answered sharply, with anger: "Your wish to travel with us is quite futile."

And when I heard this, I left them in order to return to the shelter in which I had lodged, beginning to pray as I went. Before the prayer was finished, I heard one of them, who shouted loudly after me: "Come quickly; these men are calling you."

I returned to them immediately and they began to explain to me: "Come, we will accept you in good faith. Bind yourself in friendship to us in any way you wish." Because of this I was received among them and we set sail straightaway.

And after three days we reached land. We travelled for twenty-eight days through a wilderness. They ran out of food, and hunger weakened them, and the next day the captain addressed me: "What's this, Christian? You say your God is great and all-powerful. Then why can't you pray for us? For we are in danger of dying of hunger. In fact it's doubtful if we'll see another human being." I said to them confidently: "Trust in the Lord my God and turn to Him with all your hearts[11]—since nothing is impossible for Him—that He may send you today more than sufficient food for your journey—for He has an abundance everywhere."

And with God's help, so it came about. There—right before our eyes—a herd of pigs appeared. They killed many of them, and they spent two nights in that place eating their fill of pork and recovering their strength:

for many of them had dropped out and had been left half-dead along the way. After this, they gave the greatest thanks to God, and I gained prestige in their eyes. From that point onward they had abundant food. They even found some wild honey and offered me part of it, one of them saying: "It is a sacrifice." Thank God, I tasted none of it.

That very night, when I was asleep, Satan tested me most severely: the memory of it will remain with me as long as I am in this body. It was as if a huge rock fell on top of me and I had no use of my limbs. But from what quarter came the inspiration to my ignorant spirit to call on Helias? In the midst of all this I saw the sun rise in the heavens, and when I shouted "Helias! Helias!" with all my strength—see, the brilliance of the sun came down on me and straightaway removed all the weighty pressure.[12] I believe that the Lord Christ came to my help, and that it was the Spirit Who was already crying out in me; and I pray that it will be so on the day of my troubles,[13] as it says in the Gospel: "On that day"—the Lord testifies—"it is not you who speaks, but the Spirit of the Father Who speaks within you."[14]

(And on another occasion many years later I was taken captive. And I spent the first night with my captors. However, I heard a divine announcement to me: "You will be two months in their hands." This is what happened. On the sixtieth night the Lord freed me from them.)[15]

While we were on our journey He provided us with food, fire and dry conditions until, on the tenth day, we met people. As I have indicated above, we travelled for twenty-eight days through the wilderness, and on that night on which we met people, we had truly no food left.

Another time, after a few years, when I was in Britain, my family received me as a son, and asked me whether—after such tribulations as I had undergone—they could trust me now, as a son, never to leave them again. But, while I was there, in a night vision, I saw a man coming, as it were from Ireland. His name was Victoricus, and he carried many letters, and he gave me one of them. I read the heading: "The Voice of the Irish". As I began the letter, I imagined in that moment that I heard the voice of those very people who were near the wood of Foclut, which is beside the western sea [*west of Killala Bay, in Co. Mayo*]—and they cried out, as with one voice: "We appeal to you, holy servant boy, to come and walk among us."

I was pierced by great emotion and could not read on, and so I woke. Thank God that after many years the Lord answered them according to their cry.

And another night He spoke (God knows—not I—whether within me or beside me) in words which I heard in terror, but without understanding them, except that at the end of the message He said: "He Who gave His life for you; it is He Who speaks within you." And so I woke, full of joy.

And again, I saw Him praying within me and I was as if I were inside

my own body, and I heard Him above me—that is, over my inner person—and He was praying hard with groanings. And all the while I was dumbfounded and astonished, wondering Who it could be that was praying within me. But at the end of the prayer, He spoke, saying that He was the Spirit. And so I woke, and I recollected what the Apostle had said: "The Spirit helps us in the deficiencies of our prayers, for we do not know what it is proper to pray for; but the Spirit Himself pleads on our behalf with unutterable groanings which cannot be expressed in words."[16]
And again: "The Lord, our advocate, prays on our behalf."[17]

[Patrick's trial by his seniors and his vindication]

And when I was attacked by certain of my seniors, who came and cast up my sins against my laborious episcopate; on that day I was powerfully tempted and might have fallen, now and in eternity. But the Lord showed His benign mercy to His disciple, who is an exile for His Name, and He came mightily to my support in this humiliation. Since it was not through my fault that I was brought into scandal and disgrace, I pray God that it will not be reckoned against them as sin.

They found a pretext from thirty years earlier, bringing against me words of a confession I made before I was a deacon. Because, in an anxious and melancholy state of mind, I had privately told my dearest friend about something I had done one day—indeed, in one hour—when I was a boy, before I had strength of character. I am not sure—God alone knows—if I had yet reached the age of fifteen, and I was still, since my childhood, not a believer in the living God; rather I remained in death and unbelief until I was severely chastised and truly brought down to earth, every day, by hunger and nakedness.

On the other hand, while it was not of my own choice that I arrived in Ireland at that time when I was almost a lost soul, it was a good thing for me, because I was reformed by the Lord and He prepared me to be today what was once remote from me; so that, whereas once I did not even consider my own salvation, now the salvation of others is my care and concern.

Therefore, on the day when I was rejected by the people mentioned above, that night I saw in a dream the dishonouring documents in front of me, while at the same time I heard the divine Voice saying to me: "It displeased Us to see Our chosen one in this state: stripped of honour." Nor did He say, "It displeased Me"—but rather—"It displeased Us"—(as if linking Himself with him—just as He had said: "Whoever touches you, it is if he touched the apple of My eye."[18]

For that reason, I offer thanks that He gave me strength in all matters, not hindering that departure which I had decided upon, nor also those works which I learned to do from the Lord Christ; rather, I felt all the more His great power within me.[19] And my faith was vindicated before God and men.

Therefore I tell you boldly that my conscience does not reproach me now or for the future. I have God as a witness that I do not lie in what I tell you.

But I am all the more sorry for my close friend: how did we deserve to hear such evidence given? He to whom I had entrusted my very soul! And before that case (which I did not initiate, nor was I present in Britain for it), I learned from some of the brethren that it was he who would act on my behalf in my absence. (He is the very one who had told me, with his own mouth: "Look: you should be raised to the rank of bishop"—of which I was not worthy.) But how did he come, shortly afterwards, in public, in the presence of people both good and bad, to bring me into disgrace over something which he had willingly and gladly forgiven—as had the Lord, Who is greater than all?[20]

[Patrick makes the case for his mission to the pagans]

Enough of this. Nevertheless, I must not conceal the gift of God, which He so freely bestowed on me in the land where I was a captive. Because it was at that time that I strenuously sought Him and found Him. And He has saved me from all injustices—so I believe—because His Spirit is within me and works in me to the present day. Another bold statement; but God knows that if the voice that guided me were merely human, I should have kept silent for the love of Christ.

And so, tirelessly, I thank my God, Who kept me faithful on the day I was tried, so that today I might offer to Him, the Lord Christ, the sacrifice of my living soul. He saved me in all dangers and perils, causing me to ask: "Who am I, Lord, or what am I called to, that in all Your Divinity You have shown Yourself to me, so that today I constantly lift up and magnify Your Name among the heathen, wherever I have been, not only in good times but in bad?"

So, whatever may come my way, good or bad, I equally tackle it, always giving thanks to God, Who granted me unlimited faith in Him, and Who helped me so that, ignorant as I am, I might in these final days dare to undertake this work, so holy and so wonderful.[21] It is just as if I were a follower of those whom the Lord foretold, once, in former times, who were to be harbingers of His Gospel for a testimony to all races before the end of the world. And indeed, we have seen this done. See: we are witnesses: the Gospel has been preached to those places beyond which nobody lives.

However, it would be tedious to tell in whole or in detail of my undertaking. I shall relate briefly how the most holy God frequently freed me from slavery, and from the twelve dangers which threatened my life, as well as from many snares which I cannot express in words. I do not wish to affront my readers, but God, Who knows all things before they happen, is my authority that He readily and frequently gave me His counsel, just because I am in His care, though I am poor and insignificant.

From where did this understanding come to me, who had knowledge neither of the number of my days nor of God? From where did I afterwards receive so great and so beneficent a gift—to know and to desire God, relinquishing homeland and family for Him?

They offered me many gifts, with tears and lamentation, and I offended them, as well as going against the wish of certain of my seniors, but God guided me not to agree with them or consent to them. This was no thanks to me; rather it was God Who triumphed within me and opposed them all, so that I might come to the Irish heathen to preach the Gospel and suffer the insults of unbelievers. But then!—to endure disgrace because of my departure! And many prosecutions, even to the extent of imprisonment, and to sacrifice my patrimony for the sake of others! I am ready indeed to give my life, freely, in His Name, and I choose to spend it here even until death, if the Lord will allow me.

Because I owe a great deal to God. He gave me this great boon: that through me many heathen should be reborn in God, and that afterwards they should be confirmed as Christians, so that everywhere clergy should be ordained for a population newly coming to the faith, a population which the Lord redeemed from the ends of the earth, just as He had promised through his prophets: "The nations will come to you from the ends of the earth and will say: 'How empty are the idols which our fore-fathers erected and they are of no use'";[22] and again: "I have placed you as a light among the nations so that you may bring salvation even to the end of the earth."[23]

And it is there that I choose to await His promise—in which, at least, He will never fail—as it is stated in the Gospel: "They will come from the east and from the west and will recline at table"[24] with Abraham and Isaac and Jacob: so we believe that believers will come from the whole world.

Therefore indeed it is true that there is an obligation to fish well and diligently, as the Lord commanded, saying: "Follow Me and I will make you fishers of men."[25] And again, He tells us through the prophets: "Look, I send out many fishers and hunters"[26]—says God, and so on. From which it follows most cogently that we are obliged to spread our nets so that we can catch a great shoal and multitude for God. And there should be clergy everywhere to baptise and preach to a population which is in need and longs for what it lacks, as the Lord says in the Gospel, where He admonishes and teaches, telling us: "Now therefore, go and teach all nations, baptizing them in the Name of the Father and of the Son and of the Holy Spirit, teaching them to observe all that I have commanded you, and then—see—I will be with you all days until the very end of the world."[27]

And again He says: "Going therefore out into the whole world, preach the Gospel to all of creation: whoever believes and is baptized will be saved; they who do not believe will be condemned."[28]

And again: "This Gospel of the Kingdom will be preached throughout the whole world as a testimony to all peoples; and then the end will come."[29]

And the Lord also foretells through the prophet, saying: "And in the last days", says the Lord, "I will pour out My Spirit over all flesh and your sons and daughters will prophesy, and your young men will see visions and your old men will dream dreams, and indeed in those days I will pour out My Spirit over my male servants and my female servants and they will prophesy."[30]

And in Hosea, He says: "A people that is not Mine I will call My people, and a people that has not obtained mercy I will call a people that has obtained mercy. And it will be in that place where it was said: 'You are not My people': there they will be called 'children of the living God'."[31]

So this is why it came about in Ireland that people who had no acquaintance with God, but who, up to now, always had cults or idols and abominations, are recently—by this dispensation—made a people of the Lord and are known as children of God. Sons of the *Scotti* and daughters of chiefs are openly monks and virgins of Christ.[32]

And indeed, there was a certain blessed noblewoman, of Scottic origin, mature and beautiful, whom I baptized. A few days later she had reason to come to us; she told us privately that she had received a message from an angel of God Who commanded her to become a virgin of Christ and so draw nearer to Him. Thanks be to God, just six days after that she embraced in the most excellent and eager way that which all the virgins of God follow.[33] They do not do it with their fathers' consent; on the contrary they endure harassment and false accusations from their parents. And nonetheless their numbers increase (and we do not know the number of those of our own race who were born there),[34] as well as those of widows and women living in chastity. But it is those who are held in slavery who have most to endure, even to the extent of suffering continual fears and threats. But the Lord has given grace to many of His handmaids, so that they can bravely imitate Him in spite of all prohibitions.

That is why, even if I wished to leave them so that I could visit Britain (and with all my heart I was ready and anxious for my homeland and my parents—not only that, but to go on to Gaul to visit the brethren and be in the presence of my Lord's saints—God knows how much I longed for it), I am bound by the Spirit, Whose testimony is that if I do this He will afterwards find me guilty. And I am afraid of wrecking the task I have begun—and not just I, but the Lord Christ, Who commanded me to come and live among them for the rest of my life. May it be the Lord's will to guard me against all evil, so that I may not sin against Him.

I hope, however, that I did what I should have done; but I have no trust in this self of mine so long as I am in the body. For he is powerful who endeavours every day to turn me from the faith and from the pure teachings of true religion which I hold even to the end of my life for the Lord Christ. But through the flesh the Enemy is always dragging me towards death, that is, towards what is enticing but unlawful; and I know, in part, why I have not led a perfect life like other believers. But I admit it to my Lord, and am not ashamed before Him, because I do not lie. Indeed, since I learned to know Him in my youth, the love and fear of God have grown in me, and up to now, with the Lord's help, I have kept the faith.

Let who will laugh and scoff. I will not be silent, nor will I conceal the signs and wonders which the Lord has shown to me many years before they happened—He Who knows all happenings since before the beginning of time.[35]

That is why I should give thanks to God without ceasing—because He has often been lenient with my foolishness and my carelessness. And because on more than one occasion He has not been wrathful with me, who was given to Him as a helper but who did not quickly accept the task which was made clear to me nor do as the Spirit prompted. And the Lord took pity on me countless times, because He saw that I was ready, but that I did not know how to organize myself for these matters. For there were many who hindered this mission. They even talked among themselves behind my back, saying: "Who is this fellow going into danger among enemies who do not know God?"

This was not from malice, but because they didn't like the look of it—I bear witness to that myself—and you may take it that it was because of my naïveté. And I was not aware of the grace which was within me. Now I know that I should have understood this earlier.

Now, then: I have given a simple explanation to those of my brothers and fellow servants who have believed in me because of what I preached—and continue to preach—for the strengthening and confirming of your faith. If only you too could be persuaded to do better! This will be my renown; for "it is the son's wisdom that gives honour to the father."[36]

[Patrick's declaration to his fellow workers]

You know, and so does God, how I have been among you since my youth in truth of faith and in sincerity of heart. I have kept, and will keep, faith even with the heathen among whom I live. God knows I have deceived none of them, nor even thought of doing so, lest I stir up an attack on God and His Church, and on all of us, and lest the Name of the Lord be blasphemed through me. For it is written: "Woe to the person through whom the Name of the Lord is blasphemed."[37]

For, although I lack skill in anything, yet I have tried to do whatever I

Downpatrick Head, Co. Mayo: "... even to the outermost parts beyond which there is nothing..."

could to safeguard myself in my dealings, even with the Christian brethren and with virgins of Christ and with religious women, who would spontaneously offer me gifts or throw some of their personal ornaments on the altar. These I repeatedly gave back to them, and they were offended with me, not knowing why I did so. But I did it from the hope of eternity, because of which I aimed at being careful of my integrity in all dealings, so that the unbelievers should not catch me out in any detail, and so that I would not in the smallest matter give a pretext to them to disparage or denigrate the ministry of my service.

Perhaps when I baptized so many thousands of people I was hoping for as much as a ha'penny from any of them? Tell me and I will return it to them. Or when the Lord, through my very ordinary person, ordained clergy everywhere and I assigned his ministry to each of them free of charge—if I asked any of them for so much as the price of my shoe, speak out against me and I will return it to you.

On the contrary, I spent money on your behalf, so that they would receive me. And I journeyed among you, and everywhere, for your sake, often in danger, even to the outermost parts beyond which there is nothing, places where no one had ever arrived to baptize or to ordain clergy or to confirm the people. By the Lord's grace, I achieved all these results, conscientiously and gladly for your salvation.

At times I gave presents to chiefs, apart from the stipend I paid their sons who travelled with me. Nevertheless, once, they seized me with my companions, and on that occasion they were most eager to kill me. But the time had not come. They stole everything they found in our possession, and they put me in chains. On the fourteenth day the Lord freed me from their power, and our belongings were returned to us, through the intervention of God and of firm friends whom we had had the foresight to acquire. However, you have seen for yourselves how much I have paid to the administrators of justice in all the districts I was in the habit of visiting regularly. I reckon to have distributed to them no less than the price of fifteen men, so that you could continue to enjoy me, and I you, in God. I have no regret, nor have I done with it: I still spend, and will spend more. The Lord has power to grant to me that I may continue in the future to spend my very self for the sake of your souls.

[Patrick sums up his testament]

Look: I call God into my soul as a witness, that I am not lying. Nor would I wish to write to you to ingratiate myself or to gain anything from you, nor because I look for respect from any of you. If my integrity is not clear to you, it is enough for me that I am sure of it in my heart. Moreover, He Who made His promise to the faithful, He never lies.

But I see that already, in the present, I am lifted up beyond measure by the Lord, and I was not worthy of that, nor of the way He has provided for me; since I know for certain that I am better fitted for poverty and misfortune than for wealth and luxury. But the Lord Christ too was poor for our sake. I am indigent and unfortunate, and even if I wanted wealth, I do not have it. But that is not how I estimate myself; because I expect daily to be killed, betrayed, or brought back into slavery, or something of the kind. But, because of the promise of heaven, I fear none of these things. For I have thrown myself into the hands of Almighty God, who reigns everywhere; as the prophet says: "Cast your cares upon God and He will sustain you."[38]

See: I now commend my soul to my most trustworthy God, Whose ambassador I am, in spite of my obscurity. He *accepts* no person, but He *chose* me for this task, to be one of the least of His servants.

Because of this I will repay Him for all He has bestowed on me. But what shall I say, what shall I promise my Lord, since I have no power over anything unless He gives it to me? But let Him look into my innermost being: I greatly desire and am prepared for Him to grant me that I might drink from His chalice, as He has permitted to others who loved Him.

Therefore, let God never permit me to lose the people that He has won in the ends of the earth. I pray God to give me perseverance and to deign to allow me to give faithful testimony of Him until my death, for the sake of my God.

And, if I have ever succeeded in following any good for the sake of God, Whom I love, I pray Him that, with others of His converts and captives in His Name, I may shed my blood, even though I might go without burial, or my miserable corpse might be torn limb from limb by dogs or wild beasts, or the birds of the air might devour it. I know for certain that if this should happen to me I should gain my soul along with my body, because, without any doubt, on that day we will rise again in the brightness of the sun, that is in the glory of Jesus Christ our Redeemer, as children of the living God and as co-heirs of Christ, and we will be moulded to His image, and we will then reign from Him and through Him and in Him.

For the sun is that which we see rising daily at His command, but it will never reign, nor will its splendour last forever. And all those who worship it will be subject to grievous punishment. We, however, worship the true sun, Christ, who will never perish. Nor will those who do His bidding, but they will continue forever just as Christ will continue forever, He Who reigns with God the Father Almighty and with the Holy Spirit before time and now and in eternity. Amen.

See: again and again, I would reiterate what I wish to express in my declaration. I testify, in truth and in joy of heart, before God and His angels, that I never had any reason beyond the Gospel and its promises, ever to return to that people from whom I had formerly barely escaped.

But I implore those God-fearing believers who agree to read or accept this document which the unlettered sinner Patrick composed in Ireland, that none of them will attribute to an ignorant person like me any little thing I may have done, or any guidance I may have given according to God's will. Consider, and let it be truly believed, that it may have been rather the gift of God. And that is what I have to say before I die.

SEVENTEEN

St Patrick's Letter against the Soldiers of Coroticus

I, Patrick, a sinner and unlettered, declare myself to be a bishop publicly established in Ireland.

I am firmly of the opinion that whatever I am, I have received from God. I live among barbarian foreigners, a stranger and exile for the love of God—as He is my witness. And I would not have chosen to speak as harshly and as sternly as I must; but the zeal of God compels me, and Christ's truth urges me, for love of my neighbours and children on whose behalf I gave up my parents and my homeland, and my very life until death. If I am worthy, I live for my God to teach the heathen, even if many look down on me.

With my own hand I have written and set out these words to be sent, transmitted and delivered to the soldiers of Coroticus—whom I will not call fellow-citizens of mine or of the holy Romans, but rather—because of their evil deeds—fellow-citizens of the demons. After the manner of the Enemy, they live in death, allies of the *Scotti* and of the apostate Picts. I denounce them as bloodthirsty men embrued in the blood of the innocent Christians whom I have brought to life in countless numbers for God and whom I have confirmed in Christ.

On the day after the catechumens, wearing their white robes, had been anointed (the oil shone on their brows as they were cut down and slaughtered by the swords of those I have mentioned) I sent a holy priest whom I had taught from childhood, together with some clerics, with a letter requesting that they return some of the loot and the baptized captives to us. They laughed aloud at them.

On this account I do not know whom I should lament more, those who were killed or captured, or those whom Satan has so thoroughly ensnared. For they will be consigned along with him to the eternal pains of hell, since he who commits sin is a slave and will be known as a son of Satan.

Therefore, let every God-fearing person know that they—the murderer of kin, the fratricide, the ravening wolves who devour God's people like a meal of bread—are strangers to me and to my God, Whose ambassador I am. As it is said: "The wicked have destroyed Your Law, O Lord"[1]—that law which at the end of time He has graciously planted most successfully in Ireland, so that it has been firmly founded there with God's favour.

I do not exceed my jurisdiction. I am one of those whom He called and predestined to preach the Gospel even to the end of the earth, in spite of no small persecution, although the Enemy shows his resentment through the petty tyrant Coroticus who fears neither God nor God's bishops whom He chose and to whom He gave that highest divine power, that those whom they bind on earth are also bound in heaven.

Therefore I most solemnly enjoin those of you who are holy and humble of heart to take heed that it is not permitted to show any honour to the likes of them, nor to eat or drink with them; nor ought their alms be accepted until they have done the most severe penance with shedding of tears to satisfy God, and until they free the servants and handmaids of Christ on whose behalf He died and was crucified. The Most High rejects the gifts of the wicked. He who offers sacrifice from the goods of the poor is like him who sacrifices the son in the sight of the father.[2]

It is said that: "The wealth he has accumulated unjustly will be vomited from his belly; the angel of death drags him away; he will be scourged by the rage of dragons; the adder's tongue will kill him; and an inextinguishable fire will consume him."[3]

And further: "Woe to them who fill themselves with what is not theirs:"[4] or: "What shall it profit a man to gain the whole world and suffer the loss of his own soul?"[5]

It would be tedious to analyse in subtle detail and to pick out texts on such greed from the whole of the Law. Avarice is a mortal sin.

"Thou shalt not covet thy neighbour's goods."[6] "Thou shalt not kill."[7] A murderer cannot be with Christ.

"He who hates his brother will be known as a murderer;"[8]—or: "He who does not love his brother remains in death."[9]

How much greater a criminal is he who stains his hands with the blood of those children of God whom He won recently at the ends of the earth through my unworthy preaching. Was it without God's intervention or in a purely human way that I came to Ireland? Who was it that drove me? It is by the Spirit that I am prevented from seeing any of my family again. Is it from me that the mercy comes which I show to that same people which once enslaved me and pillaged the male and the female slaves of my father's household? According to the world's reckoning I was a gentlemen, the son of a decurion. I have sold my patrimony, without shame or regret, for the benefit of others. In short, I serve Christ on behalf of a foreign people for the ineffable glory of life everlasting which is in Christ Jesus Our Lord.

And—if my own people will not give me recognition—"a prophet is without honour in his own country."[10]

Perhaps we are not of the one fold, and do not have the one God. As He says: "He who is not with Me is against Me; and he who does not gather with Me scatters."[11]

It makes no sense: one destroys; the other builds. I do not ask for what is mine. It is not my kindness, but that God has placed in my heart an urge to be one of His hunters or fishers, whom He once foretold would come in the last days.

It is begrudged to me. What should I do, Lord? I am treated with great contempt. Look: your sheep are mangled around me and are carried off, and by these robbers I have spoken of, on the orders of the hostile Coroticus. Far from the love of God is he who betrays Christians into the hands of *Scotti* and Picts. Savage wolves devour the Lord's flock, just when, by great care, it has reached its best growth in Ireland—and I cannot number the sons of the *Scotti* and the daughters of chiefs who were monks and virgins of Christ. Therefore do not accept this injury to be just; it is unacceptable all the way to hell.

Who among the holy would not be horrified at the thought of making merry or enjoying festivity in the company of the likes of them? They have filled their houses with what has been robbed from dead Christians; they live by plunder. The wretched creatures do not realise what they do, offering deadly poison as food to their children and their friends, just as Eve did not understand that she too was offering death to her husband.

So it is with all who commit evil: they bring on themselves the perpetual punishment of death.

This is the custom of the Christian Roman Gauls: they send worthy holy men to the Franks and other heathens with as many thousand *solidi* as are needed for the redemption of baptized captives. You [*Coroticus*], on the other hand, kill them and sell them to a foreign people that does not know God; you betray the members of Christ as if into a brothel. What kind of hope do you have in God, or, for that matter, does anyone who goes along with you or who speaks to you in terms of respect? God will judge. It is indeed written: "Not only those who do evil, but even those who consent are to be damned."[12]

I do not know what more I should say or tell of those dead children of God who were direly struck down by the sword. It is indeed written: "Weep with those who weep."[13] And again: "If one member sorrows, let all be sorrowful."[14]

Therefore the Church weeps and laments for those of its sons and daughters whom the sword has not yet slain but who have been carried away and transported to distant lands where open, shameless, grave sin abounds. There free citizens have been sold, and Christians have been reduced to servitude which is all the worse since they are enslaved to the vilest worthless, apostate Picts.

For that reason I shall cry out in grief and sadness. "O most beautiful and loving brethren and children whom I begot in Christ (and whom I cannot number)—what can I do for you? I am inadequate to help either God or humans. The wickedness of the wicked has overcome us. We have been transformed into strangers. Perhaps they do not believe that we have been given the same baptism, or that we have the same God. For them it is shameful that we are Irish." But the saying is: "Have you not the one God? Why have you, one and all, abandoned your neighbour?"

For that reason I grieve for you; I grieve, my most loved ones. But, then again, I rejoice within myself. I have not laboured in vain, and my exile has not been for nothing. For it is an unspeakably horrible crime that has taken place; but, thank God, it was as baptized believers that you left this world for paradise. I have a vision of you: you have begun your journey to where there will be no night nor sorrow nor death any more; freed of your bonds, you will gambol like young calves and you will trample on the wicked, and they will be like ashes under your feet. And you will reign with the apostles and the prophets and the martyrs. You will gain an eternal kingdom as He Himself has promised. He said: "They will come from the east and the west and they will sleep with Abraham and Isaac and Jacob in the Kingdom of Heaven."[15] "Outside are dogs and purveyors of evil and murderers;"[16]—and: "The lying perjurers will be allotted the lake of eternal fire."[17] It is not without reason that the apostle says: "When the just man will barely be saved, where will the sinner and the unholy breaker of the law find himself?"[18]

Where then will Coroticus and his most criminal crew—rebels against Christ—where will they see themselves, they who have distributed young Christian girls as prizes, for the sake of a wretched worldly kingdom which will pass away anyway in an instant? Like mere mist or smoke which is dispersed by the wind, deceitful sinners will perish in the face of the Lord; the just on the other hand will feast in perfect harmony with Christ; they will judge the nations and rule over wicked kings for ever and ever. Amen.

I bear witness before God and His angels that, for all my lack of learning, it will be as I have indicated. The words that I have expounded in Latin are not mine, but those of God and the apostles and the prophets, who certainly have never lied. "Whoever will believe will be saved; whoever will not believe will be condemned."[19] God has spoken.

Most earnestly, I ask whichever servant of God may be willing, to be the bearer of this letter, so that no one may for any reason withdraw or hide it, but rather so that it may be read aloud in public, and in the presence of

Coroticus himself. Because, if some time God should inspire them to come back to their sense of Him and, however late, if they should repent of such unholiness as they have committed—murder of the Lord's brethren!—and if they should release the baptized prisoners whom they had captured; so may they merit life from God, and may they be restored to wholeness now and forever! Peace in the Father and the Son and the Holy Spirit.

Dumbarton Rock (Ail Cluait)

PART THREE

Extracts from Later Writings

EIGHTEEN

The Annals

Selections, mainly of entries relating to ecclesiastical matters, have been made in the following sections from three of the sets of annals which survive as records of a long period of Irish history.

As has already been pointed out, these are not the best evidence for the fifth century, because for that period they are not true annals (which should be kept year by year, noting the main events of the previous twelvemonth). The Annals of Inisfallen, as they are preserved in the manuscript Rawlinson B.503 in the Bodleian Library at Oxford (from which they were edited by Seán Mac Airt) are true annals entered by a sequence of contemporaneous hands from 1092 until 1214. But all the entries up to 1092 in this manuscript are in a single hand; i.e. they were copied by one scribe from another source or sources. Again, after 1214, just two scribes (probably in the fourteenth century) have completed all the years from 1214. It is unusual to have even that much of contemporaneously entered annals—but a good scribe could copy a whole set of annals from the originals and leave us a useful text. The Annals of Ulster, although they exist now only in late medieval manuscripts, nonetheless in large part seem to have been fairly faithfully copied from originals, or from good copies of originals.

But the process of making annual notes of the previous year's events did not begin until perhaps the seventh century, when, among other attempts at historical record, an Irish World Chronicle was compiled. The fifth-century records are reconstructions from miscellaneous sources, done by scholars of that time or later. The Annals of the Four Masters are a *seventeenth*-century compilation, selected here (in John O'Donovan's nineteenth-century translation) as a succinct summary of the traditions and legends about St Patrick and his time that had accumulated over many centuries in Ireland.

NINETEEN

From the Annals of Ulster

[431] In the year 431 of the Incarnation of the Lord, Palladius was ordained bishop for the Irish by Celestine, bishop of Rome, and was sent to Ireland so that they might believe in Christ—in the eighth year of Theodosius.

[432] The year of the Lord 432, according to Dionysius. Patrick reached Ireland in the ninth year of Theodosius Minor, and the first year of the episcopate of Xistus, forty-second bishop of the church of Rome.[1] So reckon Bede and Marcellinus and Isidore in their chronicles.

[436] Orosius and Prosper and Cyril flourished in Christ.

<437><Finbar moccu Bardeni.>[2]

[438] The Senchus Már was written. <Or, according to another book, it is here that Secundinus and his companions should be entered.>

[439] Secundinus, Auxilius and Iserninus are sent—bishops themselves—to help Patrick.

[440] Death of Xistus, bishop of the church of Rome, who lived eight years and twenty-seven days in the episcopate of the Roman church, as Bede tells in his chronicle.

[441] Leo was ordained forty-second bishop of the Roman church.[3] Patrick the bishop was approved in the Catholic faith.

[443] Patrick the bishop was flourishing in our province in the fervour of faith and the teaching of Christ.

[444] Armagh was founded. From the foundation of the City [*Rome*] to the foundation of this city, 1,194 years.

[447] The repose of Secundinus in the seventy-fifth year of his age.

[451] The Lord's Easter was celebrated on 24 April.

[452] Some say that St Brigid was born at this time.

[455] The astronomer Victorius flourished.

[457] The Council of Chalcedon was assembled.[4]
The repose of Old Patrick, as some books tell.

[459] Auxilius the bishop rested.

[460] Pope Leo of the Roman church died.[5] He held the see of Peter for twenty-one years, one month and thirteen days, as Bede tells in his chronicle.

[461] Hilary was made forty-fourth[6] pontiff of the Roman church and lived six years.
Here some place the death of Patrick.

[465] Hilary, bishop of the Roman church, died.[7] He had occupied the see of Peter for six years, three months and ten days. Simplicius was ordained. He sat for twelve years, one month and <?> days.

[467] The repose of bishop Benignus, Patrick's successor.

[468] Iserninus the bishop dies.

[471] Some say that the second Saxon prey from Ireland was carried off this year—as Maucteus says. So I found in Cuanu's book.

[473] Repose of St Doccus the bishop, abbot of the Britons.

[481] The repose of Iarlath <Mac Threna>, third bishop of Armagh.
Felix was ordained forty-sixth[8] bishop of the Roman church and lived twelve or thirteen years.

[487] The repose of St Mel, the bishop, in Ardagh.

[489] The repose of St Cianán, to whom Patrick gave a Gospel.

[490] The repose of MacCaille the bishop.

[492] The Irish say that Patrick the archbishop died . . . < . . . and Vincent, in *Speculum Historiarum*, that Patrick was eighty years in Ireland preaching, and that God revived forty people for him. He founded 365 churches, made as many bishops, and baptized 1,200>.

[493] Gelasius was ordained forty-seventh bishop of the Roman church and lived three years.[9]
Patrick, arch-apostle <apostle and martyr> of the Irish, rested on the 17th of March, in his sixtieth year since he had come to Ireland to baptize the Irish.

[496] The repose of Mac Cuilinn, bishop of Lusk.

[497] Anastasius was ordained the forty-eighth pontiff of the Roman church and lived two years.[10]
Mo-Choí of Nendrum rested.
The repose of Cormac, bishop of Armagh, heir of Patrick.

[498] <The repose of Cuinnidh son of Cathmogha, bishop of Lusk.>

[499] Symmachus was made bishop and lived fifteen years.[11]
<Or here Mo-Choí of Nendrum, according to another book.>

[500] Death of Ibar the bishop on 23 April.
The Gospel written with his own hand by Matthew, and relics of Barnabus were found this year.

[504] Bishop Cerpán died—a bishop from Ferta Cherpáin and Tara.

[506] The repose of Mac Cairtin, bishop of Clochar.

[507] The repose of Mac Nisse, bishop of Conor.

[512] The repose of Brón the bishop.
The birth of Ciarán, son of the carpenter.

[513] The repose of Erc, bishop of Slane.
Dubtach of Druim Derb, that is the bishop of Armagh, died.

[514] Mac Nise, bishop of Conor, died.

[515] Hormisdas was ordained fortieth bishop of the Roman church and lived nine years.[12]

[516] The birth of Comgall of Bangor.

[517] The repose of Darerca of Cell Sléibe Cuilinn [*Killeevy, Co. Armagh*] on 5 July.

[519] The birth of Colum Cille on the same day on which Búite son of Brónach slept.
The repose of Darerca, called Moninna.

[520] Conláed, bishop of Kildare, died.
Comgall of Bangor was born, according to some.

[521] <Cainnech of Achad Bó [*Aghaboe, Co. Laois*] was born, according to some.>

[523] <Búite, son of Brónach, died.>
<Colum Cille was born.>

[524] The repose of St Brigid in the seventieth year of her age.

[525] John, the fifty-first pope of the Roman church, lived two years <in the see of Peter>.[13] He came to Constantinople, and when he

returned to Ravenna, Theoderic the Arian king imprisoned him and his companions. His body was brought from Ravenna and buried in the basilica of the Blessed Peter after two years, nine months and seventeen days.

[526] The sleep of St Brigid, in the seventieth year of her age.
<Ailill of the Uí Bresail, bishop of Armagh, rested.>

[527] The birth of Cainnech of Achad-Bó.
The end of St Ailbe.

[528] Felix, bishop of the church of Rome, sat for four years, nine months and fourteen days (John's seventeen days and two months, and thirteen days of Felix, add up to a fourth year) and he was buried in the basilica of the blessed Peter the Apostle.[14]

[531] The body of the holy monk Antony was found by divine revelation and brought to Alexandria and buried in the church of St John the Baptist.

[532] In this year Dionysius wrote the paschal cycles, beginning with the year of the Lord's Incarnation 520, which is the 246th of Diocletian.[15]

[533] Felix was buried in the basilica of the blessed Peter the Apostle.[15a]

[534] Rest of Ailbe of Imlech Ibair [*Emly, Co. Tipperary*]. Boniface, the Roman bishop, sat for two years and twenty-six days and was buried in the basilica of the blessed Peter the Apostle.[16]

[535] The sleep of Mochta, Patrick's disciple, on 20 August. So he wrote in his own letter: "Maucteus the priest, a sinner, disciple of holy Patrick, would offer salutation in the Lord."[17]

[536] Mercurius, known as John, of the Roman nation, sat as bishop of the Roman church for two years, four months and six days, and was buried in the basilica of the blessed Peter the Apostle.[18]

[537] <Or, here: the sleep of St Mochta, Patrick's disciple.>

[538] Agapitus, of the Roman nation, bishop of the Roman church, sat eleven months and eight days and was buried in the basilica of the blessed Peter the Apostle.[19] Boniface's twenty-six days and Mercurius's four months and six days, and Agapitus's eleven months and eight days, add up to one year, four months and ten days.

[539] <Silverius, of the Roman nation, sat one year, two months and eleven days, and died a confessor.>[20]

[540] In Rome, Vigilius, of the Roman nation, bishop of the Roman church, sat seventeen years, six months and twenty-two days. He died in Syracuse and was buried on the Via Salaria.[21]

[542] Ailbe's end.

[545] The first plague, called *Bléfed*, in which Mo-Bhí Cláirínech died.[22]

[548] Cluain moccu Nois [*Clonmacnoise, Co. Offaly*] was founded.

[549] Tigernach of Cluain Eois [*Clones, Co. Monaghan*].
A great plague, in which these met their end: Finnio moccu Telduib; Colum <ua> Cremthainn; Mac Tail of Cell Cuilinn [*Old Kilcullen, Co. Kildare*]; Sinchell son of Cennanán, abbot of Cell Achaid Druimfhata [*Killeigh, Co. Offaly*]; Colum of Inis Celtra [*Inishcaltra, or Holy Island, L. Derg, Co. Clare*].

[553] So I have found in Cuanu's book: Patrick's relics were put by Colum Cille in a shrine, sixty years after his death. Three noble relics were found in the tomb: his cup, the Gospel of the Angel, and the Bell of the Will. This is how the angel distributed the relics: the cup to Down, the Bell of the Will to Armagh, and the Gospel of the Angel to Colum Cille himself. It is called the Gospel of the Angel because Colum Cille received it from the hand of the angel.
<Or, here: the repose of David, bishop of Armagh and legate.>[23]

[554] The birth of Lugaid moccu Ochae.
The church of Bennchor [*Bangor, Co. Down*] was founded.

[556] Pelagius, of the Roman nation, sat eleven years and eighteen days. He was buried in the basilica of the blessed Peter the Apostle.[24]
(A great plague this year: the Crón Chonaill; the Buide Chonaill.)

[558] Diarmait son of Cerbél held the Feis of Tara . . .
Brendan founded the church of Clonfert.

[559] The church of Bangor was founded.

[565] The killing of Diarmait mac Cerbél <by Áed Dub son of Suibne>.

TWENTY

From the Annals of Inisfallen

[429] Loegare son of Niall held the kingship of Ireland.

[431] In the eighth year of Theodosius king of the world, Palladius was ordained by Celestine, bishop of Rome and was the first sent to Ireland, to the *Scotti*, so that it might be possible for them to believe in Christ.

Pope Celestine rested.

Augustine, sage and bishop, died in the seventy-sixth year of his age. From the Incarnation of Our Lord Jesus Christ there are 432 years to this year. From the death of the hero Cúchulainn 434. From the death of Conchubhar Mac Nessa 413.

[432] Bishop Patrick holds Ireland and begins to baptize the *Scotti*, in the ninth year of the reign of Theodosius Minor, and the first year of the episcopate of Xistus II, bishop of the Roman church, and in the fourth year of the reign of Laegare son of Niall. Here the entry ends.

(Palladius, however, stayed for this one year, in the twelfth year of the reign of Theodosius Minor.)

(Patrick truly came to the *Scotti* in his thirteenth—or as some say, his fourteenth year. Palladius therefore returned[1], but did not reach Rome, but rested in Christ in Britain.)

[432?] Patrick is sent to Ireland, in the reign of Theodosius Minor, son of Arcadius, in which year, the angel whose name is Victor summoned Patrick from the place where Patrick's Cross was erected. At that time Laegare son of Niall ruled Ireland for thirty-eight years. In the fourth year of his reign, however, Patrick came to the *Scotti*. The aforesaid Loegare was the eighteenth king from the time of the five kings who divided Ireland into five provinces; that is: Conchobar and Corpre and Tigernach Tétbannach and Dedad mac Sin and Ailill mac Mágach.

[433] Conversion of the *Scotti* to the Christian faith.

[439] Secundinus, Auxilius and Isserninus are sent to help Patrick. However the Apostolate was not theirs, but Patrick's alone.

[440] The repose of the wise Augustine.[2]

[441] The testing of holy Patrick in the Christian faith.[3]

[443] Holy Patrick was eminent in Christian doctrine.

[448] The repose of holy Secundinus.

[451] The council of Chalcedon assembles.

[453] Leo ruled, and the head of John was found.[4]

[455] Some say that holy Brigid was born in this year.

[457] Victorius wrote the Paschal cycle.[5]

[460] Auxilius slept.

[461] The repose of Pope Leo and the consecration of Bishop Hilary.[6]

[465] Iserninus slept.

[468] The repose of Bishop Benignus. . . . dies in Rome.[7]

[481] The repose of Iarlaithe, the third abbot of Armagh.[8]

[486] The birth of Brénainn, son of Finnlug.

[491] The repose of Cianán of Dam Liac [*Duleek, Co. Meath*].

[492] The repose of the bishop Mac Caille.

[496] The repose of Patrick on 17 March, in the 432nd year since the Passion of the Lord.[9]
The repose of Mac Cuilinn of Lusca [*Lusk, Co. Dublin*].

[497] The repose of Cormac, bishop of Armagh.

[498] The repose of Mochoe of Naendruim [*Nendrum Island, Co. Down*].

[499] The repose of the bishop Ibur.

[503] The repose of Domangart of Cenn Tíre [*Kintyre in Scotland*].

[505] The repose of the bishop Cerpán in Ferta Cerpáin [*near Tara, Co. Meath*].

[509] The repose of Mac Nise of Condere [*Connor, Co. Antrim*].

[511] The birth of Ciarán son of the wright.[10]

[512] The repose of Dubthach bishop of Ard Macha.
The repose of Erc of Slane.

[515] The birth of Comgall of Bennchor [*Bangor, Co. Down*].

[516] The repose of the bishop Conláed and of Dar Erca.

[521] The birth of Colum Cille and the sleeping of Búite son of Brónach.

[524] The repose of holy Brigit.

[528] The repose of Ailbe of Imlech Ibuir [*Emly, Co. Tipperary*].

[529] The discovery of the body of the monk Antony and its translation to Alexandria.

[538] The birth of Gregory.[11]

[544] The first plague,[12] called *bléfed*, in which Mobhí Cláiríneach slept.

[547] In this year Cluain Moccu Nois [*Clonmacnoise*] was founded—Nos, swineherd of the king of Connachta, gave his name to Cluain.

[548] The repose of Ciarán son of the wright; and Máel Odur on the same day.

[551] *Crom Connaill*—a great plague.

[552] The repose of Finnian of Cluain Iraird [*Clonard, Co. Meath*] and of Colum of Tír dá Glas [*Terryglass, Co. Tipperary*].

[555] The repose of Cathbad (the noble bishop of Leth Cuind) [*The northern half of Ireland*].

[556] Nicthán the leper died.

[558] The church of Benchor [*Bangor, Co. Down*] was founded.

[560] Diarmait son of Cerbhaill held the *feiss* of Tara.

[561] In which the battle of Cúil Dreimne [*north-east of Sligo town; possibly Cooldroman, Drumcliff*] is to be noted, and in which Ainmire son of Sétna and Ainnedid son of Fergus and Domnall were victorious. Diarmait, however, fled. And in this year Cluain Ferta Brénainn [*Clonfert, Co. Galway*] was founded on the angel's instructions.

[563] (Colum Cille overseas.) At Pentecost he spent his first night in Britain.

[564] The death of Diarmait son of Cerball, whom Áed Dub killed in Ráith Bec [*Rathbeg, Dunegore, Co. Antrim*].

TWENTY-ONE

From the Annals of the Four Masters

[O'Donovan's translation]

[430] The second year of Laeghaire. In this year Pope Celestine the First
sent Palladius to Ireland[1] to propagate the faith among the Irish,
and he landed in the country of Leinster with a company of twelve
men. Nathi, son of Garchu, refused to admit him; but, however, he
baptized a few persons in Ireland, and three wooden churches were
erected by him, [namely], Cell-Fhine [*possibly Cillín Chormaic, Co.
Kildare*], Teach-na-Romhán [*probably, according to O'Donovan,
Tigroni, Co. Wicklow*], and Domhnach-Arta [*probably Donard, near
Redcross, Co. Wicklow*]. At Cell-Fhine he left his books, and a shrine
with the relics of Paul and Peter, and many martyrs besides. He left
four in these churches: Augustinus, Benedictus, Silvester, and
Solinus. Palladius, on his returning back to Rome (as he did not
receive respect in Ireland), contracted a disease in the country of the
Cruithnigh, and died thereof.

[431] The third year of Laeghaire. Saint Patrick was ordained bishop by
the holy Pope, Celestine the First, who ordered him to go to
Ireland, to preach and teach faith and piety to the Gaedhil, and also
to baptize them.

[432] The fourth year of Laeghaire. Patrick came to Ireland this year, and
proceeded to baptize and bless the Irish, men, women, sons, and
daughters, except a few who did not consent to receive faith or
baptism from him, as his Life relates.
Áth Truim [*Trim, Co. Meath*] was founded by Patrick, it having
been granted by Fedhlim, son of Laeghaire, son of Niall, to God
and to him, Lomán, and Fortchern . . . .

[438] The tenth year of Laeghaire. The Seanchus and Féineachus of Ireland[2] were purified and written, the writings and old books of Ireland having been collected [and brought] to one place, at the request of Saint Patrick. These were the nine supporting props by whom this was done: Laeghaire, i.e. King of Ireland, Corc[3] and Dáire, the three kings; Patrick, Benén[4] and Cairneach,[5] the three saints; Ross, Dubhthach, and Fearghus, the three antiquaries . . . .

[447] The nineteenth year of Laeghaire. Secundinus, i.e. Seachnall Mac Ua Baird,[6] the son of Patrick's sister, Darerca, bishop of Árd-Macha [*Armagh*], yielded his spirit on the twenty-seventh of November, in the seventy-fifth year of his age.

[448] The twentieth year of Laeghaire.
The family of Patrick of the prayers, who had good Latin, I remember; no feeble court [were they], their order, and their names.
Sechnall, his bishop without fault; Mochta[7] after him his priest;
Bishop Erc[8] his sweet-spoken Judge; his champion, Bishop Mac-caerthin;[9]
Benén, his psalmist;[10] and Coemhán,[11] his chamberlain;
Sinell[12] his bell-ringer, and Aitchen[13] his true cook;
The priest Mescán,[14] without evil, his friend and his brewer;
The priest Bescna,[15] sweet his verses, the chaplain of the son of Alprann.[16]
His three smiths, expert at shaping, Macécht,[17] Laebhann,[18] and Fortchern.[19]
His three artificers, of great endowment, Áesbuite, Tairill and Tasach.[20]
His three embroiderers, not despicable, Lupaid,[21] Erca[22] and Cruim-thiris.[23]
Odhrán[24], his charioteer, without blemish, Rodán,[25] son of Braga, his shepherd.
Ippis, Tigris, and Erca, and Liamhain, with Eibeachta:[26]
For them Patrick excelled in wonders, for them he was truly miraculous.
Carniuch[27] was the priest that baptized him; German[28] his tutor, without blemish.
The priest Manach,[29] of great endowment, was his man for supplying wood.
His sister's son was Banbán,[30] of fame; Martin[31] his mother's brother.
Most sapient was the youth Mochonnóc,[32] his hospitaller.
Cribri and Lasra,[33] of mantles, beautiful daughters of Gleaghrann.
Macraith the wise, and Erc—he prophesied in his three wills.
Brogan,[34] the scribe of his school; the priest Logha,[35] his helmsman,—

It is not a thing unsung,—and Machiu[36] his true fosterson.
Good the man whose great family they were, to whom God gave a
crozier without sorrow;
Chiefs with whom the bells are heard, a good family was the family
of Patrick.
May the Trinity, which is powerful over all, distribute to us the boon
of great love;
The king who, moved by soft Latin, redeemed by Patrick's prayer.[37]

[454] The twenty-sixth year of Laeghaire. . . . Saint Usaille,[38] Bishop of
Cell Usaille,[39] in Liffe,[40] [died] on the twenty-seventh of August.

[457] The twenty-ninth year of Laeghaire. . . . Árd-Macha [*Armagh*] was
founded by Saint Patrick, it having been granted to him by Dáire,
son of Finnchadh, son of Eóghan, son of Niallán. Twelve men were
appointed by him for building the town. He ordered them, in the
first place, to erect an archbishop's city there, and a church for
monks, for nuns, and for the other orders in general, for he perceived that it would be the head and chief of the churches of
Ireland in general. Old Patrick yielded his spirit.

[467] The ninth year of Oilioll Molt. Benén,[41] son of Sescnen, Bishop of
Ard Macha [*Armagh*], resigned his spirit.

[481] The third year of Lughaidh. Saint Jarlaithe,[42] son of Tréana, Bishop
of Árd Macha, resigned his spirit.

[487] The ninth year of Lughaidh. Mel, bishop of Árd Achadh [*Ardagh*]
in Teathbha, disciple of Patrick, died.

[488] The tenth year of Lughaidh. Cianán, bishop of Doimliag [*Duleek,Co.
Meath*], died.

[489] The eleventh year of Lughaidh. Bishop Mac-caille[43] died.

[493] The fifteenth year of Lughaidh. Patrick, son of Calphurn, son of
Potaide, first primate and chief apostle of Ireland, whom Pope
Celestine the First had sent to preach the Gospel and disseminate
religion and piety among the Irish, [was the person] who separated
them from the worship of idols and spectres, who conquered and
destroyed the idols which they had for worshipping; who had expelled
demons and evil spirits from among them, and brought them from
the darkness of sin and vice to the light of faith and good works, and
who guided and conducted their souls from the gates of hell (to
which they were going), to the gates of the kingdom of heaven. It was
he that baptized and blessed the men, women, sons and daughters
of Ireland, with their territories and tribes, both [fresh] waters and

sea-inlets. It was by him that many cells, monasteries, and churches were erected throughout Ireland; seven hundred churches was their number. It was by him that bishops, priests, and persons of every dignity were ordained; seven hundred bishops and three thousand priests was their number. He worked so many miracles and wonders that the human mind is incapable of remembering or recording the amount of good which he did upon earth. When the time of St Patrick's death approached, he received the Body of Christ from the hands of the holy Bishop Tassach, in the 122nd [year] of his age, and resigned his spirit to heaven.

There was a rising of battle, and a cause of dissension in the province contending for the body of Patrick after his death. The Uí-Néill and the Oirghialla attempting to bring it to Armagh; the Ulta to keep it to themselves. And the Uí-Néill and the Oirghialla came to a certain water, and the river swelled against them so that they were not able to cross it in consequence of the greatness of the flood. When the flood had subsided these hosts united on terms of peace, i.e. the Uí-Néill and the Ulta, to bring the body of Patrick with them. It appeared to each of them that each had the body conveying it to their respective territories, so that God separated them in this manner, without a fight or battle. The body of Patrick was afterwards interred at Dún-dá-Lethglas [*Downpatrick, Co. Down*] with great honour and veneration; and during the twelve nights that the religious seniors were watching the body with psalms and hymns, it was not night in Magh-inis [*Lecale*] or the neighbouring lands, as they thought, but as if it were the full undarkened light of day. Of the year of Patrick's death was said:

> Since Christ was born, a correct enumeration,
> Four hundred and fair ninety,
> Three years add to these,
> Till the death of Patrick, chief Apostle.

[496] Mochaoi, Abbot of Aendruim [*Nendrum, Co. Down*] died on the twenty-third day of the month of June.
Cormac, of Críoch-in-Ernaidhe [*O'Donovan suggests that this is a corruption of "Críoch Loeghaire", since Cormac's church was at Trim, Co. Meath*], successor of Patrick, resigned his spirit.

[499] [*504*] The twenty-first year of Lughaidh. Cerbán, a bishop of Feart-Cearbáin [*north-east of Tara*], at Teamhair [*Tara*], died.

[500] The twenty-second year of Lughaidh. Saint Ibhar,[44] the bishop, died on the twenty-third day of the month of April. Three hundred and four years was the length of his life.

[503] After Lughaidh, son of Laeghaire, had been twenty-five years in the sovereignty of Ireland, he was killed at Achadh-farcha [*somewhere in the barony of Slane, Co. Meath*], being struck by a flash of lightning, by the miracles of God, on account of the insult which he had offered to Patrick, as this quatrain states:

> At Achadh-farcha warlike, the death of Laeghaire's son, Lughaidh [occurred],
> Without praise in heaven or here, a heavy flash of lightning smote him.

[511] The eighth year of Muircheartach. Saint Brón, Bishop of Cúil-Irra [*the parishes of Killasbugbrone and Kilmacnowen, Co. Sligo*], in Connaught, died on the eighth day of the month of June.

[512] The ninth year of Muircheartach. Saint Erc, Bishop of Lilcach, [*not known*] and of Fearta-fear-Féig [*Slane, Co. Meath*], by the side of Sidhe-Truim [*a hill to the east of Slane*], to the west, died on the second day of the month of November. His age was four-score and ten years when he departed. This Bishop Erc was judge to Patrick. It was for him Patrick composed this quatrain:

> Bishop Erc,—
> Every thing he adjudged was just;
> Every one that passes a just judgment
> Shall receive the blessing of Bishop Erc.

Dubhthach, i.e. of Druim-Dearbh [*probably Derver, Co. Louth—O'D.*], Bishop of Ard-Macha, [*Armagh*] resigned his spirit.

[513] The tenth year of Muircheartach. Saint Mac-Nisi, i.e. Aenghus, Bishop of Coinnere, [*Connor*] died on the third day of November.

[517] The fourteenth year of Muircheartach. Saint Darerca, of Cill-Sléibhe-Cuilinn [*Killeevy, Co. Armagh*], whose first name was Moninne, died on the 6th of July. Nine score years was the length of her life; of whom was said:

> Nine-score years together, according to rule without error,
> Without folly, without evil, without danger, was the age of Moninne.

[519] The sixteenth year of Muircheartach. Saint Connláedh, bishop of Kildare, Bridget's brazier, died on the 3rd of May.

[521] The eighteenth year of Muircheartach. Saint Búite mac Bronaigh, bishop of Mainister [*Monasterboice, Co. Louth*], died on the 7th of December.

> Let Búite, the virtuous judge of fame, come each day to my aid,
> The fair hand with the glories of clean deeds, the good son of
> Brónach, son of Bolar.

[523] The twentieth year of Muircheartach. Beoidh, Bishop of Árd-Carna [*Ardcarne, Co. Roscommon*], died on the eighth day of March.

[525] Saint Brighit, virgin, Abbess of Cill-Dara [*Kildare*], died. It was to her Cill-dara was first granted, and by her it was founded. Brighit was she who never turned her mind or attention from the Lord for the space of one hour, but was constantly meditating and thinking of him in her heart and mind, as is evident in her own Life, and in the Life of St. Brénainn, Bishop of Cluain-Fearta. She spent her time diligently serving the Lord, performing wonders and miracles, healing every disease and every malady, as her Life relates, until she resigned her spirit to heaven, the first day of the month of February; and her body was interred at Dún [*Downpatrick, Co. Down*], in the same tomb with Patrick, with honour and veneration. Ailill, Bishop of Armagh, who was of the Uí-Breasail, died.

[534] The seventh year of Tuathal. Saint Mochta, Bishop of Lughmhagh [*Louth*], disciple of St Patrick, resigned his spirit to heaven on the nineteenth day of August. It was of him the following testimony was given:

> The teeth of Mochta of good morals, for three hundred years, lasting the rigour!
> Were without [emitting] an erring word out from them, without [admitting] a morsel of obsonium inside them.
> Three-score psalm-singing seniors, his household of regal course,
> Without tilling, reaping, or threshing, without any work but reading.
> A man of three-score, a man of three hundred, blessed be God, how old the teeth!
> Not more has the youth under valour! How lasting the ancient teeth!

[535] The eighth year of Tuathal. The church of Doire-Calgaigh [*Derry*] was founded by Colum Cille, the place having been granted to him by his own tribe, i.e. the race of Conall Gulban, son of Niall.
Oilill, Bishop of Armagh, died. He was also of the Uí-Bresail.

[537] The tenth year of Tuathal. St Lughaidh, Bishop of Connor, died.

[539] The first year of Diarmaid, son of Fearghus Ceirrbheoil, in the sovereignty of Ireland. The decapitation of Abacuc at the fair of

Tailltin [*Teltown, Co. Meath*], through the miracles of God and Ciarán; that is, a false oath he took upon the hand of Ciarán, so that a gangrene took him in the neck (i.e. St. Ciarán put his hand upon his neck), so that it cut off his head.

[541] The third year of Diarmaid. St Ailbhe, archbishop of Imleach-Iubhair [*Emly, Co. Tipperary*], died on the twelfth day of September.

[543] The fifth year of Diarmaid. There was an extraordinary universal plague throughout the world, which swept away the noblest third part of the human race.[45]

[544] The sixth year of Diarmaid. St Móbhí Cláraíneach, i.e. Berchán of Glais-Naidhen [*Glasnevin, Dublin*], on the brink of the Liffey, on the north side, died on the second day of the month of October.

[545] The seventh year of Diarmaid. St Ailbhe, of Seanchua-Ua-nOiliolla [*Shancoe, Co. Sligo*], died.

[547] The ninth year of Diarmaid . . . St Dubhthach, abbot of Árd-Macha [*Armagh*], died. He was of the race of Colla Uais.

[548] The tenth year of Diarmaid. St Ciarán, son of the artificer, abbot of Cluain-mic-Nois [*Clonmacnoise*], died on the ninth day of September. Thirty-three years was the length of his life.
St Tighearnach, bishop of Cluain-eois [*Clones, Co. Monaghan*], died on the 4th of April.
St Mac Tail[46] of Cill-Cuilinn [*Old Kilcullen, Co. Kildare*] (i.e. Eoghan, son of Corcran), died.
St Sincheall the elder, son of Ceanannán, abbot of Cill-Achaidh Droma-foda [*Killeigh, Co. Offaly*], died on the twenty-sixth day of March. Thirty and three hundred years was the length of his life.
St Odhrán, of Leitrioch-Odhráin [*Latteragh, Co. Tipperary*], died on the second day of the month of October.
St Finnén, abbot of Cluain-Eraird [*Clonard, Co. Meath*], tutor of the saints of Ireland, died.
St Colam, of Inis-Cealtra [*Inishcaltra, Co. Clare*], died. Of the mortality which was called the Crón-Chonaill,—and that was the first Buidhe-Chonaill,—these saints died, except Ciarán and Tighearnach.

[550] The twelfth year of Diarmaid. David, son of Guaire Ua Foránnáin, bishop of Árd-Macha [*Armagh*] and Legate of all Ireland, died.

[551] The thirteenth year of Diarmaid.
St Neasan, the leper, died.

[552] The church of Bennchar [*Bangor, Co. Down*] was founded by Comhgall of Beannchar. The feast of Teamhair [*Tara*] was made by the King of Ireland, Diarmaid, son of Fearghus Ceirbheoil.

[553] The fifteenth year of Diarmaid. Brénainn of Birra [*Birr, Co. Offaly*] was seen ascending in a chariot into the sky this year. Cluain-fearta [*Clonfert, Co. Galway*] was founded by St. Brénainn.

[554] The sixteenth year of Diarmaid. St. Cathdub, son of Fearghus, abbot of Achadh-cinn [*possibly Aughnakilly, Craigs, Co. Antrim*], died on the 6th of April. One hundred and fifty years was the length of his life. The last feast of Teamhair [*Tara*] was made by Diarmaid, King of Ireland.

Curnán, son of Aedh, son of Eochaidh Tirmcharna, i.e. the son of the King of Connaught, was put to death by Diarmaid, son of Cearbhall, in violation of the guarantee and protection of Colum Cille, having been forcibly torn from his hands, which was the cause of the battle of Cúl-Dreimhne [*on the north side of Sligo town*].

[555] The seventeenth year of Diarmaid. The battle of Cúl-Dreimhne was gained against Diarmaid, son of Cearbhall, by Fearghus and Domhnall, the two sons of Muircheartach, son of Earca; by Ainmire, son of Sédna; and by Ainnidh, son of Duach; and by Aedh, son of Eochaidh Tirmcharna, King of Connaught. [It was] in revenge of the killing of Curnán, son of Aedh, son of Eochaidh Tirmcharna, [while] under the protection of Colum Cille, the Clanna-Néill of the North and the Connaughtmen gave this battle of Cúl-Dreimhne to King Diarmaid; and also on account of the false sentence which Diarmaid passed against Colum Cille about a book of Finnén, which Colum had transcribed without the knowledge of Finnén, when they left it to award of Diarmaid, who pronounced the celebrated decision, "To every cow belongs its calf", &c. Colum Cille said:

> O God, wilt thou not drive off the fog, which envelopes our number,
> The host which has deprived us of our livelihood,
> The host which proceeds around the carns!
> He is a son of storm who betrays us.
> My Druid—he will not refuse me—is the Son of God, and may he side with me;
> How grandly he bears his course, the steed of Báedán before the host;
> Power by Báedán of the yellow hair will be borne from Ireland on him [the steed].

Fráechán, son of Teniusan, was he who made the Erbhe-Druadh[47] for Diarmaid. Tuathán, son of Dimmán, son of Sarán, son of Cormac, son of Eoghan, was he who placed the Erbhe Druadh over his head. Three thousand was the number that fell of Diarmaid's people. One man only fell on the other side, Mag Laim was his name, for it was he that passed beyond the Erbhe Druadh.

[557] The nineteenth year of Diarmaid. St Bec, son of Dé, a celebrated prophet, died.
Colum Cille went to Scotland, where he afterwards founded a church, which was named after him [*Iona*].
St Aedhán O'Fiachrach died.

[558] After Diarmaid, the son of Fearghus Cerrbheoil, had been twenty years in sovereignty over Ireland, he was slain by Aedh Dubh, son of Suibhne, King of Dál-Araidhe, at Ráth-beag, in Magh-Line [*Rathbeg, Donegore, Co. Antrim*].[48]

[563] St Molaisi, Abbot of Daimhinis [*Devenish, Co. Fermanagh*], died on the twelfth of September.

Late medieval relief carving
of St Patrick, Rathmore, Co. Meath

TWENTY-TWO

The "First Synod of St Patrick"

This has been accepted by many scholars as—in the main or in part—a fifth-century encyclical. However, in its present form it would seem to be no earlier than the seventh century. While it may embody some more ancient regulations, it appears to incorporate, slightly repetitiously, statutes from several synods or councils. The attribution to Patrick, Auxilius and Iserninus cannot be taken at face value.

Here begins the synod of the bishops—Patrick, Auxilius and Iserninus.

The bishops Patrick, Auxilius and Iserninus greet the priests and deacons and all the clerics.

We prefer to give advance warning against negligence rather than to condemn what has already been done. As Solomon says: "It is better to dispute than to be angry."

Our decrees are published here and begin:

1   Should anyone of his own accord, without permission, appeal to the secular judges in the *tuath*,[1] he has merited excommunication.

2   (Finally),[2] every lector should make himself familiar with the church in which he is to read the lessons.

3   There may be no wandering cleric in the community.

4   If permission has been given to someone and a collection has been made, he may not demand more than is necessary.

5   What is left over, he should lay on the altar of the pontiff to be given to other poor people.

6   If a cleric of any order from porter to priest is seen without an under-garment and fails to cover the shame and nakedness of his lower parts; if he has not his hair cut in the Roman way; and if his wife goes

around without a veil on her head: both are to be treated by the laity as of no account and are to be expelled from the church.

7   Any cleric who fails to turn up for matins or vespers, in disregard of the rule, is to be considered a stranger—unless he is bound by slavery.

8   If a cleric has become the guarantor for a pagan, in whatever amount, and it should happen—and it would not be unusual—that the pagan should default through some trick; then the cleric must make up the surety from his own goods. But should he enter into an armed contest with him, he will rightly be considered to be outside the church.[3]

9   A monk and a virgin, each from a different place, may not stay in the same hospice, nor travel together in the one chariot from house to house nor converse together frequently.

10   If someone makes a good beginning in the liturgy, but then drops out and lets his hair grow, let him be excluded from the church unless he comes back to his former office.

11   If a cleric has been excommunicated by one, and another accepts him, both he and the one who receives him must do the same penance.

12   The alms of an excommunicated Christian are not to be accepted.

13   It is not permitted to accept alms offered to the church by pagans.

14   The Christian who commits murder or fornication or who swears before a seer like the pagans, must do a year's penance for each such crime, and at the end of the year should come with witnesses and then be absolved by a priest.

15   And he who commits theft must do half that penance—with twenty days on bread alone—and shall if possible restore what was stolen: so he may be restored to the church.

16   A Christian who believes that there is such a thing in the world as an enchantress, which is to say a witch, and who accuses anyone of this, is to be excommunicated, and may not be received into the church again until—by his own statement—he has revoked his criminal accusation and has accordingly done penance with full rigour.

17   A virgin who has vowed to God to be chaste and has then married a fleshly spouse, is to be excommunicated until she is converted. If she is converted and turns away the adulterer, she is to do penance and afterwards must not live in the same house or the same homestead with him.

18 If someone is excommunicated he may not enter the church, even on the vigil of Easter, until he has undertaken penance.

19 If a Christian woman has taken a man in lawful marriage and afterwards deserts the first man and joins herself to an adulterer, she must be excommunicated.

20 A Christian who cheats on a debt to anyone, in the fashion of the pagans, is to be excommunicated until he fulfils his obligation.

21 A Christian who has been wronged by someone and takes that person to the court and not to the church for the hearing of the case, is to be a stranger.

22 If anyone has given his daughter to a man in lawful marriage when she has made love with another; and he conspires with her and receives a bride-price; both are to be excluded from the church.

23 If any of the priests has built a church, he may not offer Mass until he has brought his bishop to consecrate it; for that is what is right.

24 A stranger who comes into a community may not baptize, nor offer the Mass, nor build a church without receiving the bishop's permission. If he relies on permission from a pagan, he shall be a stranger.

25 When the bishop on his rounds stays in the various churches, if religious people have made gifts on the day of his stay, these shall be regarded as pontifical gifts, as the people of old customarily laid down, either to be used for necessities or to be distributed to the poor, as the bishop himself may decide.

26 But if a cleric should act contrary to this and be found to be taking the gifts, he should be separated from the church because of his shameful greed.

27 Any cleric who has newly come into the *tuath* of a bishop, may not baptize or offer the Mass nor perform in any other way; otherwise he is to be excommunicated.

28 If a cleric has been excommunicated he is to pray alone—not in the same house with the brothers—and he may not offer the Mass or consecrate the Host until he has made amends. if he does not do this, he is is to be punished doubly.

29 If any of the brothers wishes to receive God's grace, he is not to be baptized until he has fasted forty days.

30 Any bishop who has travelled from his own to another's jurisdiction must not presume to ordain without permission from him who is in

authority in that place. On Sunday he may offer Mass only insofar as he has been approved; and he is to comply fully in this.

31   If there happens to be a dispute about some matter between two clerics, and one of them hires an enemy of the other who agrees to kill him, he is properly called a murderer. Such a cleric is held to be a stranger by the just.

32   If one of the clergy wishes to help a prisoner, he should use his own resources to pay his fine. But if he dishonestly frees the man, many clerics will be reviled because of one thief. He who acts in this way is to be excommunicated.

33   A cleric arriving among us without a letter may not minister, even if he should live in the *tuath*.

34   Similarly, it is fitting that a deacon of ours who decides on another jurisdiction without consulting his abbot and without a letter should not be served with food and should be punished by a penance from the priest whom he defied.

35   And it is fitting that a monk who wanders without reference to his abbot should be punished.

TWENTY-THREE

From Adomnán's Life of Columba

In the name of Jesus Christ

The Second Preface

There was a man whose life was worthy of reverence and whose memory is blessed, a father and founder of monasteries. He was given the same name as the prophet Jonah. For, although it is rendered differently in three different languages, yet it means the same in each of them: what is called *iona* in Hebrew and *peristera* in Greek, and *columba* in Latin ["*dove*"]. It is thought that a great name of such quality was not given to him without God's direction. For we are told truly by the Gospels that the Holy Spirit descended on the Only Begotten of the Eternal Father in the form of that small bird known as a dove. So in many sacred writings the special mystical significance of a dove is the Holy Spirit.

Our Saviour, therefore, according to the Gospel, told His disciples to contain in a pure heart the simplicity of doves. The dove is truly a simple and innocent bird. So it was fitting that a man both simple and innocent should be so named, since, dovelike himself, he received the Holy Spirit as a guest. What is written in the Book of Proverbs applies well to him: "A good name is rather to be chosen than great riches."[1] However, not only was our forerunner dignified, as he deserved, with this honourable name, but, long before the day of his birth—many years—the Holy Spirit showed him to a certain soldier of Christ who prophesied miraculously and called him a son of promise. For it has been passed down to us from ancient times by knowledgeable men, that a certain man who had come over from Britain, a holy person, a disciple of the blessed bishop Patrick, named Maucteus [*St Mochta of Louth*], made the following prophecy about our patron: "In the last days, a boy will be born, whose name, Columba, will achieve fame throughout all the territories of the islands of the ocean and will shine brightly at the end of the world. The cultivation plots of our two monasteries—his and mine—will be separated by the width of a single little fence. He will be a man greatly beloved by God and much esteemed by Him."

TWENTY-FOUR

From St Columbanus's Letter to Pope Boniface IV

[From a letter to Pope Boniface IV (AD 613)]

The letter concerns the "Three Chapters" controversy, which had continued for half a century, since the time of Pope Vigilius (537–555), who, under pressure from the Emperor Justinian and his Monophysite Empress Theodora, had reluctantly condemned, or half-condemned, teachings approved by the Council of Chalcedon (451): this had caused a schism in the West. In the passage quoted, St Columbanus refers back to the origin of the Church in Ireland—without reference to St Patrick, but apparently with reference to the sending of Palladius.

. . . I am sad—I must say it plainly—that the see of St Peter is touched by scandal. I know that the business is above me, and that, at first sight, as the saying is, I must seem to be placing my face among the hot coals. But what is my face to me—my public face, my reputation—when it is zeal for the faith that must be made public? My confusion will not be in the sight of God and the angels: craziness in human eyes—if it is for God—deserves praise. If my argument prevails, it will benefit all; if it is despised, it is I who will be rewarded. For I shall not speak to you as a foreigner, but as a friend, a disciple, a follower. Therefore, I shall speak freely and tell those who are—insofar as they are—our masters, the captains of our spiritual ship and our steersmen in the mysteries: "Keep watch; for the sea is stormy and whipped up by deadly gusts of wind, since it is not a single menacing wave which, just from the swell of the ocean, continuously raises crests of harmless foam on hollow ridges of water, raised up from a great distance, and drives the ship before it through liquid furrows rising from the deadly underworld; no, it is a storm in which the whole element rises up and batters from every side, threatening to wreck the mystical ship." Therefore

I—a frightened sailor—dare to cry out: "Keep watch! For water has already entered the ship of the Church, and the vessel is in danger!"

For we—all of us Irish—who live at the edge of the world, we are pupils of Saints Peter and Paul and of all the disciples who were inspired by the Holy Spirit to write the divinely directed scriptures; and we accept nothing beyond the teaching of the Gospels and the Apostles. There has been among us no heretic, no Jew, no schismatic; but our possession of the Catholic faith is unshaken: we hold it just as it was first handed to us by you, the succesors of the holy apostles. This assurance makes me strong and spurs me on to urge you to resist those who revile you, who proclaim that you tolerate heretics, and call you schismatics; so that my own vainglory, which caused me—honestly—to speak out on your behalf in reply to them, will not be useless; and that it is they, not us, who will be confounded.

For—speaking and interpreting for you, as disciples should on behalf of their master—I undertook that the Roman Church would tolerate no heretic who opposed the Catholic faith. For that reason, accept that my presumptuous intervention is necessary: receive it willingly and heed it dutifully. Whatever I have to say that is useful or sound in doctrine will be to *your* credit; for a master earns praise through his disciples' teaching and "a wise son" (through what he has to say) "maketh a glad father."[1] And the praise will be yours because it derives, as I said, from you. Purity, indeed, is to be attributed, not to the river, but to the source. And if you find, either in this letter or in the other one against Agrippinus,[2] who provoked me to write, that I have used some undisciplined and over-zealous expressions, put it down to my confusion, not my vainglory . . .

. . . But indulge me in my dealing in such rough and difficult areas—if, as an outsider, I give offence to pious ears by any of my words—since the significance of what has been happening is such as to allow me to overlook nothing in my investigation. And what makes me bold, if I may say so, is partly the freedom of speech which is the custom of my country. For among us it is not the person but the argument that carries weight. However, love for Gospel peace makes me say everything, so that both of you may be damped down, you who ought to have spoken with one voice—that, and the greatness of my concern for harmony and peace among you: "And whether one member suffer, all the members suffer with it."[3] For, as I said before, we are bound to the see of St Peter. For, although Rome is great and renowned; among us she is held great only because of that see. The name of Italy's ornament—that city which is as if it were elevated in the highest heaven, remote from the common air—that city founded long ago to the great applause of all the neighbouring peoples—has been made known far and wide, throughout the whole world and even to the bounds of the remote western reaches of the earth—unhindered, wonderful to say, by the ocean's great surge, although the waves swelled to unconscionable heights from every direction. Yet it reached as far as us only at that time when the Son of God deigned to be Man, and the Spirit of God, with that pair of ardent steeds, the apostles Peter and Paul (the possession of whose valuable relics is your good fortune), driving over the ocean of heathendom, stirred many waters, and multiplied his chariot-teams with innumerable thousands of people; while the supreme driver—who is Christ, the true father, the charioteer of Israel—came over the flow of straits, over the backs of dolphins, and over the swelling tide. Since then you are great and renowned and Rome has grown greater and more famous; and—if I may say so—it is because of Christ's pair of apostles that you are near the stars and that Rome is the head of the churches of the world—saving only the singular prerogative of the place of resurrection of the Lord[3]—I speak of those who are called "heavens" by the Holy Spirit, who "declare the glory of God",[4] to whom the words apply: "their sound went into all the earth, and their words unto the ends of the world."[5] So, just as your honour is great because of the dignity of your see, you must take great care not to lose your honour through some untowardness. For you will retain power only as long as you follow right reason. For he is the sure keeper of the keys of heaven who through true knowledge opens to the worthy and closes to the unworthy. Otherwise—if he does the contrary—he will be able neither to open nor to shut.

TWENTY-FIVE

From Bede's Church History of the English People

The Venerable Bede was a scholarly English monk, born in the north of England about AD 672. He spent most of his life in the monastery of Wearmouth-Jarrow, where a large library was built up. His scholarly work was concerned with chronology and with the church controversies of his time, in which he was an active partisan. He finished his *History* in 731. In it he has gathered together what materials he could find about the history of the Christian Church in his country down to his time, and has assembled a narrative which, among other things, asserts the superiority of his own tradition—derived from the partly unsuccessful late-sixth-century mission of St Augustine of Canterbury and the more successful seventh-century missions sponsored by Rome—over that of the Irish who had played a large part in the evangelization of northern Britain. He provides a great deal of valuable information about the insular churches in the period of monastic dominance; but he has little that is original to contribute about the earlier Christian church. His information about the origins of the church in Ireland is taken from Gildas. He seems to have known nothing of St Patrick.

1.1 . . . Here in Britain at present there are the languages of five peoples (corresponding to the number of books in which the divine law is written), each and every one seeking and proclaiming the knowledge of perfect truth and true sublimity: English, British, Irish, Pictish—and Latin, which is common to all through the study of the Scriptures. Originally only the Britons inhabited the island, which receives its name from them. It is said that having sailed to Britain from the territory of Armorica [*Brittany*] they took over the southern part of it. And it is told that after the Britons had occupied most of the island, proceeding northwards, the Pictish people of Scythia ventured onto the ocean in a few ships, were blown by the winds beyond all the shores of Britain and reached Ireland. They landed on the north coast and found there the Irish people, from whom they asked permission to settle in their country; but this was refused. Ireland, it must be said, is of all the islands the next largest to Britain, lying to the west of it. But, while it falls short of Britain to the north, to the south it extends much beyond the British coasts, as far as the latitude of northern Spain—although there is a great expanse of ocean between the two.

And, as we have already said, the Picts voyaged to Ireland and asked to be given land on which they might settle. The Irish answered that the island wasn't large enough to contain both peoples. "But", they said, "we can give you good advice as to what you should do. We know another island not far from us to the east, which we can often see in the distance on clear days. If you decide to go there, you can settle; and if anyone opposes you, you may call on our help."

And the Picts made for Britain and proceeded to occupy its northern part, the south having already been occupied by the Britons. The Picts, since they had no wives, asked the Irish for women and the Irish agreed on one condition: that wherever there was a doubt, the Picts should choose their kings from the female rather than the male line. It is well known that this is the Pictish custom to the present day.

As time went by, Britain received a third nation, following the Britons and the Picts into the Pictish country—the Irish. They were led by Reuda and came from Ireland to acquire among the Picts, by agreement or force, settlement sites—which they still hold. To the present day they are known as "Dalreuda" after that leader, "dal" in their language meaning "a part".

Ireland in extent, in healthfulness, and in serenity of climate, far surpasses Britain; since snow rarely lies there more than three days, and no one needs to make hay in summer to provide for winter, or to build stables for the beasts of burden. There are no indigenous reptiles, and no snake can live there. Serpents, often carried there from Britain, die when the ship approaches the coast and they smell the air. On the other hand, almost all things Irish are good against poison. Indeed, we have seen the scrapings of the pages of books from Ireland soaked in water, which was given to drink to persons bitten by snakes. Immediately, all the venom of the spreading poison was removed and the swelling of the body assuaged. The island is rich in milk and honey, and there is no lack of vines, fish or fowl, while it is famous for the hunting of deer and wild goats. This is the true homeland of the Irish. They left it, as we have said, and added a third nation to those of the Britons and the Picts in Britain. There is a very large inlet of the sea, breaking far into the land from the west, which anciently divided the British people from the Picts. Here there is a city of the Britons, strongly fortified to the present day, which is called Alcluith [*Ail Cluait: Dumbarton, on the Clyde*]. The Irish to whom we have referred, made their national home on the north side of this estuary when they had arrived there.

1.11–12 . . . After that, the part of Britain in which the Britons lived was exposed to depredation, all the more since its people were quite ignorant of the art of war and it had been deprived of all its armed force and military supplies and of the flower of its lively youth, who had been led away by the foolhardiness of the tyrants and were never to return. In short, the Britons were stunned suddenly by the plundering of two ferocious peoples from over the sea—the Irish from the north-west and the Picts from the north—and had cause to lament for many years. We refer to these as overseas peoples, not because they came from outside Britain, but because they were separated from the part in which the Britons lived by two intervening inlets of the sea extending far inland, one from the eastern sea, the other from the west—although they do not quite meet [*the Firth of Forth and the Firth of Clyde*]. Halfway along the eastern estuary is the city of Giudi [*not known*], while on the south shore of the western inlet is the city of Al Cluith [*Dumbarton*], which in the language of the Irish means "the rock of the Clyde", since it is beside the river of that name.

Because of the onslaughts of these peoples, the Britons sent delegates with letters to Rome, appealing with tears and prayers for help, and they promised faithful allegiance if only the enemy at their gates could be driven far away from them. A legion in arms was quickly sent to them. As soon as it arrived in the island it engaged the enemy, destroyed a great number of them, and drove the others from the territory of the allies. Having for the moment relieved the Britons in their dreadful situation, the Romans advised them to build a wall across the island between the two estuaries, which could provide a defence to protect them from their enemies. And then the legion returned home in great triumph. And the islanders did as they were told and built a wall, but with clods instead of stones, because they had no engineer who understood that kind of work; and it was useless. They constructed many miles between the two inlets already described, so that where they lacked the protection of the water they might have the wall to defend them against the enemy invasions. The remains of their work can be seen most plainly to the present day in the form of of a very wide and very high earthwork. It begins about two miles away to the west from the monastery of Aebbercurnig [*Abercorn*], in a place which is called Peanfahel in Pictish and Penneltun in English [*Kinneil*]. It extends westward and ends at Al Cluith [*Dumbarton*].

However, as soon as the former enemies saw that the Roman army had gone, they quickly sailed in their ships and swarmed in across coasts and borders, destroying everything before them, like reapers who cut down ripe corn and then trample it. As a result, delegates were sent again to Rome, begging with tearful calls for help, and pleading that their wretched country should not be totally destroyed, and that the renown of a Roman province, which they had enjoyed up to now, should not be wiped out and changed to shame through the wickedness of foreign nations. A legion was sent again and arrived at an unusual time, in the autumn. It inflicted great slaughter on the enemy and drove the survivers across the seas over which every year they had been accustomed to carry off their loot without hindrance. After that the Romans informed the Britons that they could no longer bear the burden of sending such weighty expeditions to defend them. They warned them that they must arm themselves and summon up the spirit themselves to resist their enemies—who could only prevail if they themselves were idle and lacked energy. Furthermore, wishing to help their comrades whom they had to abandon, they laid out a well-built stone wall where Severus had once constructed his rampart, in a straight line from estuary to estuary between the walled towns which had been built there from fear of the enemy. So, with public and private money, helped by the Britons, they built the famous wall which is still conspicuous: eight feet wide and twelve feet high, laid out from east to west as anyone can see today. They built this quickly and then gave some stern warnings to that indolent people and demonstrated to them how to manufacture arms for themselves. But in the south, on the shores of the ocean where their shipping was, they built towers at intervals looking out over the sea, because they feared barbarian attack. Then they bade farewell to the allies to whom they were never to return.

When they had departed to their homeland, the Irish and Picts, who knew the Romans had refused to come back, themselves immediately returned. Now they had become more confident than ever. They seized the whole northern part of the island from the natives, as far as the wall. A dispirited troop was stationed to guard the wall day and night, where they were dismayed, trembling and fainthearted. On the other hand the barbed javelins of the enemy never desisted. The cowardly defenders were dragged down from the wall and dashed miserably to the ground. What more is there to tell? They abandoned their cities and fled from the wall and were scattered. The enemy pursued, and there was quickly a massacre more cruel than all that had gone before. The wretched citizens were torn apart by their enemies, like lambs by wild beasts. They were driven out of their houses and cottages, and their response to the danger of famine was to rob and plunder one another. So they added domestic havoc to their external woes, so that the whole region was left without the sustenance of any food except what hunting could supply.

1.14 . . . In the meantime that famine already described afflicted the Britons more and more, and has left a lasting memory of its evils to posterity. It forced many to hand themselves over in defeat to the aggressive predators, but others would never do this. Rather, they trusted in God's help when human help failed them. They continually resisted from their mountains,

caves and passes. And at last they began to slaughter the enemy who had
been plundering their land for so many years. The shameless Irish marauders
therefore returned home, although they intended to come back after a
short time; while the Picts quietened down from this time onwards in the
remote part of the island, although they did not give up occasional plundering
and vexing raids on the British people . . . .

2.4 . . . Raised to the rank of archbishop, Laurence[1] made a most active
effort, through frequent pious exhortations and the continuous example
of good works, to add to the foundations of the church which he saw had
been so excellently laid, and to bring the edifice to its intended height. In
fact, not only did he devote himself to the care of the new church, with
which he had been charged by the English, but he also took on the task of
devoting himself to the pastoral care of the older inhabitants of Britain,
along with the Irish living in Ireland, the island next to Britain.

He discovered that in the homeland of the Irish, just as in the homeland of
the Britons, in Britain, life and witness fell short of church requirements in
many matters. The most serious of these was that they did not celebrate
Easter at the appropriate time but—as we have earlier explained—they
considered that the day of the resurrection of the Lord should be celebrated
from the fourteenth moon to the twentieth. With his fellow bishops he wrote
a letter to encourage them, calling them to witness and appealing to them to
maintain unity in peace and Catholic observance with that Church of Christ
which has spread over the whole world. The letter begins as follows:

> To our most dearly beloved brethren the lords bishops and abbots
> throughout the whole nation of Ireland, from Laurence, Mellitus
> and Justus, the bishops and servants of God.
> Since the apostolic see, following its normal procedure here as in
> every part of the whole world, directed us to preach to the heathen
> peoples in these western parts, it came about that it was to this island,
> which is known as Britain, that we came. Before we came to know
> them, we had the greatest reverence and respect for the sanctity of
> both the Britons and the Irish; as we became acquainted with the
> Britons, however, we thought the Irish better. But we learned, first
> from the bishop Dagan[2] when he came to this island, and then from
> the abbot Columbanus[3] when he came to Gaul, that the Irish did
> not differ from the Britons in their observances. For, when Bishop
> Dagan came to us, not only would he not take food with us, but he
> would not even eat in the same hospice.

The same Laurence, with his fellow bishops, also sent a letter, suitable for
their rank, to the priests of the Britons, in which he made every effort to

hold them to Catholic unity. But the present time shows what success he has had up to now.

2.19 . . . Pope Honorius[4] likewise wrote to the Irish people, since he had discovered that, as we explained earlier, they were in error concerning the observation of Easter. He argued skilfully, urging them not to consider themselves—few as they were and situated on the far edge of the world—to be wiser than the churches of Christ, whether ancient or modern, which were all over the world. Nor should they celebrate a different Easter, contrary to the Easter computations and the decrees of councils of the pontiffs of the whole world.

But it was John,[5] successor of Severinus (who succeeded Honorius), who sent a letter, while he was still pope-elect, which was of great authority and learning, to correct this error. And he also took pains in this letter to advise them to beware of the Pelagian heresy—which, he had come to know, had been revived among them—and to refute it. This is how his letter opens:

> To the dearest and most holy bishops Tomianus, Columbanus, Cronanus, Dimaus and Baithanus; Cronanus, Ernianus, Laistranus, Scellanus and Segenus, priests; Saranus and other Irish teachers and abbots,[6] from Hilarus, archpriest and deputy of the holy apostolic see, John the deacon elected [to the see] in God's name, John, chancellor and deputy of the holy apostolic see, and John, servant of God and counsellor of the same apostolic see.
>
> The letter which emissaries brought to the pope Severinus, of holy memory, was left without a reply to the questions it contained when he departed from this light. But—so that silence should not leave such a great matter obscure—we took over the letter, and we discovered that some people in your province were trying restore a new heresy on the basis of the old, contrary to right belief, clouding our Easter, on which Christ was sacrificed, in misty darkness, and endeavouring to celebrate it, with the Hebrews, on the fourteenth moon.

It is made plain in the beginning of this letter, both that this heresy had recently arisen among them, and that not all of that people, but only some, were involved with it.

Having explained how to calculate the observance of Easter, they added the following about the Pelagians, in the same letter:

> And we have also learnt this: that the poison of the Pelagian heresy has revived lately among you. For this reason we urge you to put out of your minds completely this poisonous crime of superstition. For you must be aware how strongly this detestable heresy has been condemned, since not only has it been done away with for the past two

hundred years, but it remains every day anathemized and buried by our perpetual condemnation. And we therefore exhort you not to take up from the ashes their weapons which have already been burnt. For who would not curse the arrogant and impious venture of those who say that people can live without sin by their own will and not by God's grace. For, in fact, it is blasphemous and stupid in the first place to say that anyone can be without sin; because it is not possible for anyone except the one mediator between God and man, Jesus Christ, Who was conceived and born without sin. For all others, born with original sin, are known to bear witness to Adam's transgression, even though they are born without actual sin, according to the words of the prophet: "Behold, I was shapen in iniquity; and in sin did my mother conceive me."[7]

TWENTY-SIX

From Cummian's Letter on the Easter Question

The letter from which this is extracted is concerned with the controversy over the calculation of the date of Easter—a matter of difficulty and concern to the early Church. The controversy itself, in this phase, belongs to the history of the sixth- and seventh-century Church; but it involves references back to the missionary period, and citations which claim to be from St Patrick. This letter has been edited and very fully discussed by Maura Walsh and Dáibhí Ó Cróinín, but they were unable to resolve finally some of the difficulties surrounding it—for example: who was its author? There are two main possibilities: that it was Cuimíne Ailbe, who became abbot of Iona in 657; or that it was Cuimíne Fota, closely associated in some way which is not clear with the monastery of Clonfert, who died in 661. The letter is addressed to Segéne, fifth abbot of Iona, from 623 to 652, and to the hermit Beccán, who is addressed as "carus carne et spiritus frater"—"beloved brother in the spirit and in the flesh"—which may mean that he was a blood brother of the author, or that he was a relation but not necessarily a brother, or (in spite of the reference to the flesh) that he was just a spiritual brother. He too can't be identified with certainty, but the likeliest candidate is a Beccán son of Lugaid, connected with Tech Conaill, near Bray, Co. Wicklow, and with Cluain Áird Mo Becóc, now Peakaun, in the Glen of Aherlow in Co. Tipperary. The background is reasonably clear. The letter of Pope Honorius (see p. 149) to the Irish churches concerning the Easter dates gave rise to the summoning of the synod of Mag Léne (north of Tullamore, Co. Offaly) in 630. The synod sent envoys to Rome to verify the Roman practice. After they had returned, in 632 or 633, Cummian's letter was written, in response to charges of heresy made by the community of Iona in connection with this matter and directed against ecclesiastics in Ireland. The matters dealt with are highly technical, and the letter shows that the author had access to extensive sources of authority, including a library of canon law. Only a few brief passages are extracted here.

Cummian the sinner sends a greeting in Christ (in supplication from the smallest to the great) and a vindication to the holy lords, venerable in Christ:

Segéne the abbot, successor of St Columba and of other holy men, and the
hermit Beccán, beloved brother in the spirit and in the flesh, with their advisers
. . .

[There follows immediately a detailed argument about the computation
of Easter dates and tables.]

. . . I find it written by the synods assembled to deal with the disagreement on this matter among the successors of the Apostles (who themselves—that is St Peter, the keeper of the keys, the evangelist of the
circumcised, and St John of the armour, the evangelist of the uncircumcised—
were harassed on all sides, as we read, and scattered through many lands,
and were unable to devise a regular cycle) that those who oppose the rules
laid down in agreement on a single Easter by the fourfold Apostolic see
(of Rome, Jerusalem, Antioch and Alexandria) "are to be excommunicated
and driven from the Church" and are to be anathema. There is also the
synod of Nicaea, of three hundred and eighteen bishops who ruled that
"the ancient canon on the observance of Easter" should be observed "so
that no remaining difference would arise among the churches, which
would all be directed correctly, and so that one and the same peace and
faith would be maintained among the churches of the East and the West."
Likewise the synod of six hundred bishops at Arles confirmed that "in the
first place we should observe Easter on the one day and at the same time
throughout the whole world", so that the universal church, as the Apostle
says, "might honour the one God with one voice . . . ."

. . . Finally, having thoroughly investigated the Easter cycles derived
from various computations, comparing the opinions given in different
languages on the course of the sun and the moon, I discovered cycles at
variance with this one which you adhere to—admittedly cycles that diverged
from yours in different ways—one in the day, another in the moon, another
in the epact, and another in the increase of the moon, which you call the
"leap". The first of these computations is that which the holy Patrick, our
papa,[1] brought to us and practised, in which the moon is regularly observed
from the fourteenth to the twenty-first, and the equinox from the twenty-
first of March . . . .

. . . Therefore, when a year had gone by, as I said before, in accordance
with Deuteronomy, I asked my fathers to shew me, and my elders to tell
me[2] (the successors, that is, of our first fathers—of Ailbe the bishop,[3] of
Ciarán of Clonmacnoise, of Brendan,[4] of Nessán[5] and of Lugid)[6] what was
their opinion of our excommunication by the Apostolic sees already
mentioned. They assembled in Mag Léne [*north of Tullamore, Co. Offaly*],
some in person, some through representatives, and they legislated, saying:

"Our predecessors, through proper witnesses (some still living, some sleeping in peace), laid it down that we should accept, humbly and without quibbling, the better and more sufficient proofs proposed to us by our source of baptism and of wisdom and by the successors of the Apostles of the Lord." Having risen together, they offered a prayer, as is our custom, that they would celebrate Easter the following year with the universal Church . . .

[Cummian goes on to explain that a further dispute arose, which was resolved by sending a deputation to Rome.]

TWENTY-SEVEN

Bishop Tírechán's Account of St Patrick's Journey

Bishop Tírechán wrote this, from the words and from the book of Bishop Ultan, whose fosterchild and pupil he was.

I found four names for Patrick written in the book of Ultán, bishop of the tribe of Conchubar: holy *Magonus* (that is, "famous"); *Succetus* (that is, the god of war); *Patricius* (that is, "father of the citizens"); *Cothirtiacus* (because he served four houses of druids).[1]

One of the druids, named Míliuc moccu Bóin, bought him. He worked for him in every kind of servitude and heavy labour, and Míliuc placed him as a swineherd in the mountain glens. Finally, however, an angel of the Lord visited him in a dream on the summits of Sliab Scirit beside Sliab Miss [*Slemish, Co. Antrim*].

The angel concluded his announcement by saying: "Look: your ship is ready: get up and make your journey!", and he left him and returned to heaven. Patrick rose and walked, as the angel of the Lord—whose name was Victor—had directed him.

It was in the seventeenth year of his age that he was taken captive and sold into Ireland. It was in his twenty-second year that he was able to abandon the service of druids. For seven further years he walked and travelled by water, through Gaul and all of Italy, and in the islands of the Tyrrhenian Sea, as he said himself in describing his work. Bishop Ultán has told me that he spent thirty years on one of these islands, which is called Aralensis [*possibly Lérins, probably Arles*].

However, you will find an account of all that happened then written in the regular history of his life. Here are his most recent wonderworks, happily performed and completed in the fifth year of the reign of Loiguire son of Niall.

Four hundred and thirty-three years are reckoned from the passion of Christ to the death of Patrick. Loiguire however reigned two (or five) years after Patrick's death.[2] Further, we estimate the full length of his reign to have been thirty-six years.

[Patrick on the plain of Brega]

In truth Patrick came with Gauls to the islands of Moccu Chor [*Skerries*]; to the eastern island known as Patrick's Island. With him there was a crowd of holy bishops, priests, deacons, exorcists, porters and lectors, as well as boys whom he ordained. Blessed by God, he came up from the sea at sunrise onto the Plain of Brega [*parts of Co. Meath*], with the true sun of marvellous doctrine, bringing light to the darkness of ignorance. The holy bishop rose over Ireland like the great bearer of light itself,[3] and his refrain from beginning to end was that of the benign Jesus Christ: "In the name of the Lord God; Father, Son and Holy Spirit." In the Irish language this is called *Ochen*.

First, then, he came to Sescnán's valley and built his first church there [*probably somewhere near Balbriggan*]. He brought away with him Sescnán's son (the bishop named Sesceneus) and he left there two of the boys from overseas. In the evening, then, he reached the mouth of the Ailbhine river [*the Delvin*] and came upon a good man whom he baptized. As well as this man he met the man's son, who pleased him and whom he named *Benignus* ("friendly"), because the boy, clutching Patrick's feet to his breast with his hands, wanted not to live with his father and his mother but cried to be allowed to live with Patrick. When they got up in the morning, Patrick finished blessing Benignus's father and began to mount his chariot. As he had one foot on the chariot and one on the ground, the boy Benignus clung to Patrick's leg with his two clasped hands and cried: "Allow me to be with Patrick, my true father!" And Patrick said: "Baptize him and lift him onto the chariot, for he is the heir to my kingdom."

(This is the bishop Benignus, Patrick's successor in the church of Armagh,[4] who carried with him the first blessed fire and the first lighted candles received from the hands of the lord Patrick, in order to produce the blessed incense for the eyes and noses of King Loiguire and his druids. For three brother druids—sons of one man—Cruth, Loch, Lethlanu, of the tribe of Runtir, barred the way and raised a great opposition to Patrick and Benignus. The druid's tunic, however, was burnt about Benignus's body and reduced to ashes. The holy boy was kept intact by his firm faith in God, in the presence of the king and his men and his druids. The tunic of Patrick's boy Benignus was placed on the druid and he was burnt within it and consumed by the fire. And Patrick said: "In this hour all the paganism of Ireland has been destroyed." And Patrick raised his hands to God about the druid Lochletheus and said: "My Lord, cast away from me this dog who barks in your face and mine. May he go to his death!"

(And all watched the druid being raised up through the night's darkness almost to the sky. Returning, his corpse, frozen solid with hail and snow mixed with sparks of fire, fell to the ground in the sight of all. That druid's stone is in the eastern part of Tara to the present day: I have seen it with my own eyes.)

On Sunday he came to Coirpriticus, son of Niall, to Tailtiu [*Teltown, near Kells*], where royal games are held. Coirpriticus wished to kill him, and had his servants flogged in the river Sele [*the Blackwater*] to make them point out Patrick to him. Because of this Patrick used to call him God's enemy. He said to him: "Your seed will serve the seed of your brothers. There will never be a king of your seed forever; and there will never be large fish in the river Sele."

Then, afterwards, he came to Conall son of Niall, in the house that he had built for himself where the Great Church of Patrick is now [*Donaghpatrick*]. Conall received him with great joy. Patrick baptized him and established his throne forever and said to him: "The seed of your brothers will serve your seed forever. And you must make an oblation to my heirs after me to the end of time; and your sons and your sons' sons must pay dues to my sons in the Faith forever."

Conall measured out a church of sixty feet with his own feet for Patrick's God, and Patrick said: "If anything is taken from this church your reign will be neither long nor secure."

At the end of Easter, when Sunday was over, he went out to the Ford of the Mill [*Athbron, near Kells*] and founded a church there. There he left three brothers and a sister. Their names are: Cathaceus, Cathurus, Catneus and their sister Catnea (who milked wild deer, as old people have informed me).

He continued on to the city of Tara, to Loiguire son of Niall again, because he had made a pact with him that he should not be killed within his realm.

(But Loiguire was unable to believe. He said: "My father Niall would not allow me to accept the Faith. Instead, I am to be buried in the earthworks of Tara, I the son of Niall, face to face with the son of Dúnlaing in Maistiu [*Mullaghmast*] in the Plain of Liphe [*the plains of Kildare*], standing like men at war because of the fierceness of our hatred for each other." For the pagans in their graves are equipped with arms at the ready.)[5] And Patrick entered the royal house. Nobody rose for him except one only; that is Erc, a heathen. He said to him: "Why did you alone rise to honour my God through me?" And Erc said to him: "I don't know what it is: I see fiery sparks rising from your lips to mine."[6] The holy man spoke too, saying: "Will you accept the baptism of the Lord, which I have to offer?" He replied: "I will accept it."

And they went to the well called in Irish Loigles, in our language, "Calf of the Cities" [*apparently on the Hill of Tara*]. And after he had opened his book and baptized the man Erc, he heard men behind his back laughing among themselves at his action; for they didn't understand what he had done. And on that day he baptized many thousands.

And as he was completing the baptismal formulas he heard talk. Notably two noblemen were conversing behind him, and one said to the other: "Is it true that you said this time last year that you would come here in these days? Please tell me your name and your father's name and the name of your land and territory and where your home is." He replied: "I am Énde

St Patrick's journeys west of the Shannon, according to Tírechán

son of Amolngid son of Fiachrae son of Echu from the western parts of Mag Domnon and the Wood of Fochloth" [*on the western shore of Killala Bay*].

When Patrick heard the name of the Wood of Fochloth, he was overjoyed and he said to Énde son of Amolngid: "I will go out there with you if I live, since the Lord has told me to go there." And Énde said: "You will not go out with me or we may both be killed." The holy man replied: "On the contrary, unless I come with you, you will not arrive alive in your country, and you shall not have eternal life; since it is because of me that you have come here—as Joseph came before the Children of Israel."

Énde then said to Patrick: "Give baptism to my son, since he is of tender age. However, I and my brothers can't believe in you until we reach our own people, for fear of being laughed at."

Conall therefore was then baptized, and Patrick gave him his blessing. He took him by the hand and gave him to Bishop Cethiacus. Bishop Cethiacus fostered him and taught him, as did Cethiacus's brother Mucneus, whose relics are in the Great Church of Patrick in the Wood of Fochloth [*probably Kilmoremoy, now the graveyard at Patrick's Well on the outskirts of Ballina*]. For this reason Cethiacus committed his church to Conall, whose family owns it to the present day—because when Cethiacus died, Conall was a layman.

Now, six sons of Amolngid came before Loiguire with a case for judgment. Énde, with his tender son, was alone in opposing them. Patrick was present. They examined the case of their inheritance, and Loiguire and Patrick passed judgment that they should divide their inheritance into seven parts. And Énde said: "I give my son and my part of the inheritance to Patrick's God and to Patrick." (Because of this some say that we are servants of Patrick to the present day.)[7]

Under the aegis of Loiguire son of Niall, Patrick and the sons of Amolngid, with the assembly of the laity and the holy bishops, made a pact to undertake a journey to Sliab Aigle [*Croagh Patrick*]. And Patrick paid the price of fifteen souls, as he states in his writing, in gold and silver, so that no evil persons should impede them as they travelled straight across the whole of Ireland. For it was necessary for them to reach the Wood of Fochloth before the end of a year—by the following Easter—because of the children whose voices he had heard crying loudly from their mothers' wombs: "Come, holy Patrick: save us!"

[Patrick's journey to the Shannon]

Patrick founded a church at Áth Segi [*place unknown*], and another church for holy Cinnena at Áth Carnoi, on the Boyne [*probably Carnes, near Dunboyne*]; and another above Coirp Raithe [*Carbury?*]; and another on the rath of Dallbrónach [*near Edenderry?*].[8]

He founded another in the Plain of Echredd; another in the Plain of Tadcne, which is called Cell Bile (it now belongs to the community of Scire) [*these places are not identified*]; another in the Plain of Echnach [*Donaghmore, near Navan*], where Cassanus the priest had his place; another in Singite [*unknown, possibly near Tara*]; another in the plain of Bil beside the Ford of the Dog's Head [*Áth Chinn Con, in Co. Westmeath near Ballynagore*]; another in Carmell's Head in the Plain of Telach [*Fertullagh*], where St Brigid received the veil from the hands of Mac Caille in Uisnech [*near Killare, Co. Westmeath*] in Mide [*Mide approximates to Co. Westmeath*].

He stayed beside Coithrige's Rock [*not known: probably near Moyvore*]. But some of his people from overseas were killed around him by a son of Fiachu son of Niall, whom he cursed, saying: "There will be no king of your seed; but you will serve the seed of your brothers." And he founded another church in Art's Head in the country of the Corcu Roide [*Corkaree, Co. Westmeath*] in which he erected a stone altar; and another in Cúl Corrae [*not known*].

And he came across the river Ethne [*the Inny*] into the two Tethbhas. And he consecrated Mel as bishop [*Mel's church was at Ardagh, Co. Longford*]. And he founded the church of Bil [*not known*], and ordained Gosacht son of Míliuc moccu Bóin whom he had fostered during his servitude of seven years.[9]

And he sent Camulacus of the Commienses [*a tribe of the region of Ballycowan in Offaly*] to Mag Cumi [*west of Tullamore?*], and, from the hill of Granard, pointed out the place to him—that is, the church of Rahan—with his finger.

And he came to Mag Réin [*south County Leitrim*], and ordained Bruscus as priest and founded a church for him. (Marvellously, Bruscus, after his death, said to another saint, who was in the monastery of the family of Cothirbe [*not known*]: "It is well for you. You have your son. I, however, am in a church in a wilderness, a church abandoned and empty, and no priests say Mass near me." The saint had this dream for three nights. On the third day, he got up, took an iron spade and excavated the grave. He carried the bones away with him to the monastery where they now are. Bruscus afterwards remained silent.)

Patrick, sending Nieth Brain—a barbarian of his company, who spoke wonders in God's truth—to the earthwork of Slecht [*Darragh Fort in Co.*

Darragh Fort

Cavan] . . . [10] . . . Patrick then came down to the basin of the Shannon to a place where his charioteer Boidmal had died. He is buried there in a place called "Boidmal's Wood" to the present day [*unknown*]. The place had been given to Patrick.

Here ends the first book, concerning what was enacted in the territories of the Uí Néill.

[Tírechán's protestation]

Here begins the second book, concerning what happened in the regions of Connacht.

All the matters I have told so far from the beginning of this book are known to you, since they happened in your regions—apart from a few items that I derived in the course of my work from numbers of my elders and from the same Ultán bishop of moccu Conchubair, which I have recounted.

However, my heart within me is perturbed with love for Patrick, since I see disputants and bombasts and warriors of Ireland who hate Patrick's ecclesiastical jurisdiction—because they have stolen from him what was his. And, further, they are afraid: since, if the heir of Patrick were to claim his territory, he could have almost all the island brought into Patrick's domain. Because, i: God gave him the whole island, with its people, through the angel of the Lord; ii: and he taught them the Lord's law; iii: and he baptized them with Christ's baptism; iiii: and he showed them Christ's Cross; u: and he announced his resurrection. But they don't love his community, because, i: it isn't lawful to swear against him; ii: or to overswear him; iii: and it is unlawful to draw lots against him. Because all the primitive churches of Ireland are his and he overswears all oaths.[11]

In my book up to this point I have written only in broad general terms. Everything from now on will be detailed and exact.

[Patrick crosses the Shannon]

Holy Patrick then crossed the bed of the Shannon at the Ford of Two Birds [*Snám dá én, a place where cattle were swum: probably by the bridge at Drumsna*] towards the Plain of Aí [*between Castlerea and Tulsk*].

(However, when the druids of Loiguire son of Niall, Calvus ["bald", or "tonsured"] and Capitolavium, who had fostered the two daughters of Loiguire, fair Ethne and red Fedelm, heard what had been done, they feared that the girls might go the way of the holy man. They became very angry, and they brought down nocturnal darkness and dense mist over the whole of Mag Aí.[12] We don't know by whose power this was done but we do know that this night lasted for three days and nights. The holy man immediately commenced a fast of three days, and with a hundredfold prayers and pros-

*Snámh dá Éan: the Shannon
at Drumsna, Co. Leitrim*

trations beseeched God, the king of kings. All the evil magic of darkness disappeared from Mag Aí, and Patrick said: "Thanks be to God.")[13]

And they crossed the bed of the Shannon—which is known as "Goddess"—to the Mound of Grad [*Doogarry, Co. Roscommon*], where he ordained the holy Ailbe as priest. He pointed out to him a marvellous altar on the Mountain of the Uí Ailello [*Curlew Mountain*]—for he was among the Uí Ailello—and he baptized Maneus, whom Brón son of Icne—God's servant and Patrick's companion—ordained.

They came to Mag Glais, and there he founded a great church, which is called Kilmore [*Kilmore Moyglass, at Ballintober, Co. Roscommon*]. There he left two barbarians, his monks Conleng and Ercleng.

Then he went to Assicus and Bitteus, and to the druids who were of the tribe of Corcu Chonluain, the brothers Hono and Ith. One welcomed Patrick and his holy people and gave Patrick his own house. And he went out to Hono's Imbliuch [*Emlagh, near Elphin*], and Patrick said to him: "Your seed will be blessed, and from your seed will spring priests of the

The well of Elphin,
Co. Roscommon

Lord, and heads of churches worthy to receive my dues and your inheritance."
And he placed there Assicus, and Betheus the son of Assicus's brother, and
Cipia the mother of Bishop Betheus.

The holy bishop Assicus was coppersmith to Patrick and he made altar
plate—shrines, and our saint's altar vessels in honour of Bishop Patrick.
And of these I have seen three rectangular patens: a paten in the church of
Patrick in Armagh; another in the church of Elphin; and a third in the
great church of Seól [*Donaghpatrick, by Lough Hackett, Co. Galway*], on the
altar of the holy bishop Felartus.

This was the same Assicus who retreated into the northern region to
Sliab Liacc [*Slieve League, Co. Donegal*], and who spent seven years in a
hermitage called Rochuil beyond Sliab Liacc. And his monks searched for
him and found him in the mountain valleys with his craftwork. They
dragged him away and he died in their company among the lonely mountains.
They buried him in Ráith Cúngai on Mag Sereth [*Racoon Hill, Co. Donegal*].
After his death the king gave to him and his monks, as a grant in perpetuity,
the grazing of a hundred cows with their calves and twenty oxen; for he
said he wouldn't return to Mag Aí where they had lied about him.

His bones are in Ráith Cúngai on Mag Sereth. He was Patrick's monk
but both the monks of Colum Cille [*i.e., of Iona and Durrow*] and the monks
of Ardstraw laid claim to him.

Patrick went from the well of Elphin to the Mound of the Uí Ailello, and he founded a church there which is called the Old Church of the Mound to the present day [*Senchell Dumiche: Shankill, Tirerrill, Co. Sligo*]. There he left the holy men Macet and Cétgen and Rodanus the priest.

And a blessed young woman named Mathona—a sister of Patrick's successor Benignus—made a journey to him there, and received the veil from Patrick and Rodanus. Having become a nun with them she went across the Mountain of the Uí Ailello [*Curlew Mountain*] and founded a free church at Tamnach [*Tawnagh, Tirerrill, Co. Sligo*]. She was honoured by God and men, and she swore a compact of friendship on the relics of Rodanus, and her successors and his entertained each other, turn and turn about.

Afterwards however, they appointed bishops to the holy church of Tamnach, whom Patrick's bishops Bronus and Bitheus consecrated. They asked nothing but friendship of the community of Dumech [*the Old Church of the Mound, i.e., Shankill*]; but the community of Cluain [*Clonmacnoise*] now makes a claim—as they hold many of Patrick's places by force since the recent plague.

[The Daughters of Loiguire][14]

Afterwards, then, before sunrise, holy Patrick came to the well that is called Clébach [*Ogulla well, near Tulsk, Co. Roscommon*] on the eastern slopes of Cruachu. They sat down beside the well, and suddenly there appeared the two daughters of King Loiguire, Ethne the fair and Fedelm the red. These had come, as is the women's custom, to wash in the morning. They found the holy gathering of bishops with Patrick by the well, and they had no idea where they were from or what was their nature or their people or their homeland; but they thought that maybe they were men of the *si* [15] or of the gods of the earth, or phantoms.

The girls said to them: "Are you really there? Where have you come from?"

Patrick replied to them: "It would be better for you to confess faith in our true God than to ask questions about our origin."

The first girl asked: "Who is God, and where is God, and whose God is he, and where is his house? Has your God sons and daughters, gold and silver? Is he alive forever? Is he beautiful? Have many people fostered his son? Are his daughters dear and beautiful to the men of this world? Is he in heaven or on earth, in the sea, on mountains, in valleys? Give us some idea of him: how he may be seen, how loved; how he may be found—is he found in youth or in old age?"

In his reply, Patrick, filled with the Holy Spirit, said:

"Our God is the God of all people, the God of heaven and earth, of the sea and of the rivers, the God of the sun and the moon and of all the stars, the God of the high mountains and of the deep valleys. He is God above

The well of Clebach
(Ogulla Well, near Tulsk, Co. Roscommon)

heaven and in heaven and under heaven, and has as his dwelling place heaven and earth and the sea and all that are in them. His life is in all things; he makes all things live; he governs all things; he supports all things. He kindles the light of the sun; he builds the light and the manifestations of the night; he makes wells in arid land and dry islands in the sea, and he set the stars in place to serve the major lights. He has a son who is coeternal with him and of like nature. The Son is not younger than the Father nor the Father than the Son; and the Holy Spirit breathes in them. The Father, the Son and the Holy Spirit are not separate. Truly, now, since your are daughters of an earthly king, I wish that you will believe and I wish to wed you to the king of heaven."

And the girls said, as if with one voice and from one heart:

"Teach us most diligently how we may believe in the heavenly king, so that we may see him face to face. Direct us, and we will do whatever you say."

And Patrick said:

"Do you believe that you cast off the sin of your father and mother through baptism?"

They replied:

"We believe."

"Do you believe in penance after sin?"

"We believe."

"Do you believe in life after death? Do you believe in the resurrection on the Day of Judgment?"

"We believe."

"Do you believe in the unity of the Church?"

"We believe."

And they were baptized, and a white veil placed on their heads. They demanded to see the face of Christ, to which the saint said:

"Unless you taste death, and unless you receive the sacrament you can't see the face of Christ."

They replied:

"Give us the sacrament, so that it will be possible for us to see the Son, our bridegroom."

They received God's Eucharist, and slept in death. Their friends laid them both in one bed, covered with their clothes, and raised a lament and a great keen.

The druid Caplit, who had fostered one of them, came and wept. Patrick preached to him, and he believed, and the hair of his head was shorn. And his brother Máel came and said: "My brother believed in Patrick, but I don't. I will convert him back again to heathenism."

And he spoke harsh words to Patrick and Mathonus.[16] But Patrick preached to him and converted him to God's penance. The hair of his head was shorn. Its style had been that of the druids—"*airbacc giunnae*", as it is called. From this comes the most famous of Irish sayings, "Calvus [*bald*, i.e. *Máel*] and Caplit: the same difference"—they believed in God.

When the days of keening the kings' daughters came to an end they buried them beside the well of Clébach and made a round ditch in the fashion of a *ferta*. That was the custom of the heathen Irish. But we call it *relic*,[17] that is, the remains of the girls.

And the *ferta* was granted in perpetuity to Patrick and his heirs after him, along with the bones of the holy girls. He built an earthen church in that place.

[Patrick in eastern Connacht]

Then Patrick came to Mag Cairetho [*not known*] and they camped in that place. He founded a church in Ardd Licce, which is called Sendomnach [*not known*] and placed in it the deacon Coimanus, his holy monk, a boy dear to Christ and Patrick.

Patrick held Árd Senlis [*Sid Nento, Ballintobber, Co. Roscommon*] and placed there the holy virgin Laloca. And he had a church in the Plain of Nente.

And they went out with the holy bishop Cethiacus to his own home country [*i.e., to Tirerrill, Co. Sligo*]; for his father was of the Uí Ailello. His mother was of the tribe of Saí of the country of the Cianachta [*mainly in Co. Louth: the barony of Keenaght*], from Domnach Sairigi [*Donaseery, Duleek, Co. Meath*], near the Stone House of Ciannán [*Dom Liacc: Duleek, Co. Meath*]. It was Bishop Cethiacus's custom to offer the Sacrifice in Corcu Saí on Easter Sunday. On the second day of Easter he would stay in the church of holy Comgella at the Ford of Two Forks (that is, Dá Loarcc, near Kells). For, according to Cethiacus's community, Comgella was a nun of his.

They left behind them a certain holy deacon—little more than a boy—named Iustus, who held Fidarte [*Fuerty, Co. Roscommon*]. Patrick gave him the books of baptism. He baptized the Uí Maine, and in his fortunate old age he baptized Ciarán the wright's son,[18] when he was an old man in the fullness of his days.

(There intervened between the death of Patrick and the birth of Ciarán, according to the experts in chronology, a hundred and forty years.)[19]

And Ciarán was baptized, from Patrick's book, by the deacon Iustus in full view of the people.

Patrick's Franks, indeed, deserted him—fifteen brothers and one sister. I don't wish to give their names, except those of the two leaders, Bernicius and Hernicius. And the sister's name was Nitria. Many church sites were given to them, of which I know the name of only one, where the Basilica of the Saints is [*Baslick, Co. Roscommon*]. For holy Patrick showed them the qualities of each location and pointed it out to them with his finger from the summit of Gair [*near Oran, Co. Roscommon*] when they came to ask him choose for them among the places they had discovered. Cethiacus founded the church of Brer Garad [*Oran*]. There was a certain girl there who crossed the river Suck and her feet and shoes remained dry.

Patrick came to Selc [*between Rathcroghan and Tulsk, Co. Roscommon*], where the sons of Brión had their halls. They camped on the ramparts of Selc and made their bed and seat among the stones. His hand wrote letters on the stones which we saw today with our own eyes.

(With him were: Bishop Brón; Sachelus; Cassanus; Brocidius; Lommán his brother; Benignus the successor of Patrick; and Benignus the brother of Cethiacus of the tribe of Ailill, who held Benignus's Cell [*Kilbennan, Co. Galway*] in . . . ; Brónach the priest; Rodanus; . . . from Patrick from Cethiacus; Bishop Felartus of the tribe of Ailill and his sister, and another sister who was in a retreat in the Mare Conmaicne [*Connemara*] that is called Croch Cuile [*Cruanakeely, Co. Galway*]).[20]

And he continued on to the confines of Gregrige [*southeastern Co. Sligo*] and founded a church at Drummae [*by Lough Gara*]. He dug a well there.

It is always full although no stream flows either into or out of it.

There are patens and a chalice of his in the church of Adrocht daughter of Talan [*Killaraght, Co. Sligo*] who received the veil from Patrick's hand.

And he continued to the land of the Sons of Ercc [*Moylurg, in Co. Sligo*]. He was in that place where millstones are made[21] at Ess Macc nErcc [*probably Assylin, near Boyle, Co. Roscommon*], when they stole his horses. He cursed them, saying: "Your seed will serve the seed of your brother." And that has come true.

And he returned to Mag Airthic [*Tibohine, Tullanarock, Elphin*] and founded the church of Senes [*Shankill, Elphin*] in that plain. And he blessed a church in the Hill of the Rocks [*Tullanarock*].

And he went out to Drummut Cerrigi [*Tullanarock*], where he came upon two men fighting. They were the two sons of one man, at odds with each other after the death of their father, who had been a coppersmith of the tribe of the Ciarraige Airnen. They hadn't agreed how to divide their inheritance. The stick of contention had been placed in position. This the pagans call "*caam*" (in battlefield custom it is displayed set in the earth). They stood tensely, grasping lethal swords in outstretched hands, brother about to kill brother. When Patrick arrived he saw them from afar—about a furlong's distance. He opened his mouth and said: "Lord, I pray you, restrain the hands of the brothers and prevent one from harming the other!" And they were unable to extend or withdraw a hand, but stood rigidly there like wooden images. He blessed them and instructed them, saying: "Make friendship, since you are brothers. Do what I tell you: sit down!" They sat down as Patrick told them, and they granted the land and goods of their father to Patrick and to the God of heaven. He founded a church there, in which is [*the grave of*] the craftsman Cuanu, brother of Sachellus, bishop of Basilica.

He continued his journey through the wastelands of the Ciarraige Airni to the southern plain, that is, to Nairniu [*on the Roscommon-Mayo border*]. He came upon holy Iarnascus under an elm with his son Locharnach. Patrick wrote an alphabet for him and spent a week or more with him, with nine or twelve men. He founded a church there and accepted Iarnascus as abbot; and he was indeed filled with the Holy Spirit.

Afterwards a man joined Patrick, coming from Irlochair in the south [*Pobble O'Keefe, Duhallow, Co. Cork*], a man named Medbu. He studied in Armagh and was ordained there. He was Patrick's deacon. He was of the tribe of Mache and was a good priest. He founded a free church at Imgoe Már Cerrigi [*Dunamon, Co. Roscommon*].

And Patrick went on to the well called Mucno [*Tobar Makee, Drumtemple, Co. Roscommon*] . . .

(. . . and built the cell that is known as Senes . . .)[22]

. . . and there was Secundinus alone and apart under an elm with rich foliage. There is a cross in that spot to the present day.

He came through the wastelands of the Sons of Énde to . . . Aian [*not known*], where Lommanus Turrescus was.

After a long time Senmeda, daughter of Énde son of Brion came and received the veil from Patrick's hands. She gave him her ornaments—bracelets and anklets that are called *aros* in Irish.[23]

[Patrick's journey to the Reek]

He continued his journey to the land of the Conmaicne of Cúl Tolith [*southeastern Co. Mayo*] and founded rectangular churches there. I know one large church among them, that of Árd Uiscon [*not known*] . . . the middle cell, in which he left the sisters of Bishop Failart of the tribe of Ailill; another cell, Sescinn . . . two barbarians . . . their names . . . [24]

And he came to Mag Cáeri [*north of Ballinrobe, Co. Mayo*] and camped at Cúl Core [*not known*]. He founded a church in that place and baptized many.

Afterwards he went out into the Plain of Foimsen [*not known*], and there he came on two brothers, Luchte and Derclaid, sons of a man named Conlaid. Derclaid sent his bondsman to kill Patrick. Luchte however saved him. Patrick said to him: "There will be bishops and priests among your descendants. But your brother's family will be under a curse and will soon die out." And in that place he left the priest Conán.

And he went out into the waste lands to the well of Stringell [*Ballintober, Co. Mayo*]. He spent two Sundays there and then went on to Mag Rathen [*northwest of Lough Carra*] and on from there to the men of Humal [*The Owles, Co. Mayo*], to Achud Fobuir [*Aghagower*], where bishops are consecrated. There came to Patrick a holy girl who received the veil from him. He ordained Senachus, her father's son, and gave him a new name, that is "Lamb of God", and made him a bishop. He made three requests of Patrick: that he would not debase his priestly order by sin; that the place would not be known by his name; and that the length of his life should be diminished to add to the length of the life of his son, named Óengus. Patrick wrote an alphabet for Óengus on the day Senachus was ordained.

Patrick consecrated a church in that place, at the dwelling of the virgin named Mathona. He said to them: "There will be good bishops here, and from their seed in this see there will be blessed people forever." That is Achad Fobuir, and they accepted the Mass of Patrick.

And Patrick travelled on to Sliab Aigli [*Croagh Patrick, "the Reek"*], to fast there for forty days and forty nights, following the example of Moses, Elias and Christ. His charioteer died at Muiriscc Aigli [*Murrisk, Co. Mayo*], that is, on the plain between the sea and Aigle. There Patrick buried his charioteer Totus Calvus [*Totmael*], gathered stones together for his cairn, and said: "So let him be forever; and he will be visited by me at the end of the world."

And Patrick went on up to the summit of Crochán Aigli and stayed there for forty days and forty nights. And he was tormented by birds gathering towards him so that he couldn't see the sky or the sea or the land . . . .

. . . Because God said to all the holy people of Ireland, of the past, the present and the future: "Holy ones, climb to the top of the mountain that rises above and is higher than all the mountains of the sun's West, that the people of Ireland may be blessed, that Patrick may see the fruit of his labours."

Because the choir of all the saints of Ireland came to him, to visit their father.

And he founded a church on Mag Humail.

[Patrick returns to the Wood of Fochluth]

He came to the territory of Corcu Temne [*not known*], to the well of Sine [*Robeen, Co. Mayo*], where he baptized many thousands of people and founded three churches.

And he came to the well of Findmag, that is known as "Slán" [*near Castlebar, Co. Mayo*], because he had been told that druids honoured the well and made votive offerings in it as if to a god. The well was square, and there was a rectangular stone in its mouth. The water came out through the stone—that is, it oozed out of its cementing, forming, as it were, a damp trail.[25] And the unbelievers said that a certain seer had made a casket for himself under the stone in the water so that it would always bleach his bones; for he was afraid of being consumed by fire. For this reason they worshipped the well as a god.

Patrick was told the reason for this adoration. But he had divine zeal derived from the living God. He said: "It is not true what you say, that the well was 'king of the waters'"—the name they had given it. The druids and the heathens of the district—a very large crowd—gathered at the well, and Patrick said: "Lift the stone and let us see what is there, whether or not there are bones. For I tell you that there are no human bones under it, but possibly a trace of gold and silver through the cementing of the stones, the residue of your disgraceful offerings." They were unable to lift the stone. Patrick, with his servants, blessed the stone, and he said to the crowd: "Move back a distance for the moment, so that you may see through me the power of my God who lives in heaven." And he lifted the stone in his hands from the mouth of the well and placed it on the opposite side of the well, where it remains always. They found nothing in the well but water alone, and they believed in the high God.

A certain man called Cáeta or Cata sat beside the stone, which Patrick had set in the ground some distance away. He blessed this man and baptized him, saying: "Your seed will be blessed forever."

Cell Tog in the country of Corcu Teimne [*Ballynew, Co. Mayo*] was Patrick's. Bishop Cainnechus—Patrick's monk—founded it.[26]

And Patrick crossed the plains and came to the country of Macc Ercae, in Dichuil and Aurchuil [*near Ballina*]. And in Dichuil Patrick came to a great tomb, of marvellous size, remarkable in its length, which his community had found. They were amazed that it measured a hundred and twenty feet in length, and they said: "We don't believe this: that a man so tall could have existed."[27]

Patrick answered, saying: "If you wish you will see him"—and they said: "We do so wish." He struck the top of the stone with his staff, and signed the tomb with the sign of the cross, saying: "Lord, open the tomb"—and it opened. And a huge man, sound and whole, rose up and said: "I wish you well, holy man, since you have raised me, even if only for an hour, from many torments." And he burst into most bitter weeping, and said: "I will go with you." They said: "We can't have you come with us on our way, because people couldn't look on your face for fear of you. But believe in the God of heaven and accept the Lord's baptism, and you will not go back to where you were. Tell us who your people are."

"I am the son of the son of Cas son of Glas, who was a swineherd of Lugar chief of Hirota [*Uí Rota: not known*]. In the reign of Coirpre Niath Fer— exactly a hundred years ago—the warrior band of the son of Macc Con killed me.[28] He was baptized and fell silent. He was laid again in his grave.

(Patrick came to Findmag [*in the barony of Athlone, Co. Roscommon*] in the country of the Uí Maini and came there upon the cross of Christ and two new graves. From his chariot the holy man said: "Who is it that is buried here?" And a voice replied from the grave: "I am a pagan." The saint answered: "Why has the holy cross been set up over you?" And he answered again: "Because the mother of the man who is buried beside me asked that the symbol of the cross be placed at her son's grave. But a silly and stupid man placed it at mine." Patrick sprang from his chariot, seized the cross and, lifting it from the pagan mound he placed it over the head of the baptized man. He mounted his chariot and silently prayed to God. When he had said "Deliver us from evil"—his charioteer said to him: "What was that about? Why did you address the unbaptized heathen man? I am distressed that a man should be unbaptized. It would have been better in the eyes of God to bless him, as if in baptism, and to pour the baptismal water over the dead man's grave." Patrick didn't answer him. I think myself that he left him as he was because God didn't wish to save him. But let us return to our narrative.)[29]

Then indeed he crossed over the Muada [*the river Moy, in Co. Mayo*]. The druids of the sons of Amolngid learned with alarm that the holy man was coming down on them into their own territory. A great number of them assembled about the chief druid, Recradus by name. He wished to kill holy Patrick, and came towards [*Patrick and his companions*] with nine druids clad in white garments and with a druid host. From afar Patrick and Énde son of Amolngid and Conall son of Énde saw him, while Patrick was baptizing a great crowd. When Énde saw him he got up and took arms, preparing to drive away the druids. For the druids were separated from them by a very great body of water, about . . . miles. However, Patrick sent Conall son of Énde to meet the druids, to identify the chief druid for fear they would kill someone else. As a signal, the boy stood beside the druid.

And the holy man, Patrick, stood up, lifted his left hand to the God of heaven, and cursed the druid, who dropped dead in the midst of the magicians. As a sign of punishment he was consumed by fire in the sight of all.

The people scattered all over Mag Domnon [*in Tirawley, west of Killala Bay*] when everyone saw that miracle, and Patrick baptized many that day.

He ordained holy Mucneus, brother of Cethiacus, and gave him the seven books of the Law—which he bequeathed to Macc Erce son of Macc Dregin—and he founded a church beside the Wood of Fochluth [*on the outskirts of Ballina*], in which are the holy bones of Bishop Mucnoe (for God told him to leave the law aside and ordain bishops, priests and deacons in that country).

And he blessed Amolngid son of Fergus, Énde's brother, because it was on his land that he performed the miracle.

A certain man, Macc Dregin by name, with seven pagan sons, came to them and asked Patrick for God's baptism. Patrick blessed him and his sons and chose one of them, named Macc Ercae, wrote him an alphabet and blessed him with a priest's blessing. The boy's father said to him: "It will grieve me if the boy goes away with you." Patrick said: "No, it will not be like that. I shall commit him to the care of Brón son of Icne and to Olcanus." He extended his arm and with his finger pointed out to Macc Ercae the distant place where his bones now are. He erected a cross there.

And two girls came to Patrick and took the veil from him, and he blessed a place for them beside the Wood of Fochlut.

Now Patrick went on to a piece of land known as Foirrgea of the Sons of Amolngid [*Farragh, Co. Mayo*], to divide it between the sons of Amolngid. There he made a square earthen church of mud, because there was no wood nearby.

They brought him a sick woman who was with child. He baptized the son in the mother's womb, the amniotic fluid being the water of baptism. They buried her below the bank of the church enclosure. The seat of the holy man himself is beside the church to the present day.

And he built a church for a certain community on a bay of the sea, that is, Ros of the Sons of Caitne [*Ross Point, near Killala*].

[Patrick completes his circuit]

And he returned to the river Muada and crossed over from Vertriga [*Bartragh, Co. Mayo, on the western shore of Killala Bay*] to Bertriga [*Bartragh, Co. Sligo, on the eastern shore of Killala Bay*]. He erected a stone marked with the sign of the Cross of Christ, and said: "Behold, at the end of the world water will be found here, and I shall remain here."

He founded a church beside the rath of Rigbairt [*Carrowmagley, Co. Sligo*]. And he came to Muirisc [*Murrisk, in Tireragh, Co. Sligo*] to the place of Brón son of Icne, and he blessed his son, that is, Bishop Macc Rime. They wrote an alphabet for him and for Bishop Muirethach, who was on the bank of the river Braith [*not known*].

And Patrick and Brón, and Macc Erce Maicc Dregin with them, crossed the Strand of Authuile [*Ballysadare Bay*] into the territory of Ira [*Tireragh, Co. Sligo*], to the plain—that is, to Ros Dregnige, where Brón's chasuble is [*probably Killasbugbrone—"Bishop Brón's Church"—near Strandhill*]. While they were sitting there Patrick's tooth fell out. He gave the tooth to his dear Brón as a relic and said: "Look: the sea will cast us out of this place in the last times, and you will go out to the river of Slicech [*Sligo River*] and to the wood."

He went out across the Mountain of the Uí Ailello [*Curlew Mountain*], and founded a church there, that is Tamnach [*Tawnagh*—see p. 163]; and Echenach [*Aughenagh, Co. Sligo*]; and Cell Angle [*Killanly, Tirerrill, Co. Sligo*]; and Cell Senchuae [*not known*].

And he went out into the country of Callrige of the Three Plains [*Calry*] and built a church by Druim Léas [*Drumlease, Co. Leitrim*]. He baptized many and climbed to Ailmag and founded a church there, that is, Domnach Ailmaige [*Donaghmore, Dromahaire, Co. Leitrim*]. For Patrick spent three days and three nights there.

He went on to Mag Áine [*not known*] and founded a church there. Then he turned to Euoe [*Magerow, Co. Sligo*] and to Mag Cetni [*not known*]. And he cursed the river that is called "Black" [*the river Duff, Co. Donegal*], because, although he asked, they would give none of their fish to the saint. On the other hand he blessed the Drowes, in which large fish are now caught. Whatever way the fish species has been produced, the river Drowes formerly had no fish: but since then it yields a harvest to fisherman.

(He cursed other rivers too, for example the rivers Oingae [*the Nanny water in Co. Meath*] and the Sele [*the Meath Blackwater*]—for two of his boy disciples were drowned in the Sele. It was done because of that; to preserve the memory of his miraculous power.)

He went on, even to enter Mag Sereth, across the river [*Erne*] between Es Ruaid [*Assaroe*] and the sea. He founded a church in Ráith Argi [*Rath Ara, Assaroe*], and camped in Mag Sereth [*Kildoney*]. He came upon a certain good man of the tribe of Lathru, whom he baptized along with his young child Hinu, or Ineus, whom the father carried in the hood of his cloak at the back of his neck—for he had been born on the way, while his father came down from the mountain. Patrick baptized the boy, wrote him an alphabet and blessed him with a bishop's blessing. Later Hinu gave hospitality to holy Assicus and his monks in Ard Roissen, that is, in Ráith Congi [*Racoon Hill, Co. Donegal*] in Mag Sereth, in the time of kings Fergus and Fothad.

He founded a church in Mag Latrain [*not known*] and the great church of Sirdruimm [*not known*], which was held by the community of Daminis [*"Ox Island"; not known; not the Devenish in Lough Erne, Co. Fermanagh*] on [*the river*] Doburbar [*the Ulster Blackwater*].

And he proceeded through the Pass of the Sons of Conall [*the Barnesmore Gap, Co. Donegal*] to Mag Itho and founded a great church there [*Donagh-more, Raphoe*].

He went out to Mag Tochuir [*Glentogher, Inishowen, Co. Donegal*] and built a church there [*Carndonagh*]. To that place there came a certain bishop, of the tribe of Corcu Theimne [*located somewhere between Westport and Castlebar in Co. Mayo*] from Cell Toch in the country of Temenrige in Cerae in the far west. His sister came with him and they were monk and nun of Patrick. The community of Cluain [*Clonmacnoise*] now holds their church, to the grief of the men of the place.

(Patrick crossed the Shannon on three occasions, and he spent seven years in the west.)

From Mag Tochuir he came to Dul Ocheni [*a plain by the Moyola river?*], where he built seven churches. He came to Ardd Sratho [*Ardstraw*] and consecrated Mac Ercae bishop. He went out to Ardd Eólurg [*by the river Foyle*] and to Ailgi [*in Firlee, north of Limavady*] and to Lee Bendraige [*Firlee*].

Then he crossed over the river Bandae [*the Bann*], and blessed the place where the cell of Cúl Raithne [*Coleraine*] in Eilne now is, where there was a bishop. He built many other churches in Eilne. He made a passage across the river Buas [*the Bush*] and he sat on a rock in Dún Sobairche [*Dunseverick*] which is "Patrick's Rock" to the present day.

He consecrated as a bishop holy Olcanus whom he had fostered, and he gave him a share of the relics of Peter, Paul and others, along with a reli-quary to preserve them. Then he returned to the plain of Eilne and built many churches which are owned by the the the Coindiri [*the people of Connor*].

He climbed up Sliab Miss [*Slemish*] of the Bonrige, because it was there he fostered the son of Míliucc moccu Bóin, whose name was Gosacht, as well as two daughters of the same man, while he was in slavery for seven years. He taught them, but swore them to silence for fear of the druid. But one night the druid Míliucc saw sparks of the divine word[30] from the mouth of Succetus [*that is, Patrick*] rising to the lips of his son—setting his whole body ablaze—and then going from his mouth to the mouths of his sisters.

"Why, slave"—he asked—"did you do evil to my son last night?" Succetus replied: "What did you see, master?" "You filled my son's mouth with fire and he filled the lips of my daughters. They were all reduced to cinders and their ashes brought life to many. They flew like birds with you, and they vomited up their vitals in a trick of deception." Succetus replied: "It was indeed deception that they vomited up—that is, their druidic heritage—for I gave into their mouths the words of my God on high."

And he went out to Sliab Scirte, to the location of the rock on which he had seen the angel of the Lord standing at the time the angel rose up to heaven, his feet extended from one mountain to the other—the faint trace of his foot is still there. And the angel said: "Look: your ship is ready. Get up and go!"

The holy man, then, came through Toome to the country of Uí Tuirtri [*west Derry and Tyrone*] to Collunt [*not known*]; and he baptized the Uí Tuirtri.

Leaving Armagh he came on into Maugdornai [*Mourne*]. He consecrated Victoricus bishop of Maigen[31] and founded a great church for him there [*Donaghmoyne*].

And he arrived in the country of Loiguire and Conall, the sons of Niall.

Having completed the circuit, he went out and built a church for the priest Justanus beside Bile Torten [*not known*], which is with the community of Ardbraccan. He built another in eastern Tortiu in which there is a tribe from Cerpanus's House [*"Tigh Chirpáin"—not known—perhaps near Stackallen*], but it is free always.

And he arrived at the confines of Leinster, and there established the House of the Martyrs [*not known*], as it is called, which is situated on the great road in the valley. Patrick's Rock is on the way.

He went out to Mag Lifi [*the plain of northern Kildare*] and established a church there [*probably "Auxilius's Church", Cell Usaille, now Killashee, near Naas, Co. Kildare*], and ordained the exorcist Auxilius—a fosterling of Patrick—and Eserninus and Mac Tail[32] in Cell Cuilinn [*Kilcullen, Co. Kildare*].

He ordained Fiacc the Fair in Sléibte [*Sleaty, Co. Laois*], and he baptized the sons of Dúnlang. Then he went up by the Pass of Gabrán [*Gowran, Co. Kilkenny*].

And he founded a church in Roigne of the House of Martyrs [*not known*] and he baptized the sons of Nie Froich in the land of Munster on Cothrige's Rock[33] in Cashel.

TWENTY-EIGHT

Muirchú's Life of St Patrick

[Summary and table of contents]¹

In the name of the king of the heavens, the saviour of this world. Here begins the prologue to the life of the Confessor, Saint Patrick.

From the passion of Jesus Christ our Lord, 436 years are reckoned to the death of Patrick.

I found four names for Patrick written in the book of Ultán, bishop of the tribe of Conchubar: holy Magonus (that is, "famous"); Sucestus . . . the same is Patricius; . . . because he served in the houses of four druids, and one of them bought him, whose name was Miluch moccu Bóin, the druid, and he served him for seven years. Patricius the son of Calfornius had four names: Sochet when he was born, Contice [*read "Cothriche"*] when he was a slave, Mauonius when he was a student, Patrick when he was ordained.³

[PART ONE]

Of Patrick's origin and his first captivity.

Of his voyage with pagans and their distress in a waste land; the obtaining of food from heaven for himself and the pagans.

Of his second captivity, which he endured for sixty days at the hands of enemies.

Of his reception by his parents when they recognized him.

Of his age when, wishing to learn wisdom, he journeyed to behold the apostolic see.

Of his finding of holy Germanus in Gaul, as a result of which he travelled no farther.

Of his age when the angel visited him and he came here.

Of his return from Gaul and of the consecration of Palladius and of Palladius's death soon afterwards.

Of his consecration by Bishop Amathorex on the death of Palladius.

Of the pagan king living at Tara when holy Patrick came bringing baptism.

Of his first journey in this island, to redeem himself from Míliucc before
    dragging others from the devil.

Of the death of Míliucc and Patrick's words on his descendants.

Of Patrick's weekly visit from an angel.

Of holy Patrick's advice when the celebration of the first Easter was being
    decided.

Of the first celebration of the Easter sacrifice in this island.

Of the pagan festival at Tara on the same night on which holy Patrick
    celebrated the first Easter.

Of King Loiguire's journey from Tara to Patrick on Easter night.

Of Patrick's summons to the king and of the faith of Erc son of Daig [and]
    of the death of the druid that night.

Of the anger of the king and his followers with Patrick and of God's wrath
    upon them and of the transformation of Patrick in the eyes of the pagans.

Of Patrick's arrival at Tara on Easter Day and of the faith of Dubthach
    moccu Lugir.

Of Patrick's contest with the druid that [day] and of his miraculous works.

Of the conversion of King Loiguire and of Patrick's words concerning the
    future of his kingdom.

Of holy Patrick's teaching, baptism and miracles after the example of Christ.

Of Mac Cuill and his conversion by Patrick's word.

Of the story of Dáire and his horse and the granting of Armagh to Patrick.

Of the pagans working on Sunday contrary to Patrick's teaching.

Of fertile land turned to marsh by Patrick's word.

Of the death of the Saxon girl Moneisen.

Of the fact that holy Patrick saw heaven opened and the Son of God and his
    angels.

Of St Patrick's conflict with Coirthech, king of Aloo [*Ail Cluaid, Dum-
    barton, on the Clyde*].

[Prologue]

At the command of Áed, bishop of the city of Slébte [*Sleaty, Co. Laois*],
Muirchú moccu Machteni put together these small items from the lore of
holy Patrick and his miracles.

My lord Áed,[4] many people have attempted to reconstruct this history,
following the tradition they received from the fathers—who were indeed
ministers at the beginning—but they have found discrepancies in the story
so often—and so many have expressed doubts—that they have never arrived
at a coherent narrative of events. Therefore it would not be wrong for me
to say that (like the boys in our proverb, on their first introduction to the
public arena) I have taken a child's skiff out on this most dangerous and
deep sea of sacred history and have ventured boldly on the swell of

mountainous waters among the most acute perils, into an unknown ocean previously entered and experienced by no boat except one only—that of my father Cogitosus. But, rather than seem to be trying to make much out of little, I shall—reluctantly and in pious obedience to the command of your loving and holy authority—attempt to relate some few of holy Patrick's many deeds; although with little skill, from uncertain sources, from an unreliable memory and weak judgment, and inelegantly. Yet my intent is wholly pious.[5]

[St Patrick's birth and his captivity in Ireland]

Patrick, also known as Sochet, a member of the British nation, was begotten in Britain by Cualfornius, a deacon, who was, as he tells us himself, the son of Potitus, a priest, of the village of Bannavem Thaburniae, not far from our sea. This village we have established, solidly and without doubt, to be Ventre [*see p. 88*]. His mother was named Concessa.

Captured, along with others, as a sixteen-year-old boy, he was taken here to this island of barbarians to be held in slavery by an obdurate pagan chieftain. He served (as in Hebrew custom) for six years, with many vigils and prayers, in fear of God and trembling (as in the words of the Psalmist). He prayed a hundred times a day and a hundred times a night, rendering to God what is God's and to Caesar what is Caesar's, as he began to fear God and to love the almighty Lord. For until that time he had not known God; but now the Spirit seethed within him.

After enduring many tribulations there; after hunger and thirst; after cold and nakedness; after tending flocks; after numerous visits by the angelic Victoricus sent to him by God; after the great miracles (which are known to almost everyone); after receiving divine messages (which I shall illustrate by only one or two—"You do well to fast; soon you will return to your homeland" and, another time: "See your ship is ready"—which, however, was not nearby but was about two hundred miles away by a journey he had never made); after all these things, which hardly anyone could recount in full, he left that despotic pagan person to his ways, and joined the holy company that owes fealty to the heavenly and eternal God. In the twenty-third year of his age he obeyed the divine command and sailed to Britain in the ship that was prepared for him, with lowborn pagan barbarians who worshipped many false gods.

Having spent three days and nights at sea (like Jonas) with the wicked; afterwards he journeyed wretchedly (like Moses although in a different manner) for twenty-eight days through a waste land. Forced by the heathens who were complaining (like the Jews) that hunger and thirst had almost destroyed them; incited also by the captain to pray to his God that they should not perish; touched by their mortality; compassionate of their common nature; sympathising with them in spirit; adorned with merit; glorified by

God; he provided with God's help plenty of food from a herd of pigs sent to him from God (like the flock of quails).[6] Wild honey also provided sustenance (as it once did for John; but pork replaced locusts: which accorded better with the merits of the evil pagans). He himself however tasted none of these foods, since they had been offered in sacrifice; yet he remained unharmed, suffering neither hunger nor thirst.

On that very night, as he slept, Satan tried him grievously, conjuring up huge rocks as if they were smashing his limbs; but when he called twice on Helias[7] the sun rose for him and shone brightly, expelling the dark shadows, and his powers were restored to him.

(And, after many years again, suffering capture by foreigners he was deemed worthy on the first night to hear the voice of God saying to him: "You will be with them two months" <that is, with your enemies>. And so it happened. On the very sixtieth day the Lord released him from their hands and provided him and his companions with food and fire and shelter daily until the tenth day, when they met people.)

[Patrick in Britain and Gaul]

And after a few years he rested once more, as before, in his own country with his parents, who received him as their son and begged him never for the rest of his life to part with them again after so many tribulations and trials. However, he did not agree with this. And he was shown many visions there. At thirty years, he had come, according to the apostle, to perfect manhood, the same age as the mature Christ.

He set out to visit and pay honour to the apostolic see, to the head of all the churches of the whole world, so that he might learn and understand and fulfil the divine wisdom and the holy mysteries to which God called him, and so that he might preach and give divine grace to remote nations, bringing them to believe in Christ.

Therefore, having navigated the sea south of Britain, he began to journey through Gaul, intending to fulfil the wish of his heart and ultimately to cross the Alps. He had the supreme good fortune to come upon the lord Germanus, the most holy bishop of the city of Auxerre. He delayed with him for a long time (like Paul at the feet of Gamaliel). A virgin in body and spirit, and in full subjection, patience and obedience, he learned, cherished and practised knowledge, wisdom, chastity and every good of spirit and soul, in great fear and love of God and with goodness and simplicity of heart—such was the whole desire of his soul.

After he had spent many years there (some say forty, some thirty) there appeared to him in frequent visions the one named Victoricus, who had been true to him in the past and who had foretold all that was to happen when he was held in slavery in Ireland. He told him now that the time was at hand for him to go fishing with the net of the Gospel for the wild and barbarous people God had sent him to teach. And it was said to him in a vision there: "The sons and daughters of the wood of Focloth call you, etc."

Consequently when the appointed time had come he set out, accompanied by God's help, to do the work for which he had long prepared, that of the Gospel. And Germanus sent an elder with him, the priest Segitius,[8] so that he would have a witness as companion, because he had not yet been consecrated bishop by the holy lord Germanus.

For they were certain that Palladius, archdeacon of Pope Celestine, bishop of Rome (who then held the apostolic see as the forty-fifth successor of St Peter the apostle)[9] had been consecrated and sent to be established in this island of wintry cold in order to convert it. But no one can receive from earth what has not been given by heaven: Palladius was denied success. For these wild and obdurate people did not readily accept his doctrine and he himself did not wish to spend a long time in a foreign country, but to return to him who had sent him. He left here, and having crossed the first sea and begun his land journey, he ended his life in the confines of the Britons.

Palladius's disciples, Augustinus, Benedictus and others, as they returned, reported his death at Ebmoria.[10] Patrick and those in his company made a detour to visit a wonderful man and great bishop named Amathorex[11] who lived nearby. Patrick, who knew what was about to happen, had the grade of bishop conferred on him by the holy bishop Amathorex. On the same day on which holy Patrick was consecrated, Auxilius, Iserninus and others received lower orders.

When they had been blessed and everything was completed according to custom, and when the verse of the Psalmist had been sung, specially and appropriately for Patrick ("Thou art a priest forever after the order of Melchisedech"); then, in the name of the Holy Trinity, the venerable traveller boarded a waiting ship and arrived in Britain. And then, since nobody seeks the Lord sluggishly, he avoided any digressions other than the ordinary vicissitudes of the road, but with all speed and with a following wind he hastened across our sea.

[Patrick's return to Ireland]

While these events were taking place in the regions already mentioned, there was reigning at Tara, which was the capital of the Irish, a great king, fierce and pagan, an emperor of barbarians, whose name was Loiguire son of Niall. He belonged to the lineage that held the kingship of almost all of this island. He had druids and learned men, soothsayers and enchanters, and inventors of all the black arts who, by their practice of heathenism and idolatry, were able to know and foresee all things in advance. Among the others, two were pre-eminent, namely Lothroch, otherwise Lochru, and Lucet Mael, otherwise Ronal. Through their magical craft these two frequently foretold the coming of a foreign tradition, a new form of rule as it were, with a strange and troublesome doctrine brought from far beyond the sea. A few would proclaim it; many would accept it; all would honour it; it would overthrow kingdoms; kill the kings who resisted; subvert the common people; and destroy all their gods; and, having cast aside all the works of their culture, it would rule forever. They also described him who would bring and advocate this tradition, foretelling him in the following words in verse form, which these two frequently repeated (especially in the two or three years before Patrick's coming). These are the words of the verse—which are not too clear because of the style of their language:

> Adze-head[12] will come, with his curve-headed stick;
> he will chant wicked incantations from his gap-headed house,
> from his table in the front end of his house;
> all his household will answer, "so be it, so be it."

This can be expressed more clearly in our words:

> When all these things happen, therefore, our rule, since it is pagan, will not endure.

And so it came to pass later: with the arrival of Patrick the cult of idols was overthrown and the Catholic faith in Christ spread throughout our country. Enough of this; let us return to the subject.

So, at the conclusion and completion of the holy voyage, the saint's worthy ship, with its overseas wonders and spiritual treasures, made its appearance in a harbour in the territory of Cualu, a port well known to us which is called Inber Dee [*the mouth of the Avoca river at Arklow, Co. Wicklow*]. There nothing seemed more urgent to him than that first of all he should redeem himself from slavery. Accordingly he headed northward, to that pagan person Míliucc, by whom he had once been held captive, bringing to him twice the cost of his redemption—an earthly price and a heavenly one—to liberate the man whom he had once served as a captive. He first directed the prow of his boat to an island which down to the present day bears his name [*St Patrick's Island, Skerries, Co. Dublin*].

Then, leaving Brega [*part of Co. Meath*] and the territories of Conaille [*part of Co. Louth*] and of the Ulaid [*part of Louth and Down*] on his left, finally he passed through the strait known as Brene [*Strangford Lough, Co. Down*]. And he and his company disembarked at Inber Slane [*Slaney Water, Strangford Lough*] and, hiding their little boat, they went inland a short distance to rest there. They were discovered by the swineherd of a man who was naturally good, although a pagan, whose name was Dichu. He

d Patrick's [*Saul, Co. Down*].
robbers or thieves, departed
hout their knowledge. Dichu
of St Patrick the Lord changed
d the faith to him. And there
ck, and the holy man stayed

visit Míliucc, the man already
som, and perhaps to convert
with Dichu and made his way
ni until he reached Sliab Miss
tain, a long time before, when
the angel Victoricus leave the
another mountain and ascend

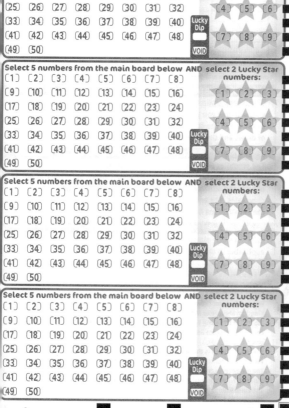

Slemish, Co. Antrim

about to arrive in his presence
ch he had no desire at the end
t to his own slave he followed
to the flames: having gathered
in the house in which he had
. St Patrick then stood on that
lope of Sliab Miss from which,
which he had gained such grace

as a slave. (A cross to the present day marks his first view of the district.) From there he contemplated, right under his eyes, the fiery funeral pyre of that chieftain. Dumbfounded by this, he uttered not a word for two or three hours; then, sighing and weeping he spoke these words: "God knows—not I—that this human king who committed himself to the fire, did it rather than believe at the end of his life and serve eternal God. God knows—not I—that none of his posterity will sit on his throne as king of his kingdom from generation to generation to come; furthermore that his seed will forever serve others."

Having said this he prayed; then armed himself with the sign of the cross and straightaway turned round and went back to the land of the Ulaid by the way by which he had come. He arrived again in Mag Inis [*Lecale, Co. Down*] and came to Dichu. He stayed there many days, and made a circuit of the whole plain, singling it out for his love; and the faith began to grow there.

But to return to the narrative. The angel came to him on the seventh day of every week and Patrick enjoyed conversation with the angel as if with a man. Even when he was captured at the age of sixteen and spent six years as a slave, the angel had joined him for about thirty meetings and he had enjoyed angelic company and counsel before he travelled from Ireland to the Latins. Once, he lost some swine he was tending, and the angel came and showed them to him. Once again, the angel told him many things in conversation, and, having spoken to him, placed his foot on Scirit [*Skerry, near Slemish, Co. Antrim*] at Sliab Mis and ascended before him. And the mark of the angel's foot may be seen on that rock down to the present day. And it is in that place that the angel spoke to him thirty times, and it is a place for prayer. And it is here that the prayers of the faithful obtain the most happy results.

[Patrick's journey to Tara]

At that time, as it happens, Easter was approaching. It would be the first Easter for God in this island—our Egypt—like the celebration <in Egypt> long ago recorded in the Book of Genesis. Among the pagans to whom God had sent him, they discussed where they should celebrate this first Easter. After many suggestions had been made on the matter, at last it seemed to Patrick—inspired by God—that this major festival of the Lord (the principal feast of all) should be celebrated on the great plain of Brega, where there was the greatest of these tribal kingdoms—because it was the head of all paganism and idolatry. There he would shatter, as the Psalmist says, the dragon's head. An invincible wedge would be struck, as it were, by the hammer of powerful faith in the spiritual hands of holy Patrick and his companions, into the head of all idolatry so that it could never again rise against the faith of Christ. And so it came to pass.

So they launched their ship on the sea, and, leaving that good man Dichu behind in full faith and peace, they departed from Mag Inis. Now they had on their right, all that had formerly been on their left, and proceeded to the completion of their ministry. After a favourable voyage they arrived at Inber Colptha [*the mouth of the river Boyne*]. They left their ship and went on by foot through the great plain (as had been foretold) until, late in the evening, they arrived at the Burial Mounds of the Men of Fiacc [*the Boyne tumuli, at Slane*]. (It is said that Ferchertne, who was one of the nine druidic prophets of Brega [*part of Co. Meath*] said that these "men of Fiacc" were the slaves who dug the graves.) Having pitched his tents there, Patrick with his company made the due offering and Sacrifice [of the Mass] in honour of the most high God, with all devotion of spirit; so fulfilling the words of the prophet.

[The Paschal Fire]

Now, it happened that the heathen that very year were holding another ceremony with many spells and conjurings and other idolatries. The kings, governors, leaders, princes and nobility of the nation gathered. Furthermore, the druids, magicians, soothsayers, clairvoyants and teachers of every art and skill, summoned by King Loiguire to Tara—their Babylon—as once to Nabuchadonosor,[13] planned to take action.

On the same night on which Patrick celebrated Easter, they conducted their festival of heathen worship. Moreover, they had the custom—proclaimed to all—that whoever in all the country, far or near, should kindle a fire before the fire in the king's house was lit (that is, in the palace of Tara) should be put to death by his people.

Patrick, then, lit the divine fire—truly bright and blessed—which was seen by the people living throughout the plain. It happened that it was seen from Tara, and at the sight they gazed and wondered. Calling together the elders, the king said to them: "Who is it who has dared to commit this crime in my kingdom? He must die." And they all replied that they didn't know who had done this. The druids answered:

> "Eternal life to you, king! The fire that we see, which has been lit tonight before the fire was kindled in your house: unless it is extinguished on this same night in which it was lit, it will not be put out forever. It will indeed rise above all our customary fires; and he who has lit it—along with the kingdom that is arriving through his kindling of the fire tonight—will overcome us all and will lead astray all the people of your kingdom; and all the kingdoms will yield to him, and his realm will expand over all, and he will rule forever and ever."

When he heard this, the king—like Herod once[14]—was greatly alarmed, and all Tara with him. He replied, saying:

> "It will not come to pass in that way; but we will go and see an end to this business: we will seize and kill those who commit such a crime against our kingdom."

He ordered twenty-seven chariots (following the teaching of the gods) and took with him the two druids most preeminently fitted for confrontation, Lucet Mael and Lochru. Late in the night Loiguire made the journey from Tara to the Grave Mounds of the Men of Fiacc, turning the faces of the men and the horses to the left, in accordance with their tabu.

On the way, the druids said to the king:

> "King: do not go yourself to where the fire is, lest perhaps you might then do honour to him who lit it. Rather, stay outside nearby. We will summon him to you, so that he will do reverence to you and you will dominate him; and we and he will then dispute in your presence, king: and so you will test us."

And the king replied, saying: "You have hit on a good plan. I will do as you have advised." They arrived at the predetermined place and dismounted from their chariots and their horses. They did not enter the circle of the firelight but sat nearby.

The holy Patrick was summoned to the king outside the illuminated space. And the druids said: "Let us not rise when he arrives; for whoever rises at his coming will believe in him afterwards and do him reverence." When Patrick finally appeared and saw how many chariots and horses they had, he chanted with his lips and from his heart an appropriate verse of the Psalmist: "Some trust in chariots and some in horses; but we will go in the name of our God"[15]—and he came among them. They did not rise when he arrived, except for one, who was so assisted by the Lord that he refused to obey the druids' instructions. That is Erc, son of Daig, whose relics are now venerated in the city which is called Slane. He rose to his feet and Patrick blessed him; and he believed in the eternal God.

Then they began their disputation. The druid called Lochru, on hearing Patrick, was contumacious in his presence, calumniating the Catholic faith with arrogant words. However, as he spoke in this way, Patrick, with flashing eyes, showed a measure of power and said in a loud voice (as Peter once said of Simon): "Lord, Who have sent me here, You who can do all things and have all things in your power: may this impious man who profanes Your name be lifted now out of here and may he perish forthwith." At these words the druid was raised into the air, and let fall again from above.

Coming down, he smashed his skull on a rock, and died right before them; and the heathen were afraid.

The king, along with his followers, was enraged with Patrick at this, and wished to kill him. He said: "Seize that man who is destroying us!" Seeing that the impious heathen were about to attack him, Patrick rose and said clearly and loudly: "May God come up to scatter His enemies and may those who hate Him flee from his face."

And at once darkness fell, accompanied by a kind of horrible commotion, and the impious ones fought among themselves, one against the other. There was a great earthquake, which caused the axles of the chariots to collide and drove them with such force that the chariots and horses hurled themselves headlong across the level plain until in the end a few arrived barely alive at the mountain of Mogdurn [*Mogdurn Breg: near Ardagh in north Co. Meath*].

By this disaster, caused by Patrick's curse in the king's presence because of the king's order, seven times seven men fell; until in the end there remained only four people: the king himself and his wife, and two of the Irish; and they were greatly afraid. The queen approached Patrick and said to him: "Just and powerful man: do not destroy the king; because he will come and go down on his knees to worship your Lord." And the king, driven by fear, came and bent his knees before the holy man, to whom he pretended to do reverence (although his intention was otherwise). After they had parted, the king, going a short distance away, invited Patrick to come. His words were mendacious: he intended to kill him by one means or another. Patrick, however, understood the most evil king's design. He blessed his companions in the name of Jesus Christ and came with them to the king: eight men and a boy. The king was numbering them as they approached; but suddenly they disappeared before his eyes. But the heathen saw what appeared to be eight deer and a fawn going into the wilderness. And King Loiguire returned to Tara at dawn, with the few survivors, in dread, fear and disgrace.

[The contest at Tara]

On the following day, that is, Easter Day, when the kings, princes and druids were reclining at table with Loiguire, eating, and drinking wine (for this was their greatest festival day), some of them discussing, some thinking about, what had happened, holy Patrick, with no more than five companions, arrived, and passed through the closed doors (as the Scriptures tell of Christ).

He intended to defend and preach the word of the holy faith in Tara before all the peoples. Then, as he entered the banquet hall of Tara, none of them rose for his arrival save one only: that is, Dubthach maccu Lugir, the great poet. With him at that time was a youthful poet named Fiacc, afterwards a wonderful bishop, whose relics are venerated in Slébte [*Sleaty, Co.*

Laois]. As I have said, this man Dubtach was the only one of the heathen to rise in honour of Patrick—and the holy man blessed him; and on that day he was the first to believe in God. It was reckoned to him for judgment.

On the arrival of Patrick, the heathen invited him to eat with them— intending to test him in what was to transpire. However, he knew what was to come; yet he did not decline the invitation to eat with them. While they were all feasting, that druid Luchet Máel, who had been in the previous night's confrontation, was, even today, after his colleague's destruction, determined to engage with Patrick. He began the proceedings, while the others watched, letting fall a drop from his vessel into Patrick's goblet—to see what Patrick would do. Patrick, knowing to what kind of test he was being put, blessed his goblet in the view of the whole assembly: the liquid froze like ice. Then he turned the goblet upside down. There fell out only the drop which the druid had put in. He blessed the goblet again. The liquid resumed its nature; and all were astonished.

After a little while the druid said: "Let us work wonders over this great plain." And Patrick answered: "How?" And the druid said: "Let us cause snow to fall over the land." To which Patrick replied: "I do not wish to cause anything to happen contrary to God's will." And the druid said: "I will bring it about in the presence of all." Then, reciting magic spells, he brought down snow over the whole plain, to the depth that would reach a man's belt. And all saw this and were struck with wonder. The holy man said: "Look: we see this. Now remove it." The druid answered: "I can't remove it before this time tomorrow." And the holy man said: "You can do evil but not good. Not so I." Then he blessed the plain all around and, instantly at his word—without any rain or mist or wind—the snow vanished. The crowds cried aloud. They were greatly astonished and their hearts were pierced.

A little while later, in a display of magic, the druid invoked demons and brought about a dense fog over the land; and all the people murmured. The holy man said [to the druid]: "Cause the fog to disperse." But, just as before, he was unable to do it. The holy man, however, prayed and gave his blessing, and suddenly the fog cleared and the sun shone. All cried aloud and gave thanks.

When all this had been transacted between the druid and Patrick in the king's presence, the king said to them: "Place your books in water, and we will do reverence to him whose books are retrieved undamaged." Patrick replied: "I will do it." But the druid said: "I do not wish to go to the judgment of water with him, for water is one of his gods." (Undoubtedly he had heard that Patrick administered baptism with water.) Answering him, the king said: "Try fire then." And Patrick said: "I am ready." But the druid refused again, saying: "This man worships in alternate years now water, now fire as a god." And the holy man said: "It is not so. But: you yourself shall go into a closed and partitioned house. You will wear my garment and my boy will wear your garment, and fire will be set. You will be judged in the sight of the Highest."

This proposal was accepted and a house was made for them, half of green wood and half of dry. The druid was placed in the green part, and one of St Patrick's boys—named Benignus—was placed in the dry. The house then was closed up from without and was set alight in the presence of all. And through the prayers of Patrick, what occurred at this time was that the flames of fire consumed the druid and the green half of the house, leaving only Patrick's chasuble to remain intact, untouched by the fire. On the other hand, happily, Benignus, along with the dry half of the house, was not touched at all by the flames (in which matter this story is like that of the three boys);[16] but he was not frightened nor did he suffer any harm; but at God's command only the robe of the druid, which he wore, was burnt.

And the king was greatly enraged at Patrick because of the death of his druid. He attempted to attack him, wishing to kill him; but God prevented this. For, when Patrick raised his voice in prayer, the wrath of God descended on the impious people and many of them died. Holy Patrick said to the king: "If you do not believe now, you will die on the spot; for the wrath of God descends on your head." And the king, shaken in his heart, feared greatly, as did the whole city with him. King Loiguire summoned his elders and his whole council, and said to them: "It is better for me to believe than to die." And he took the advice of his company and followed it: he believed on that day and turned to the eternal Lord God. Many others also believed on that day.

[The conversion of Monesan]

Holy Patrick now, following the precept of the Lord Jesus, left Tara and went out to teach all peoples, baptizing them in the name of the Father, the Son and the Holy Spirit. He preached everywhere, with the cooperation of the Lord, Who confirmed his words by the miracles that followed. So, the Lord willing, I shall try to recount a few of the miracles of Patrick, who was, if I may so describe him, the bishop of all Ireland and the most outstanding teacher.

To begin: at that time, when all of Britain froze in the cold of unbelief, the illustrious daughter (named Monesan) of a certain king became filled with the Holy Spirit. Although she was sought in marriage she refused. The more she was wet through with drenchings of water, the less she could be compelled against her will. Indeed, between floggings and dousings with water, she still contrived to ask her mother and her nurse if they knew who made the wheel by which the world is provided with light. From the answer given to her she came to this knowledge: that the maker of the sun is He Whose throne is heaven. When she was repeatedly urged to join in the bonds of marriage she was enlightened by the shining of the Holy Spirit, and said: "I will never do that." For it was by merely natural means that she sought to discover the maker of all creation—in which she followed the example of the patriarch Abraham.

Her parents, in impassioned argument, took counsel, and heard of Patrick, who was reported to be visited by God every seventh day. Accompanied by their daughter, they went searching the lands of the Irish, and found Patrick, the object of their quest. On their arrival he began to question them. The travellers cried out, saying: "We are forced to come to you by our daughter's great desire to see God!" Then he, filled with the Holy Spirit, lifted his voice and asked her: "Do you believe in God?" She said: "I do." Then he laved her in the sacred font of the water of the Spirit. At once, she fell to the ground and yielded her spirit into the hands of angels. She was buried in the very place where she died. Then Patrick prophesied that after twenty years her body would be borne from that place, with due honour, to a nearby church. This is what was done later. The relics of the girl from beyond the sea are venerated there to the present day.

[The destruction of Corictic]

I shall not pass over in silence a certain marvellous achievement of Patrick's. He was informed of the most evil act of a certain British king named Corictic, an ill-disposed cruel tyrant. He was indeed the greatest persecutor and murderer of Christians. Although Patrick tried to call him to the way of truth by means of a letter, he laughed at the salutary admonition. When this was reported to Patrick, he prayed to the Lord, saying: "Lord, if it can be done, drive this man out of both this world and the next." Not much time passed before Corictic, listening to the music of a certain bard, was told in the course of the verse that he must abandon his royal seat. And those most dear to him joined their voices in the song. Then, before their eyes, in the middle of the gathering, the very man wretchedly was transformed into the shape of a little fox. Since that day and hour he has never appeared again.

[Patrick's vision of heaven]

I will make known in a brief account a certain miracle of the Lord's apostle Patrick—of him of whom we treat—a miracle performed when he was in the flesh. It is something written of him and of Stephen, and of almost none other. Once, long ago, when he went to his customary place to pray through the watches of the night, he looked at the wonders of the heavens, which were familiar to him. And he spoke to his beloved and faithful acolyte (the holy boy), wishing to test him, saying: "O my son, tell me, I beg you, if you observe what I observe." Then the little boy—Benignus by name—said without hesitation: "I already know what you observe. For I see heaven open, and the Son of God and His angels." Then Patrick said: "Now I know that you are worthy to be my successor." Without delay they walked quickly to his accustomed place of prayer. As they prayed standing in the middle of a stream, the little boy said: "I can't continue to endure the cold of the water!" for the water was too cold for him. Then Patrick told him to move downstream. But now again he was unable to stay very long—because, as he testified, he found the water too hot. So, unsuccessful in standing any longer where he was, he went up onto dry land.

[The conversion of Mac Cuill]

There was a certain man in the country of the Ulaid in Patrick's time, Mac Cuill moccu Greccae. This man was a very wicked and fierce tyrant—such that he was called "Cyclops". His thoughts were crooked; his words were immoderate; his deeds were evil; his spirit was bitter; his soul was wrathful; his body was oafish; his mind was cruel; his life was heathen; his conscience was vain. He was so far sunk in wickedness that one day, as he sat in a wild mountainous place on Druim moccu Echach [*Dromore, Co. Down*] where he daily exercised his tyranny (displaying most wicked emblems of cruelty and murdering, in cruelly evil ways, strangers who passed by) he determined to kill Patrick. He had seen the holy man walking along his intended path, shining with the bright light of faith and radiant under a nimbus of celestial glory with unshaken faith in his doctrine. He said to his gang: "Look: this man is coming who leads people astray; his custom is to play conjuring tricks in order to deceive people and seduce them. Let us go now and put him to the test, to find out if that God in whom he glories has indeed any power."

So they designed their test for the holy man in this fashion: they had one of their number—who was in good health—lie down in their midst, covered with a cloak and pretending to be mortally ill. They wished to try the holy man by this deceit. They called his miracles tricks and his prayers venomous outpourings or spells. When Patrick and his disciples arrived, the heathen said to them: "Look: one of us has just become ill. Come here, therefore, and chant some of your spells over him: perhaps he may recover." Holy Patrick, however, knowing all their deceits and subterfuges, resolutely and firmly answered: "And it would be no wonder, should he turn out to have been ill." When the companions of the man who was feigning illness uncovered his face, they found that he was dead. The heathen, stupefied and astonished by so great a miracle, said to one another: "In truth, this man is of God. We did wrong to test him." And so holy Patrick turned to Mac Cuill and said: "Why did you want to try me?" And the cruel tyrant replied: "I am sorry for what has been done. I will do whatever you tell me; and I yield myself now to the power of the High

God Whom you preach." The holy man said: "Believe, then, in God, my Lord Jesus, and confess your sins, and accept baptism in the name of the Father, the Son and the Holy Spirit." He was converted there and then, and believed in the eternal God, and was baptized.

Then Mac Cuill further said: "I confess to you, my holy lord Patrick, that I had planned to murder you. Judge me therefore, and assess what penalty is due for such a great crime. Patrick said:

> "I can't judge you, but God will judge. Now go out, unarmed, to the sea, and cross quickly over from this region of Ireland, taking nothing of your goods with you, except one mean scrap of cloth which can barely cover your nakedness. Neither eat nor drink any produce of this island; and bear on your head the sign of your sin. And, after you reach the sea, chain your feet together with an iron fetter, and throw the key of the lock into the sea; board a coracle made from one skin, without steer or oars; and be ready to go wherever wind and sea may guide you. Wherever divine providence may direct you: live in that land. And follow the commandments of God."

Mac Cuill said: "I will do as you have told me. But what do we do about this dead man?" And Patrick said: "He will live and will rise painlessly from the dead." And Patrick raised him there and then, and he came to life in good health.

In the confidence of unshaken faith Mac Cuill departed without delay and travelled to the sea south of Mag Inis [*Lecale, Co. Down*]. On the shore he fettered himself and threw the key into the sea, as he had been told to do. He put to sea in a coracle. And the north wind blew on him and bore him southward to the middle of the sea, casting him ashore on the island called Euonia [*The Isle of Man*]. There he came upon two men, very wonderful in faith, brilliant in religious learning. They were the first to teach the word of God and bring baptism to Euonia; through them the people of the island were converted to their teachings and to the Catholic faith. Their names are Conindrus and Rumilus.

These were astonished when they saw the man dressed only in his single clout. They took pity on him, lifted him from the sea, and received him joyfully.[17] As for him: having found his spiritual fathers in the region granted to him by God, he followed their rule with mind and body and passed his life with those two holy bishops until he became their successor in the episcopate. He is Maccuill, bishop of Man and prelate of Arda Huimnonn [*not known: probably St Maugholds, Isle of Ma*n].

[Patrick punishes Sunday work]

Again, on another occasion, when holy Patrick was taking his Sunday rest above the sea, near a marsh which is a short distance to the north of Collum Bovis [*Muin Daim, near Saul, Co. Down, by the river Quoyle*], he heard the hubbub of heathens working on the Lord's Day to dig the fosse of a rath. Patrick summoned them and forbade them to work on Sunday. But they rejected his words, even mocking him with laughter. And holy Patrick said: "Mudebroth!"[18] No matter how much you labour, you will achieve nothing. So it came to pass. The following night a great wind rose and agitated the sea: the storm destroyed all the work of the heathens, in fulfilment of the holy man's words.

[Dáire and the grant of Armagh]

There was a certain wealthy and honourable man in Airthir [*Orior: eastern Airgialla; part of Co. Armagh*] whose name was Dáire. Holy Patrick asked him to give him a place for the exercise of religion. The rich man said to the holy one: "What place do you want?" "I ask"—said the holy man—"that you give me the hilltop known as Druim Sailech [*Armagh*], and I will build a church there." But he did not wish to give the hilltop to the holy man; but he gave him another place on lower ground, where is now Fertae Martar, beside Armagh [*"Burial mounds of the martyrs:" the church of this place was in what is now Scotch Street in Armagh*]. Patrick settled there with his people. After some time there came an ostler of Dáire's, leading his horse to graze it in the Christians' meadow. The pasturing of the horse on his land annoyed Patrick, who said: "It was stupid of Dáire to place brute animals in the small place he has given to God, to disturb it." But indeed the ostler behaved as if he were deaf and dumb, neither listening nor opening his mouth to answer; but he left the horse there for the night and went away. The following morning the ostler came back to tend to his horse, but found that it was now dead. He went home sadly and reported to his master: "Look: that Christian has killed your horse. The intrusion on his church annoyed him." And Dáire said: "Then he must himself be killed. Go now and kill him." Just after they had gone out, sudden death struck Dáire—more quickly than it can be told. His wife said: "This death is caused by the Christian. Someone go out quickly and curry favour with him for us; and you will be saved. Those who have been sent to kill the Christian must be stopped and called back." Two men went out, who spoke to Patrick (concealing what had happened) and said: "Look: Dáire is ill. He may be restored to health if we bring him something from you." Holy Patrick, however, knew what had happened. "Indeed?"— he said. He blessed water and gave it to them, saying: "Go: sprinkle some of this water on your horse, and take it with you." And they did; the horse came back to life and they took it with them. When Dáire was sprinkled with the holy water he was brought back to life and health.

After this, to honour holy Patrick, Dáire came carrying a marvellous cauldron (imported from overseas) which held a triple measure. He said to the holy man: "Look: this cauldron is for you." And holy Patrick said: "Grazacham."[19]

When Dáire arrived home he said: "This man is a fool, who can find nothing better to say than 'Grazacham' for such a marvellous cauldron of triple measure." Then he added, speaking to his slaves: "Go and bring back that cauldron to us." They went back and said to Patrick: "We will take away the cauldron." Patrick said little more than on the previous occasion: "Grazacham. Take it." And they carried it away. Dáire questioned his people, saying: "What did the Christian say when you repossessed the cauldron?" They answered: "He said 'Grazacham.'" Dáire responded to this, saying: "'Grazacham' for the giving. 'Grazacham' for the taking away. His saying is so good a one that for these 'Grazachams' the cauldron will be brought back to him again." And Dáire himself came along this time and bore the cauldron to Patrick, saying to him: "Let this cauldron now be yours. You are a stubborn and imperturbable man. Furthermore, I now give you that piece of land that you previously asked for—in so far as it is mine. Live there." And that is the city now called Armagh.

And the two of them, Patrick and Dáire, went out to inspect the marvellous donation, the pleasing gift. They climbed to that hilltop—and they came on a doe with its little fawn lying in the place where is now the northern altar of the church in Armagh. Patrick's companions wished to catch the fawn and kill it; but Patrick refused to permit this; instead he caught the fawn himself and carried it on his shoulders, and the doe followed him like a gentle loving sheep until he released the fawn on another hillside to the north of Armagh where, as the learned recount, certain signs of the miracle remain to the present day.

[Patrick makes a field barren by his curse]

The learned tell that a certain man who was very hard and equally greedy, lived in Mag Inis [*Lecale, Co. Down*]. One day, when the pair of oxen that drew Patrick's car, after their holy work, were resting and grazing in this pasture, he fell into such folly and greed—this vain man—that in the presence of holy Patrick he violently and capriciously drove away the cattle. Angry with him, Patrick said—cursing: "Mudebrod![20] You have behaved wrongly. May this field of yours never prosper—not only for you but for your seed forever; from now on it will be useless." And so it came to pass: for indeed on that very day a tidal wave swept up and overwhelmed and washed away the whole field, and—as the prophet said—fertile land was changed to salt-marsh by the evil of those who live there. From the day Patrick cursed it to the present day it is sandy and barren.

[PART TWO]

1   Of Patrick's diligence in prayer
2   Of the dead man who spoke to him
3   Of the illumination of Sunday night, and the finding of the horses
4   Of the time when an angel forbade him to die in Armagh
5   Of the angel in the burning bush
6   Of Patrick's four petitions
7   Of the day of his death and of his term of life: thirty years
8   Of the stopping of nightfall, and of the suspension of darkness for twelve nights
9   Of the sacrament received from Bishop Tassach
10 Of the angels' vigil on the first night by Patrick's body
11 Of the angel's counsel regarding his burial
12 Of the fire which sprang from his tomb
13 Of the tide of the sea that rose to prevent a battle for his body
14 Of the beneficial misleading of the people

[Patrick's diligent praying]

We shall try to write a few of the many things that could be told about his diligence in prayer. He repeated daily all the psalms and hymns and the Apocalypse of John and all the spiritual songs of the Scriptures, whether he stayed in one place or travelled. A hundred times, at every hour of day and night, he made the sign of the triumph of the cross, and wherever he saw a cross he would leave his chariot and go aside to pray at it.

[A dead man speaks to him]

So it happened that one day when he was on the road, he passed by a wayside cross without seeing it. However, his charioteer saw it. When they had arrived at a certain lodging which was their destination and had begun to pray before their meal, the charioteer said: "I saw a cross that was erected beside the road we travelled." At this, Patrick left the guest-house and returned by the way he had come, and prayed. He saw a grave there and spoke to the dead man buried in the tomb, asking him how he had died and whether he had lived in the faith. The dead man replied:

> "I lived a pagan and was buried here. However, a certain woman living in another province had a son who had had dwelt far away from her and who died and was buried in her absence. And after a number of days the mother came, lamenting the son she had lost. She made a mistake, confusing a heathen's grave with her son's, and she erected the cross over the pagan."

And Patrick said that this was why he had not noticed the cross, because it was located over a heathen tomb. And from this there arose the great marvel: that the dead spoke, that the man who had died in the faith was located and was well served in that the emblem of the sweet cross was replaced in its true position over his grave.

[Patrick's fingers provide light to search for missing horses]

It was a custom of Patrick's that he would not continue a journey between Saturday evening and Monday morning. One Sunday he was interrupting a field-trip in this way in honour of the sacred period, when, overnight, there was a heavy storm of rain. But, although the rain fell heavily on the dwellings of the whole country, it was dry in the place where Patrick was spending the night (as happened in the case of Gideon's trumpet and his fleece).[21]

The charioteer came to him and told him that he had lost the horses—lamenting for them as he would for dear friends, because he was unable to see in the all-enclosing darkness and couldn't search for them. At this, Patrick's feelings of affection were aroused to those of a loving father, and to the weeping charioteer he said: "God, Who helps in difficulties and when things go wrong, will be quick to come to your aid: you will find the horses whose loss you are bewailing." Thereupon he pulled up his sleeve and raised his outstretched hand; and his five fingers, like lamps, so lit up all the surroundings that the charioteer found the horse he had lost and ceased his lamentation. But the charioteer—his attendant—kept this miracle secret until after Patrick's death.

[The angel in the burning bush]

After such great miracles, described in other writings and celebrated by the world in the talk of the faithful, the day of his death drew near. An angel came to him to tell him of his death. So, because of this, he sent word to Armagh, the place he loved best in the world, that many men should come to conduct him there, the place to which he wished to go. Then, with his company, he began the journey he desired to make to that place—Armagh—that he longed for. But, by the wayside there was a burning bush, which was not consumed (as had happened in the past to Moses).[22] In the bush was the angel Victor, who had been a frequent visitor to Patrick. Victor sent another angel to Patrick to forbid him to go where he wished to go, who asked him: "Why do you set out on the road without Victor's counsel? Victor is summoning you about this. Turn aside and go to him." And he digressed as he had been instructed, and he asked what he should do. The angel answered him, saying:

"Go back to where you came from (that is, Saul), and the four requests you have made are granted to you. (1) The first request: that your primacy will be in Armagh. (2) The second request: that whoever, on the day he is departing from the flesh, sings the hymn composed about you, will have you as judge of the penance due for his sins. (3) The third request, that the descendants of Dicu, who kindly received you, will earn mercy and will not be lost. (4) The fourth request: that on the day of judgment all the Irish will be judged by you (as it is said to the apostles—'and you shall sit in judgment on the twelve tribes of Israel'), so that you may sit in judgment on those whose apostle you were. Go back, therefore, as I tell you; and you will die and go the way of your fathers."

This occurred on the 17th of March, the years of his whole life numbering one hundred and twenty; and it is commemorated throughout the whole of Ireland every year.

[Twelve days without night]

(And You will set a limit to the night.) For on that day of his death no night fell; it did not wrap its black wings around the earth; and the evening did not send the darkness which carries the stars. The people of Ulaid say that to the very end of the year in which he departed, the darkness of the nights was never as great as before. There is no doubt that this was testimony to the merit of so great a man. And if anyone wishes, in disbelief, to deny the suspension of nightfall and denies that night was not seen through the whole province during the short time of the mourning for Patrick, let him learn and study carefully how Ezechias when he was sick unto death was shown—as a sign of his recovery—how the sun went back ten degrees on the sundial of Acaz—so that the length of the day was nearly doubled—and how the sun stood still upon Gabaon and the moon in the valley of Achilon.[23]

[Patrick receives the sacrament from Bishop Tassach]

As the hour of his death drew near he received the sacrament from Bishop Tassach, as his viaticum—as the angel Victor informed him—for his journey to the life of beatitude.

[Angels keep vigil by his body]

On the first night of his wake, angels kept watch by his blessed body with customary prayers and psalms. All those who had come for the vigil slept on that first night. On the other nights, however, it was humans who guarded the body, praying and chanting psalms. After the angels had returned to heaven, however, they left behind a most delightful scent as of honey and a sweet fragrance like wine, to fulfil what was said in the blessings of the

Downpatrick, Co. Down (Dun Lethglais), the reputed burial place of St Patrick

patriarch Jacob: "Behold: the scent of my son is as the scent of a harvest field blessed by the Lord."[24]

[The angel advises on Patrick's burial]

When the angel came to him he advised him about his burial: "Let two untamed oxen be picked and allowed to go wherever they will with the waggon carrying your body; and wherever they pause to rest, there let a church be built to honour your body." And, as the angel had directed, two frisky young bullocks were chosen: they pulled steadily under the yoke and drew the cart bearing the holy body. It was in a place called Clochar, to the east of Findubar, and from Conal's herds that the choice was made which gave renown to these cattle [*possibly Clogher, Co. Tyrone, with which and with a nearby Findubar Patrick reputedly was connected; possibly places in Co. Down: see Hogan,* Onomasticon, *252*]. And under God's direction they went out to Dún Lethglaisse [*Downpatrick, Co. Down*], where Patrick is buried.

[Fire bursts from his tomb]

And [the angel] said to him: "Let a cubit's depth of earth be placed on your body, so that relics will not be taken from it." In recent times it was shown that this was done at God's command; because when a church was being built above the body, the men who were digging in the earth saw fire bursting forth from the grave, and they drew back in fear of the flaming fire.

[An inundation ends fighting over Patrick's body]

A dreadful conflict, extending even to war, arose at the time of his death—about his relics. It was between former friendly neighbours, now deadly enemies, the Uí Néill and the Airthir on the one hand and the Ulaid on the other, wrathfully arrayed for battle. But the inlet of the sea called Muin Daim [*near Saul, Co. Down*] swelled up with a curving undulation—through Patrick's merit and God's mercy to prevent the shedding of blood—and the cresting waves frothed into the empty air; while the seas surged in conflict, now high mountains breaking into foam, now dark valleys. It was as if the fury of the sea rose up to restrain the animosity of the fierce tribes—such as these indeed are—and prevented the peoples from fighting.

[Renewed fighting is ended by an illusion]

However, later, when Patrick had been buried and the swelling of the sea had subsided, the Airthir and the Uí Néill hastened to do battle with the Ulaid. Sedulously prepared and armed for war they forced their way to the place where the blessed body was. But happily they were misled by an illusion. They thought they had found two oxen and a waggon and imagined themselves to be carrying off the holy body. They reached the river Cabcenne [*not known*] with the body and with all their force and armament; then the body disappeared from their sight.

For peace would have been impossible in the quarrel about so great and blessed a body had God not permitted this vision to delay things—so that innumerable people should not be turned away from salvation to destruction and death. So long ago the Syrians were blinded lest they kill the prophet Elisha and were led by him (through divine providence) as far as Samaria.[25] This delusion too was brought about for the sake of harmony among peoples.

Saul, Co. Down

TWENTY-NINE

A misplaced list from the Book of Armagh

This list of ecclesiastics and churches appears to have been misplaced because the leaf on which it was written was bound in by mistake with Tírechán's text and then copied by a scribe as part of the text (see p. 155). It most likely consists of notes compiled by an editor or redactor of Tírechán rather than by Tírechán himself. It is set out in three columns, here reduced to one. It appears to include all the names the compiler could find which derived from the first century of Christianity —although Palladius, known for certain to have preceded Patrick as bishop, is omitted. However, Ibor—a traditionally "pre-Patrician" saint—is included as one of "Patrick's bishops" along with others whose connection with Patrick is almost certainly quite artificial.

The number of bishops he ordained in Ireland was four hundred and fifty. We cannot reckon the number of priests because he baptized people every day and read letters to them and wrote them alphabets. He made bishops of some and priests of others who received baptism and were baptized at a mature age.

Bishops

Benignus; Bronus; Sachellus; Cethiacus; Carthacus; Cartenus; Connanus; Firtranus; Siggeus; Aeternus; Sencaticus; Olcanus; Iborus; Ordius; Nazarius; Miserneus; Senachus; Secundinus; Gosachtus; Camulacus; Auxilius; Victoricus; Bressialus; Feccus; Menathus; Cennanus; Nazarus; Melus; Maculeus; Mactaleus; Culeneus; Asacus; Bitheus; Falertus; Sesceneus; Muirethacus Temoreris, who founded the holy church of Cairech, which the community of Cluain Auiss [*Clones, Co. Monaghan*] held; Daigreus; Iustianus mac Hii; Daimene; Olcanus; Domnallus—and very many others.

Priests

Anicius; Brocidius; Amirgenus; Lommanus; Catideus; Catus; Catanus; Broscus; Ailbeus; Trianus the bishop.

The names of the Franks of Patrick the bishop: three: Inaepius; Bernicius; Hernicius the sub-deacon.

Seman; Semen; Cancen; Bernicius the deacon and Ernicius: fifteen Frankish men, with one sister, or six or three.

Cassanus; Conlang; Erclang; Brocanus; Roddanus; Brigson; and another Roddanus, who founded the church called Senes of the Ui Ailello [*Shankill, Co. Sligo*], which was held by Patrick's monks Genget and Sannuch.

Deacons

Iuostus the deacon who baptized Ciarán the carpenter's son from the book of Patrick; Coimmanus the deacon, dear to Patrick, who was in the great church of Ard Licce [*otherwise Sendomnach: not known: in the Roscommon– Mayo area*]; Olcanus the monk who was in the great church of the Moy as priest [*Kilmore Moy, at Ballina*]; we know of two exorcists with him: the exorcist Losca in Druim Dairi [*at Armagh*] in the territory of Uí Tuirtri; another exorcist in the plain of Liphi [*Co. Kildare*].

Churches

Churches which he founded in the plain of Brega [*mainly Co. Meath*]: 1: at the Summit [*not known*]; 2: the church of Cerne [*on the Boyne, near Navan, Co. Meath*], in which Erc was buried, who bore the great plague; 3: on the Height of Aisse [*Ard Aisse, near Ashbourne, Co. Dublin*]; 4: in Blaitiniu [*Platten, near Duleek, Co. Meath*]; 5: in Collumbus [*uncertain; possibly Skreen, Co. Meath*], where he ordained the holy bishop Eugenius; 6: the church for the son of Laithphi [*not known*]; 7: in Brí Dam [*Brí Dam Dile?: somewhere in Meath*]; 8: on Argetbor [*not known*], where Kannanus the bishop was, whom Patrick ordained on the first Easter at the burial mounds of the men of Fiacc [*Slane, Co. Meath*].

From the notes to Tírechán's narrative in the Book of Armagh

There are pages of notes and jottings in the Book of Armagh, some of which are supplementary to Tírechán's narrative. Most of the material has to do with Armagh's case for primacy, and relates to the seventh, eighth or ninth century, and concerns judicial and jurisdictional claims or contests dealing with property and primacy: much of it is not relevant to the present purpose. The extracts here translated may, in some small part, include material derived from genuine information about Patrick's time.

[Summaries and fragments prefaced to Tírechán's narrative]

Patrick brought with him across the Shannon fifty bells, fifty patens, fifty chalices, altars, books of the law, and Gospel books, and he left them in the new churches.

Patrick was baptized in his sixth year, he was taken captive in his twentieth, he served for fifteen, he studied for forty, and he taught for sixty-one. His total age then was one hundred and eleven.[1] So Constans discovered in Gaul.[2]

Patrick came from the plain of Arthicc [*Tibohine, Elphin, Co. Roscommon*] to Drummut Cerrigi [*Tullanarock, Co. Roscommon*] and to Nairniu [*on the Roscommon-Mayo border*], to Ailech Esrachta [*probably Ailech Airthicc in Cenel Enda, somewhere towards the northwest-Roscommon-Mayo border*], and the people saw him accompanied by eight or nine men, with tablets in their hands, like Moses, with writing on them. The heathen shouted at the people to kill the holy men, and said: "They have swords in their hands for murdering people. By daylight these seem to be pieces of wood, but we judge them to be iron swords for the shedding of blood." The huge crowd was intent on harming the holy men; but there was a merciful man among them, Hercaith by name, the father of Feradach, of the race of Nothi. He believed in Patrick's God, and Patrick baptized him and his son Feradach.

He gave Patrick his son, who went with Patrick to study for thirty years. Patrick ordained him in the city of Rome and gave him Sacellus as his new name. He gave him a book of the Psalms—which I have seen—and he brought from him a part of the relics of Peter and Paul, Lawrence and Stephen, which are in Armagh.[3]

   Caetiacus and Sacellus therefore ordained bishops, priests, deacons and clerics in the plain of Aí [*north Co. Roscommon, near Cruachu*] without the advice of Patrick. Patrick reproached them and sent them a letter and imposed penance on them. They went to Patrick in Armagh and did the penance of monks as two biddable servants of Patrick. And he said to them: "Your churches will not be great."[4]

Great Britain in the early sixth century

THIRTY-ONE

"Sayings of Patrick"

The four sayings attributed to Patrick (possibly simply because they were believed to be very old) were probably gathered from ecclesiastical folklore—a source much used by hagiographers, as several of them inform us.

I had the fear of God to guide me on my journey through Gaul and Italy and in the islands of the Tyrrhenian Sea [*"the islands of the Tyrrhenian Sea" may refer to the monastic island of Lérins, closely connected with the metropolitan church of Arles and with the episcopal promotion of the monastic movement in the late fifth century*].

You have sought to go to paradise from heathenism.

Thanks be to God.

The church of the Irish; rather the church of the Romans: for in order to be Christians as the Romans are, you should recite the praiseworthy chant "Kyrie eleison, Christe eleison" in your congregations at every hour of prayer. Let every church that follows me sing: "Kyrie eleison; Christe eleison; thanks be to God!"

From further fragments in the Book of Armagh

The further fragmentary pieces appended to Tírechán's narrative are largely concerned with the rights or claims of the church of Armagh in the monastic period. Some refer back to events of St Patrick's time.

[The two Patricks]

. . . In the thirteenth year of the emperor Theodosius, Patrick the bishop was sent by Celestine the bishop, pope of Rome, to teach the Irish. Celestine was the forty-fifth bishop since the apostle Peter in the city of Rome. The bishop Palladius was sent first (who was also called Patrick) but suffered martyrdom among the Irish, according to the tradition of the saints of old. Afterwards the second was sent—Patrick—by God's angel Victor and by Pope Celestine. All of Ireland believed through him, and almost all was baptized by him . . . .

[St Lommán of Trim]

. . . When, then, Patrick arrived in Ireland from his holy voyage, he left St Lommán at the mouth of the Boyne to guard his ship for forty days and forty nights. Afterwards, Lommán remained a further forty days beyond what Patrick had instructed. Then, following his master's orders, he travelled in his ship upstream, guided by the Lord, as far as Áth Truim [*Trim, Co. Meath*], to the sward[1] at the gate of Fedelmid son of Loiguire. In the morning, Foirtchern son of Fedelmid discovered him proclaiming the Gospel. Foirtchern admired the Gospel and believed in it there and then. A spring appeared on the spot, and he was baptized as a Christian by Lommán. And he stayed with Lommán until his mother came looking for him. She was delighted to see Lommán because she [too] was British. And she too believed, and went back again to her home and told her husband all that had happened to her and to her son. Fedelmid also was pleased at the cleric's arrival, because his mother was British—a daughter of the king of the Britons, that is, Scoth Noe. Fedelmid greeted Lommán in the British language, and questioned him closely about his belief and his people. He replied to him: "I am Lommán, a British Christian, a disciple of Patrick, the bishop who has been sent by God to baptize the peoples of Ireland and convert them to the faith of Christ. It was he who followed the will of God and sent me here." Fedelmid and all his family believed at once. He granted to Lommán and to Patrick possession of his territory, along with all his property and all his offspring. He granted all this to Patrick, to Lommán and to his son Foirtchern until the day of judgment. Fedelmid transferred across the river Boyne to Cluain Lagen [*Clonlyon, Kilmore, Co. Meath*], while Lommán remained in Trim with Foirtchern until Patrick came and built a church with them, twenty-five years before the foundation of the church of Armagh.

(Lommán was British by race; that is, he was a son of Gollit. His mother was Patrick's sister. His brothers are as follows: Munis, bishop in Forgnide of the Cuircni [*Forgney, Co. Longford*]; Broccaid in Imbliuch Ech among the Ciarraige of Connacht [*Emlagh, Co. Roscommon*]; Broccán in Brechmag among the Uí Dorthim [*Breaghy, Co. Longford*], Mugenóc in Cell Dumi Gluinn in the south of Brega [*Kilglinn, Co. Meath*]. This lineage is Patrick's by blood as well as by grace, faith, baptism and teaching; and they granted everything which they had acquired of land, territories, churches and all other gains, to Patrick forever.)

After some time Lommán's death drew near. He went, with his disciple Foirtchern, to see his brother Broccaid. However, as they were setting out he committed his holy church to St Patrick and to Foirtchern; but Foirtchern refused to take his father's inheritance which he had granted to God and Patrick, until Lommán said: "You will not have my blessing unless you accept the governance of my church." After his master's death he held that office for three days until he arrived at Trim; then, straightaway he handed over the church to the pilgrim Cathlaid . . . .

[Patrick disciplines the churches of Mag Aí]

. . . Foreseeing through the Holy Spirit that it would undergo turmoil of every kind, St Patrick brought together his community in the territory of the Ciarraige (the bishop Sacellus and Broccaid and Loarn and the priest Medb and Ernascus) in eternal peace and in the liturgy of one faith and one mind, under the one rule of his heir in the apostolic see of Armagh, and under his blessing.

[Patrick founds a church for Binén]

Binén son of Lugu, scribe, priest and anchorite, was the son of the daughter of Lugaith son of Netu. He consecrated and granted to Patrick his inheritance of land from his mother's people, in which he founded a church for God. St Patrick marked out the site for himself with his staff, and he was the first to offer the body and blood of Christ, after Binén had been ordained by him. Patrick blessed Binén and left him there in his church.

[Patrick baptizes St Mac Cairthin]

Patrick came to the country of the Calrigi [*north Co. Sligo and part of Leitrim*] and baptized Mac Cairthin and Caichán. After he had baptized them, Mac Cairthin and Caichán granted a fifth of Caichán's holding to God and Patrick, which the king allowed for God and Patrick . . .

. . . After it had been granted to him Patrick held Druim Lias [*Drumlease, Co. Leitrim*] in Druimm Daro. He left his pupil there—Benignus—and he was there for seventeen years. Lassar daughter of Anfolmith, of Caichan's family, received the veil from Patrick. She was there for sixty years after Benignus . . . .

[The mission of Iserninus]

. . . Patrick and Iserninus were with Germanus in the city of Auxerre. Germanus directed Iserninus to go and preach in Ireland. He was willing to obey and preach in whatever place he might be sent—except Ireland. Germanus asked Patrick: "Will you too be disobedient?", and Patrick said: "Let it be as you wish." Germanus said: "This is what will be the distinction between you. And Iserninus will not be able to avoid Ireland." Patrick came to Ireland. Iserninus indeed was sent to another country, but an unfavourable wind drove him to the southern half of Ireland.[2]

<Then he came to his cure, a small tribe in Cliu [*in Idrone, Co. Carlow*], named Catrige. He went from there to found Toicuile [*not known: near Ballon, Co. Carlow*]. He left a saint of his community there. He went on to found Ráith Foalascich [*not known*]. He left another saint there. From there he went to Láthrach Dá Arad in the Two Plains [*Larah, near Ballon, Co. Carlow*]. In that place the seven sons of Cathboth came to him. He preached to them and they believed and were baptized; and he went southward with them to their home. Énde Cennselach proclaimed them for believing before everyone else. Bishop Fith[3] went to exile with each of them separately. Then Patrick came, and the seven sons of Dúnlang believed through him. Patrick went on to Crimthann, son of Énda Cennselach, who professed the faith at Raith Bilech [*Rathvilly, Co. Carlow*]. When he had baptized him Patrick asked him to reprieve the sons of Cathboth along with Iserninus, and his request was granted. Then the sons of Cathboth went home; so it is said: "Féni for Fith." And they joined Patrick and Crimthann son of Énde at Scé Patric [*not known*]. Crimthann offered

some of Ulba of Grian Fothart [*not known*] from Gabur Life [*the hill country by Ballymore Eustace, Co. Kildare*] to Suide Laigen [*Mount Leinster, on the Carlow–Wicklow border*]. Iserninus yielded to Patrick in respect of his monastery and his church of first fruits; Patrick then granted them to Bishop Fith, and he granted them to the sons of Cathboth and with them founded Áth Fithot [*Aghade, Co. Carlow*].>

[Patrick baptizes Fiacc of Sleaty]

Patrick travelled from Tara [*Tara Hill, near Gorey, Co. Wexford*] into the country of the Lagin. He and Dubthach moccu Lugir met at Domnach Mór Criathar [*Keilin, Domnach Mór Maige Criathar; Donaghmore, north of Cahore Point, Co. Wexford*] in Uí Cennselig. Patrick asked Dubthach for someone from among his Leinster disciples suitable to become a bishop: a freeman of good family, without liability, neither too poor nor too rich: "I want a man with one wife and only one child." Dubthach answered: "The only one like that among my people is Fiacc the Fair of the Lagin, who has gone from me to the lands of Connacht." As they spoke of him they saw Fiacc the Fair coming to them. Dubthach said to Patrick: "Pretend to tonsure me; then this man will dutifully take my place and be tonsured instead of me." So Fiacc replaced Dubthach and Patrick tonsured and baptized him. He consecrated him as a bishop, and he was the first bishop to be ordained in Leinster. Patrick gave Fiacc sacred valuables: a bell, a reliquary, a staff and a writing tablet. And he left seven of his community with him: Mo-Chatócc of Inis Fáil [*Beggary, near Wexford*], Augustine of Inis Becc [*also Beggary*], Tecán, Diarmait, Naindid, Pool, Fedelmid.

Afterwards Fiacc founded the church of Domnach Féicc [*not known: near Carlow*], and was there until sixty of his community died around him. At this, the angel came and told him that: "West of the river in Cúl Maige [*Sleaty, Co. Laois*] is the place of your resurrection": and that they should place their refectory where they found the boar and their church where they found the deer. Fiacc told the angel that he would not go there until first Patrick should mark out the ground for him and consecrate it; and that it is from him he would receive the site. Patrick then came to Fiacc and marked out and blessed the land and established Fiacc there. It was Crimthann who granted the place to Patrick, for it was Patrick who had baptized him. And Crimthann was buried in Sleaty.

Afterwards Sechnall [*Secundinus*] went to reprove Patrick about a chariot of his. At this, Patrick sent the chariot to Sechnall without a charioteer but with angels to drive it. When Sechnall had it for three nights he sent it on to Manchán, who also had it for three nights. He then sent it to Fiacc, who secured it from them. They went three times round the church and the angel said: "It is to you Patrick has given it, since he knows your need."

THIRTY-THREE

Cogitosus's Life of St Brigid the Virgin

[Prologue]

Brothers, you press me to begin an account of the miracles and works of the virgin Brigid, of blessed memory. I am to take heed of the example of men of learning and to consult written documents as well as people's memories.

This task which you have imposed on me involves a difficult and delicate subject, and I am poorly equipped for it because of my inadequacy, my ignorance and my lack of capacity to express myself. However, God has the power to make much of little, as when he filled the poor widow's house from a drop of oil and a handful of meal.

I must therefore be content to do as I am told, since I undertake this at your bidding. So—to avoid the fault of disobedience—I propose to try to rescue from obscurity and ambiguity some small part of that extensive tradition which has been passed down by people who are greater and more learned than I am.

In this way, all eyes may see clearly the great qualities of that virgin, who flourished in virtue. Not that my memory, my indifferent talent and my rustic style of writing are adequate for the performance of so great a task; but your cheerful faith and sustained prayer can help to make good the author's deficiencies.

The woman of whom I tell, then, grew in virtue, remarkably, and the fame of her good deeds attracted innumerable people of both sexes to come from all the territories of Ireland and gather to her, willingly making their votive offerings. Because of this, she established a monastery—on the firm foundation of the faith—in the open expanses of the plain of Life [*north Co. Kildare*]. It is the head of virtually all the Irish churches and occupies the first place, excelling all the monasteries of the Irish. Its jurisdiction extends over the whole land of Ireland from sea to sea.

Her interest was to provide in all matters for the orderly direction of souls, and she was concerned about the churches which adhered to her in many territories. Taking thought, she decided that she could not make her foundation without a high priest who could consecrate churches and confer orders on the clergy. She called on a famous hermit, distinguished in every way, a man through whom God made much goodness manifest, to leave his hermitage and his solitary life and to come and join her in that place, so that he might rule the church with her in episcopal dignity, and so ensure that nothing of the priestly office would be lacking in her establishments.

And afterwards, this anointed principal of all the bishops, and Brigid, most blessed head of all the women, built their church in happy partnership, guided by virtue. Their episcopal and feminine see, like a fertile vine expanding everywhere in growing branches, spread throughout the whole island of Ireland.

She continues to rule (through a happy line of succession and a perpetual ceremonial) venerated by the archbishop of the Irish and by the abbess, as well as by all the Irish abbesses. In conclusion, therefore (under pressure from the brothers, as I have said) I shall try to tell of this virgin Brigid; both what she accomplished before she came to her princely office and what were her marvellous attainments afterwards. I shall make every effort to be succinct, even though my brevity may lead to some confusion in the order in which I narrate her wonderful works.

THE LIFE OF ST BRIGID

[Her parentage]

The holy Brigid, whom God knew beforehand and whom he predestined to be moulded in his image, was born in Ireland of noble Christian parents stemming from the good and most accomplished tribe of Eochu.[1] Her father was Dubtach, her mother Broicsech. From her childhood she was dedicated to goodness. Chosen by God, the girl was of sober manners, modest and womanly, constantly improving her habit of life.

Who could give a full account of the works she performed at an early age? From the innumerable instances I shall select a few and offer them by way of example.

[A wonderful supply of butter]

In course of time, when she came of suitable age, her mother sent her to the dairy, to churn and make butter from cows' milk, so that she too would serve in the same way as the women who were accustomed to engage in this work.[2] For a period she and the other women were left to themselves. At the end of the period they were required to have produced a plentiful return of milk and curds, and measures of churned butter. But this beautiful maiden, with her generous nature, chose to obey God rather than men. She gave the milk to the poor and to wayfarers, and also handed out the butter. At the end of this period the time came for all to make a return of their dairy production; and it duly came to her turn. Her co-workers could show that they had fulfilled their quota. The blessed virgin Brigid was asked if she too could present the result of her labour. She had nothing to show, having given all away to the poor. She was not allowed any extension of time, and she trembled with fear of her mother. Burning with the fire of an inextinguishable faith, she turned to God in prayer. The Lord heard the voice of the maiden raised in prayer and responded without delay. Through the bounty of the divine will, He who is our help in adversity answered her faith in him by providing a plentiful supply of butter. Marvellous to behold, at the very moment of the maiden's prayer, not only was her quota seen to be filled, but her production was found to be much greater than that of her fellow workers.

And they, seeing with their own eyes such a mighty marvel, praised the Lord, who had done this, and thought it wonderful that such faith should have its base in Brigid's virginal heart.

[She takes the veil]

Not long afterwards, her parents, in the ordinary way of the world, wished to betrothe her to a man. But heaven inspired her to decide otherwise: to present herself as a chaste virgin to God. She sought out the very holy bishop Mac Caille, of blessed memory. He was impressed by her heavenly longings, her modesty and her virginal love of chastity, and he veiled her saintly head in a white cloth. She went down on her knees in the presence of God and the bishop, and she touched the wooden base that supported the altar. The wood retains to the present day the wonderful effect of that gesture long ago: it is as green as if the sap still flowed from the roots of a flourishing tree, and as if the tree had not long ago been felled and stripped of its bark. Even today it cures infirmities and diseases of the faithful.

[A wonderful supply of pork]

It seems right not to pass over another marvel which this outstanding handmaid in the divine service is said to have worked.

Once, when she was cooking pork in the boiling trough, a dog came fawning and begging, and she gave him the food out of pity. But when the pork was taken from the trough and divided among the guests (just as if its quantity had not been reduced), the amount in the trough was found to be still undiminished. Those who saw this marvelled at the girl, so full of merit, so outstanding in her devotion to the faith, and they rightly spread abroad fitting praise of her wonderful works.

[Her crops remain dry in a rainstorm]

Once she gathered reapers and other workers to glean her crops, but as they assembled, a storm of rain came on the harvest. The rain poured down in torrents all over the surrounding territory, and streams of water gushed through the gulleys and ditches. Her crops alone remained dry, undisturbed by rain or storm. While all the reapers throughout the surrounding region were unable to work because of the day's downpour, her harvesters, unaffected by cloud or shadow of rain, carried on their work from dawn to dusk, through the power of God.

[A wonderful supply of milk from one cow]

Among her other achievements, this one seems a cause for wonder.

It so happened that some bishops were coming as her guests, and she had not the wherewithal to feed them. But the manifold grace of God gave her abundant help when she needed it. She milked a cow three times in one day, contrary to what is normal. And the amount of milk she would normally obtain from three of the best cows, she drew on this extraordinary occasion from the one cow.

[She hangs her cloak on a sunbeam]

I retail here another episode which demonstrates her sanctity; one in which what her hand did corresponded to the quality of her pure virginal mind.

It happened that she was pasturing her sheep on a grassy spot on the plain when she was drenched by heavy rain, and she returned home in wet clothes. The sun shining through an aperture in the building cast a beam inside which, at a casual glance, seemed to her to be a solid wooden joist set across the house. She placed her wet cloak on it as if it were indeed solid, and the cloak hung safely from the immaterial sunbeam. When the inhabitants of the house spread the word of this great miracle among the neighbours, they extolled the incomparable Brigid with fitting praise.

[Stolen sheep are miraculously replaced]

And this next work must not be passed over in silence.

St Brigid was in the fields with a flock of grazing sheep and was absorbed in her pastoral care, when a certain evil youth, who knew her reputation for giving away her charges to the poor, skilfully and surreptitiously stole and carried off seven wethers in the course of one day, and hid them away. But towards evening, when the flock was driven as usual to the sheepfold and was counted most carefully three or four times, marvellous to relate, the number was found to be whole and complete, without deficiency. Those who were in the know were overwhelmed at the goodness of God made manifest through the maiden, and they returned the seven wethers to their flock. But the number in the flock was then neither greater nor less than before, but was restored exactly to the original tally.

The most renowned handmaid of God was, not surprisingly, famous everywhere for these and innumerable other wonders: she was seen to be worthy of the highest praise.

[She turns water into beer]

On another extraordinary occasion, this venerable Brigid was asked by some lepers for beer, but had none. She noticed water that had been prepared for baths. She blessed it, in the goodness of her abiding faith, and transformed it into the best beer, which she drew copiously for the thirsty. It was indeed He Who turned water into wine in Cana of Galilee Who turned water into beer here, through this most blessed woman's faith.

[She miraculously ends a pregnancy]

When, however, this miracle is told, it provides a wonderful example.

A certain woman who had taken the vow of chastity fell, through youthful desire of pleasure, and her womb swelled with child. Brigid, exercising the most potent strength of her ineffable faith, blessed her, causing the foetus to disappear, without coming to birth, and without pain. She faithfully returned the woman to health and to penance.

[She makes salt from rock]

And afterwards, since all things are possible for those who believe, even things that are outside the range of ordinary everyday possibility, she performed innumerable miracles.

One day, when a certain person came asking for salt, just as other poor and destitute people in countless numbers were accustomed to come to her seeking their needs, the most blessed Brigid supplied an ample amount. She made it from a rock, which she blessed at that moment in order that she might be able to give the alms. And the suppliant went home joyfully from her, carrying the salt.

[She miraculously cures blindness]

And it seems to me that this further, most divine, wonder-work of hers should be added to the list. For, following the example of the Saviour, she worked in God's name a superlative marvel.

Following the Lord's example, she opened the eyes of a person who was born blind. The Lord gave His followers licence to imitate His works since, as He said, "I am the light of the world", He also said to His apostles, "Ye are the light of the world", and, speaking to them, He also affirmed, "The works that I shall do they do also; and greater works than these shall they do".[3]

Brigid's faith, like the grain of mustard seed, worked on the one born blind and, just like the Lord, she produced by a great miracle eyes with normal sight. By such remarkable works, through the humility of her heart and the purity of her mind, and through her temperate ways and spiritual grace, she earned the great authority that came to her, and the fame which exalted her name above the virgins of her time.

[She cures a child of dumbness]

And, on another day, a woman from outside the community came to visit, bringing along her twelve-year-old daughter, who was dumb from birth. With the great veneration and reverence that all were accustomed to show to Brigid, the woman bowed down and bent her neck to Brigid's kiss of peace. Brigid, friendly and cheerful, spoke to her in words of salvation based on divine goodness. And, following the example of the Saviour who bade the little children come to Him, she took the daughter's hand in hers and—not knowing that the child was mute—she proceeded to ask the girls's intentions: whether she wished to take the veil and remain a virgin or whether she preferred to be given in marriage. The mother intervened to point out that there would be no response, at which Brigid replied that she would not relinquish the daughter's hand until the girl had answered. And when she put the question to the girl the second time, the daughter responded to her, saying: "I wish to do nothing but what you wish." And, after her mouth had been freed of the impediment to her speech, the girl, released from her chain of dumbness, spoke quite normally.

[A dog guards meat for her]

And this further work of hers, of which everyone has heard: who is left wholly unmoved by it?

Once, when she went into a trance, as was her custom, her soul in celestial meditation, sending up her thoughts from earth to heaven, she left down by a dog, not a small amount but a large quantity of bacon. After a month, the meat was looked for and was found just where the dog was—intact. Not only had the dog not dared to eat what the blessed virgin had put down; but, as docile guardian of the bacon, he was tamed by divine power and was seen to act against his nature.

[Her mantle is not stained by raw meat]

The number of her miracles grew daily, so that it is almost impossible to count them, so much did she devote herself to the duty of pity and to ministering to the poor people's need of alms, in and out of season.

For example, when a certain indigent person asked her for something from the food supply set aside for the poor, she hastened to those who cooked the meat so that she could obtain something for alms. One boorish servant among the meat-cooks slopped uncooked meat into the fold of her white garment. She carried the meat to the poor man and gave it to him, but her mantle was neither ruffled nor discoloured.

[A cow accepts another cow's calf at her behest]

Nor indeed is this particularly remarkable among her holy acts.

Among the poor and the strangers from every quarter who thronged to her, drawn by the reputation of her great deeds and the excess of her generosity, there came a certain wretched leper, who asked that the best cow of the herd, with the best of all the calves, be given to him. Far from spurning this request, she soon willingly gave the best possible cow from the herd, along with another cow's calf that had been chosen as the best, to this importunate afflicted person. From pity, she sent her chariot along with him, so that in his long weary journey across the wide plain he would not be troubled with concern about the cow. She directed that the calf be placed beside him in the chariot. And so the cow followed, licking the calf with her tongue as if he were her own, and attending to him, without any drover, until they reached their destination.

See, dearest brothers, how brute beasts obeyed her, even contrary to their nature.

[A river rises up against cattle rustlers]

After some time had passed, some wicked thieves, who had regard for neither God nor man, came on a robbing expedition from a certain territory. They crossed the wide bed of a stream on foot, and they stole her cow. But, as they returned by the way they had come, a sudden flood created a great river, whose onrush overwhelmed them. That river, however, stood like a wall, and allowed the blessed Brigid's cow to cross back over it; but it bowled over the thieves and carried them along with its flood, freeing other stolen cattle from their possession. These returned, with the thongs hanging loosely from their horns, to their proper pastures.

[Her chariot is drawn by one horse]

See how the power of God is revealed.

One day certain business required that the most holy Brigid attend an assembly of the people. She sat in her chariot, which was drawn by two horses. As was her custom, she meditated while in her vehicle, practising here on earth the way of life of heaven, and she prayed to her Lord. One of the horses stumbled, and the other, in the alarm of a dumb beast, sprang from the chariot and, extricating itself from the harness and from the yoke, ran away in fright across the plain. But God's hand held up the yoke and kept it suspended without falling. Brigid sat praying in the vehicle drawn by one horse, and arrived safely at the assembly in full view of the crowd, who followed along after this display of divine power. And when she addressed the gathering with words of salvation, her teaching was reinforced by these marvels and by the signs of the divine protection she enjoyed.

[A hunted wild boar joins her herd]

And it seems to me that this work of hers is particularly worth considering.

Once a solitary wild boar which was being hunted ran out from the woods, and in its wild flight was brought suddenly into the most blessed Brigid's herd of swine. She observed its arrival among her pigs and blessed it. Thereupon it lost its fear and settled down among the herd. See, brothers, how brute beasts and animals could withstand neither her bidding nor her wish, but served her tamely and humbly.

[Wolves act as swineherds for her]

Among the many people who offered her gifts was a man who came once from a distant territory. He said that he would give her fat pigs, but asked that she send some of her people with him back to his farm to collect the pigs. The farm was far away, situated at the space of three or four days' journey. She sent some of her workers with him as travelling companions; but they had in fact gone barely a day's journey (as far as the mountain known as Grabor, which forms a territorial boundary) [*not known; possibly a mistranscription: there was a Sliab Gabuil in the plain of Life; possibly Gabur Life*] when they saw his pigs, which they had thought to be in distant parts, coming towards them on the road, driven by wolves which had carried them off. As soon as he realized what had happened, the man recognized them as his pigs. Truly, the wild wolves, because of their enormous reverence for the blessed Brigid, had left the great forests and the wide plains to work at herding and protecting the pigs. Now, on the arrival of the people she had sent—who were astonished to see such swineherds—the wolves, leaving the pigs there, gave up their unnatural activity. The next day, those who had been sent to collect the pigs gave an account of the marvellous event and returned to their homes.

[A wild fox takes the place of a king's pet]

It seems to me that this should be the last of her miraculous deeds to be passed over.

On another day, a certain person, not knowing the circumstances, saw the king's fox walking into the royal palace, and ignorantly thought it to be a wild animal. He did not know that it was a pet, familiar with the king's hall, which entertained the king and his companions with various tricks that it had learned—requiring both intelligence and nimbleness of body. He killed the fox in the view of a large crowd. Immediately, he was seized by the people who had seen the deed. He was accused and brought before the king. When the king heard the story he was angry. He ordered that, unless the man could produce a fox with all the tricks that his fox had had, he and his wife and sons should be executed and all his household be committed to servitude.

When the venerable Brigid heard this story, she was moved to such pity and tenderness that she ordered her chariot to be yoked. Grieving in the depths of her heart for the unhappy man who had been so unjustly judged, and offering prayers to the Lord, she travelled across the plain and took the road which led to the royal palace. And the Lord, instantly, heard her out-poured prayers. He directed one of his wild foxes to come to her. It immediately made all speed, and when it arrived at the most blessed Brigid's chariot it sprang aboard and sat quietly beside Brigid under her mantle.

As soon as she arrived in the king's presence, she began imploring that unfortunate man, who had not understood the situation and was held prisoner as a victim of his own ignorance, should be set free and released from his chains. But the king would not heed her prayers. He affirmed that he would not release the man unless he could produce another fox with the same tricks as his, that had been killed. In the middle of this she introduced her fox. And, in the presence of the king and of the crowd, it went through all the tricks that the other fox had performed, and amused the crowd in exactly the same way. The king was satisfied. His nobles, and the great applauding crowd wondered at the marvel that had been worked. The king ordered that the man who had been under sentence of death should be set free. Not long after St Brigid had procured that man's release and had returned home, the same fox, bothered by the crowds, skilfully contrived a safe escape. It was pursued by large numbers of riders and hounds, but made fools of them, fled through the plains and went into the waste and wooded places and so to its den.

And all venerated St Brigid, who excelled more and more in her great works. They marvelled at what had been achieved through the excellence of her virtue and through the prerogative of so many gifts of grace.

[Wild ducks come to her]

On another day the blessed Brigid felt a tenderness for some ducks that she saw swimming on the water and occasionally taking wing. She commanded them to come to her. And, as if they were humans under obedience, a great flock of them flew on feathered wings to her, without any fear. Having touched them with her hand and caressed them, she let them go and fly away through the air. She praised highly the Creator of all things, to whom all life is subject, and for whose service—as has been said—all life is given.[4]

And from these examples it is plain that the whole order of beasts, flocks and herds was subject to her rule.

[A band of murderers is deceived by a miracle of glamour]

Now this miracle of hers, one to be celebrated in all ages, must be told to the ears of the faithful.

Once, as was her custom, she was spreading abroad among everyone the seed of the Lord's word, when she observed nine men belonging to a certain peculiarly vain and diabolical cult. They were deceived and corrupted in mind and soul, and at the instigation of the ancient Enemy who ruled among them, they had bound themselves—since they thirsted for the spilling of blood—and resolved with evil vows and oaths to commit murder before the beginning of the forthcoming month of July. The most revered and kindly Brigid preached to them in many gentle phrases, urging them to abandon their mortal errors, to humble their hearts and through true penance to renounce their sinfulness. But they were profane of mind, they had not fulfilled their wicked vow, and they continued their ways, resisting her appeal, and in spite of the abundant prayers which the virgin had poured out to God in her desire (following her Lord) that all should be saved and know the truth.

The criminals went on their way, and met with what they thought was the man they had to kill. They pierced him with their spears and beheaded him with their swords, and were seen by many to return with bloody weapons, as if they had destroyed their adversary. Here was the miracle: they had killed nobody—although it seemed to them that they had fulfilled their vows. When, however, no person was missing in that territory in which they thought they had triumphed, the fulness of the divine favour granted through the most holy Brigid became known to all. And they who had formerly been murderers were now turned back to God through penance.

[She cures a man of overeating]

Words cannot adequately describe St Brigid's devotion to God, through which the divine power of holy religion was shown in the following work.

There was a certain man called Luguidam, a strong man for sure, and one of the bravest. When he was of a mind, he did the work of twelve men in a single day all by himself. At the same time, he ate enough food to feed twelve men (as he could do the work singlehanded, so could he consume the rations). He implored Brigid to pray to almighty God to moderate his appetite, which caused him to eat to such excess, but he asked that he should not lose his former strength along with his appetite. Brigid blessed him and prayed to God for him. Afterwards, he was content with the sustenance of one man, but, just as before, when he worked he could do the labour of twelve. He had all his former strength.

[The miraculous transport of a huge tree]

Among all her famous works we should recount the following to all—one which is extraordinary and is well verified.

A huge and magnificent tree, which was to be used for certain purposes, was cut down and trimmed with axes by skilful craftsmen. Its great size caused such difficulty in manouevring it that a gathering of strong men was summoned to transport the tree with its awkward branches through difficult places. Aided by the craftsmen's tackle, they proposed to haul it with many oxen to the place where it was to be dealt with. But in spite of the large number of men, the strength of the oxen, and the skill of the craftsmen, they were unable to budge the tree; so they drew back from it. But the Master teaches through the medium of the heavenly Gospel that it is possible for faith to move mountains; and—through Brigid's stalwart faith (like the grain of mustard seed)—they carried this weightiest of trees without the slightest difficulty, through the divine mystery of the power of the Gospel and without any mortal aid, to the place designated by St Brigid. This display of the excellence of God's power was made known through all the territories.

[Through the miraculous recovery of a brooch she vindicates a woman accused of theft]

And it comes to mind that we should not omit the following manifestation, which, among innumerable other miracles, was worked by the venerable Brigid.

There was a certain nobleman, with the deviousness of a man of the world, who lusted after a particular woman. He exercised his cunning on ways to seduce her. He entrusted a silver brooch to her safe-keeping; then deviously filched it from her without her knowledge and threw it into the sea. This meant that, when she was unable to produce it on demand, she would be forfeit to him as his slave, and so must submit to his embraces to be used as he wished. He contrived this evil for no other reason than to be in a position to demand this ransom. If the silver brooch were not returned, the woman herself must be given to him instead in servitude, because of her failure, to be subject to his wicked lust.

This chaste woman fled in fear to St Brigid, as she would fly to the safest city of refuge. When Brigid learned what had happened, and how and why; almost before she had heard the story out she summoned a certain person who had fish that had been caught in the river. The fishes' bellies were cut and opened, and there in the middle of one of them was revealed the silver brooch which that most cruel man had thrown into the sea.

Then, easy in her mind, she took along the silver brooch and went with that infamous man to the assembly of the people for the case to be heard. She showed the assembly the brooch, and many witnesses gave testimony, people who were able to identify the brooch as the same one that was concerned in this accusation. Brigid took the chaste woman into her own company, and freed her from the clutches of that most cruel tyrant. Indeed he afterwards confessed his fault to St Brigid and submissively prostrated himself before her. Everyone admired her for the performance of this great miracle, and she gave thanks to God (for whose glory she had done everything) and went home.

[She miraculously replaces a calf and a loom]

In the telling of these wonders, we may compare to her hospitality that of another woman.

For St Brigid came to her dwelling while making a journey on God's business across the wide plain of Brega [*mainly in Co. Meath*]. She arrived as the day was declining into evening, and she spent the night with this woman, who received her joyfully with outstretched hands and gave thanks to God for the happy arrival of the most revered Brigid, Christ's virgin.

The woman was too poor to have ready the wherewithal to entertain such guests, but she broke up the loom on which she had been weaving cloth, for firewood. Then she killed her calf, placed it on the heap of kindling and, with a good will, lit the fire. Dinner was eaten, and the night was passed with the customary vigils. The hostess (who had taken the calf from her cow in order that nothing should be lacking in the reception and entertainment of St Brigid) rose early. The cow had discovered another calf, in the same form exactly as the calf she had previously loved. And a loom was to be seen, exactly in the same shape and form as the other.

So, having accomplished this marvel, and having bidden farewell to the people of the house, St Brigid continued on her pontifical way and went cheerfully on her journey.

[She divides a silver dish exactly into three]

Her miracles are great, but this one is especially admired.

Three lepers came, asking for alms of any kind, and she gave them a silver dish. So that this would not cause discord and contention among them when they came to share it out, she spoke to a certain person expert in the weighing of gold and silver, and asked him to divide it among them in three parts of equal weight. When he began to excuse himself, pointing out that there was no way he could divide it up so that the three parts would weigh exactly the same, the most blessed Brigid herself took the silver dish and struck it against a stone, breaking it into three parts as she had wished. Marvellous to tell, when the three parts were tested on the scales, not one part was found to be heavier or lighter by a breath than any other. So the three poor people left with their gift and there was no cause for envy or grudging between them.

[She receives a bishop's vestments from Christ in place of those she had given to the poor]

She followed the example of the most blessed Job and never allowed a poor person to leave empty-handed. Indeed, she gave away to the poor the foreign and exotic robes of the illustrious bishop Conláeth, vestments he wore in the course of the liturgy of the Lord and the apostolic vigils. When in due course the time for these solemnities came round, the high priest of the people wished to change into his vestments. It was to Christ—in the form of a poor person—that St Brigid had given the bishop's clothing. Now she handed the bishop another set of vestments, similar in all details of texture and colour, which she had received at that very moment (draped over a two-wheeled chariot) from Christ, whom, as a beggar, she had clad. She had freely given the other clothes to the poor. Now, at the right moment, she received these instead. For, as she was the living and most blessed instrument of the sublime, she had power to do what she wished.

[She divines a supply of honey]

After this, a certain man, finding himself in particular need, came to her to ask for a sixth of a measure of honey. She was distressed in her mind, because she had no honey ready that she might give to the person who was asking for it, when the humming of bees was heard underneath the paved floor of the building in which she was. And when that spot from which the buzzing of the bees was heard, was excavated and examined, there was found a sufficient quantity to meet the man's requirements. And he, receiving the gift of enough honey for his needs, returned joyfully to his village.

[She miraculously moves a river]

In the following episode too she performed a miracle.

The king of her country (the region in which she lived) issued a decree for all the tribes and places under his rule. All the people were to come together from his territories to build a wide road. It was to be solidified with tree branches and stones in the foundation, it was to have very strong banks and deep impassable ditches, and it was to run through soggy ground and through a swamp in which a full river flowed. When built it should be able to carry four-wheeled cars, horsemen, chariots, wagon-wheels, and the traffic of people as well as that of forces to assault enemies on all sides.

When the people had gathered in from every quarter, they divided up the road they had to build into sections, by septs and families, so that each tribe or family would build the section assigned to it. The most difficult and laborious section was that with the river, and it was assigned to a certain tribe. These people decided to avoid the heavy work, so they used their strength to force a weaker tribe (that to which St Brigid belonged) to labour on the difficult section. Choosing an easier section for themselves, this cruel tribe could do their construction without facing the hazard of the river.

St Brigid's blood-relations came and prostrated themselves at her feet. It is reliably reported that she told them: "Go. God has the will and the power to move the river from the location where you are oppressed by hard labour to the section that they have chosen."

And, when at the dawn of that day the people rose to work, the river which had been complained of was found to have left its former valley and the two banks between which it had flowed. It had transferred from the section in which St Brigid's tribe had been forced to labour to the section of those powerful and proud people who had unjustly compelled the smaller and weaker tribe to work there. In proof of the miracle, the traces of the river which transferred to a different place, and the empty channel through which it flowed in past time; these may still be seen, dry and without any trickle of water.

[She continues working miracles after her death]

Many miracles were performed in her lifetime, before she laid down the burden of her flesh; many later. The bounty of the gift of God never ceased working wonders in her monastery, where her venerable body lies. We have not only heard tell of these marvels; we have seen them with our own eyes.

[A millstone is miraculously brought to the mill]

For example, the prior of the great and famous monastery of St Brigid (of the beginnings of which we have made brief mention in this little work) sent masons and stonecutters to look in suitable places for a rock fit for making a millstone. They made no provision for transport, but went up a steep and difficult road, reached the top of a rocky mountain and chose a great stone at the summit of the tallest peak. And they carved it all over to a round shape and perforated it to make a millstone. When the prior arrived, in response to their message, with an ox-team, he was unable to drive the oxen up to pull the stone; he was barely able to ascend the very difficult track with a few of them following him.

He and all his workers pondered this problem: by what means could they remove the millstone from the highest ridge of the mountain when there was no way in which the oxen could be yoked and burdened in that high and precipitous place? They came to the despairing conclusion (some of them even giving up and descending the mountain) that they should abandon the stone and regard as waste the labour they had put into fashioning it. The prior, however, taking prudent thought and consulting his workers, said confidently: "By no means let it be so; but manfully lift this millstone and cast it down from the high peak of the mountain in the name—and calling on the power—of the most revered St Brigid. For we have neither equipment nor strength to move the millstone through this rocky place, unless Brigid, to whom nothing is impossible (all things are possible to the believer), will carry it to a place from which the oxen can pull it." So, with firm faith, they first gradually raised it from the mountain top and then cast it into the valley. When they flung it down, it found its way; sometimes avoiding rocks, sometimes springing over them, rolling through damp places high on the mountain in which neither men nor cattle could stand, and, with marvellous noise, it arrived quite unbroken at the level spot where the oxen were. From there it was transported by the ox-team as far as the millhouse, where it was skilfully matched with the other stone.

[The millstone refuses to grind a pagan's corn]

There is another, previously untold but quite outstanding, miracle to add to the story (now known to everyone) of the millstone that was moved in the name of St Brigid. A certain pagan, living near the millhouse, sent some grain from his house to the mill, employing a simple and ignorant man so that the miller who did the work there did not know that the grain was his. And when that grain was spread between the millstones, nothing could budge them—not the power of the water, and no exercise of strength or skill. When the people who observed this sought its cause, they were quite perplexed. Then, when they learned that the grain belonged to a druid, they had no doubt at all that the millstone upon which St Brigid had performed the divine miracle had refused to grind the pagan man's grain into flour. And immediately they removed the heathen's grain and placed their own grain, from the monastery, under the millstone. Straightaway the mill machinery resumed its normal course without any impediment.

[Her millstone remains intact in a fire]

And after an interval of time it happened that this very millhouse caught fire. It was no small miracle that, when the fire consumed the whole building, including the other stone which was matched to St Brigid's millstone, the flames did not dare to touch or scorch her stone. It remained unaffected by the fire in the conflagration that destroyed the millhouse.

And afterwards, since note was taken of this miracle, the stone was brought to the monastery and placed near the gate, inside the cashel that encloses the church where many come to venerate St Brigid. It was given a place of honour in that gate, and it cures diseases of the faithful who touch it.

[The miraculously rebuilt church]

Nor must one be silent about the miracle of the rebuilding of the church in which the bodies of that glorious pair, the bishop Conláeth and this holy virgin Brigid, lie right and left of the ornamented altar, placed in shrines decorated with a variegation of gold, silver, gems and precious stones, with gold and silver crowns hanging above them.

In fact, to accommodate the increasing number of the faithful, of both sexes, the church is spacious in its floor area, and it rises to an extreme height. It is adorned with painted boards and has on the inside three wide chapels, all under the roof of the large building and separated by wooden partitions. One partition, which is decorated with painted images and is covered with linen, stretches transversely in the eastern part of the church from one wall to the other and has two entrances, at its ends. By one entrance, placed in the external part, the supreme pontiff enters the sanctuary and approaches the altar with his retinue of monks. To these consecrated ministers are entrusted the sacred vessels for Sunday use and the offering of the sacrifice. And by the other entrance, placed on the left side of the above-mentioned transverse partition, the abbess, with her faithful virgins and widows, equally enters to enjoy the banquet of the body and blood of Jesus Christ.

And another partition, dividing the floor of the church into two equal parts, extends from the east in length as far as the transverse wall. The church has many windows, and an ornamented door on the right side through which the priests and the faithful of male sex enter the building. There is another door on the left through which the virgins and the congregation of the female faithful are accustomed to enter. And so, in one great basilica, a large number of people, arranged by rank and sex, in orderly division separated by partitions, offers prayers with a single spirit to the almighty Lord.

When the ancient door of the left-hand entrance, through which St Brigid was accustomed to enter the church, was set on its hinges by the craftsmen, it did not fill the new entrance of the rebuilt church. In fact, a quarter of the opening was left unclosed and agape. If a fourth part, by height, were added, then the door could be restored to fit the opening.

The artificers deliberated and discussed whether they should make a completely new, and larger, door which would fill the opening, or whether they should make a timber piece to attach to the old door, to bring it to the required size. The gifted master, who was in all these matters the leading craftsman of the Irish, gave wise advice. "We ought"—he said—"in this coming night, alongside St Brigid, to pray faithfully to the Lord so that she may indicate in the morning what we should do." And so he spent the whole night praying before St Brigid's shrine.

And, having sent on his prayer, he rose in the morning and brought the old door and placed it on its hinges. It closed the opening completely. There was no gap, no overlap. And so St Brigid extended the height of the door so that it filled the opening, and no aperture could be seen except when the door was pushed back to allow entry to the church. And this miracle of the Lord's power is plain to the eyes of all who see this doorway and door.

[Brigid's city]

But who could convey in words the supreme beauty of her church and the countless wonders of her city, of which we would speak? "City" is the right word for it: that so many people are living there justifies the title. It is a great metropolis, within whose outskirts—which St Brigid marked out with a clearly defined boundary—no earthly adversary is feared, nor any incursion of enemies. For the city is the safest place of refuge among all the towns of the whole land of the Irish, with all their fugitives. It is a place where the treasures of kings are looked after, and it is reckoned to be supreme in good order.

And who could number the varied crowds and countless people who gather in from all territories? Some come for the abundance of festivals; others come to watch the crowds go by; others come with great gifts to

Kildare

the celebration of the birth into heaven of St Brigid who, on the First of February, falling asleep, safely laid down the burden of her flesh and followed the Lamb of God into the heavenly mansions.

[Epilogue]

I beg the indulgence of the brothers and of readers of these episodes, since I had no pretension to knowledge but was compelled by obedience to skim over the great sea of St Brigid's wonderful works—something to be feared by the bravest—and to offer in rustic language these few narratives of the greatest miracles.

Pray for me Cogitosus Ua hAedha, who am worthy of blame. I urge you to commend me to the good Lord in your prayers; and may God grant you the peace of the Gospel.

Here ends the life of St Brigid the virgin.

The Three Orders of the Saints of Ireland

[The first order]

The first order of saints was in the time of Patrick. They were all bishops, eminent and holy and filled with the Holy Spirit, numbering three hundred and fifty. They were founders of churches, who worshipped one head, Christ, followed one leader, Patrick, had one tonsure and one liturgy of the Mass, and celebrated one Easter (that is, after the spring equinox). What was excluded from the communion of one church, all excluded. They did not reject the government and the company of women because, since their foundation was the rock, Christ, they did not fear the wind of temptation. This order of saints lasted through four reigns: that is, from the time of Loeguire son of Niall, who reigned thirty-seven years, and Ailill surnamed Molt, who reigned thirty years, and Lugaid, who reigned seven years. And this order of saints lasted until the end of the time of Tuathal Maelgarb.[1] They all continued to be holy bishops, and for the greater part they were of Frankish and Roman and British and Irish origin.

[The second order]

The second order of saints was as follows. In this second order there were in fact few bishops but many priests, to the number of three hundred. They worshipped one God as their head. They had diverse liturgies and diverse rules of life, but they celebrated one Easter (that is, on the fourteenth of the moon), and they practised one tonsure, from ear to ear. They shunned the company and the services of women and excluded them from their monasteries. This order lasted as far as four reigns, that is, from the end of the reign of Tuathal Maelgarb through the thirty years in which Diarmait son of Cerbél reigned, through the time of the two descendants of Muiredach,[2] who reigned for seven years, and through the time of Áed son of Ainmere,

who reigned thirty years.[3] These accepted their ritual of the Mass from
holy men of Britain: St David and St Gildas and St Doc. And their names are:
Finnian, Énda, Colmán, Comgal, Áed, Ciarán, Columba, Brendan, Brichin,
Cainnech, Cóemgen, Laisren, Lugid, Barra, and many others who were of the
second rank of saints.

[The third order]

The third order of saints was as follows. They were holy priests, few of
them bishops, to the number of one hundred, and they settled in uninhabited
places. They lived on herbs and water and on the alms of the faithful; they
despised all earthly goods and they utterly avoided every murmur and
distraction. They had diverse rules and liturgies, and even differences in
the tonsure: some shaved the top of the head; others wore their hair long.
And they varied in their celebration of Easter, some calculating from the
fourteenth of the moon, others from the thirteenth. This order lasted
through four reigns: through the time of Áed Allán, who reigned just three
years; through the time of Domnall, who reigned thirty years; through the
time of the sons of Máel Cobo; and through the time of Áed Sláine.[4] And
this order endured until the time of the famous great plague.[5] Their names
are as follows: Bishop Pertran; Bishop Ultán; Bishop Colmán; Bishop Áedán;
Bishop Lommán; Bishop Senach. These were all bishops, and there are
many more. These indeed are the priests: the priest Fechín; Airendán; Faelán;
Cummíne; Colmán; Ernán; Crónán—and many more priests.

[The hierarchy of the orders]

Note that the first order was the holiest, the second holier than the third,
the third holy. The first blazed like the sun in the heat of love; the second
shone with a paler light like the moon; the third glowed like gold. The
blessed Patrick, taught by heavenly inspiration, discerned these three
orders when—in his prophetic vision—he saw the whole of Ireland filled
with flames of fire; then, afterwards, the mountains as if they were burning;
then lighted lamps in the valleys. This is taken from the old Life of Patrick.

[The disciples of St Finnian]

Note: These are the disciples of St Finnian of Clonard: the two Ciaráns—
Ciarán son of the Wright and Ciarán of Saigir; Columba son of Crimthann
and Colum Cille; the two Brendans—Brendan son of Findlug and Brendan
of Birr; Mobhí Clárínech; Lasrén son of Nad Froích; Sinell son of Máenach;
Cainnech, son of ua Dalann; Ruadán of Lorrha; Ninnid Lámderc [*"red-
hand"*]; Mogenóc of Cell Cumili, and Bishop Senach.

THIRTY-FIVE

The Life of St Ailbe

St Ailbe was one of those reputed in the medieval ecclesiastical tradition to be "pre-Patrician". The church of Emly, in other words, did not acknowledge Patrick as its founder but claimed that Munster (of which it was for a time the chief ecclesiastical centre) had been converted by Ailbe. In mythology, Ailbe was the name of a divine war-hound, who guarded the boundaries of the province, or nation, of Leinster, and he appears less consistently elsewhere in Ireland as a boundary guardian. Inevitably, in the storytelling, mythological tales and attributes of the hound have attached themselves to the bishop. The name Albeus is perfectly plausible for a fifth/sixth-century bishop; but unfortunately there are no contemporary records to inform us about him. The chief interest of this late Latin Life is that it shows the persistence into the Middle Ages of the tradition of non-Patrician foundation. The association of Ailbe with "Bishop Hilary" in the Life has no historical value. The hagiographers tended to connect their hero-saints with the one or two early Continental ecclesiastics whose names they knew, and the name of "Bishop Hilary" occurs from time to time. This may be Hilary of Arles, briefly Leo the Great's vicar in the West, with whom Leo came into conflict on the issue of authority and hierarchy. It may be Pope St Hilary (461–468), Leo's immediate successor, who also intervened in the affairs of the Church in Gaul and Spain, but did his best to maintain the church of Arles as a primatial see in the West. It is not impossible that either might have been concerned in the appointment of a bishop to Munster; but the death of Ailbe is entered in the Annals of Inisfallen at 528 and in the Annals of Ulster at 527, 534 and 542 (when the annals are beginning to be approximately reliable)—and, assuming that he died in the second quarter of the sixth century, he lived too late to have been an active contemporary of either Hilary.

THE LIFE OF ST AILBE, ARCHBISHOP OF EMLY

[The birth of St Ailbe]

Ailbe, bishop of the men of Munster, most blessed father, and second patron of the whole island after Patrick, came from the eastern part of the region of Cliach, which is in Munster. His father, who was named Olcnais, was in the household of King Crónán in the region of the Artrige [*Araid Cliach; in north-eastern Co. Limerick*]. There he went in by night to the king's slave-woman—named Sanclit[1]—and slept with her. Olcnais, then—St Ailbe's father—knowing that the slave-woman had conceived by him, and fearing that the king might kill him, fled. She, however, afterwards gave birth to his son, the holy Ailbe. Seeing his slave-woman's son, the king Crónán said: "This boy now born to the slave-woman will never live under my roof; nor will he be fostered with my sons."

[He is fostered by wolves]

And the king told his slaves that the boy should be killed. But the Holy Spirit inspired the slaves not to kill the boy; instead they hid him under a certain rock and left him there; and his name is honoured there to the present day. There lived under this same rock a wild wolf, who loved the holy boy and, like a gentle mother, fondly nourished him among her own cubs.

One day however, while this wild beast was out hunting prey in the woods, a certain man named Lochán son of Lugir, a man of natural goodness, saw the boy among the wolf-cubs under that rock and took him out and brought him with him to his own home. As soon as the wild beast returned and saw that the boy was missing, she searched frantically, with breathless anxiety, for him. And as Lochanus approached his home, the animal seized his cloak and would not let him go until she saw the boy. At which Lochanus said to the beast: "Go in peace. This boy will no longer be among wolves, but will stay with me." Then that wild animal, weeping and howling, returned sorrowfully to its cave.

[He is fostered by Britons and baptized by Palladius]

This Lochanus son of Lugir gave the holy boy to certain Britons, who were with him in eastern Cliach, and they faithfully fostered him; they gave him the name Albeus because he had been found alive under the rock.[2] And the grace of God was with him.

After this, there came a certain Christian bishop,[3] sent from the Apostolic See to the island of Ireland many years before Patrick, to propagate the faith of Christ there. The Irish, however, were then pagans, and they did not receive him nor—except for a few—did they believe in his teaching. When he arrived in Munster, he came upon the holy boy Ailbe, who was praying in the open, gazing at heaven, who earnestly asked him to bring him the true faith, saying: "I pray that I may know the Creator of all, and believe in Him Who made heaven and earth and all creatures; since I know for certain that all of nature was made without human art and that no human craftsman could have created it." And when the holy boy Ailbe spoke these words, the bishop, who was nearby, heard them and greeted the boy. He fulfilled the boy's heart's desire by teaching him about all these matters, and baptized him, giving him his name, Albeus.

[He travels to Britain and Gaul]

Afterwards, however, the Britons who had fostered Ailbe decided to return to their own country. Ailbe journeyed with them to the coast, since he desired to make the voyage with them. But they didn't wish him to accompany them, and they left him alone at the harbour. However, they were tossed by wind and waves for a whole day, and eventually were driven back to the same place where they had left him. Then, when they saw the holy boy at the harbour, they understood why they had been battered about dangerously among the waves. They took him on board and together they sailed safely as far as Britain.

Afterwards the blessed Ailbe wished to travel to Rome to study the Divine Scriptures. And when he reached the Sea of Icht, which is between Britain and Gaul, he came upon men proposing to set sail; and they did not allow him to go with them. Then one of them said to him—mocking him: "Go in this ship which is there before you."

The ship, however, was an old broken wreck which had been lying there a long time. Straightaway at the man's word, holy Ailbe boarded the ship and, miraculously, through God's guidance and steering, he began the passage. Then the man shouted after him: "Don't sail in my ship!" Ailbe didn't wish to be in the ship without the mariner's permission. He spread out his cowl on the sea, sat on it, trusting in God, and blessed the ship, which returned empty to its owner. Ailbe, however, praying to the Holy Trinity while seated on his cowl, miraculously crossed the sea.

[He works cures, and tames lions in a legionary camp]

Afterwards St Ailbe arrived at a military post occupied by Roman troops. His reputation had gone before him, and they tested him by sending three men to him to be cured, the first of blindness, the second of deafness, the third of dumbness. St Ailbe, seeing their distress, invoked Divine clemency on them and healed all three.

But when God saw how those unworthy sceptics were attempting to harm His saint, He sent a great snowfall down on their camp. Then all of them, shrivelling in the extreme cold, cried out to St Ailbe, begging him to remove that infliction of snow from them. Ailbe took pity on them. He raised his hands and prayed to heaven. Straightaway the bright sun appeared and warmed the camp, and all most joyfully blessed the Lord and St Ailbe.

Then there came from the forest three mighty lions. They raided the camp: one of them killed a man and the other two killed two of the king's horses. They were eager to devour them, and seized their prey in their fangs. Everyone fled in terror of the lions. But St Ailbe saw the anguish and said to the lions: "You have been bold enough to kill those when we weren't looking; now you may not eat their bodies before our eyes." And in truth, the lions at once dropped the bodies obediently from their mouths and ran tamely to St Ailbe and—as if they were asking pardon for having killed them—they meekly licked the feet of the saint. Through the prayers of St Ailbe the dead man then returned to life. Then the king said to Ailbe: "Saint of God! I know that nothing is impossible for your God! Therefore I implore you, in the name of the Omnipotent, to revive my pair of horses, whom I loved." St Ailbe heeded his prayer in the name of Almighty God, and he blessed the horses with the sign of the Cross and thereupon brought them back to life. He also blessed the lions who had licked his feet, and they gently brushed the feet of holy Ailbe with their manes, as if with linen cloth—although his nature was alien to theirs. The king said to the saint of God: "Make those lions stay away from here." At which the blessed Ailbe replied to him: "I don't wish to send them away hungry from your presence to their own place. Look: by God's grace your horses, which they were hungry to eat, were snatched from their mouths. Allow them then some form of food, so that they may stay away from your territory for good." At which the king said: "I have nothing to hand that I would like to offer them." Then St Ailbe took the king's steward with him up on a nearby mountain. There he prayed with him to the Lord; at which a dark cloud came down from heaven to earth, and it bore with it food fit for lions. Then the saint of God said to the lions: "Take this away with you to your wilderness, and eat it there." And the lions did as he bade them. This caused the crowd to cheer loudly at such a miracle, praising the Lord and holy Ailbe with one voice. And St Ailbe blessed them all along with the king and departed from them.

[He studies with Bishop Hilary in Rome]

After this St Ailbe arrived in Rome, where he studied the Divine Scriptures with the bishop Hilary. And there, dearest brothers, the Divine power produced great and marvellous miracles—in the following way—for the credit, the love and the honour of the holy archbishop Ailbe. For, when he stayed in Rome with Bishop Hilary in order to advance in virtue, the first of his master's commands—which he obeyed—was to herd swine in a nearby wood. That wood, as it happened, was so crowded with animals that it had been stripped of acorns and other fodder. However, Almighty God granted this boon to His servant, the holy Ailbe: that each year, although lacking the fruit of the woods, his swine throve and grew fat. And each day when St Ailbe went into the City, where he was studying with Hilary, he drew a mark on the earth with his crosier around the swine; and the swine didn't dare to cross the line traced by the crosier—nor could thieves or wild beasts harm them. And this continued so long as he was their swineherd.

[He reaps corn miraculously]

One year a hundred measures had been sown in a cornfield of St Hilary's. But when harvest time came, and the crop was full and ripe, workers could not be found to reap the corn. Then St Hilary said to Ailbe: "Look for harvesters, my son, so that we won't lose the brothers' corn."

At his master's command the holy disciple immediately rose and went to examine the corn. It was then almost nightfall; St Ailbe's whole mind was directed to prayer; and he prayed a long time. In the first vigil of the night, angels of God came to converse with St Ailbe; and on that night, in his presence, they reaped all the corn and gathered it neatly in one place. And when St Hilary saw this miracle performed through his servant and disciple, he glorified the name of the Lord and blessed his holy disciple Ailbe.

[He produces a miraculous shower of apples]

One day St Hilary said to the blessed Ailbe: "Look, our orchard is barren this year and we have no apples." St Ailbe replied: "It is for good men, not for my wretchedness, to pray against the will of God. And He Who made all out of nothing can give us apples without restoring the fruit of our orchard." God the Father Almighty, hearing the humble expression of St Ailbe, fulfilled his prophetic saying by raining down such an abundance of apples that the whole monastery within its walls was filled with them; and they tasted of honey. And all who saw this wonderful thing gave thanks to God and marvelled at St Ailbe.

[He miraculously escapes poison]

A certain man of St Hilary's community offered a chalice of poisoned wine to St Ailbe, because of hatred and envy. Then the blessed Ailbe, filled with the grace of the Holy Spirit and with a spirit of prophecy, brought his lips down to the chalice and made the wine solidify and remain in the vessel. The poison fell to the ground and immediately assumed the form of a serpent, which saw the man who had given the poison to St Ailbe. It hastened to him and entered into him. He died on the spot. When St Ailbe saw that the man was dead, he recollected the precept of the Lord which says: "Return good for evil." He prayed over the dead man and brought him back to life in the presence of all. That man spoke great praises of St Ailbe; and the serpent turned back into poison so that it would do no further harm to people.

[He visits the Pope and is joined by many Irish]

St Hilary observed the great sanctity of St Ailbe and the marvellous wonders which God worked through him, and knew that he had passed the test in all forms of wisdom. He sent him to the lord pope, to be ordained bishop by him. And the holy pope was overjoyed at his arrival. He stayed with him a year and fifty days. After St Ailbe, there then came to Rome fifty holy men from Ireland. When they arrived where the holy pope and Ailbe were, the pope gave them each a cell, and he sent St Ailbe to them. Many of them shared the same names—so there were twelve Colmáns, twelve Comangens and twelve holy Fintáns—and the most blessed Declán among the others. The pope indeed sent to these saintly guests of his beautiful breads, wine, oil and other good comestibles. Then St Ailbe asked Saints Declán and Colmán: "Who will serve us the food in this feast?" And they replied: "We are all tired: we can't serve." At once holy Ailbe rose and ministered to them, rejoicing in his heart, because he wished to do this task himself. The Lord Jesus Christ conferred such grace on St Ailbe that thereafter each day the brothers found before them just such sustenance as the holy pope had first sent them. For St Ailbe every evening divided up the meal for his brothers, and similarly he afterwards distributed the empty plates to the poor—who found them full the following morning. And similarly with drink; for many days. When the holy pope heard of this great work, he gave thanks to God and he honoured holy Ailbe and his brothers.

[The pope consecrates St Ailbe, who is blessed by angels]

Another time, many saintly men implored the pope to ordain St Ailbe as a bishop, and to send him to preach to the Irish; since up to then they were heathens. The holy pope answered: "I would like to ordain him; but I hesitate to place my hand on his head because of the greatness of the spiritual grace which the Almighty Lord has bestowed on him so abundantly." These words much dismayed St Ailbe, and he didn't wish to accept the Order, since he was gentle and humble of heart. The holy pope spoke again, saying: "Let what you wish be done; but this cannot be performed until the festival of the apostles Peter and Paul, for God's angels have spoken to me and so instructed me; and on that day, after his ordination, we will see the angels of God blessing him." Indeed this prophecy of the holy pope's was fulfilled. For, on the feast day of the apostles Peter and Paul, God's angels, in full view of the blessed pope and of the whole people of the apostolic see, blessed Ailbe. After this benediction, all who saw it gave glory to God and joined with the angels in blessing St Ailbe.

[He produces a miraculous feast to celebrate his consecration]

Afterwards St Ailbe spoke to the apostolic bishop, asking: "Where will this crowd find food?" Knowing well that the blessed Ailbe had food and drink supplied without stint in his cell, the pope answered him: "On the day of your ordination it is fitting that you should provide for all." Ailbe said: "That is not difficult for my Lord Jesus Christ, and, with His help, I will feed you."

Thereupon the whole populace followed his apostolic holiness to the hospice. Almighty God then caused five showers to fall for St Ailbe into his store-room—a shower of honey, a shower of oil, a shower of fish, a shower of the whitest bread, and a marvellous shower of wine. And from these the people of Rome, along with the holy pope, were abundantly supplied for three days and three nights, praising and blessing the Lord and honouring His servant, St Ailbe. So that was the ordination feast of St Ailbe. St Ailbe lived for a long time among the Romans, and they loved him greatly.

[He miraculously supplies water in a dry land]

After this, St Ailbe was sent from the apostolic see to the heathen, to be an apostle and preach the Gospel of Christ to them, and through him a numerous heathen people came to believe in the Lord and was baptized. That people lacked water. Then the blessed Ailbe took pity on them, since they had no water and they had made their resulting misery plain to him. He went up a nearby mountain until he found a huge rock, which he struck four times with his staff. Straightaway, four streams flowed from the rock, and replenished the province, in four divisions of land. Afterwards, when they saw so great a miracle wrought by the man through whom they had come to believe in God, they gave thanks to God and were strengthened in the Catholic faith. St Ailbe built a monastery in that region, in which he left the holy sons of Goll.[4] Further, he blessed the whole region, and then he departed from them.

[He miraculously repairs St Samson's chalice]

Afterwards St Ailbe arrived at the city called Dolo Moir [*Dol, in Brittany*], at the furthest limits of Letha [*Armorica, or Brittany*], where he and his people stayed in a hospice. And when the bishop of that city —Samson by name—had begun to offer the Body of Christ at a public Mass, it happened that his chalice and his oil-flask were broken at the same time. The bishop was greatly dismayed at this, and a cry began to rise up from all the people in the church. At this point St Ailbe entered the church, and asked the cause of their uproar. Once he understood the cause of their clamor, he took the fragments of the chalice and oil-flask and blessed them. They were reconstituted, so that not a broken fragment of them remained. And all who saw this glorified the Lord—through His servant Ailbe.

[He restores his slanderers to life]

In the same region a most evil man and woman sinned against holy Ailbe, disparaging him in public without cause. For this they were punished by execution. Ailbe, however, hearing that they had been put to death, was greatly grieved. He went to them, prayed for them to God, and brought them back to life in the presence of all, although it was for the sake of his honour that they had been condemned to death. All then glorified God at seeing so great a wonder.

[He prophesies about St David]

At this time St Ailbe came upon a priest in a certain church, who was standing before the altar intending to offer the Sacrifice but was unable to do so, because his tongue was rigid. At this, Ailbe looked about at the congregation in the church, and noticed among them a pregnant woman. Then the spirit of prophecy filled St Ailbe, and he said to the priest: "This is why you are unable to speak: God wished that first you would hear the news of the infant whom that woman carries in her womb. He will indeed be a chosen one of God, a renowned bishop, and he will be called David. And the sign of this for you will be as follows: once the congregation here present has heard these words, you will chant in a clear voice." And so it was: once the people had heard the prophecy, the priest sang the Mass; and the whole congregation, with one voice, blessed the saintly Ailbe, who, through the grace of God, had revealed this hidden matter. Later, that boy was born. His father gave him to Ailbe, to foster him in God. He is David, the holy bishop, whose relics rest in the city of Cell Muni [*St Davids, in Wales*], which is in Britain.

[He returns to Ireland and brings a stream from a rock]

After this, St Ailbe, befriended by God, returned to his homeland, Ireland, like a most wise bee laden with honey. When he reached the sea, he blessed it, and he and the whole of his people crossed the sea in a wretched vessel, in the most perfect calm and without any mishap. They made port in the north of Ireland. And there, on St Ailbe's order, one of his family, Colmán by name, built a church which is called Cell Ruaid [*Kilroot, Co. Antrim*]. Since, however, the place had no water, holy Ailbe blessed a certain rock in the name of Almighty God, and immediately a little stream of water began to flow from it. At which Colmán said to Ailbe: "There's very little water in it." Ailbe replied: "However little it is, it will never dry up, and that little stream will flow forever—until the end of this world." From which the brook is called Buanann Chelle Ruaid; that is, "the permanent stream of Kilroot".

[He raises the three sons of King Fintán from the dead]

Afterwards, in those days, the king of that region—which is called Dál Aride[5]— who was of the same kin as St Ailbe,[6] was making war against the Connachta when he was defeated in a great rout, and his three sons were killed. He came with their bodies to Ailbe, saying: "See how I, miserable man that I am, come to you, God's saint, hoping for your help; for I have heard that you work great wonders." That king was named Fintán, and he was a pagan. Ailbe said to him: "If you will believe and accept baptism, I will ask for divine help for you and for your sons." At that, the king accepted the faith and was baptized. Truly then St Ailbe went to where the sons were and prayed for them to the Lord Jesus Christ. And they were returned alive from the dead to their father, and all of them were confirmed in the faith of Christ. Thereupon Ailbe blessed them and said to them: "Because you have believed in Christ, you will overcome your enemies." At that, following the words of St Ailbe, the king went to war with the Connachta and had his revenge on them. He took hostages and returned home in great triumph, rejoicing.

[He acknowledges the primacy of Patrick]

St Ailbe indeed made a circuit of the whole of Ireland, preaching baptism; and he converted many there, but not all; for Almighty God willed that the blessed bishop Patrick, who came to Ireland later than Ailbe, should convert all the Irish to the faith. And so it came to pass. For Bishop Patrick converted all Ireland from heathenism to the faith and brought all to baptism. When blessed Ailbe heard that Patrick had converted to Christ the king of Munster, Óengus mac Nad Froích, and that he was with him in the royal city of Cashel, he came to greet them. The king and Patrick were joyful indeed at Ailbe's arrival, and he rejoiced to see them. Since he was very humble, he gladly accepted Patrick as his master. Then King Óengus and Patrick decreed that the archiepiscopal primacy of Munster should be forever with the city and see of St Ailbe.

[He identifies the adulterous father of a child]

One day a certain woman who had secretly given birth as the result of adultery was brought before Patrick to confess who the child's father was; but she refused to tell. Then blessed Patrick said to St Ailbe: "An angel told me that this question can be answered through you." St Ailbe replied: "I will obey your angel's word." And he went on: "Let all the men who live in the same homestead with her be brought to me." And all but one came. St Ailbe said to them: "There is one man in the field, who didn't come with you." It was true: he was a charioteer. And all the people marvelled at such soothsaying. When he came, the infant boy was brought to St Ailbe, and he baptized him. He said to him: "Go now to your father and show him to us." Straightaway the little baby stood up and went to the charioteer, saying to the people: "This is my father." And that man then confessed that his child had told the truth. Then all the people glorified God for this revelation.

[He takes precedence over Bishop Ibar]

One day, when Ailbe and Bishop Ibar were travelling across the plain of Femin [*the plain of south-eastern Co. Tipperary, between Cashel and Slievenamon*], coming to Cashel to converse with Bishop Patrick and King Óengus there, St Ailbe said to Ibar: "You go ahead of us, father, and receive greetings from the people as the master." Ibar replied to him: "So be it—if that is what is better." At which an angel spoke to St Ibar, saying: "The precedence is not yours, but Ailbe's." St Ibar had hardly gone one pace ahead when he lost the sight of his eyes. Then he said to Ailbe: "Bless my eyes and I will see the light." And, holy Ailbe, blessing his eyes, said: "May God, Who is One in Three, heal you and restore the light of your eyes." Immediately his eyes opened and he saw the light. And after that, with St Ailbe leading, they arrived in Cashel.

[He obtains the grant of Aran from King Óengus for St Enda]

Now, when St Ailbe was leaving Cashel, he met the abbot Enda, who said to him: "Come back with me to Cashel and ask the king on my behalf to give me that island which is known as Aran, so that I may build a monastery there in the name of the Lord." So St Ailbe returned to the king and greeted him, saying: "Give us that island which is situated in the ocean sea, so that we may build a monastery there." The king replied: "I have neither seen nor heard of any such island; therefore I won't give it to you, until first I know what and where it is." At this, the divine power enabled the king to see, across a vast extent of land, the whole of that island; and he could see what and how large it was. The king therefore granted the island of Aran; and—under St Ailbe—St Enda built a remarkable monastery there; and the island is known by one name; that is, Aran. And that island is great: it is an island of saints— since no one, except God alone, can tell how many saints are buried there.

[He visits St Brigid]

St Ailbe went out to visit St Brigid, who was in the plain of Liffe [*north Co. Kildare*] and he stayed for some days with her, leaving aside the divine mysteries while they had daily converse about Godly matters. One day, while St Ailbe and St Brigid were so engaged in a certain place, a glass vessel full of wine fell from heaven between them—but closer to St Ailbe. Ailbe accepted it and gave it to St Brigid. Then they both gave thanks to God. And then, with St Brigid's permission, the blessed Ailbe came to Munster.

[He restores to life the son of Mac Dara]

However, when St Ailbe approached the river Barrow, which is in the land of Leinster, a good man named Mac Dara came to him, weeping and lamenting, and said: "Man of God, have pity on my misery! Look: just now my only son has been drowned in that river; and because of that my heart is in torment. I pray you, therefore, in the name of Jesus Christ, in Whom we believe, to intercede for him; and my hope is that God, through you, will restore him." When the holy man heard him, and saw his sorrow, his bowels were moved to pity, and he said to him: "I will pray for you because of your faith; and God will do what He sees to be best for you." Then St Ailbe went down on his knees and prayed earnestly to God, and, through God's help, that man rose live and well from the dead before all. From this, that place is called to the present day Áth Dara—that is, the Ford of Dara, where he had been drowned [*somewhere near Leighlinbridge, in Co. Carlow*].

[He miraculously returns a stolen bronze vessel to St Sinchell]

At that time, when St Ailbe was in the place called Cluain Damdaim [*Clonduff, in Co. Kildare*], there came to him the holy man, Sinchell, asking St Ailbe to acquire a dwelling place for him. At this, St Ailbe said to his eminent follower Cianán: "God has sent St Sinchell to us. Let us give him our church and all that we have here; and God will supply us with another in its place." Thereupon Cianán gave St Sinchell the whole church together with everything that was in it. Afterwards St Ailbe came there, and he directed his disciples to take nothing with them from that church. However, one boy, heedless of St Ailbe's orders, secretly carried off a small bronze dish. When they had reached a certain place, St Ailbe asked that boy: "Why did you commit theft among us?" The boy remained silent and the blessed Ailbe said to him: "Give me the dish you stole from among holy Sinchell's vessels." At this, prostrating himself at the saint's feet, the boy placed the dish before him. St Ailbe took the dish in his hands and then placed it on the ground again. He was very downcast, because it was such a long way from where he was to where the dish had been stolen. Almighty God saw that St Ailbe's mental distress arose from the fervor of his love, and he caused that vessel to fly away across a great tract of country, all the way to its proper place. All those who saw this miracle gave thanks to God. They feared St Ailbe indeed, and they loved Christ.

[An angel guides him to Emly]

After this an angel of the Lord came to St Ailbe and said: "Come, follow me, and I will show you the place of your resurrection." When they arrived at the place where the tomb of the most holy Ailbe now is, the angel of the Lord said to him: "Here you will be buried; and in this place there will be a very great city in your honour; and here, through you, God will work many miracles, both after your death and in your lifetime." And so saying, he vanished from his sight. St Ailbe fasted there for three days, and at the end of the fast he said to St Cianán: "Go to the right and bring me whatever you find there." When he did so he found a meal sent by the

Lord, consisting of the whitest of bread and a dish of roast fish; accepting this, they gave thanks to God. Afterwards the angel came to St Ailbe and led him to the place where there now stands the high cross that is called "the Cross of the Angels"—because angels conversed there so often with St Ailbe—and said to him: "Remain here, and build God a church; for there will be a great city here in your name, which will be known as Imbliuch Iubair" [*Emly, Co. Tipperary*]. And what the angel said came to pass.

[He works a miracle of glamour on a robber]

One time, when St Ailbe was travelling in Uí Cairbre [*Uí Cairbre Aedhbha—the territory around Bruree and Kilmallock, Co. Limerick, extending to the Shannon*] and Uí Conaill [*Uí Conaill Gabhra—in south-western Co. Limerick*] he visited some nuns, who received him happily and offered him their church, that is Achad Cáerech [*not known*]. Now, these religious virgins had fostered a boy named Cummíne son of Eochaid. His manner of life was contrary to God and to the holy virgins. For, once he approached manhood, he had left the nuns and had become a great bandit and a member of a war-band. The holy nuns therefore asked St Ailbe to preach the Word of God to him and see if he could convert him from the error of his ways. Ailbe preached the Divine Word to him, and he answered: "Allow me to go my own way today; and tomorrow I will behave as you have told me to." He was given leave accordingly, and he went on an expedition that day with his comrades. It seemed to him that, out in the country, they had come upon enemies of theirs. They cut off the heads of their enemies—as they thought—and brought them away with them. But on their return they discovered that they were carrying blocks of wood—which they had thought to be heads—and similarly, tree-trunks had appeared to them to be bodies. That man said: "I know now that, through holy Ailbe, God caused logs to approach us as men walking; therefore I will do as Ailbe tells me." And he threw himself at Ailbe's feet and granted his land to him. And afterwards he became respectable.

[He and St Mac Creiche produce a miraculous spring]

Another time St Ailbe visited a certain hermit called Mac Chire [*Mac Creiche*],[7] who said to him: "In this neighbourhood we have no water." At that, Ailbe and the hermit went outside and, when they prayed, a clear spring of water flowed from the ground; and it continues to flow to the present day. After that, giving thanks to God, the two saints went in again.

[He restores a dead scribe to life to complete his work]

The most holy virgin Scietha daughter of Mechar sent a message to St Ailbe asking him to send her a scribe to copy the Four Gospels. He did so, and the scribe wrote two of the Gospels; but then he fell ill and died. Hearing that he was ill, the blessed pontiff Ailbe hastened to him, but found him dead. St Ailbe and St Scietha prayed for him, and St Ailbe said to him: "Now rise, brother. God has granted your soul to us so that you may write the two Gospels which you have not copied. But it is decreed that immediately after that you will die." At this word the man rose. Then he copied those two Gospels; whereupon he died. Ailbe's disciples, however, removed his body and buried it in Ailbe's monastery, which is in the city of Imbliuch.

[A man who tries to kill Ailbe's oxen is struck down]

A holy man named Modán, whose monastery is Tuam Dindach [*not known*], asked St Ailbe for two plough-oxen. Ailbe sent him two very beautiful beasts—white, with red ears. The oxen, indeed, went straight—with no one driving them—of their own accord to Modán. So, every year, without a drover, they came to Modán in the ploughing season. But it happened one day that a certain man decided to kill them. However, as soon as he lifted his arm, his spear shattered in his hand, and a fragment flying from it pierced his eye. After that he did penance and gave his land to Ailbe. The oxen, meantime, went safely on their way from him.

[He saves a captive from execution by the king of Connacht]

Again, when St Ailbe was travelling in Connacht at that time, the king of that region decided to kill a captive whom he had in chains. At this, Ailbe sent one of his followers to the king, asking that the king release the captive into his custody. But the king spurned St Ailbe's emissary and ordered that the captive be executed. But it proved to be quite impossible to carry out the order and put that man to death; while, at the same time, the king's son died. Ailbe was immediately summoned to the presence of the king, who gave him the man, and land as well, on which churches of God might be built; and he asked that his son might be restored to life. The saint prayed for the son, who was instantly revived. And many in that place believed in Christ through St Ailbe and were baptized.

[Ailbe's prayer provides fish in a Connacht river]

In the same country of Connacht there was a river barren of fish. The local people requested St Ailbe to bless the river in the name of the living God. Holy Ailbe blessed the river in the name of the Father Almighty, and showed them five places along the stream in which they might catch fish. And that very day the river was filled with an abundance of fish. The people were confirmed—by St Ailbe—in the Catholic faith, and they built five churches in honour of St Ailbe.

[The servant Gobbán is restored to life to fulfil Ailbe's promise]

At that time St Ailbe sent two holy men, Lugid and Sailchin, to Rome to plead a case, and with them a good servant, Gobbán, who is the patron of the monastery known as Cenn Sali [*Kinsale, Co. Cork*]. They said to St Ailbe: "May our request be granted by you: that is, that we may return safe and sound to Ireland." This St Ailbe promised in Christ's name—that they would so return. It so happened, however, that on their voyage their servant Gobbán died. Then St Lugid said: "We will not eat any food until Ailbe's promise in Christ's name is fulfilled for us." After they had fasted for three days and three nights, the servant Gobbán came back to life, and told them much about St Ailbe, saying: "God returned my soul to its body because of St Ailbe's promise." Afterwards, safe and sound, they returned from Rome to Ireland.

[His breath after fasting intoxicates King Scanlán]

Another time St Ailbe went out into Osraige [*Ossory—a territory in south-west Leinster to which the present diocese more or less corresponds*], and he rested there alone for three days and nights. On the fourth day, the chief of that territory came to him. When he greeted him, the perfect odour from St Ailbe's mouth so inebriated the king that somnolence overcame him and he slept for three days and nights. Then, when he was awake again, St Ailbe said to him: "Up to now you have never fasted for three days: that is how this affected you." The king promised to lead a pious life—as he did. It was he, Scanlán, who granted that place—Imbliuch—to holy Ailbe.

[A miracle worked by nuns causes envy among his disciples]

When Ailbe was travelling in that same region there were nuns in his company, including Brige and Berach. It happened on the way that a nun among them fell ill. She implored them for milk to drink. No milk was to be had there, but they saw a doe coming out of the forest. Brige called the doe and she came, tamely and submissively. Brige said to one of the nuns: "Go and milk the doe: her milk will cure our sister." As soon as she drank the doe's milk, the virgin rose from her sick-bed. At this, St Ailbe's disciples murmured against the virgins—because of the miracle. But an angel of the Lord came to Ailbe and said to him: "You must not be jealous of the virgins, as your disciples are. If you willed it, that mountain over there would move immediately from one place to another; and no miracle under heaven is impossible for you." And he went on: "Christ, the Son of God, promised this to His servants: and you are a proven servant of God." Having said this, the angel withdrew. The nuns, and the others who were with holy Ailbe, gave thanks to God.

[His charity protects his servant from burning by live coals]

One day, when it was extremely cold, guests arrived. St Ailbe, hearing that they were very cold, in mercy told his servant, who was before him: "Quickly carry burning coals to the guests, so that we may show them pity in Christ's Name." At his master's word, the dutiful disciple, who had no utensil immediately available, took up the coals in his bare hands and gathered them to his breast. Divine Grace was so extended to him that, not only were his hands and his clothes not burnt, but the fire did not touch even the end of a thread of his garment.

[King Óengus prevents him from making a retreat in Thule]

St Ailbe, when he saw how honoured he was among all people, and how many churches were under his jurisdiction, decided to flee from company and sail to the island of Thule [*perhaps Iceland*], situated in the Ocean, and to live there alone with God. But at the prompting of God, Óengus, king of Cashel, forbade this; and the same king ordered his guards to watch all the maritime ports, so that St Ailbe might not desert those whom he had made his children through preaching and baptism.

[He advises Nessán on the receipt of gifts]

One time the eminent and most holy deacon Nessán[8] came to St Ailbe to question him on certain matters [whether it was proper to receive gifts from people]. It was St Ailbe's custom to remain in solitude from the ninth hour until the third hour of the following day, devoting himself to prayers to God; and no one dared to approach him then except the steward of the guesthouse. When the blessed Ailbe was told by this servant that Nessán had arrived, he said to him: "Go to Nessán and recite this verse in the Irish language to him, and tomorrow I will speak with him." And the steward came and recited:

> Dánae Dée nis frithchoirthi,
> Selba forru niscorthi;
> Attoberthar na gabae,
> Secht nit muide nud chéle.

> [*Do not reject God's gifts;*
> *Do not refuse to possess them;*
> *You may take what is offered*
> *—But it makes you no greater than another.*]

The following day St Ailbe and St Nessán discussed God's mysteries, and he answered Nessan's questions. After some days, Nessán, with permission, returned to his place.

[He disperses a troublesome flock of cranes]

Another time, numerous cranes congregated in the one great flock, and did great harm to people by eating much grass and corn. Then the people of that place appealed vociferously to Ailbe, saying: "Help us, for these cranes have devastated our country and there is nothing we can do to prevent them." Then Ailbe, on hearing of this outlandish business, sent his servant, named Buairnén, to take the cranes into custody. He went out and drove the cranes before him like sheep, holding them in open imprisonment. On the following day, St Ailbe went out and greeted the cranes, saying to them: "Leave these parts, and disperse your great multitude, and go to different places." They obeyed him right away, and divided themselves into flights going this way and that, just as St Ailbe had commanded them.

[He saves a she-wolf and her cubs from hunters]

One time the people of his region—that is, Araid [*north-eastern Co. Limerick*]—went hunting with their chief, to drive wolves from their territory. One she-wolf, however, pursued by horsemen, made her way straight to the place where Ailbe was, and placed her head in his bosom. Ailbe truly said to her: "Do not be afraid. For not only will I save you, but your cubs also will go safe." And so it came to pass. And Ailbe said: "As an infant I was fostered by your people, and you did well to come to me in my old age. For, each day you will take bread with me at my table, and no one will harm you." So the wolves came daily to St Ailbe, and ate with him, returning afterwards to their own places. And no one harmed them, and they harmed nobody.

[The tide does not inundate his seat]

When St Ailbe was in the part of his region which is called Corcumruad [*north Co. Clare*] he had a seat by the sea, in which he prayed to God and discovered God's wonders. The flowing tide each day circled Ailbe's seat and surged high above him, but never dared to enter the place in which St Ailbe sat.

[He is visited by an Otherworld ship]

Another time, when St Ailbe sat in the same region on the seashore, they saw a spectral ship, with a veil about it, coming towards them from the sea, and heard from it the voices of a choir of singers; but then the ship stopped and stayed far from them on the sea. Thereupon St Ailbe sent one of his disciples out to greet them; but he received no reply. In the same fashion, one after one, they all sailed out to the ship, and not one of them could get a response. Finally, the blessed Ailbe, walking in his sandals over the sea, went out to them; and the veil was drawn aside for him. He boarded the ship, and straightaway it put out to sea. Indeed Ailbe's disciples lamented greatly on seeing this, until an angel of the Lord said to them: "Don't be dismayed. The servant of God, your patron Ailbe, will return to you." When the brothers had waited barely three hours, they saw the ship returning towards them. Ailbe immediately disembarked, carrying in his hand a fruiting vine; and for three years that vine was held in honour by Ailbe. After that the Lord's angel took the vine from St Ailbe and said: "Ailbe, soldier of Christ, go to your city of Imbliuch, for the time of your departure from this world has come, and it is there that you will be buried, as the Lord foretold to you."

[His death in Emly]

Then the blessed Ailbe came to the city of Imbliuch, and immediately he fell ill. However, while St Ailbe was happy, truly all the Irish grieved. Then God's angels appeared before the whole clergy and announced that holy Ailbe had carried out all of God's commands by day and night. And the same holy Ailbe, having baptized many peoples, and converted many tribes to the Christian faith and built many churches in the Lord's Name; having chastened himself in nightly vigils and three-day fasts and assiduous prayers, departed, among choirs of angels sweetly singing canticles, to the Lord Jesus Christ, to Whom is honour and glory for ever and ever. Amen.

Emly:
"St Ailbe's Stone"

THIRTY-SIX

The Life of St Declan of Ardmore

[His origins and ancestry]

The most blessed bishop Declan was descended from the noblest Irish kin. During a very long period of time his ancestors vigorously held the kingship of all Ireland in the city of Temoria [*Tara*]—as in due course his genealogy will make plain to you, dearest brothers. For Eochu Fedlach, from whom we trace his lineage, was a very powerful king, who extended his realm from Tara over all Ireland. He had three sons, Bres, Nar and Lothar (known as "the three Finns of Emain" [*i.e., of Navan Fort, near Armagh*]). Numerous kings of this line reigned over Ireland from Tara for many years, both before and after the coming of the Faith. The three sons of Eochu—Bres, Nar and Lothar—slept with one of their sisters—Clothra by name—but no one of them knew that either of the others had done so. Nor did she tell them; but afterwards it was revealed. She conceived of them and gave birth to a beautiful son in whom the three conceptions were assorted in order. That boy had three rosy rings about his body, dividing it in a manifestation of the triple conception. He is hence called Lugaid Reoderg, because he had those three ruddy bands about him. He was handsome in appearance and manly in his strength, and from his infancy great things were expected of him. He began his reign in the year in which Gaius Caesar was killed, he ruled for twenty-six years in Tara, and in the year in which Peter and Paul were put to death by Nero he was killed by the Leinstermen. He had a son named Crimthann, who reigned for just ten years and then died. Crimthann had a son named Feradach Finn Fechtnach, who reigned in Tara for thirty years. Feradach was the father of Fiachu Findfholadh, who ruled for thirteen years and was killed at Tara. Fiachu Find begot a son who was called Tuathal Techtmar (because he was a powerful ruler of different regions), who reigned for twenty-three

years at Tara and was killed by the Ulstermen. Tuathal Techtmar begot
Fedelmid Rechtaid, who passed important laws during his reign and ruled for
nine years. He had three sons: Conn Cétchathach, Eochaid Finn and
Fiacha Suigde. Conn ruled for twenty years; but his fame will endure until
the end of the world for the fertility, peace and goodness of his reign. He
was killed by Tibraide Tíreach, chief of the Ulstermen, in Magh Cobha
[*western Co. Down*]. His descendants reigned for centuries at Tara. Eochaid
Finn, the second son of Fedelmid, proceeded to the province of Leinster,
where his descendants continue to live in various places, among them many
chieftains and men of power who were numbered among the Leinstermen. Fiacha Suigde held the very region around Tara but died without
achieving the kingship of Ireland. He had three illustrious sons, named Ross,
Óengus and Eógan, who were warriors and were outstanding in battle.
Óengus especially was a hero irresistible in his fury and strength.

[Cormac mac Airt's wounding by Óengus son of Fiacha]

When Cormac son of Art, son of the Conn already mentioned, was reigning
at Tara and wanted to make peace with a certain powerful nobleman, who
was an enemy of the king, the man would have none of it unless the king
would give him the same Óengus, with his brothers, as a bodyguard. At
first Cormac was not willing; then he changed his mind. And, when the
king agreed that Óengus should be his defender, that man came and made
peace with him. But some days later, Cellach, King Cormac's son, seized
the man without his father's permission, and put out his eyes. Hearing
this, Óengus was filled with fury, and instantly made all speed to Tara
where Cellach was with his father the king; and no one had the strength
to prevent him. But at the sight of a numerous armed force approaching
Tara, led by the mighty Óengus, the king ordered that the rampart gates
be closed, saying: "Truly, Óengus comes at the head of his brothers to
take vengeance on us for the betrayal of his guarantee." The hearts of all
who heard the king's words shrivelled with fear, since they knew and
dreaded the ferocity of that man. And, when Óengus saw the rampart gates
closed against him, his rage, his daring and his agility were such that he
sprang through the air to land on the highest part of the fort, and leaped
from rampart to rampart until he was in the centre of Tara with his
weapons. He entered the palace, where the king was, demanding the king's
son Cellach so that he might kill him without delay. The king's son, however,
while everyone fled this way and that, stood before his father the king,
determined to defend him and himself. And the governor of Tara, a brave
man, also determined on is own account to defend the king. He came and
placed himself between the king and his son. But Óengus thought nothing
of their opposition. He cast his poisoned spear at them so that it struck

the breast of Cellach, the king's son, and went through him and through the governor's chest to pierce the eye of Cormac the king. The king's son and the governor were felled instantly by the spear. Not only did it kill them; its force carried it to penetrate the king's head. So, with one cast Óengus killed Cellach the king's son and the governor of Tara and pierced King Cormac's eye. When he wished to go on to finish off the king, Cormac appealed to him in the name of their gods and of their kinship to spare him. For they were heathens, whose beliefs led them to be worshippers of gods—or rather, idols. And when Óengus saw the king's son dead, along with the proud governor, his rage began to calm; and, for the sake of kinship he spared the king and departed from Tara in great triumph.

[The expulsion of the Dési]

Afterwards, Cormac, king of Ireland (who ruled for forty-two years), grieving greatly at the death of his son and his governor and at the loss of his own eye, assembled an army of no mean size and expelled Óengus with his brothers from their territory—the district of Tara which is known as "the Dési" [*Upper and Lower Deece, Co. Meath*]—and, not satisfied with that, he drove them from all of the northern half of Ireland. He feared them greatly, since they had as much right to the kingdom as he had. And on their side, for some time they fought bravely and fiercely for their status, engaging in seven wars in which Óengus and his brothers did great slaughter; but in the end they were vanquished and many of them were killed. Afterwards, unable to resist the large armies summoned by the king from various parts of Ireland, they abandoned their homeland—that is, the region of Mide— and came to the province of Leinster; and a year later they arrived in Munster. But the Osraige, whose territory is in the western part of Leinster, near Munster, attacked them on their passage. They came to the king of Munster, Ailill Aulomn, who had as wife a most beautiful and glorious queen— who by nature was of the greatest goodness—Sadb, daughter of their uncle, Conn Cétchathach.

[The conquests of the Dési in Munster]

The king treated them most honourably and granted to them that they might win part of the enemy territory and have part of Munster too, by waging war from within Munster against the Connachta or the Leinstermen, or against their own homeland of Mide. They refused, however, to accept any territory from him except what they would win with their own swords. And they chose to go to war against the Osraige, to avenge the injury done to them. They fought four battles for the extensive and excellent land on the borders of Munster and Leinster, round about the river Súir—two against Leinster (that is, against the Osraige) and two against the Munstermen—in which Óengus was preeminent and irresistible. They drove the Osraige from the middle of the plain of Femin [*south-eastern Co. Tipperary*] to the bank of the Linnán [*a stream flowing into the Suir near Carrick*], which is subsequently the boundary of Munster and Leinster in that area, dividing the land of the Dési [*territory in Co. Waterford and around the Suir valley*] from that of the Osraige. And, from the middle of that plain of Femin, they drove the inhabitants of the region once called Tír na Féned, subsequently Fir Maige [*the area around Fermoy, in eastern Co. Cork*], as far as the little plain in which lies the city of Brí Gobban [*Brigown, near Mitchelstown, Co. Cork*]. And they expelled the inhabitants of the region of Uí Liatháin [*south central Co. Cork*] after a fierce battle, and drove them from the river once called Nem, later however known as Abha Mhór [*the Munster Blackwater*] as far as the place known as Cell Cobthaigh [*not known*], which is now on the border of the Dési and Uí Liatháin. So, after those four great battles, they had obtained a territory fertile in land and water, extending north to south from the river Luasc [*probably the Munster river, on the Kilkenny–Tipperary border north-west of Callan*] to the sea, and west of Miledach [*the river estuary from the confluence of the Nore and the Barrow to the confluence of the Suir and the Barrow: otherwise "Comar na dtrí nUisce"*], which subsequently separates Munster and Leinster—that is, the Dési from Fir Gáilián. And the three brothers, Ross, Eógan and Óengus, in great amity, divided that territory between themselves—plains, mountains and woods. The territory bears their names to the present day. The chiefs of the Dési down the ages, the descendants of those who were first called "Dési" in the neighbourhood of Tara, have been of the seed of Eógan son of Fiacha son of Fedelmid Rechtaid. His son was Cairbre Rigruad, the powerful leader of the Dési, who begot Conra Cathbuadach (called "Cathbuadach" [*"battle-victor"*] because of his triumphs in war). Conra was father to Cuana Cambretach [*"Cuana of crooked judgment"*], who was unfair in his judgments; his son was Mess Fore. He begot Moscegrai, father of Moss Corp, who begot Ard Corp, whose son was the second Eógan, father of Brian, father of Niath, father of Lugaid, father of Trén, father of Erc, who was St Declan's father. Such are the rulers of the Dési, from the time they came from Tara down to the birth of St Declan.

[The birth of St Declan]

Erc, chief of the Dési, St Declan's father, was invited to the house of a relation of his named Dobranus, and came with many of his people, including his wife, whose name was Dethidin (which means "solicitude"). She, as it happened, was pregnant with Declan, and her time was now at hand. And she gave birth instantly and without pain, through the sanctity of the child in her womb. Just as she had decided to stand up, she gave birth to a beautiful infant, who fell out before her and struck his head on a large rock. And it was immediately made manifest that the miraculous grace of God was with St Declan even from his mother's womb. As the prophet wrote: "And before thou camest forth out of the womb I sanctified thee, and I ordained thee a prophet unto the nations."[1] For the most blessed Declan, as you will learn, came to the heathen as a prophet inspired by God, to convert the people of many localities from paganism to Christ. When he fell, the very tender crown of his head, as has been said, struck that hardest of rocks; and a hollow indentation, shaped like his crown, was made in the stone, while his head was not harmed in the least. Those who were present saw the miracle and marvelled greatly at the boy. This happened when Ireland was given over to heathenism; and in that time there was hardly a single Christian who could be found there who was secure from persecution. The rock on which St Declan was born, which is now out of doors in the enclosure, is called today "Declan's Stone"; and when rainwater filled the depression made by St Declan's head, it is a powerful cure for pains and diseases, through the operation of Divine grace.

[A miraculous light from heaven greets his birth]

On the same night on which the most blessed Declan was born, another major miracle occurred in that place. A ball of fire was seen by many of the people living in the neighbourhood, rising from the roof-ridge of the house in which St Declan was born, up to heaven. And angels were seen ascending and descending about that fireball, singing sweet psalms and climbing a ladder just like that which the holy patriarch Jacob saw in his dream. Seeing and hearing this, the people were overjoyed at the mystery which they did not understand then. For the heathen at that time did not know that from the very moment of his birth, Almighty God was working miracles for His servant, His future saint, who had just then been born on this earth.

[St Colmán baptizes him as an infant and foretells his greatness]

When people were told this story in the presence of a certain Christian, named Colmán, who was a holy and pious priest and later was to be a most eminent bishop, he came full of a great joy, and of the spirit of prophecy, to the place in which the holy infant Declan had been born. And he preached to the boy's parents the faith of Christ, Who had extended His grace to the child before their eyes; he prophesied the glory and honour which their son would have before God and men; and he foretold the future course of his life in this world. Inspired by God, the parents gave their son to him that he might baptize him. Thereupon St Colmán baptized the most holy infant Declan, giving him his name. And after the baptism, he announced in prophecy to the boy in the presence of all: "You, truly my son—rather my master—will be exalted and honoured in heaven and earth by God and men; the fame of your holiness, your love and your goodness will fill all four quarters of Ireland; and you will bring the peoples of the Dési from diabolical error to the way of Christ. And I will claim brotherhood with you right away, and I now commit myself to your holiness." Having said and done so much, the blessed Colmán returned to his own place, recommending that the holy child should be fostered with care and should in his seventh year be sent to school in order that he might be instructed as a Christian. And great happiness showed in the face of the child in the presence of the blessed man who had baptized him, so that all the people present felt that he was rejoicing in his inward spirit.

[He is fostered for seven years by Dobrán]

Hearing and seeing all this, Dobrán—the relation of the chief, Erc, St Declan's father, who has already been mentioned—pressed St Declan's parents hard to give him the child in fosterage, since St Declan had been born in his household. And St Declan was given to him to foster. That place in which St Declan was born was formerly called Ráith Dobráin, but subsequently is known as Ráith Decláin [*not known*]. The same Dobrán, St Declan's foster-father, gave that place to St Declan, and moved his own fort to another place. There, much later, when he was bishop, St Declan built a church of God. It is in the southern part of the land of the Dési, in the east of the plain which is called in Irish Mag Scéith, that is "the plain of the shield" [*south of the Blackwater*]; and the famous city of St Carthach, known as Liss Mór [*Lismore, Co. Waterford*] is not far from it. So for seven years St Declan was fostered with great care by the same Dobrán, whom he knew as a father and whom he greatly loved. In those years of the holy boy Declan's childhood, God worked great miracles through him. And in the same years, marvellously inspired by the grace of Christ, the holy boy avoided all forbidden heathen rituals as if he were a pious and instructed Christian.

[He is taught by St Dimma]

When he was seven years old St Declan was given by his parents and foster-parents—as the blessed Colmán had laid down—to St Dimma, a religious and wise man, tested in the faith of Christ, who was to teach him his letters. This man, having become a faithful Christian, had recently returned to Ireland where he was born and had built a church in that region. Declan, the holy boy, was sent to him as a pupil. And another boy, named Cairbre son of Colum, who was later a saint and a venerable bishop, was given at the same time to the blessed Dimma to learn his letters. And the pair of them devoted themselves to learning from him.

[Seven men of Mag Scéith are inspired to give him church sites]

Among others, seven men who lived in Mag Scéith witnessed the heavenly ball of fire, already mentioned, which appeared on the night of the birth of St Declan; but they were singled out from the others by God, Who instilled in them a spirit of prophesy. The seven came to St Declan and took him as their lord and master, foretelling publicly that he would be a bishop and prophesying, saying: "The day will come, dear boy, servant of the Great God, when we will give both ourselves, and land for churches, to you." Indeed they became believers in God and were made most holy men; and they built seven famous churches of God within Mag Scéith.

[He studies in Rome and is made bishop by the pope]

The most blessed Declan studied for a long time with the aforementioned St Dimma, imbibing many a draught of varied Scriptural teaching, by which he was made shrewd and wise and eloquent. Many people then, observing the nobility of St Declan, and seeing and hearing his sanctity, piety and charity in all matters, came to him and voluntarily submitted themselves to his rule. Then, he was inspired to go to Rome, where he might learn the ways of the Church, graduate in learning, obtain from the Roman see a licence to preach, and be accepted and placed under the rule according to the Roman system. So, taking into his entourage certain chosen disciples, he sailed, and travelled to Rome, where he stayed for a long time. In those days, St Ailbe had been in Rome for many years as a disciple of the holy bishop Hilary, at whose prompting and request Ailbe had been consecrated bishop by the blessed pope. He was overjoyed at the arrival of St Declan when he came to Rome with his disciples, and he made known Declan's nobility and sanctity to the Roman people. And, once they had understood his goodness, the most blessed Declan received only great honour and goodwill from the people and clergy of Rome. For St Declan was beautiful in appearance, noble in his bearing, humble in manner, sweet in discourse, sound in counsel, cheerful in love, liberal in giving, holy in habit, prodigal in miracles. After a long time, at the urging of many, St Declan was ordained bishop by the lord pope. Afterwards he was given books and rules and sent to his homeland, Ireland, to preach there. The holy bishop Declan received the permission and the blessing of the apostolic bishop and of the people of the church of Rome and set out on this journey to Ireland. Many followed him, intending to live under his rule on their pilgrimage. Among them there came the son of the king of Rome, Lunanus by name, whom St Declan greatly loved. On the way, in Italy, St Declan and St Patrick (who was later sent by Pope Celestine to preach to the Irish, and who is the archbishop of all Ireland) met each other. Greeting each other in peace they entered into mutual brotherhood.

With that kiss of peace, St Declan came to Ireland; St Patrick meantime travelled on to Rome.

[A bell is sent to him from heaven]

In a church on his way, the pontiff Declan was offering the Sacrifice when God sent him down from heaven a small black bell, which came to him through the window of the building and rested before him on the altar. St Declan received this joyfully and gave thanks to Christ; and through this gift his resolution was strengthened against the barbarous ferocity of the heathens. And he gave it to Lunanus, son of the king of the Romans, already mentioned, that he might carry it and be its custodian. The Irish called this bell "Duibín Decláin" ["*the Small Black of Declan*"], giving it that name because of its colour and because it belonged to Declan. Down to the present day many signs of God's grace have been worked through it by the sanctity of him who possessed it, and it remains in honour in the city of St Declan [*Ardmore, Co. Waterford*].

[He makes a miraculous crossing of the English Channel]

Afterwards, the holy pontiff Declan with his disciples was prevented from crossing the Sea of Icht, which divides Gaul from Britain, because the shipmen asked too high a fare of him. Seeing this, the holy man took in his hand the bell already described, and struck it, calling for help on Christ Almighty. And immediately, by Divine instigation, they saw an empty ship, without any humans on board and without sails, coming towards them from wave to wave. And St Declan said to his followers: "In the name of Christ, let us board that ship; and He Who sent it to us will cause it to carry us safely on a calm passage of the sea." At the saint's word, they boarded, and by God's direction it put out to sea again and took them swiftly across the ocean swell. And speedily and calmly it arrived in a part of the nation of Britain. When the holy bishop Declan disembarked at the harbour with his followers, the ship returned to the place from which it had come. Understanding that they had witnessed a great miracle, the saints glorified Christ the Son of God among themselves: so was fulfilled the saying of David: "God is wonderful in His saints."[2]

[The four saints who preceded Patrick]

Afterwards, St Declan, who possessed the discretion of the serpent and the modesty of the dove, reached Ireland and began to sow the seed of life there. Indeed on his homecoming he was full of the sweet marrow of the Scriptures, like a wise bee laden with an offering of honey. There were four most saintly bishops who were in Ireland with their disciples before Patrick, preaching there and converting many to Christ. They were Ailbe, Declan,

Ibar and Ciarán. And these drew many to Christ with the net of the Gospels, but nevertheless it was St Patrick who converted most (and the most important) of the people of Ireland to the faith; and in time he held the supreme archbishop's see of Ireland. St Ailbe, St Declan and St Ibar joined themselves and their successors together in brotherhood even to the end of the world in heaven and on earth, each pledging love to the others. But St Declan and St Ailbe in particular drew together in such brotherly love that they would have wished to be joined forever, but that they were persuaded by their disciples of the need to part. So St Declan came to his own people—the Dési—and began to preach faith in the Holy Trinity to them, and to baptize them in the name of the Father, the Son and the Holy Spirit, and to turn them away from the devil to the One God Almighty. And he founded many churches of God, establishing some of his disciples in them to serve Christ and to direct the heathen from the worship of the devil to the Gospel of Christ.

[The seven saints of Mag Scéith visit him]

Finally, St Declan visited the place in which he had been born. He stayed there forty days and founded there a church for men of religious observance. Then he was visited by the seven saints—already mentioned—who had remained in Mag Scéith [*south of the Blackwater, near Lismore, Co. Waterford*], who had prophesied about him when he was a boy and had given themselves and their followers and their churches to him. These are the names of the seven saints: Mochellóc, Riadain, Colmán, Lachlán, Móbí, Findlug and Camín. Afterwards they lived a most religious life under St Declan's direction, and God worked many signs through them.

[Patrick, not Declan, baptizes the king of Munster]

The most blessed father Declan wished to preach to Óengus son of Nad Froích, the king of Munster, who reigned in the city of Cashel, and he travelled to that city. Now, St Declan had two uterine brothers—that is sons of his mother but not of his father—who were children of the same Óengus, king of Cashel. They were called Colmán and Eochu. Colmán, inspired by Divine grace, came of his own accord to the holy bishop Ailbe, and was baptized, and received from him a cleric's robe; he stayed with him, studying diligently, and became a holy and wonder-working man. Eochu however remained a layman, hoping to be king after his father. The same Eochu now asked his father the king to show respect to his brother Declan. The king did so, and did not prohibit Declan from preaching; he was satisfied with both the religion and the teaching of the saint, but in the end he accepted neither faith nor baptism from him. Some say that the reason the king didn't wish to be baptized by St Declan was that St Declan was of the blood of the Dési, a people which was always at enmity with the king's people, the Eóganacht, by whom Munster was ruled. He was not willing to have a patron from that people—not because of his unbelief, as is to be seen in what follows. For the same king, hearing that the archbishop Patrick was on his way to him—who was born of the British nation, a people against whom the king had neither grievance nor enmity—not only believed through him, but went joyfully out of his city to meet him on his way, and, professing his belief without delay, was baptized by him. St Declan, however, having spread the word of salvation there, returned to his own nation, who believed through him, and baptized it—except for the chief and some of his retinue, who daily promised to believe and to accept baptism, but were inspired by the devil from day to day to put it off.

[St Declan's three visits to Rome]

The people say that St Declan went to Rome many times, but we have found accounts of no more than three visits in the ancient writings. On his return from one of these he came to the holy bishop of the Britons, named David, who was in his city Cell Muni [*St Davids, in Wales*]— which is by the shore of the sea that separates Ireland and Britain—and was received there with honour. At the invitation of St David, St Declan stayed there for forty days, and celebrated the Mass every day. In the name of Christ the two pontiffs, Declan and David, confirmed brotherhood forever between them and theirs. And after forty days he received the blessing and the leave of the most holy bishop David, his brother, with the kiss of peace; he boarded ship and commenced his voyage to Ireland.

As was the custom of the community, St Declan's bell (of which it has already been told that it had come down from God in heaven to him through the window onto the altar) had subsequently been in the custody of that Lunanus to whom he had entrusted it from the beginning. But that day Lunanus gave the bell to a member of the community—the son of Testa—to bring to Declan on the ship. However, the son of Testa was occupied with another matter, and when he came to the shore he left the bell down on rock, thinking he would remember later to take it to the ship; but he forgot it, until the ship, its canvas swelling with wind, was already sailing in the middle of the sea. When St Declan heard that the bell, dear to him, which had been given to him by God, had so been mislaid on the shore, he was sore at heart, as well all his companions. So the man of God looked up to heaven and prayed silently to Christ. Shortly after he had completed his prayer, he said to his sorrowing disciples: "Brothers, lay aside your sorrow; God Who gave us that bell can bring it miraculously to us in our ship." Oh how beautifully the created thing then obeyed the creator, contrary to the deepest qualities with which He had endowed it in the creation! For the rock, which in full truth was made of the hardest and heaviest stone, at the divine command entered the sea and lightly floated, guided with the greatest speed, most directly after the ship, carrying his bell. And after a short space of time, the men of God who were on board marvelled at the wonder being performed at Divine instigation before their eyes; and they were filled both with the love of Christ and with respect for their own master. Then the holy bishop Declan, filled with the spirit of prophecy, said to them: "Steer the ship on a course directly behind that stone. And wherever it comes ashore; my city will be there—and my bishop's see will remain there. From there I shall travel to Christ, and it is from its earth that my resurrection will come." The stone, indeed, went before the ship swiftly until it was a long way ahead; however, it did not move in such a way that the ship was unable to follow it. The rock directed its course to Ireland and floated to the southern coast half way between one inlet and another.[3] And the ship was steered in its wake as the holy man had ordered. And when that stone reached a certain sea-girt island in the southern part of the territory of the Dési, it came to harbour on its shore. So, at the same time, as St Declan had instructed, the ship arrived. The holy man came ashore and thanked God that he had reached the place of his resurrection. On this island there was a conspicuous hill, which gave the place its name—Ard na gCáerach—which means, in Latin, the height of the sheep. For the sheep of the chief of that region were pastured on the island; and it was their custom to sow the land after it had been grazed. One of St Declan's followers, seeing from the hill that the island was close girt by the sea, said to him: "How could this small hill sustain your people?" St Declan replied: "My son, this hill will in no way be called small, but rather 'the great height'." And so the Irish ever after called Declan's city, which was founded on that spot, "Ard Mór", which means "the great height" [*Ardmore, Co. Waterford*].

[He miraculously links Ardmore to the land]

After this the holy pontiff Declan went to the chief of the Dési to ask him for that island. The chief granted it to him straight away. On his return, the holy bishop Declan arrived at Ráith Breasail [*not known; not the Ráith Breasail south of Cashel but somewhere close to Ardmore*] where there were ships to take him to the island. But his intention of settling on the island greatly displeased the local people, and they hid their boats to thwart the saint and prevent him from going to the island. Then St Declan's disciples said to him: "Father, as we see it, there will often be a need, while you are alive, to sail backwards and forwards across the sound; but after you have gone to heaven, the passage must be made many more times. Therefore we beseech you, in words that come from the heart, to abandon this island, or to pray to the Father through His oneness with the Holy Spirit (since the Son of the same God has said: 'Whatsoever ye shall ask of the Father in my name, he will give it to you')[4] that this strait may be moved from its present position into the ocean and that its position should be occupied by dry land before your city. For the place can't be settled easily or well because of this strait. Certainly it is not possible to have a city there, and hardly even a church." The holy man replied, saying: "How can I abandon the place of which God has foretold to me that I will die and be buried in it? What you tell me about the difficulty of settling there is already known to me as well as to you—and even better known to God. I am not prepared to pray for the removal of the sound if that is contrary to the will of God. But let me go so far, at your urging, as to offer a prayer to the Lord; and what pleases God, my Creator, He will do of His own accord." And when the man of God rose from his prayer, his followers said to him: "Father, take your staff, and, following the example of Moses, strike the water with the rod, and afterwards, as you have said, let God do as He wills." And the disciples prayed to God with their master; they were indeed holy and proven men. When the staff was given into his hand, the holy pontiff Declan touched the water with it in the name of the Father, the Son and the Holy Spirit, blessing it with the sign of the holy cross of Christ. And immediately, at the most high Divine instigation, the water began to recede from that place into the ocean in the presence of God's saint, like a torrent from a mountain glen. The monsters of the deep could barely swim fast enough to keep up with the rushing water, while many fish were left thrashing about in the mud of the shore which was deprived of their accustomed water. The servant of Christ, the holy pontiff Declan, holding his staff in his hand, followed the retreating waters, and his disciples followed him. There was a great uproar from the sea-monsters and from the sea. However, when the holy pontiff reached the point which now marks the end of the land and the beginning of the ocean, a pious boy who followed in St Declan's footsteps, by the name of Manchín, was in fear of the marine animals who were fleeing with the water of the sound and were crawling about on the strand displaying their gaping jaws horrendously. He said to Declan: "Oh, holy father, you have driven the sea far enough from its bed: we are threatened by the sea monsters!" And at his words the sea stopped immediately and withdrew no further. When the holy pontiff Declan saw this he was displeased, and he struck the boy lightly on the nose and said: "It was not I who drove back the sea, but my God Who did so by His great power; and if you had not said what you just said He would have driven it back much farther." Three drops of blood fell from the boy's nose to the ground in three different places. Seeing this, the saint blessed the boy's face and the bleeding stopped at once. Under the feet of the man of God three little springs of clear fresh water appeared in the three places where the boy's blood had spilled. They are there to the present day, and, as a sign of that miracle, they sometimes appear in the form of fountains of blood. The area from which the water of the sound was expelled is a mile wide and of considerable length, and is fruitful land good for grass and crops, which supports the city of the holy father Declan all round the former island. So, as in the Psalmist's words, dry land without water appeared from the expulsion of the sea.[5]

And that staff which in St Declan's hand drove back the strait is known in Irish to the present day as "Fertach Decláin" ["*Declan's Wonderworker*"], that is, "Declan's miraculous staff"—because at all times many miracles are worked through that staff by the sanctity of the most blessed Declan. We will describe one of those miracles to you in another place below.

[He founds Ardmore and many other monasteries]

The holy pontiff Declan and his followers rejoiced at the elimination of the strait of the sea—which made his name known in the various regions of Ireland. Then he began the construction of a great monastery on the west bank of a stream which had flowed from the centre of the island to the vanished sound, but now flowed directly to the sea. And in the same place a famous city rose, along the stream, in St Declan's honour. In the Irish language it is called Ard Mór (it has already been explained what this name means in Latin). Many communities, drawn from various regions of Ireland by the fame of the sanctity of the most blessed pontiff Declan, came to him and offered themselves to Christ, body and soul, under the yoke of St Declan's rule. And the holy father Declan built many monasteries and churches throughout the whole territory of the Dési; not only there, for he also founded churches of God in other parts of Ireland. So, many thousands, of both sexes, lived a life of great joy in those many places under the care and the rule of their holy patron Declan. Some of his disciples he consecrated as bishops and established them in some of these churches, already mentioned, to further the Christian cause. The holy pontiff Declan's piety, gentleness and equal dealing, person to person, were apparent to all; so that his disciples preferred to be with him under his guidance than to live as their own masters in other churches.

[St Patrick arrives and meets the pre-Patrician saints]

In the meantime, the most glorious archbishop Patrick was sent by Pope Celestine and came to Ireland; and God submitted the hearts of most of the people of Ireland to his teaching. And, as we have already told, the king of Munster, Óengus son of Nad Fróich, came to meet him and, with great ceremony, conducted the holy archpontiff Patrick to his city of Cashel, where St Patrick baptized and blessed him and his kin and his city. When the most blessed bishop Patrick heard that up to now the chief of the territory of the

Dési was still pagan, and had put off accepting the faith from St Declan, he came to preach God's word to him. The four bishops, already mentioned, who were in Ireland before Patrick (sent, like him, from Rome), that is, Ailbe, Declan, Ciarán and Ibar, were not of one mind with Patrick, but differed—although in the end they all made their peace with him. For Ciarán gave all deference, friendship and obedience to St Patrick, both in his presence and in his absence. Ailbe, however, when he saw that most of the people of Ireland were following Patrick, came to St Patrick in the city of Cashel and there, in the presence of King Óengus, accepted his primacy with all humility —although that is not what he formerly had in mind. For those bishops had previously acknowledged the same Ailbe as their master and primate; therefore he came before them to St Patrick, so that they would not deny Patrick's primacy on his behalf. Indeed Ibar would in no way come to terms with St Patrick, nor was he willing to defer to him; for he held that Ireland should not have a foreigner as its patron. Now, Patrick was of British birth; but he was captured in his youth and fostered in Ireland. And, at the beginning, Ibar and Patrick quarrelled greatly; but later, when an angel persuaded them, they made peace, harmony and brotherhood between them. Declan, however, did not wish to oppose St Patrick— because he had previously entered into brotherhood with him in Italy—not indeed that he thought himself to be his inferior, since he himself had the apostolic dignity—but he had so been directed by the angel, to go to Patrick and do his will.

[He saves the Dési from Patrick's curse]

For God's angel came to St Declan and said to him: "Go quickly now without any delay to St Patrick and prevent him from cursing your people and your country. For tonight he is fasting in the place called Inneoin [*Mullaghnoney, Co. Tipperary*] against the chief of your tribe; and if he curses your people they will be cursed forever." Then St Declan, following the angel's instruction, made all speed to this place Inneoin, which is in the middle of Mag Femin in the north of the country of the Dési, trav- elling all night over Sliab Cua [*Slieve Gua—the Knockmealdown mountains in Co. Waterford*] and across the river Suir, and by morning he reached St Patrick. Now, when St Patrick saw St Declan arriving, he was overjoyed, because he had heard that Declan didn't wish to come to him. And when St Declan reached Patrick, he was received with honour by St Patrick and his people, and St Declan bowed down before Patrick and asked him to curse neither people nor the country of the Dési; and he promised to do his will. St Patrick answered him: "Since you agitate for them, I will, on the contrary, bless them." Then St Declan went to the chief of the Dési, who was nearby with his army, and who had refused to accept the faith from him and had dealt evilly with St Patrick. He asked the chief, beseeching him, to come to St Patrick to accept the faith and baptism from him; but in no way and by no persuasion would he submit to God's saints. And he said angrily that the brothers and relations of St Declan would not cause him to yield, since there were very few of them with him. This chief, who persisted in his unbelief, was called Ledbán. When St Declan saw that this man was remaining in his allegiance with the devil, he feared that because of him St Patrick might curse his people. He turned to the other Dési and said: "Abandon this evildoer, so that you may not be cursed for your unbelief, you whom I have blessed with the holy water of baptism; and follow me, so that St Patrick, who was sent to us by God and whom we have chosen as archbishop of all Ireland, may bless you along with me. For, because of who my father was, I have just as much right as Ledbán to be your chief." At these words, all the rest of the Dési (except their unbelieving chief along with some of his own household) followed St Declan, who said to the blessed Patrick: "Look, the Dési people abandon their unbelieving ruler and take me as their chief. They come, father, to submit to you, ready to honour and glorify you; they have already received baptism from us; they now ask your blessing." Patrick at this, with his holy followers, duly blessed the people of Dési— and not only the people, but also the woods, land and water of their country. The princes and nobles of the Desi asked the holy bishops: "Now who will be our chief?" St Declan replied to them, saying: "I am just now your chief; and St Patrick will bless him whom I appoint and will bless us all; and that man will be your chief." Then St Declan chose a young man named Fergal son of Cormac, of the royal blood of the Dési— that is, of St Declan's kin—and he led him among them to be their chief. All were pleased. Then that young man was blessed by God's saints and was inaugurated chief of all. That same chief, Fergal son of Cormac, was very acceptable to the holy bishops. After his blessing, St Patrick said: "This young man is handsome in appearance and brave in battle, and his kingdom will prosper. And so it will be with the chiefs of the Dési through time." (This prophecy about the Dési chiefs continues to be fulfilled.) Then St Declan, Fergal the chief, and the people of Dési gave much land, there in Mag Femin [*south-eastern Co. Tipperary*], to St Patrick—from which his successors have had great service—and a place near the river Suir in the same plain, where there is a large clear-water spring, known as "St Patrick's Well", which St Patrick greatly loved. After acquiring these grants, St Patrick returned to the city of Cashel, to King Óengus, and St Declan left with him.

[St Patrick heals St Declan's wounded foot]

Now we wish to narrate to your worthiness a certain miracle performed at the gathering described above. As St Declan was hurrying there from his people to St Patrick, he carelessly passed a place where there lay an iron implement which gashed his foot so badly that he bled copiously and began to hobble along. When the holy bishops saw this they were greatly dismayed; that is, Ailbe, St Declan's beloved friend and companion, and Seachnall [*Secundinus*], St Patrick's disciple, a most wise and saintly man, of whom it is said that he was the first bishop to be buried in the soil of Ireland. They informed St Patrick, and when he learned of it, Patrick was dismayed too, just like them, and said: "Lord, heal the foot of Your faithful servant, who has put the talents You have given him to great service on Your behalf." Then St Patrick examined St Declan's foot, blessed it with the sacred Sign, gazed on heaven and prayed. At once the flow of blood ceased and the edges of the wound drew together and were sealed with skin; and a scar appeared. St Declan rose, sound and well, without hurt in his leg. The saints gave thanks to Christ, and the crowd raised a cheer in praise of God and of His servants.

[St Declan is declared bishop and patron of the Dési]

While St Patrick, St Ailbe and St Declan, with many of their followers, stayed in the city of Cashel in the presence of King Óengus, they laid down many good rules of Christianity. It was there that King Óengus and St Patrick, together with the whole populace, decreed that the archiepiscopate of Munster should be in the city and see of St Ailbe [*i.e., in Emly, Co. Tipperary*], who was then consecrated archbishop by them forever. And for St Declan they decreed that those whom he had converted from heathendom—that is, the Dési—should belong to his episcopal diocese, which is large and eminent, and that the Dési should serve their patron, St Declan, just as the Irish in other parts served St Patrick. Then St Patrick, archpontiff and patron of all Ireland, recited the following verse in the Irish language to define the status of the bishops. (Neither the community of St Ailbe nor that of St Declan wished to translate this stanza into Latin for themselves, but they preferred to write it in Irish to preserve its integrity. Nevertheless we shall give some indication of its meaning for the benefit of those ignorant of Irish.) This is how the verse goes in Irish:

"Ailbe humal Pátric Muman, mo gach ráth;
Declán Pátric na nDési, na Dési ag Declán go bráth."

[*Ailbe the humble is the Patrick of Munster, the greatest surety;
Declan is the Patrick of the Dési; the Dési are Declan's till Doom.*]

In this it is decreed that Ailbe should be a second Patrick and patron of Munster, while Declan should be second to Patrick and patron of the Dési and that the Dési should form his diocese to the end of time. Afterwards the holy bishops saluted and blessed King Óengus, exchanged among themselves the kiss of peace, and with joyful hearts returned to their divine task of spreading the faith.

[He establishes Christian rules among the Dési]

Then the holy pontiff Declan met with the young man Fergal, chief of the Dési, along with the muster of the Dési, in the place already mentioned, Inneoin [*Mullaghnoney, Co. Tipperary*] and they established Christian laws in his kingdom. The deposed chief, Ledbán, who had denied the name of Christ, was expelled by all and went into oblivion—as the Scripture says of God's enemies: "Their memory perished with their name."[6] Then St Declan and the chief, Fergal, and the magnates of the Dési laid it down that the chiefs of the Dési should be inaugurated in that place, Inneoin, in which the saints had appointed Fergal. And it is reported from ancient times that formerly the chiefs of that people were acclaimed in the same place.

[He revives hostages who had died of the plague]

At this time there was a severe pestilence in Munster, which was worse in the city of Cashel than elsewhere. It first turned people yellow; then it killed them.[7] Now, King Óengus had seven noble hostages under guard in a certain fort situated on the western side of the city of Cashel in a place called Ráith na nIrlann, that is, "the rath of the lances" [*not known*]. One night all seven of the hostages died of the pestilence. When the king heard of their deaths, he was most perturbed, for they were sons of powerful chiefs at the extremes of his kingdom who might, he feared, now bring serious trouble to his territory. So he ordered the deaths of the hostages to be concealed. The very next day St Declan arrived in the city of Cashel, for he wished to talk with the king. When King Óengus heard that he had arrived, he was much pleased, and summoned him immediately to his presence. In the presence of his friends he said to Declan: "We beseech you, holy bishop, servant of the living God, that in the name of Christ (in Whom we believed as the result of your preaching) you bring back from the dead our seven hostages who died last night from this mortal plague. We fear that great evil may come to our kingdom from their parents, who are saying that their sons were brought to death through our fault; and this greatly shames us." The holy pontiff Declan answered: "O dear king, it is not for our human infirmity to bring back flesh from the dead; for such a task is fitting only for the power of God. But since you have appealed to us in the name of Christ, we will go to view their corpses, and we will pray to the Lord on their behalf; and what seems good to Him to do, that will be done." Then the holy pontiff, together with some suitable disciples of his, was brought by the king's servants to where the wax-like bodies of the dead lay. And the king followed in the footsteps of the bishop, who viewed the corpses before him. Entering the chamber in which the dead lay, the man of God sprinkled them with holy water, prayed briefly, and said, before those who were present: "My Lord Jesus Christ, only-begotten of the living God, for the glory of Your name resuscitate these dead men, so that these new Christians, through our ministration, may be strengthened in their faith in You." After that, the holy pontiff knew in his soul that their life had been granted to him by God, and said to them, even as they fluttered their eyelids: "In the name of Jesus Christ, the Saviour of all, rise up to us, praise God and give Him thanks." At his words, they rose at once from the dead and greeted all who were present. And the holy pontiff Declan handed them over alive and well, in the presence of the people, to the king, Óengus son of Nad Froích. The witness of so great a miracle led all to glorify the name of Christ, and the sanctity of His servant Declan was proclaimed through all the towns and districts of Ireland. Then King Óengus joyfully granted that fort—Ráith na nIrlann—with its attached land in the city, to St Declan forever.

[He banishes the plague]

Afterwards the people of the city of Cashel begged St Declan that he should bless the city to banish the plague, and appeal to Christ on behalf of the many people who were suffering from the pestilence. The holy man, since he saw their faith, prayed to God on their behalf and blessed the air in all four quarters with the Sign of the Cross. Then was made manifest what the Lord told His disciples as He ascended into heaven: "They shall lay hands on the sick, and they shall recover."[8] At that moment, after the most holy Declan had made the Sign with his hands, those who were stricken by the pestilence, not merely in the city, but wherever the plague was in the whole province, were relieved of the disease and returned sound and well to their people. The infection of the plague was then banished completely from the whole region; and everyone marvelled even more at this than at the raising of the dead. Seeing and hearing this, the king, firstly on his own behalf and secondly on behalf of all the kings of Cashel forever, granted a great tribute to St Declan and his successors; and he handed over to him in the presence of many witnesses from among the nobility of Munster the freedom of his city and his diocese. Afterwards, the glorious pontiff Declan blessed King Óengus with his city and his people, and returned to his own region.

[He detects dogflesh served as mutton]

Once St Declan was a guest in the southern part of Mag Femin [*south-eastern Co. Tipperary*] in the house of a certain pagan. This man, who was rich, was named Dercán. He wished to fool the Christians; so he ordered his serfs to kill a dog secretly, to bury its head and paws in the ground, to cook its flesh well, and afterwards to offer it to St Declan's disciples to eat. And, since it was a plump dog, he ordered that they were to entice the disciples to enjoy the meat, passing it off as mutton. And when this dish was brought to the table with breads and other food, St Declan, who had been dozing on the side, was wakened so that he might bless the meal. He looked silently at the table. When his disciples said: "Father, bless our food," he said

Ardmore: "St Declan's House", reputed burial place of St Declan

to them: "Truly I see the devil's doing in this meat." When he questioned the servants, asking them what the meat was and how it had come to be killed, they answered him: "Our master ordered us to kill a fat hogget for you; and so we did." Then the holy bishop Declan said in the presence of all: "My faithful Lord Christ, show me why I see the devil's business on our table, and do not let Your servants eat what is forbidden." Then, guided by God, the holy man saw the claw of a dog among the morsels of meat. Unknowingly, the servants had cooked one of the four paws of the dog, thinking all had been buried. St Declan said: "This is not a sheep's hoof but a dog's claw." When the servants saw it they hurried to tell their master, Dercán. He, when he heard how it had come about, immediately came to St Declan. He accepted the faith and he offered himself and his posterity and his farm to St Declan in perpetuity. He was baptized with his people and was overjoyed. He asked St Declan to bless something on his land, which would ever after be called by his name. So, there and then, St Declan blessed a rock there, which from then to the present day has been known as "Dercán's

Rock." And St Declan told him: "If the chief of the Dési or a kinsman is going to war with enemies, or to take revenge on other people for an injury done, let them go round this stone: they will return unbeaten and they will have victory over their enemies." And so it has always come to pass. But certain miscreants among that kin refuse, from pride, to circle the stone, and so fail to achieve victory. That homestead was then called "Tech Dercáin" [*Dercan's house*]; later "Con Inga" [*"hound's claw" is intended: a folk etymology*] from that canine claw. Holy men arrived here—Conán, Mochoba, Ultán son of Erc, and the son of Lasrén—all at the same time, and came to Declan, submitting themselves to God and to the government and rule of St Declan. He founded a monastery in that farmstead of Dercán—Con Inga—and established those holy men, with others, in that place; but later he arranged for St Ultán to be with him.

[He returns to the land of his forebears]

Afterwards St Declan returned to the region of Brega [*largely Co. Meath*], to the first home of his forefathers. He received great honour from the king of Tara and from the magnates of Brega (for Tara is in that territory). From there he then traced out the origins of his people. And they esteemed St Declan because of the ancient blood relationship. On land given to him there he built a monastery of canons, which bears his name. And there he left with his community a famous Gospel book which he had with him. That Gospel book was kept in the place and held in great honour: miracles are performed by its means. Afterwards he blessed the place and returned to Munster.

[People in Osraige suffer for their ill-treatment of him]

On his way through the country of the Osraige he turned aside to spend the night resting in a certain fort. But the people there not only refused him hospitality; they drove him away contemptuously and by force of arms. The saint, however, prayed with his people to the Lord, and there came to them what is told in Holy Scripture: "Vengeance is mine; I will repay . . . "9 The inhabitants of that place, to the number of sixty, all died on that one night, with the exception of two men and the women who had been opposed to the treatment of the man of God by the others. These men and women came humbly the following day to St Declan and told him of the wretched deaths—of which he already knew. And by the way of penance they gave him their place with their land, and other gifts. And when the dead had been buried, St Declan founded a famous monastery there, which is called Cell Coluim Deirg [*not known*]. He placed there one of his disciples, a holy, pious and wise man who came from the eastern part of Leinster—from Dál

Messincorb—who was called Colum the Red, after whom the monastery is named. St Declan blessed that place and afterwards returned to the land of the Dési.

[Ráith Breasail is destroyed]

Another time, the holy pontiff with his people arrived late in the day at a place already mentioned, Ráith Breasail [*not known; near Ardmore*] but the inhabitants of that place would not allow the holy man into their fort. The same people had previously refused the use of their ships, to prevent St Declan from crossing over to his island—for they hated God's saint for no reason. But at that time Almighty God, in the words of the Psalmist, "turned the sea into dry land"[10] because of the sanctity of His servant who prayed to Him, and in recompense for the patience of Declan. You have heard of this long since. He spent the night in an empty shed by the wayside, in which he could not obtain even a spark of fire from them. Then they received their just retribution from God. To them who would not out of pity give fire to the servants of God, fire came from God about dawn, and all were burnt within their fort—which is empty and deserted down to the present day, under a curse, as it is written: "Thou hast destroyed their cities."

[He yokes a stag to his chariot]

One day when the holy pontiff Declan was making a journey again in Sliab gCua in the territory of the Dési [*the Knockmealdown mountains*] one of his chariot horses went lame and was unable to continue. At that point St Declan noticed a herd of deer on a mountain some distance away. He ordered one of his serving people to use a halter and bring him a strong stag from the herd and yoke it in place of the horse. The man went at once about the business, never doubting to find the deer tame, just as the man of God had said. And the herd received him most submissively, while he chose a very strong stag from among them. And all day long that stag powerfully and deftly drew the chariot of the man of God, until they reached Mag Femin. When they reached the guest house St Declan ordered the stag to return to its own kind. At the words of the man of God, the stag turned in the presence of all and made its way back. That man who had brought the stag from the mountain to St Declan was called Dormanach. Declan blessed him and granted him the village of Mag Gabra [*not known*] in the northern part of the Dési country beside the land of the Eóganacht. His descendants live there to the present day honourably serving St Declan.

[A man called Dualach cures a broken leg at his bidding]

Another time, when St Declan was walking in the midst of a large crowd, as was his custom, one of the brothers fell on the path so that his leg was broken in two. When St Declan saw the dreadful accident he gave orders that someone among them should bandage his leg so that he would not bleed to death. At that, a man from the crowd, named Dualach, came up to him boldly and jokingly and said: "In the name of Christ and of our patron Declan, I will be the leg's doctor." He said this in mockery. Nevertheless he carefully bandaged the leg, blessing it in the name of God and of St Declan. Immediately the brother began to recover, by degrees, and after a short time the wound closed and the brother was healed and felt no pain. When he directed that the bandage be unbound, a scar was to be seen on the leg: the broken bones were united again by flesh and skin. All present gave thanks along with him to God and St Declan, and Declan said to the man, Dualach, who had bound the brother's leg: "You promised in the name of Christ and in my name to be doctor to his leg; and Christ, when you duly bandaged the brother, healed him by His power. Therefore, from this time onward you will be a true doctor, and your descendants even to the end of time will be worthy and respected doctors. And if they make the sacred Sign over any sick person, in the name of God and in my name, and if they have no evil desire for excessive payment, and no ill will, then the grace of God will help that patient through their medicine." All his descendants are as the holy bishop said, except that their clerics and their women are not skilled in the art of medicine. They honourably serve the successors of St Declan through their medical knowledge.

[He baptizes St Ciarán son of Eochu]

Once when the holy bishop Declan was journeying in the western part of Mag Femin, by the river Suir [*that is, somewhere near Caher, Co. Tipperary*], he met people who were carrying a small infant to a certain priest, to be baptized. On seeing the group the holy bishop was filled with the spirit of prophecy, and said to them: "Wait here! For it is I who will baptize that holy child." The people were astonished that the bishop should so speak of the baby, for they hadn't shown him the infant, nor had they told anyone the purpose of their journey. They pointed out to him that in that place they could find neither a water vessel nor salt for the baptism. St Declan said to them: "We have a vessel which is both wide and long—that is, the river. Salt, however will be wonderfully given to us through the miracle of Christ. For that infant will be holy and wonderful in the sight of God and men, and through him many miracles will be worked by God." (They came from distant farms on the bank of the river Suir in a place called Erend [*not known*].) The holy pontiff Declan took mud in the palm of his hand and spat in it. He prayed mentally and made the Sign of the Cross. And instantly, before their eyes, there was dry white salt in the hand of the servant of God. While both groups of Christians, marvelling, gave thanks and blessing to their bishop, the holy prelate Declan baptized the infant on the spot, and gave him the name Ciarán. After the baptism the holy bishop said to them: "Foster this spiritual son of mine diligently, and at the appropriate time give him to Catholic men to be taught. He will be a notable pillar of Christ's Church." That infant is the most holy Ciarán son of Eochu, who migrated to heaven after a venerable old age, after working many miracles in Christ's name and after founding many holy churches of God. And he lies in his renowned monastery, which is called Tibrada (which means "wells") and is in St Declan's diocese, in the western part of the country of the Dési, in the country of the people known as Uí Fathid, between the prominent mountains Cua and Crot [*Tubbrid, Co. Tipperary, south of Caher*].

[A woman steals from St Declan and is swallowed up by the earth]

The bondswomen of a certain steward came, in the course of her servile business, to St Declan's monastery; but shortly she stole from the city a large hide,[11] part of the holy pontiff's rents, wrongly intending to give it to others. But—in the presence of wayfarers—the earth swallowed her up, avenging by divine intervention the wrong that she had done earlier, and continued to do, to the holy bishop's good monastery. But, even as the earth devoured her, it flung the hide up from her arms, and this instantly appeared to all who were present in the form of a stone. The holy bishop in his monastery saw all this with his spiritual vision, and he told the story to his brothers. The people, in great fear, carried to him the stone into which the flying hide had turned, and they told everyone what they had seen. The name of St Declan was greatly magnified by all, and they were afraid of him both in his presence and in his absence. That stone remains always in St Declan's graveyard in his city of Ard Mór, in a high place, as a monument to the great miracle by which the hide turned to stone.

[He makes a barren woman fertile]

A certain rich man named Fintán was without offspring, because his wife was barren. And, since she had almost reached old age, he came with her to St Declan, and asked him to pray to God on their behalf, that they might have issue. They promised in return to give alms and do works of piety. Further, they said they were certain they would have offspring if St Declan appealed to God for them. Thereupon the saint blessed them, saying: "Do what you promise; by God's gift you will have issue." They went home with their people, rejoicing in the blessing and promise of the holy bishop. That night when Fintán slept with his wife, she conceived. She gave birth to two sons, named Áed and Fiachna. They bound themselves, with their posterity, in tribute to St Declan until the end of the world.

[When St Ailbe is about to die he goes to meet Declan]

The blessed Ailbe, archbishop of Munster, when he knew his death was near, said to his people: "Before I die, brothers, I wish to visit and see my dearest comrade and fellow-servant of Christ, Declan the bishop." Then he set out to go to St Declan. And an angel of the Lord came to St Declan, to tell him that his holy friend, the aged Ailbe, was on his way to him. When he learned this from God's angel, the saintly pontiff Declan instructed his people to make ready for the reception of holy guests. And he set out from his city to intercept St Ailbe, travelling as far as a place called Druim Luchtri [*not known; probably near Lismore, Co. Waterford*]. When St Ailbe arrived there, he was received with honour by St Declan and his people. St Ailbe stayed with St Declan for fourteen days in which they rejoiced in fullness of love, in devotion to the divine mysteries, enjoying sacred bliss and spiritual exultation. At the end of those days the aged St Ailbe returned to his city, named Imbliuch [*Emly, Co. Tipperary*], which is situated on the plain of Munster. St Declan, accompanied by no small company, came with St Ailbe as far as the place already mentioned, Druim Luchtri, where St Ailbe told him to return now to his own city. Since the aged saints Ailbe and Declan knew that they would not see each other again in this world after that, they shed copious tears, from their great love for each other. And they renewed the old perpetual brother-hood between them and theirs; their pious prayers were answered by Christ. Afterwards, St Ailbe blessed the city, the people and the clerics of St Declan, and received in return similar benedictions from him. Then, exchanging the kiss of peace, the most holy pontiffs Ailbe and Declan, with their disciples, separated and returned from there to their own churches, in holy sorrow but in true delight at the nearness of God.

[His staff saves the chief's fort from fire]

Once, the fort of the Chief of the Dési—who was named Cainnech—caught fire and began to burn fiercely. At this, the aged and most holy Declan, went towards the fort and was so dismayed at the sight of the conflagration that he took in his hand his wonder-working staff (which we have mentioned in connection with the miraculous driving back of the sea) and threw it from where he was to the fort. As if on divine wings, the staff soared through the air, and fell into the middle of the fort at the edge of the flames. And far from continuing to burn for hours, the fire did not last for a moment; but it was totally extinguished instantly, leaving half the fort destroyed. Now, there were many miles between the place from which St Declan cast his staff and the location of the fort, and in between there was a high wood called "the grove of Curt" [*not known*]. When he saw this, the chief, Cainnech, wondering, like all others, at this miracle of miracles, gave thanks to God of his own accord and so satisfied St Declan's intention. That fort is not far from the river Suir, on the southern side, in a place called "Firm Ridge" [*Druim Buan?: not known*]. However, the place from which the holy pontiff flung his staff is beside a ford of that river opposite the monastery of the most holy virgins—daughters of the same chief, Cainnech—which is called "the Plain of the Lake" [*Mag Locha, near Ardfinnan, Co. Tipperary, south of Caher*]. A stone cairn, with a cross, was made in that place to mark the miracle, which is called "Ullath Decláin", that is, "Declan's cairn".

[He has Ultán sink a hostile fleet with a "left-handed blessing"]

Once a fleet came in from the sea towards St Declan's monastery, intending to plunder the church, and carry off both people and property. The seafarers were heathens. Everyone ran to the aged bishop Declan, begging him to pray to Christ for help against the pagans. Declan, however, was aware of the favourable quality, the goodness, and the saintly love of his most holy disciple Ultán (already mentioned) and, praying to God, he bade him make the Sign over the fleet, against the pagans. At his most saintly master's word, the holy brother Ultán, holding back his right hand, made the Sign with his left hand against the fleet. And at once the sea swallowed up the ships as if they were bags of lead. Further, indeed, the drowned sailors, re-emerging, were turned into great rocks, which are in the inlet of the sea not far from the shore, and always are seen above the surface. All the Christians, seeing this, were filled with joy and faith in the Trinity. And they glorified God's saint, their preacher and bishop, whom they had seen work this and many other miracles. There was a pious dispute between the holy bishop Declan and his blessed pupil Ultán about this miracle. For the disciple ascribed it all to his master, the master to the disciple. But to the present day, the Irish, when they hear or see some imminent danger, say: "Ultán's left hand against it!" God's grace is abundantly manifest in these words. And the same Ultán, after St Declan's death, was outstanding as a holy abbot and the wonder-working father of many monks; his distinguished life shines with bright miracles.

[He restores a disciple of St Patrick to life]

The most blessed Patrick, archbishop of the Irish, sent one of his disciples as an emissary to St Declan; but when this man reached the southern part of the country of the Dési, he was drowned in a river called Luch [*the Licky river, flowing into the Blackwater a short distance above Youghal, Co. Cork*]. When the holy pontiff Declan heard of his death, he was much dismayed, and sadly said: "Truly I am sorrowful at heart, that the most blessed man's disciple, who had been sent to me, should meet such an untoward death in my country, and cannot bring back my message to his holy master. Set me quickly in my chariot therefore, so that I may tend to his obsequies, and that his master, our holy father Patrick, may hear that we did our duty for him." It was a distance of two miles from St Declan's city to the stream in which St Patrick's disciple had drowned. He was placed on a bier and was borne by his people towards St Declan to be buried. On the way they encountered the holy pontiff with his disciples. He told them to lay the body on the ground. All thought that the holy bishop wished to chant the office of the dead on the spot. But he approached the bier and drew back the shroud from the dead man's face. When he saw how swollen and wax-like it was (as is usual with the drowned), he shed tears and prayed—but the company couldn't hear the old man's words. After a short space of time, he said in the hearing of all: "In the name of the Trinity and undivided Unity of the Father, the Son and the Holy Spirit, rise before us, for Christ has granted me your life!" At these words of the most holy bishop, he sat up on the bier and blessed the holy old man and all the others. St Declan embraced him, raised him and kissed him—as his disciples did afterwards. And that brother, who had previously been infirm of body, was as a man freed from ill. Afterwards, in good health, he proceeded with St Declan to his city and stayed with him there for some days in unfeigned love. And there was great rejoicing in that city at this miracle; and the name of Christ and the sanctity of His servant were glorified far and wide through those regions. That disciple of St Patrick was called Baillín. He returned joyfully to St Patrick and told many people what had happened to him. The glorious archprelate Patrick himself, when he heard the story, bore full and eminent witness publicly to the merits of St Declan, and afterwards offered praise and glory to Christ.

[He sends for St Mac Liag before his death]

After telling of that remarkable wonder, we bring to an end the account of his miracles, leaving aside many, since the others may be inferred from the few we have recounted. We pass over all the blind he made see, how many lepers he made clean, how many cripples and lame people he cured, all the deaf he made hear, and how many various diseases Declan, the most blessed bishop of Christ, healed in a variety of places as he sowed the seed of life among the heathen. There are too many to tell, and the writer tires and wishes to weary neither the reader nor the hearer. So: when our holy elder, Declan, knew that the time of his reward was approaching, there was summoned to him the holy bishop Mac Liag (a dear foster-son of his, whose monastery was beside the inlet of Miledach [*the estuary of the Barrow above the confluence of the*

Suir], opposite the country of the Fir Gáilián to the east of the Dési country) that he might receive the body and blood of Jesus Christ from his hand at the moment he yielded up his soul. He informed the holy elders of the day of his death. He directed that he should be borne to his city, so that from there he could depart to Christ. For he was in his cherished little cell, which he had built with his own hands, between the mountain and the ocean in a narrow hidden cleft over the inlet, through which a clear brook ran down from the hill to the sea, surrounded by beautiful trees—the place known as "Declan's little hermitage". It was just a few miles from there to his city. There the holy pontiff Declan used to retreat to devote himself to God alone, in vigils, fasting and prayer; but he could only spend a little time there, because his disciples and the community of the faithful, Christ's poor, and pilgrims constantly sought him. For he was generous, pious and merciful; and because of this, as we learn from his disciples of old, there was usually a great army of people in his company. He greatly loved that little cell, in which he could, for short intervals of time, devote himself to meditation on God. It is always religious men who live there.

[His death]

When, therefore, the glorious pontiff, deprived of bodily strength but strong in faith, hope and charity, came to his city, he preached the divine word to the clergy and people gathered there. He counselled them to live well among themselves after his death; to obey his successors—who were to follow in his footsteps in charity and in other matters—and, if it should so be, he commended the guardianship of his city to the grace of God. When the people and clergy heard these words, their cry rose in a great lament, for they knew that their holy patron had decided to go from them to Christ. And the holy father duly offered them consolation. Afterwards he was carried to his hut, as wonder and fear spread through the city at the absence of its holy bishop. Afterwards the bishop Mac Liag, already mentioned, came, and our most holy bishop and preacher Declan received from his hand the body and blood of Our Lord Jesus Christ, Son of the Living God. He was of cheerful mind and surrounded by the saintly retinue of his worthy disciples. Having blessed them, with the kiss of peace, our saintly elder and patron, Declan, who had destroyed the temples and the idols, who had brought the heathen to the Faith, who had won many peoples for Christ, who had founded many churches of God, and consecrated and ordained many ecclesiastics, departed in most holy and happy fashion in his venerable old age, escorted by a chorus of angels, on the 24th of July, to the kingdom of heaven. Vigils were held and solemn Masses celebrated, signs and wonders were seen, a conclave of saints gathered in from every side and the Dési people gathered around their apostle; then his holy body, with due honours, was buried in his city of Ard Mór, in the cemetery which he himself, at the bidding of the angel, had designated. There great signs and miracles are worked through him at all times, through the intervention of Our Lord Jesus Christ, to Whom is honour, glory and power with God the Father in Unity with the Holy Spirit for ever and ever. Amen.

THIRTY-SEVEN

The Life of St Ciarán of Saigir

[The birth of Ciarán]

The blessed pontiff Ciarán was of Irish ancestry. His father, Lugne, was of the nation of the Osraige. His mother, Lidán, was of Munster. Even before she carried the holy burden in her womb, his mother dreamed that a star entered her mouth. The woman was troubled, wondering what this was, or what it foretold; and when she had failed to find out anything about it otherwise, she consulted druids. They answered her and said: "Indeed, you will conceive and bear a son, and his name, as if bestowed by the will of heaven, will not dim in the course of time." And behold: substance followed semblance. For she conceived and gave birth at last to a male infant—in whom God was pleased to dwell.

[His childhood]

The boy so chosen by God was full of virtue in his fosterage. By the shining light of his example, like the sun rising on the world, he drove away the shadows from people's minds. As he was saintly in his heart, so he was chaste in his body. So it came about that everyone marvelled at him: how in childhood he showed the wisdom of age, and in boyhood the strength of a man; and how in a human breast he possessed the discernment of an angel. It is no wonder; for the eternal God had made His tabernacle holy so that He might dwell among humankind, and because he was a vessel chosen to carry His name among the heathen who lived pagan lives. For at that time all his people were pagans. Once, when he was staying in his parents' house, he saw a small bird taken by a hawk. He prayed earnestly to God that the hawk should release from its talons the prey it was carrying off. The Lord heard the appeal of His beloved one; and straightaway the predator returned and released the little captive bird to the man of God. The Son of the Holy Father allowed it to depart safely into the air.

[He is consecrated bishop in Rome]

For many years up to this time, Ciarán had remained in Ireland, innocent of spirit and clean of heart, but still unbaptized. The fame of the Apostolic See had reached him, however, and he had heard that it was the head of the world and the apex of the Catholic Faith. He longed to hasten there, like a hart to springs of water. So, when he satisfied his desire to travel to Rome, and begged in full faith to be washed in the baptismal font there, he gained that which he desired. He remained for twenty years as a most diligent student and a painstaking collector of sacred writings. So, when shrewd judges observed that he was strong in virtue and prodigal of miracles, it came about that he was summoned to the supreme pontiff and raised to the dignity of a bishop.

[He is sent to Ireland and converts many]

And once he was appointed to this office, he was directed to return all the way to his native land—a country not yet sown with the seed of the Gospel—and to uproot the briers of sin and plant the corn of good works and faith. He had a prosperous voyage and arrived there. God inspired him to live in the place called Saigir [*Seirkeeran, Co. Offaly*]. When the eternal Father of the Household saw that the harvest was great and the reapers few, he did not permit the cruse to be overwhelmed by the brimming measure. On those who lived in that territory in the shadow of death, a light rose. Without pause people of both sexes and of all ages thronged to him from near and far. When they heard his sound teaching, they became firm Catholics. The error of heathendom was weakened and the Catholic Faith was strengthened, and she who was formerly reckoned barren gave birth now to many children of life. And Ciarán, holy and just as he was before God, was their teacher and chief, their father and precursor.

[He saves an abducted nun]

His mother Lidán, who shared the fruit of life with humankind, was blessed by her son, and gathered about her a group of women in a convent some little distance from his monastery, all of whom followed the example of the saints and menially served the needs of other people. One of them, named Brunech, was a noble and most beautiful girl. A certain petty chief, called Dimma, carried her off by force and for some days claimed her as his wife. St Ciarán, who condemned the barbarity of this crime and sought to undo it, came to the house of the impious man to obtain the return of the girl from him. When he demanded in the name of God that he return his captive to him, the predator (who was deranged by his desire) rejected his demand, answering: "If you can arrange to have me wakened from sleep tomorrow morning by the voice of the cuckoo—then you can have your

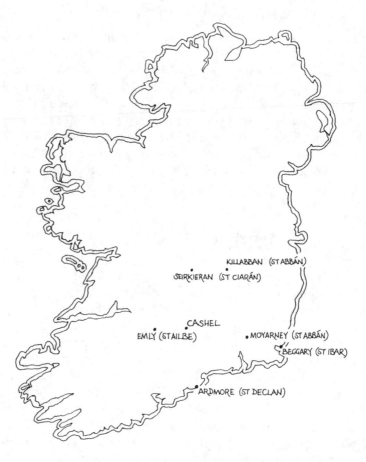

KILLABBAN (ST ABBÁN)
SEIRKIERAN (ST CIARÁN)

CASHEL
EMLY (ST AILBE)   MOYARNEY (ST ABBÁN)
                         BEGGARY (ST IBAR)

ARDMORE (ST DECLAN)

"The pre-Patrician saints"

disciple back." He said this because it was then winter. That night, although its snowed over the whole country he would by no means offer hospitality to Ciaran. Then truly, as the day dawned, behold: a cuckoo called on the roof of that man's house. And when Dimma was wakened from his sleep by this, he was overwhelmed by fear and trembling at this great miracle, but for a long time he was unable to decide whether to release the girl or not; for fear urged him to do so, while desire prevented him; but finally he was forced by the extremity of his terror to hand her over—although he did so reluctantly and regretfully. While the man of God was returning to the monastery, the girl told him that she had conceived in her womb. The zeal for justice of the man of God made him unwilling that the viper's seed should be given life. He made the Sign of the Cross on her belly and the conception vanished.

[The same girl is attacked again, dies, and comes back to life]

It happened after this that the same chieftain, troubled by his desire for the girl and forgetful of his salvation, came to the convent again to abduct her. But God, Who foresees everything, inspired His emissary to warn the girl in advance. And then, at the word that this criminal was coming, the girl was so greatly dismayed and her breast was so agitated that she died. When he arrived shortly afterwards he found her dead. Seeing that the girl's life had ended he flew into a rage and promised that he would do what harm he could to the man of God. But when Ciarán heard, his heart was greatly touched, as that of a father, at the untimely demise of the girl. He stormed the Heavenly One with his prayers, asking that He, Whose power had made her soul from nothing, would cause the animating principle to return to the body it had left. As he completed his prayer the girl, who had been dead, was restored to the full vigour of her life.

[He saves Dimma's son from burning]

After this that petty chief returned home full of fury, only to discover that his village with all his goods had been gutted by fire. In one of the houses, his son, whom he loved, had been left asleep. The boy's foster-father despaired of his life and cried out: "Son, I commit you to the care of St Ciarán!" Oh, what a great miracle—recalling the three children [*in the fiery furnace*]![1] For—see!—that house in which the boy slept was reduced to ashes, but through St Ciarán's name the boy was kept safe from the fire and was unhurt. Afterwards the father, seeing that this had been done by the invocation of St Ciarán's name, hastened to offer him, and another of his sons, to the man of God. And he, leaning more to pity than to condemnation, accepted his offering. And the chief said: "Holy father, because you have cast all my sins behind your back, therefore I offer you my service and that of my descendants in perpetuity." Having said this, he departed in peace with the blessing of the man of God.

[King Óengus is blinded for insulting him]

Meanwhile, as time's chariot hurried by, the blessed Patrick was ordained archbishop by Pope Celestine and appointed to Ireland, equipped with apostolic authority. And, when he had surveyed the land in which he was to preach, to baptize and to heal various ills, he arrived in the province of Munster and baptized Óengus, the king of that country. It happened after this that a horse, necessary for Patrick's business, was killed by a man of the Osraige. When the man was convicted of this crime, he was brought as a prisoner before the king to be punished by a fitting penalty. St Ciarán, meantime, was asked by his kinsmen to go to the king and request an alleviation of the penalty. In response to the supplications of these people, the pious father agreed to hasten to the king to intercede on behalf of the prisoner. When his appeal was unsuccessful there, he was able to make good the fine. He offered gold to the king for the release of the prisoner, and so obtained his freedom. The saint departed, but soon the wrongly acquired gold vanished before the king's eyes. However, the king, judging that he had been deceived by Ciarán, sent after him with orders to return and pay in real gold. The saint returned and was much chided and bullied by the king because of the phantom gold. But God did not allow the insult to St Ciarán to go unavenged. For shortly after, the king fell to the ground and lost the sight of his eyes. Then St Ciarán was earnestly beseeched by a disciple of his named Carthach (who was the king's grandson) to forgive his ignorance and to restore his sight. The pious master was moved by the prayers of his holy disciple to remit the punishment, and he restored to the king's eyes the light they had lost.

[King Ailill too is punished for insulting him]

Another king of Munster, named Ailill,[2] one day abused the man of God with insulting words. But, since it was by humiliating words that he had sinned against the saint, he was for seven days tormented by being deprived of the use of speech. Then, when his infirmities were increased, in the end he hastened to beg forgiveness; which was mercifully granted to him when he humbly applied for it.

[He foretells the death of King Óengus and his queen]

Among the other gifts with which God enriched Ciarán was the spirit of prophecy; he often foretold the future with as much certainty as he spoke of the present. One day in autumn, when he observed a certain bramble bush bearing the most beautiful blackberries, he wrapped it neatly in a linen cloth and in this fashion held it in safekeeping. Later, the king of the Osraige—Concraid by name—who was powerful and famous, prepared a great feast for the princes and magnates of the land. The king, Óengus, who has already been mentioned, was invited to the banquet with his wife Ethne Uathach. When the queen Ethne saw how outstandingly beautiful Concraid was, she was wounded by an arrow of inordinate desire, and she made known the nature of her distress to Concraid. He did not want to violate the royal bed, and he refused what she openly asked of him. Because she felt scorned by her beloved, she pretended to be ill and claimed that she could be cured only by a dish of blackberries; and she declared that if it were not possible for her to eat them her death was near. It was, however, the month of April, and at that time blackberries would not normally be found. When he heard of the woman's wishes—deranged as they were—the same Concraid who had invited the king and his wife to the feast was greatly concerned about her and he turned to place his whole trust in St Ciarán's protection; he asked him to satisfy the woman's desire, offering in return his own perpetual service. The man of God was moved by the supplicant's prayers and gave him the blackberries which, through Divine providence, had been kept since the autumn. Concraid accepted the precious gift of these miraculous blackberries, and then brought them back to the queen, who ate them and was relieved of her love sickness. She soon recovered her health. Mindful of the favour she had received, the queen went to the revered father and humbly confessed to him her deceit and her affliction. The man of God spoke to her in prophecy: "You should rather grieve for your untimely death and that of your husband than because of your unchaste love for another man. Truly, the time is coming when Illann,[3] king of North Leinster, will engage in fierce battles against Óengus, your husband, and his people, in which, in a great slaughter of the Munstermen, you too will perish along with your husband." So said Ciarán; and so it came to pass.

[He prevents a battle at Saigir]

It happened at another time that the king of Tara and the king of Munster were about to engage in battle. They made their camps the night before-hand near St Ciarán's city of Saigir. He—the begetter of peace and the smoother of dissension—went to them to dissuade them from conflict and to ask them to make peace. In the eyes of the haughty kings his request was regarded with derision. When they spurned the servant of God and were eager for mutual slaughter, God heeded His saint's appeal and pre-vented the enterprise of the pagans as follows. For a nearby wood was suddenly uprooted and strewn across the paths to impede them, while a river which lay between them rose in flood and overflowed its banks; so that the impenetrability of the trees and vast extent of the water prevented them from meeting in battle as they intended. And then the flooding river brought joy to the just and fear to the enemy, who was forced to retreat.

[He feeds the Munster army miraculously]

While the others hurried home, the king of Munster extended his encamp-ment into Ciarán's neighbourhood. The man of miracles fed the army with one cow and a pig, through the power of Him Who fed five thousand people with five loaves. And—just as then—many fragments were left over. And all those who were present gave praise to God and offered His saint the honour which he deserved.

[He saves a band of robbers]

Another time, a certain lord of the land was in pursuit of a band of robbers. They lost hope, certain they were about to fall into the hands of their pursuers, and they fled to St Ciarán—whose fame was then abroad in the land—and appealed to his protection. If he would agree to snatch them from the jaws of death, they said they would enslave themselves to him. With one voice they cried out: "Help us, father—Ciarán—help us in our misery and insignificance!" And behold: suddenly the Father of mercy, the God of all consolation, sent a column of fire in honour of His saint—it impeded the pursuers and protected the pursued. Mindful of the boon they had received, they hastened to throw themselves at Ciaran's feet to display their gratitude. They told their deeds one by one, and, following Christ, put on the new man, dedicated themselves to the monastic life and renounced with all their hearts the shows of Satan.

[A robber who steals his calf is drowned]

Another robber—to give him the same description as those men although his lot was different—who stole a cow from St Ciarán's herd, didn't get away with it safely. For shortly afterwards he was drowned in a river and lost both the animal and his life. The cow returned to the herd; while he went to hell.

[His disciple Carthach is tempted to sin with a nun]

Carthach, St Ciarán's disciple, was smitten by a grave temptation. He fell in love with one of St Lidán's virgins, and by mutual agreement they met in a place where they might commit sin. The Spirit of God revealed this to the holy pontiff Ciarán, who was provoked to anger by the act of his son and daughter. But He was present Who is the standby in time of temptation and He sent down a flame of fire, which separated them from one another. It struck the virgin with incurable blindness, and, returning home, she did penance. The youth, truly sorrowing in his heart, confessed humbly to the man of God that the fault was his, for which he pledged himself to set out on a penitential pilgrimage.

[He miraculously heats a cold stream and produces a fish for Carthach]

A long time afterwards, the aged St Ciarán, with just one companion, entered a stream by night, to pray. And, after they had spent a long time praying in the icy water, the brother admitted to the holy father that he was overcome by the cold. Ciarán shortly blessed the water in the name of Him Who produced a stream from a rock, and at once, losing its frigidity, the water became hot. And when the brother was telling another person how remarkable this wonder was, St Ciarán said to him: "Brother Germanus" (for so he was called) "put in your hand and seize the fish that swims underneath you; then bring it with you and use it to supply my dear disciple Carthach, whose arrival here tomorrow will fill me with joy." Then Germanus heard and obeyed; he thrust his hand into the water and took out a large fish. The following day Carthach indeed arrived, and his presence brought great joy to the father of the household.

[St Ciarán of Clonmacnoise appeals to him for help]

There was a petty king in the land—very rich—named Furbaide,[4] who commited his treasure to the care of St Ciarán, abbot of Clonmacnoise, that he might guard it carefully. When the faithful servant Ciarán distributed the treasure for the use of the poor, the king considered what to do, and then ordered Ciarán the abbot to be brought before him in chains, while his followers looked on. He spoke sarcastically and insultingly to Ciarán, saying: "Good abbot, if you wish to be released from your bonds, bring me seven hornless cows with red bodies and white heads. If you can't find the like, you will have to suffer the punishment for dispersing the treasure." The man of God, confident that he was acting on the Lord's behalf, answered: "All is possible to the true believer, because for the God in Whom he believes no word is impossible. And since, in the course of nature, every creature obeys its creator, I believe, in the presence of Him Who has the power to make the children of Israel from stones,[5] that it is possible for me to find what you want—not in order to escape your bonds, which I deserve, but so that I may show you the magnificence of my God." And then, when he was released on oath, on condition that he return, he hastened to the elder St Ciarán so that he might the more easily obtain what he had promised.

[He prophesies the doom of a man who scorns his miraculous meal]

At that time, two most holy men, both named Brendan, were there. In the presence of the holy men, he told the reason for his journey and explained his remedy for the king's avarice. But, when the hour came for refreshment of the body, the hospitaller came hurrying to the elder Ciarán and said that he had no suitable food to provide for such men; and he placed what he had—a little pig's lard—before Ciarán. Then the man of God, confiding in the goodness of the Lord, blessed this and distributed it to those who were reclining at table. Like magic, the pork drippings were turned into sweetly delicious food, as if it were another manna, and took on the flavour of the food which each of the diners most enjoyed. Further, Ciarán blessed the water which had been placed in the brothers' ladles and they confirm that it was changed to the sweetness of wine. However, there was one among them—dressed in the habit of a convert [*to the Church*] but a pervert in his heart—who refused the food on the grounds that it was dirty; since he knew it was prepared from pig's lard.

The elder saint said to him—not to justify the food, but in prophecy: "Understand that you will revert to your nature and put off that habit; and at the time you have eaten your fortieth dinner you will be beheaded and will go to hell." This the saint stated in prophecy. Not a detail, not an iota, of what he said failed to come to pass.

[He finds miraculous cattle to pay the fine for the younger Ciarán]

On the following day, the men of God—that is, the two Ciaráns and the two Brendans—entered into a perpetual pact of brotherhood among themselves. The junior St Ciarán said farewell to the brothers and departed in peace. At which, as was his custom, the senior St Ciarán accompanied him a little part of the way; and both asked the Almighty for the cows promised to the king. Truly—once their prayer was complete—behold! seven cows appeared, with red bodies and white heads, just as the evil king had demanded. The father abbot Ciarán drove these to the tyrant, and afterwards returned to his own place. When he had left, the miraculously produced cows vanished.

[His seven handmaids]

St Ciarán, shining with the light of these and many other miracles, had always with him seven handmaids. These were: humility as his lover; discretion as his hospitaller; generosity as his servant; chastity as his spouse; faith as his supporter; hope as his strengthener; perfect love as his governor. From which it can be said of him fittingly that in the words of Isaiah: "Behold, says the Lord, I gave you for a light of the Gentiles, that you may be my salvation even to the ends of the earth."[6]

[His death]

Ciarán lived in this life, poor in worldly matters, rich in divine matters, a balance of law, a coffer of justice, a teacher of youth, a leader of the old, and an inimitable communal example for all, for almost three hundred years; and finally, in the ripeness of his old age he blessed his people and said: "O God: commit these people to Your power, and all who perform our rituals." He even obtained from the Almighty that God would bring to bliss whoever would celebrate his feast day. Finally, on the 5th of March, the Lord led him into the vineyard of his inheritance, and planted him on the mountain of his heritage—the heavenly Jerusalem, which is our mother. Now, brothers!— make the festival of the most holy Ciarán a day of celebration; let the voice of praise resound in the tents of the just, because the right hand of the Lord wrought great strength in this man. Inasmuch as Jesus Christ, through the merits of His servant Ciarán, deigns to work here among us, so may we be worthy to enter the mansion of our eternal heritage. Amen.

THIRTY-EIGHT

The Life of St Darerca, or Moninna, the Abbess

[Her childhood and her baptism by St Patrick]

The venerable virgin named Darerca, also known as Moninna, descended from the Conaille [*in north Co. Louth*]. Her father was an excellent man named Mocteus.[1] She was born in Mag Coba [*the plain of Coba, in north-western Co. Down*], and fostered, as was befitting, in the care of conscientious parents. By the inspiration of God's grace, she determined at a tender age to preserve the unfading flower of virginity, from infancy for as long as she might live. Some years after her birth it came to pass that St Patrick arrived in the province in which she had been born. There, when numbers of people had been brought to him through the good offices of devout men, to be washed at the baptismal font and confirmed in faith by the imposition of hands, one of the gathering crowd was St Darerca, who came and made herself known to the bishop. The saintly pontiff was filled with the Holy Spirit: he observed her closely and understood her fervent desire to serve God. Having distributed his blessings, along with suitable counsel, he received her—who was already confirmed by her own virginal state—at the pool of Bríu [*not known: some-where in Mag Coba*], whose name, translated into Latin, means "generosity" or "abundance". This signifies that she was to be a fountain of living waters of the spirit from which many measures of life would be drawn.

[St Patrick forms a community of pious women]

The same pontiff, then, having commenced her instruction in the way of salvation, approved her virginal style of living as a worthy one, and directed her to come together with other virgins to whom she should teach the fear of God, so that—supported by their help and encouraged by their comfort—she could better bring to a conclusion the good work that she had under-taken. Then he entrusted the responsibility of protecting them and teaching them the psalms,[2] to a devout priest who lived near her parents. She spent a little time under this master, understanding what she was told without any difficulty because of the natural subtlety of her intelligence, and tenaciously retaining what she was taught because of the capacity of her memory; and within a short space of time she had learnt a great deal. There were with her at first, as they tell, eight virgins, as well as one widow who had a small boy named Luger. Darerca adopted the child as her foster son and when she had thoroughly accustomed him to the ways of the church, she raised him to the high dignity of a bishop. He crowned his good works as leader of the whole of his people—the Conaille—by building the church of Rúscach [*Rooskey, Cooley, Co. Louth*] in honour of God.

[She goes to stay with St Ibar]

So this virgin lived for some time with her parents; but since she could find no convents of nuns in her own country—although it had been converted to the Faith—she decided to leave her parents and relations and go away. In fact she did not wish to have her devout intentions vitiated through empty discussions and inept conversations with lay people or through frequent encounters with her parents. Therefore the virgin of Christ, placing her trust in the Lord, set out, along with the eight other virgins and the widow—together with some others—to make her way to the reverend pontiff Ibar, who was settled in the western islands of Ireland; for that is what she had longed to do. When St Darerca with her company reached the man of God, she spent a long time under his rule with many other virgins.

[She visits St Brigid]

Afterwards this bishop moved from those islands, crossed the south of Ireland, and arrived at the island they call "Little Ireland" [*Beg Ériu, now Beggary, at the mouth of Wexford Harbour*] (where finally he died). Christ's sheep followed their shepherd. When they had arrived in the country of the Lagin, the people told them of the fame of the holy virgin Brigid. Learning this, St Darerca, with her virgins, obtained their master's permission and turned aside to visit St Brigid. And it is said that she spent some time with her, accepting no honour but always acting with humility. She lowered herself to such an extent that God raised her correspondingly so much above all others—through the merit of her wonderful works—so that she is even reckoned second only to Brigid for holiness, for worthy practices and for her gift of virtue.

[She receives gifts and gives them to the poor]

Then, in her obedience to the regulations of the nuns, she was made keeper of the guesthouse, on the instructions of the abbess. And she performed the duties of this office diligently, and was agreeable in all matters. The All-Highest indeed conferred on her the grace to bring health to the sick and to expel demons from those who were possessed. Such reputation for signs and wonders did she have among the ordinary people, that she was revered by all, so much so that every day, because of her sanctity, many came to her with food and offerings; but, placing her trust in God, she kept none of this to herself, but gave it all, for Christ, to the poor who approached her.

When the sisters complained that she gave all for the use of the poor, and kept nothing back, she replied (relying on God): "My sisters, those who possess Christ in firm faith, if they are fed and clad, will have everything they need. Those, on the other hand, who give way to the temptations of the devil and want to be rich will never be free of care and anxiety. Christ acts through His members and you blame me for what I have done every day; but He can, whenever He wishes, restore to you what you have condemned me for, and alleviate the hunger and nakedness of my sisters."

Having said this, trusting in God she went to her accustomed bed, and she discovered twelve superb garments—although none such had been there before. When Christ's virgin saw these, she understood that they had been sent by God and she brought them to St Brigid, saying: "O Lady Brigid, look what God has given to meet your poverty." St Brigid answered her, saying: "These garments were sent by the Lord to you to be divided among your sisters at your will: they are needed more for them than for us." It is told that another great miracle was performed by the same virgin: that is, that a certain boy who had the temerity to deny that these garments were given to St Darerca by God, was suddenly struck dead but was restored to life through her prayers.

[She returns to St Ibar]

After this, she went on to the bishop, Ibar, and lived under his direction in Ard Conais [*not known; presumably near Wexford*]. There were many virgins and widows in the community there, as well as queens and noble matrons who gathered round her, to whom she was mistress, showing them by word and deed how to live well in all goodness.

[She produces a spring in a drought]

It happened, another time, that in summer too much sunshine caused the land to dry up so much that the springs and wells ceased to flow. Since they had no water, St Darerca's sisters complained in front of their mistress about this drought. God's handmaid then, concerned about their complaint, asked God in her prayers for a well flowing with water for them. Even while she was intent on her prayer, the water burst out in an unceasing flow, enough not merely for the nuns but also for those who lived in the surrounding homesteads. When this miracle became known, not only women but men too wished to come into her presence, and this was granted—with proper formality—since it was reckoned a great thing to be worthy of receiving the most holy virgin's blessing.

[She prophesies about an unworthy girl,
who causes the community to move]

Among other graces of the Holy Spirit, the spirit of prophecy shone in her soul, as the following miracle shows. The holy bishop Ibar sent a certain girl from the district in which the nuns lived to the blessed and most faithful Darerca, to be fostered and trained in the monastic discipline. St Darerca saw within her soul the future of that girl and said: "This little girl will be the future cause of our having to leave this convent in which we live." And the course of events showed this to be quite true. The same girl, when she arrived at the age of young womanhood, was inflamed by the fires of envy and persuaded by the devil, and she inspired her relations to hatred of St Darerca. When the daughter of peace observed this, she said to her sisters: "See: what God revealed to us in the beginning about that little girl is now out in the open. If we must suffer like this while I am alive, it will not be possible for you to live here after my death. Let us therefore hand over our place to her who envies us, and leave all our belongings—which the envious desire—to her people, saving only the clothes we wear. Our God will provide another place for us to live in."

[Their journey is impeded because a nun has taken
a bunch of garlic with her from Ard Conais]

Having said this, the beloved of God and of humans set out on her journey, with fifty nuns. They came to a certain river, which up to then was fordable by women and boys; but on their arrival it flooded suddenly and prevented them from crossing. God's handmaid saw this and said to the sisters: "My sisters, observe and be aware that it is in retribution for our sins that this inundation prevents our passage. Let us therefore examine our consciences, so that if we are at fault through any transgression of ours, we may confess it duly and be relieved from punishment." And at this one of the sisters answered her and said: "As I was leaving the monastery, I saw garlic drying, and I carried off one bunch, which I thought to belong to us." St Darerca said to her: "Bring it back immediately to the place from which you took it. For we should no more take away the smaller items than the bigger ones, without the permission of those with whom we left the larger." And when the nun, obeying the command of her superior, returned the bunch of garlic to the place they had left, the river soon reduced its flood to its former level and allowed the nuns to pass.

[St Brigid blesses them]

Afterwards they turned aside to go to St Brigid and they spent some days with her. When they were enlightened and confirmed in the faith by her admonitions, they set out on their journey. And when, for their comfort on the way, they asked St Brigid for her blessing, she answered: "May God protect you on the road you follow; and may He guide you to the dwelling place you wish for."

[St Brigid gives her a silver vessel,
which is miraculously returned to her]

After the blessing, she gave St Darerca a certain silver vessel (of the type called *escra* in Irish), from which the nobility used to drink. And since the daughter didn't dare to speak against her mother, although she didn't wish for anything beyond the blessing, she accepted the vessel reluctantly. She bade farewell to the other sisters and as she hastened on her way, she hid this gift in a certain secret place and then departed. When St Brigid's girls presently discovered this vessel and brought it to the holy mother Brigid, she said: "What we gave to God we may not receive" and she directed that it should be thrown into the nearby river Liffey. The vessel, which was accordingly thrown into the river —which flows eastward into the sea—was found, through the workings of God's power, contrary to the normal way of nature, at the mouth of the lake which is known in Irish as the Head of the Beach [*Cenn Trágha: not known*] by the holy bishop Herbus, Darerca's brother—so it is said. And he made no delay in giving the vessel to St Darerca, whose monastery was situated beside that lake. St Darerca's monastery, indeed, was four leagues from St Brigid's monastery.

[She turns water into wine]

Afterwards the virgin of Christ left for the northern part of Ireland to visit her relations, like the lost sheep of the house of Israel. At the end of her journey she came at last to the plain of Muirtheimhne [*in Co. Louth*], where the dwelling place of her people formerly was. This people, endowed in ancient times more than the neighbouring tribes with skill in the magical arts, had nevertheless become Christian, by God's grace operating through St Patrick. Then—it is told with complete certainty—when the virgin of Christ lived here, she never looked at a man. If she had to leave her cell for some compelling necessity, such as, for example, to visit the sick, or to free a captive from prison, either by persuasion or by paying a ransom, she made her journey by night; and it was her custom to keep her face veiled in case she might encounter someone on the way.

At that time she came one night to certain handmaids of God, the daughters of Campán. When she—the spouse of Christ—with her company, was being fed from their store, she, by her own hand through God's grace, supplied what was deficient in their supplies—that is, drink, fitting for the entertainment of such a company. For she blessed a vessel full of water and God so worked through her that the water was turned into the best of wine. It is further told that when she was the guest of one of her neighbours, named Dénech, she worked a most remarkable miracle. The host, who was a man poor in goods but rich in love, had killed a calf to provide the meal. Next day, either the same calf or an identical one was found with its mother.

[She restores Dénech's supply of beer]

Time went by, and later, it is said that the same Dénech was patrolling his land when he came on Darerca with her sisters, weary and perspiring from a night journey. (For it was the custom of the spouse of Christ to travel by night rather than by day, so that the sight of the everyday affairs of humanity would not distract her little doves.) This man, then, asked the handmaid of God to be gracious enough to turn aside and accept his hospitality. He obtained his request, for the lover of piety yielded to his entreaties. And when they came into the house, the faithful man cheerfully served them with food and drink from his small store. When the meal was served, the holy virgin blessed the house and its contents, but in particular the vessel in which beer had been brought to them. The little amount of beer remaining in the vessel straightaway increased and filled up until it brimmed over. Then she spoke to the host and said: "You can be sure that from this vessel, which barely held enough for one, you can now supply drink to all your guests. And God, Who returns all good, will greatly increase the small amount of property you have had up to now, both for you yourself and for your posterity. For you have tried to be hospitable to the servants and handmaids of Christ even beyond the capacity of your store." And when she said this, she departed.

After the handmaid of Christ had left, it happened that the king of Conaille was passing by that same man's house and was invited to a meal. The king, however, knew of the man's poverty, and at first declined the invitation. But, the invitation was pressed so earnestly that in the end he accepted. When he and his people reclined at table, a meal was laid before them, and beer was poured freely from the vessel which the holy virgin had blessed. And in truth, this beer, blessed by St Darerca, was sufficient to supply the whole crowd in the king's company for two days and two nights. And indeed, the same man who had been given the blessing, increased in prosperity day by day, and his descendants rose to the leading place among his people for many years.

[She spends a time at Faughart and moves to Killeevy]

It is said that when the holy virgin returned (as we have already told) to her native province, she first lived on the mountain of Facharta [*Faughart, Co. Louth*]. In that place she faithfully served God with her sisters, to the number of one hundred and fifty. One night she heard the sounds of a wedding feast and feared the large number of voices she seemed to hear. In the end she crossed over to a certain place situated on the slope of the mountain of Culind [*Slieve Gullion, in Co. Armagh*], so that there she could listen to the sweet discourses of her Spouse without any earthly impediment. And there she laid the foundations of her church for the handmaids of Christ [*Cell Sléibe Cuilinn; Killeevy, Co. Armagh*].

It is said that, like a daughter of John the Baptist, or the prophet Elijah, she waged war most strenuously in this desert place, clad in sack-cloth like a stern hermit, while bound indissolubly to her sisters by their most steady love and support. It is not to be doubted, indeed, that, like a taper placed on a candlestick, shining with the light of her miracles, she drove away by the effect of her devoted prayers the foul clouds of northern darkness. It is not possible, however, to reckon up or to know in full how many the prayers and vigils, how great and how frequent the manual works she imposed on herself, or how fierce the battles in which she sweated to overcome demons, or how brilliantly she shone through her miracles. For she did her best, as far as she could, to conceal the good deeds she did from public notice, except for those which dire necessity compelled her to

Killeevy, Co. Armagh, from a mid-nineteenth-century photograph

reveal. She followed in the footsteps of the earlier hermits to such an extent that she dug the earth and sowed it with her own hands: she contained within her woman's body a manlike spirit. The hoe she used for digging was kept for many years after her death in her monastery in her honour. They also kept for a long time, with great reverence, her badgerskin garment—more precious than gowns of silk—and the wooden comb with which, once a year (on the Feast of the Lord), it was her custom to comb her hair.

[Through her prayers, wolves return a calf]

Another time, wolves came running in from the woods and suddenly attacked the nuns' calves, which were grazing on the mountain beside the monastery. The calves ran away but the wolves seized one of them. And when the nuns woefully told Darerca what had happened, she said: "Don't worry about this. He Who brought the prophet Daniel safely from out of the jaws of the lion will restore the calf intact from the fangs of the wolves that have seized it." True: next day the wolves returned the calf, unharmed, back to its pasture.

[A rock is changed to salt]

Then, when more time had passed, certain robbers passing near the monastery encountered a little woman on the way and asked her where she was from and where she was going. She answered: "I come from nearby and I am going to holy Darerca." Making fun of her, they said: "Let Darerca know that we're not rich, and—seeing that she receives presents from everywhere—now she should condescend to receive alms of some kind from us, brought to her by you. For we think it will be of lasting use to her." Then they took one of the rocks which lay around and placed it in the arms of the little old woman, who was trembling, telling her that she was to carry it as far as the holy virgin Darerca and not to lay it down until she was in her presence. Then they let her go. When the woman had done as she was told, and laid down the rock before the virgin, it was immediately turned to salt.

[Thieves who steal from the monastery are lost in the woods]

A certain handmaid of Christ was living in a private cell near the monastery leading the life of an anchoress. Her daily food was sent to her from the monastery. One day, when her meal had been sent to her with one of the nuns, the bearer encountered robbers, who stole the food from her and allowed her to return empty-handed. And when she told her mother what had happened, she comforted her and said: "The reward of your work is intact, and God can return to you, untouched, what was stolen from you."

And indeed those robbers, after they had stolen the food, were confused by the power of God so that they lost the track they were following, and they wandered, lost, for three days in woods with which they were very familiar. At length they came to their senses and understood that they had to make good the wrong they had done; and they promised to do whatever penance the judgment of the holy virgin should impose on them if they found the right way. And since God is quicker to show mercy than condemnation, once they had acknowledged their fault he opened their eyes, and showed them the way to the monastery, which was close by. When they arrived at the monastery, they presented themselves to the holy virgin and returned what they had stolen; and, throwing themselves down, they humbly begged forgiveness and voluntarily offered themselves to perform such penance as might be imposed. And they renounced robbery and returned to a life of amendment.

[She sends the nun Brignat to Whithorn for a while]

It is said that a certain virgin named Brignat, among other handmaids of God, lived with the holy virgin. Darerca, contemplating the signs of this woman's future sanctity, was inspired to send her to the island of Britain to follow the rules of the community of the monastery of Rosnatense [*Whithorn, in Galloway*]. Brignat, since she was subject to holy obedience, set out without delay and arrived at the designated place without any pause on the way. She was careful to comply with the direction of her holy mother, and she stayed in that monastery, in a certain little lodging in which she read the Psalms and other necessary books. To fulfil holy obedience, with God's help she made the return voyage safely just as she had made the outward passage, and came back to her abbey.

[She revives a novice who died suddenly]

After this, St Darerca, by her devoted prayers, was found worthy to bring to life a certain girl, a novice, who had been suddenly struck dead. And the girl lived for many years after that.

[A nun who accepted shoes from a man causes the visits of angels to cease in Killeevy]

Furthermore, as is proven to be true by the witness of those who knew her, angels often visited her and held familiar conversation with her. This is shown with certainty by the following miracle. For one night, when the sisters were coming in to celebrate Matins but had not yet begun the sacred office, she clapped her hands and called for silence, saying: "O blessed Lord, we must not pass over in silence what has happened to us tonight! For our prayers up to now could barely rise above the ridge of the church roof before angels would come as guests to visit us; now, however, tonight I don't see them. I have no doubt that this has happened to us because of sins we have committed. Let us examine our consciences as best we can." Hearing this, the terror-stricken nuns, trusting more in their mistress than in themselves, threw themselves to the ground. One of the widows, who had only lately come from worldly society, stood up and said: "Oh, mistress, I admit that my sin is the cause of this business. I confess that I accepted a pair of shoes from a man with whom I was unlawfully joined. I forgot that I had not your permission, and I have them on my feet because of the cold." The holy prophetess said to her: "It would be better that these shoes should be dropped into the depths of the sea rather than that we should suffer the absence of the angels because of them." And one of the sisters—the same Brignat whom we mentioned a short while ago—supported by some of the others, said to St Darerca: "Go and hide those shoes in some abyss, where no one could find them." While they went to follow this advice, the other nuns completed the vigil. At the end, the blessed virgin said: "We should give thanks to God from devout hearts, because now our prayers, with nothing to impede them, can reach heaven, and because our dear guests are no longer unwilling to be present—since that which met divine displeasure has been disposed of." From this it is plain that she understood the principle of keeping morally pure, how she perceived clearly that her prayers were being impeded by minor sins, and how she was as quick to see to the correction of small matters as she was to prevent the growth of major faults.

[The nun Briga sees angels in St Darerca's cubicle]

The sisters already mentioned completed their task, and when they returned and knocked on the door of the oratory, they discovered that the office of Matins had been concluded. A virgin named Briga said to the others who were with her: "You, before the day breaks, go into the dormitory for a little sleep." When they had entered the dormitory, the same virgin Briga made her way to the cubicle where St Darerca was accustomed to pray and to converse with angels. As she approached it seemed to her that she had seen two swans flying from it. She watched them closely, and when she sensed that something hidden lay beyond what she saw, she did not dare to watch any longer. Struck by the fear of this marvellous vision, she fell to the ground, earnestly praying that she might not perish. At length she rose, trembling, and gently knocked on the half-door, and told that she had done as she was bidden and had been so frightened that she could hardly retain the spirit in her body. St Darerca said to her: "Bless yourself with the Sign of the Cross. It may be that you have been driven into delusion by bestial or demonic visions, such as are common with hermits." And she said: "No, lady, it is not so; but

I saw a pair of swans—of the purest white colour—rising up from your compartment, and it is from this marvellous vision that my terror comes." Then the mother said to the daughter: "Now I know why God, Who reveals His mysteries according to the merits of people, has thought you worthy tonight to enrich you by His grace. For He has found it fitting to show to you the sight of His ministering angels—which He has denied to others. The time, therefore, has come for you to settle in the land of your birth and to serve others according to the grace that has been bestowed on you." Then she added: "Furthermore, you will in future be without those eyes with which you have seen angels; but in their place you will have better, with which to contemplate God. Further: tell no one about your vision as long as you live." So that handmaid of Christ, obeying the order of her superior, travelled to her homeland, and having located a place suitable for the dwelling of nuns there, one league distant from the monastery of St Darerca, remained there—without bodily sight—as long as she lived.

[She speaks to her people on her death-bed]

After these happenings, as the day approached on which St Darerca was to pay the ultimate debt of nature, the worsening of her illness, which had long been hidden, was made known and caused enormous grief in the surrounding populace. As a result the king Eugenius son of Conaille,[3] who at this time ruled over three territories—Muirtheimhne [*north Co. Louth*], Cuailgne [*the Cooley peninsula in north-east Co. Louth*] and Cobha [*north-west Co. Down*]— along with the magnates of other peoples, and with great crowds, came as far as the immediate vicinity of the monastery, all having the same wish to visit her. And they all appealed to the bishop Herbeus, whom we have already mentioned, to go to the virgin Darerca, and faithfully to convey to her the message of the whole people, saying as follows: "Lady, we appeal to you on the grounds of our common blood" (many of her own people were there, the king Eugenius himself being of the Conaille on his mother's side) "through which we have an affinity both in the flesh and in the spirit, to go so far as to grant us the space of one year in which you will live still with us on this earth. And that you will not orphan us by dying this year. For we are quite certain that whatever you ask of God you will straightaway obtain. In fact, anyone among us who is a man of substance will give a handmaid free to the Lord in exchange for your life. And every man at arms will gladly give a cow of full age."

To them she replied, through the bishop: "May you be blessed by the Lord Who made heaven and earth, you who lowered yourselves to come and visit me in my infirmity. If you had asked this yesterday or the day before yesterday, perhaps God's mercy would have granted your request, but today I am unable to accede to you. Venerable guests who are listening to our dialogue, Peter and Paul, have been sent to guide my soul worthily to God,

Ireland in the early sixth century

and they are now here present with me. I see them holding between them a
kind of linen cloth, made with marvellous art and interwoven with gold. I
must go with them to my Lord Who sent them for me. But Almighty God,
to Whom a ready good will is as good as the deed, will return you suitable
compensation. God further will grant to you what you asked for me—that
my life be redeemed—but will give a life instead to one of you. Bless you in
the name of the Lord Who created heaven and earth and all things; bless you,
I say, and your wives and children and your possessions. I leave you my
badgerskin garment and my rake and some other tools. Have no doubt that
if you carry these with you against enemies who come to plunder your
territories, God will grant you, through them, to be victorious. But do not
presume to cross your borders in order to ravage other territories (unless
perhaps you are compelled by superior power) or the just punishment of God
will descend upon you. Do not be sad at my departure. For I believe that

Christ, with Whom I now go to stay, will give you whatever I ask of Him in heaven no less than when I prayed to Him on earth."

[Her death]

Having passed on these and similar words through the bishop Herbeus, she said farewell one by one, calling each person by name. But the populace, hearing this, cast away their weapons, lamenting and keening, and raised an enormous wail to the sky. Finally, comforted by the address of the bishop, they returned to their own homes. Having arranged everything for the future of her monastery, and having foretold, by the spirit of prophecy, the sequence of many things that would happen in time to come, then, on the day on which these things were concluded, that is the 6th of July, the octave of the feast of the blessed apostles Peter and Paul—her good fight fought and her course happily completed—she migrated to Christ, with Whom she reigns for ever and ever. Amen.

[Taunat has a vision of St Darerca and goes to join her]

Three days after her death, one of the sisters, whose name was Taunat, was impelled (it is not known why) to leave the dormitory at night, after Compline. She stood praying by the cross which was erected near the monastery, when she was summoned by a bodily vision. Taunat, not knowing who it was, directed her steps there and said: "Lady, what would you have me do?" And she answered: 'Return to your dormitory and instruct the sisters to be extra diligent, in such a time, to observe the strict law of silence; let them take pains not to have their voices heard outside the dormitory. Why have they broken the rule, since its provisions may on no account be overstepped? My daughters: you should not be careless in small things, for fear you would then, in similar fashion, be negligent in major matters. But you, yourself: when a week has gone by, you will come to me. Therefore, in the interval, make yourself ready for your journey." Happy to have received such a promise, she accompanied her mother as far as the well which is situated in the northern part of the monastery, where she vanished before her eyes.

When this woman returned to the house, she told the sisterhood everything that had happened. Hearing of so great a vision, they were overwhelmed by a mixture of joy and fear and threw themselves down on the ground. The same Taunat, when a week had passed, received the Viaticum, then bade farewell to her sisters, entered her cubicle, stretched out and arranged her limbs, and rested in Christ.

[St Darerca in heaven moves a tree for Abbess Derlasra]

After the death of St Darerca, Bia was abbess, as Darerca herself had directed; then Indiu; then Derlasra, who was forty years at the head of the monastery. In her time a famous miracle occurred. She had almost finished a work which she had begun—the building of a church, in the style of the Irish nation, of planed planks, with careful workmanship, in the monastery of St Darerca. However, a timber was missing up to now: the piece called *spina* in Latin [*"spine", that is,"druimm"—"ridge-pole"*], the member which was placed on the apex of a building to join together the two planes of the pitched roof. The craftsmen had to go into the woods to find a suitable piece to solve this problem. They found it at last, but in a remote and difficult place. There was no way in which they could remove the felled tree because of the impracticability of the place. The abbess knew of this and was losing hope of getting the timber to the monastery; so she applied to St Darerca as advocate, and said: "St Darerca, then, for whom this house is being built on earth, is now living in heaven. She can help us if she will."

The very next day the ridge-pole already mentioned was discovered, located on a level spot beside the monastery, where harm could come neither to beasts of burden nor to humans. Afterwards, the carpenters were curious to see if there were any traces along the way of the passage of this pole: they found some broken branches near the top of the tree-trunk. From this it is to be understood that divine power, through the service of angels, had done what was beyond human power. That tree, found on the highest crags, could not have been brought over the terrain from so steep and high a place by human art, but was borne down through the air without difficulty by the art of angels.

[Water from St Darerca's well provides beer for St Finbarr]

Another time, a bishop of venerable life, commonly called Finbarr (his name was Finnian) made a journey to the said monastery and was seen when he was making his way down from the mountain which was situated opposite the monastery. Knowing in advance of his arrival, the same abbess, Derlasra by name, said to her serving girl: "Draw water from St Darerca's well and use it to fill containers in which there are small amounts of yeast. Then shut everyone out and remain on your own, demanding by your prayers the help of St Darerca with the filled containers." When she had done this, the fermenting water was turned into the best beer, through the blessing she gave in St Darerca's name. And there was adequate refreshment for those who drank that beer.

Tables of Dates

TABLE OF EMPERORS

Constantine the Great	AD 311–337
Constantine II	337–340
Constans	340–350
Constantius	350–361
Julian the Apostate	361–363
Jovian	363–364
Valentinian I (Western)	364–375
Valens (Eastern)	364–378
Gratian (Western)	375–383
Valentinian II (Western)	383–392
Theodosius the Great (Eastern; after 392 Western)	379–395
Maximus	383–388
Eugenius	392–394
Arcadius (Eastern)	395–408
Honorius (Western)	395–423
Theodosius II (Eastern)	408–450
Valentinian III (Western)	425–454
Marcian (Eastern)	450–457
Petronius (Western)	455
Avitus (Western)	455–457
Majorian (Western)	457–461
Leo I (Eastern)	457–474
Severus (Western)	461–465
Anthemius (Western)	467–472
Olybrius (Western)	472
Glycerius (Western)	473–474
Julius Nepos (Western)	473–475
Leo II (Eastern)	473–474

Zeno (Eastern)	474–491
Romulus Augustulus (last Western Emperor)	475–476
Anastasius I	491–518
Justin I	518–527
Justinian the Great	527–565

TABLE OF POPES

Melchiades	AD 311–314
Sylvester I	314–335
Marcus	336
Julius I	337–352
Liberius	352–366
(Felix II, antipope)	355–365
Damasus I	366–384
(Ursinus, antipope)	366–367
Siricius	384–398
Anastasius I	398–401
Innocent I	402–417
Zozimus	417–418
Boniface I	418–422
(Eulalius, antipope)	418–419
Celestine I	422–432
Xistus III	432–440
Leo I	440–461
Hilary	461–468
Simplicius	468–483
Felix II	483–492
Gelasius I	492–496
Anastasius II	496–498
Symmachus	498–514
(Laurence, antipope)	498–505
Hormisdas	514–525
John I	523–526
Felix III	526–530
Boniface II	530–532
(Dioscurus, antipope)	530
John II	533–535
Agapetus I	535–536
Silverius	536–?538
Vigilius	?538–555
Pelagius I	556–561
John III	561–574

TABLE OF KINGS OF TARA

Niall Noígiallach	?
[Nath I ?]	?
Loeguire son of Niall Noígiallach	Died AD 461?
Ailill Molt son of Nath I	461–482
Lugaid son of Loeguire	482–507
Muirchertach Mac Ercae son of Muiredach	507–536
Tuathal Maelgarb son of Cormac Cáech	536–544
Diarmait son of Fergus Cerrbél	544–565

Croagh Patrick, Co. Mayo

Notes and References

The Spread of Christianity to the West (pp. 8–13)

1 Máire MacNeill's book, *The Festival of Lughnasa* (1962), explores the Irish evidence in depth.

The Church in Gaul and Britain (pp. 14–22)

1 Salvian, *De Gubernatione Dei*, 6, 39. F. Pauly, ed., *Salviani Presbyteri massiliensis Opera Omnia* (*Corpus Scriptorum Ecclesiasticorum*, 8) (1883), 136.

2 C.H. Turner, *Ecclesiae Occidentalis Monumenta Iuris Antiquissima*, 1 (1899), 120–121; 196–197.

3 G.S.M. Walker, *Sancti Columbani Opera* (1970), 48.

4 Migne, *P.L.*, 54, 879–882.

5 See the discussion in Malcolm Todd, *Roman Britain 55 B.C. – A.D. 400* (1981), 228.

6 See M. Hassall, "Britain in the Notitia", in R. Goodburn and P. Bartholomew, ed., *Aspects of the Notitia Dignitatum* (*British Archaeological Reports*, 15) (1976), 103–118. Charles Thomas, "Saint Patrick and Fifth-century Britain; an historical model explored", in P.J. Casey, ed., *B.A.R.*, 17 (1979): *The End of Roman Britain*, 81–101; also, *Christianity in Roman and Sub-Roman Britain to A.D. 500* (1979).

7 St Jerome, Letters, no. 133, *Ad Ctesiphontem*; I. Hilberg, ed., *Sancti Eusebii Hieronymi Epistulae* (1918), 2, 225. Attributed to Porphyry in A.W. Haddan and W. Stubbs, *Councils and Ecclesiastical Documents relating to Great Britain and Ireland* (1869), 1, 12–13. St Jerome was responding to Porphyry, who had argued, in his work *Against the Christians* and elsewhere that God was worshipped differently in different countries; if He had wanted to reveal Himself in the same way to all, He would have done so all at once. "The chief fruit of piety", wrote Porphyry to his wife (*Letter to Marcella*, 18), "is to honour God according to the laws of our country, not deeming that God has need of anything, but that He calls us to honour Him by His truly reverend and blessed majesty" (trans. A. Zimmern, with introduction by David Fideler, *Porphyry's Letter to his wife Marcella concerning the life of Philosophy and the Ascent to the Gods*, 1986). See Amos Berry Hulen, *Porphyry's Work Against the Christians: an Interpretation* (Yale Studies in Religion No. 1) (1933), 50–51.

8 See M. Todd, op. cit., 239–241.

9 See p. 71.

10 See p. 79.

11 See E. Schwartz, *Acta Conciliorum Oecumenicorum: Concilium Universale Ephenisum*, I fasc. 2 (1925–1926), esp. pp. 31 ff; also A.J. Festugière, trans., *Ephèse et Chalcedoine: Actes des Conciles* (1982).

12 René Borius, ed., *Constance de Lyon, vie de Saint Germain d'Auxerre* (1965).

13 The later Pope Leo the Great was at this time archdeacon in Rome, and he too was involved in the organization of the Council of Ephesus through correspondence with Cyril of Alexandria. The correspondence, although calendered, is lost. See Migne, *Patrologia Latina*, 51 (1861), 1217–1218 ("*De epistolis perditis*", 1). It is probable that Leo would have been involved in the arrangements for appointing Palladius to Ireland.

14 See also E.A. Thompson, *St Germanus of Auxerre and the End of Roman Britain* (1984), 6.

15 Constantius, *Vita Germani, M.G.H.*, VIII, 258.

16 H. Hess, *The Canons of the Council of Sardica A.D. 343* (1958), 68.

17 C.H. Turner, op. cit., 118–119; H. Hess, op. cit., 68.

18 H. Hess, op. cit., 111 ff.

19 H. Hess, op. cit., 119.

20 See E.A. Thompson, op. cit., 24; 31; 80.

21 E.A. Thompson, op. cit., 47–54.

22 See Borius, op. cit., 154.

23 Celestine, Letters, 14.5, Migne, *P.L.*, 50 (1865), 434. See also the letters of Pope Siricius, *P.L.*, 13 (1845), 1143, and of Pope Leo, *P.L.*, 54 (1881), 673.

Ireland in the Fifth Century (pp. 23–37)

1 Marie-Louise Sjoestedt, *Gods and Heroes of the Celts* (trans. Myles Dillon) (1949; reissued 1994), 93.

2 A. and B. Rees, *Celtic Heritage* (1961), 118–172.

3 D. Sproule, "Origins of the Eóganachta", *Ériu*, 35 (1984), 31–37.

Gaulish and British Bishops in Ireland (pp. 38–45)

1 St Jerome, Letters no. 133: Hilberg, *Sancti Eusebii Hieronymi Ep.*, 2, 255.

2 St Augustine, second sermon on Psalm 101: "'This Gospel', he says, 'will be preached.' Where? 'Throughout the whole world.' To whom? 'As a witness to all peoples.' Afterwards, what? 'And then the end will come' [Matthew 24: 14]. Have you not seen that by now that there are no peoples to whom the Gospel has not been preached?" D.E. Dekkers and J. Fraiont, ed., *Sancti Aureli Augustini, Ennarationes in Psalmos CI-CL* (1956) (*Corpus Christianorum, Series Latina, Aurelii Augustini Opera*), 1444.

3 St Augustine (*ad Hesychum*) "*De fine saeculi*", Letters, no. 199: A. Goldbacher, ed., *S. Aureli Augustini Hipponiensis Episcopi Epistulae*, 2 (1911), 285–286.

4 It is a commonplace in the early tales for kings and chiefs to be represented as having British mothers, often described as captives taken in raids (and by no means always Christian). See the story about St Lommán, pp. 203–204.

5 See J. Carney, *The Problem of St Patrick* (1961), *passim*.

6 These legends have been incorporated, along with much other late material, in the Annals of the Four Masters. See p. 126.

7 T.F. O'Rahilly, *The Two Patricks, a lecture on the history of Christianity in fifth-century Ireland* (1957), 19; 16.

8 See p. 179.

9 See pp. 57–58.

10 See p. 59.

11 L. Bieler, *The Works of St Patrick* (1953), 6.

12 E. Schwarz, *Concilium Universale Ephenisum*, I fasc. 2 (1925–1926), 27.

13 See p. 63.

14 J. Carney, op. cit., 31–48.

15 See p. 259.

16 See the discussion in Carney, op. cit., 40 ff. Also E. MacNeill, "The Hymn of St Secundinus in honour of St Patrick", *Irish Historical Studies*, 2 (1940), 129–153.

17 H.J. Lawlor and R.I. Best, "The Ancient List of the Coarbs of St Patrick", *Proceedings of the Royal Irish Academy*, 35C, 316–562.

18 See p. 227; also C. Plummer, *Vitae Sanctorum Hiberniae*, 1, xxx ff.

19 See p. 167.

20 K. Meyer, "*Feacht n-aile luidh Sechnaill*", *Zeitschrift für Celtische Philologie*, 8 (1912); L. Bieler, *Patrician Texts*, 178.

21 See Carney, op. cit., 46.

22 See p. 135.

23 See p. 174.
24 See p. 205.
25 Carney, op. cit., 33 ff.
26 Bede, *Church History of the English People*, 1.29; 2.105.
27 See p. 149.
28 See *Chronicon Scottorum* for the year 493.
29 See p. 204.
30 Bieler, *Patrician Texts*, 66–168.

The Council of Arles (pp. 53–56)

1 C. Munier (*Concilia Galliae*, 238) suggests amending this to "Veneticus".
2 This entry appears on only one copy of the list.

The Council of Orange (pp. 57–58)

1 This may have been directed against crypto-Manichees, who opposed the drinking of wine and received communion in one kind only. Leo I, who became Pope in 440, used this as a test for discovering Manichean tendencies in his congregation at Rome. See Prosper's *Chronicle*, p. 83.
2 See p. 40.
3 See p. 40.

The Council of Vaison (pp. 59–60)

1 See p. 40.
2 The province was Vienne.
3 The text is defective and confused here.

The Synod of May, 451 (pp. 61–63)

1 See p. 41.

The Council of Vannes (pp. 66–69)

1 Matthew 5:32.

Prosper of Aquitaine on Pope Celestine and the Pelagians (pp. 70–71)

1 Pelagianism.
2 St Augustine, Bishop of Hippo.
3 2 Timothy 2:19.
4 Pope Innocent I (402–416).
5 An associate of Pelagius and a leader of the Pelagians.
6 Celestine. Prosper's account is disingenuous. See p. 19.

The Chronicle of Prosper of Aquitaine (pp. 72–87)

1 He was Bishop of Avila, in the province of Lusitania.
2 The Frankish general Arbogast had been dismissed by him but refused to go. Valentinian, a boy, had been left under Arbogast's care and guidance by Theodosius, whose trust was betrayed. He was probably murdered by the general's supporters.
3 Bishop Julian of Eclanum, a Pelagian.
4 Later Pope Leo the Great.
5 There is a hiatus in the text here.
6 Aëtius.

St Patrick's Writings (pp. 88–95)

1 Charles Thomas, "Saint Patrick and Fifth-century Britain" (*B.A.R.*, 71) (1979), 81–101; *Christianity in Roman and Sub-Roman Britain to A.D. 500* (1979).
2 Christine Mohrmann, *The Latin of St Patrick* (1961), suggests the influence of northern Gaul on St Patrick's tongue.
3 F.X. Funk, *Didascalia et Constitutiones Apostolorum* (1905), 2, 30.
4 J.B. Pitra, *Juris Ecclesiastici Graecorum Historia et Monumenta* (1864), 1, 451–454.
5 Siricius, letters, 1.9: *P.L.*, 13, 1142–1143.
6 E.A. Thompson, *Who Was St Patrick?* (1985), 61 ff.
7 Canon 19 of the early-fourth-century Council of Elvira prohibits clergy from travelling about on business. C.F. Hefele, *Histoire des Conciles* (1907), I, 1, 232.
8 Hamilton Hess, *The Canons of the Council of Sardica, A.D. 343* (1958), 71.
9 See his Letter (p. 110) and the Declaration (pp. 106–107).
10 Hefele, loc. cit.
11 Thompson, op. cit., 125–143.

St Patrick: Declaration (pp. 96–108)

1 Psalm 50:5, ". . . But unto the wicked God saith, What hast thou to do to declare my statutes, or that thou

shouldst take my covenant in thy mouth . . .".

2 Tobit 12:7.

3 Psalm 5:6.

4 Wisdom 1:11.

5 Matthew 12:36.

6 Ecclesiastes 10:12.

7 Isaiah 32:4—i.e., with the coming of the righteous kingdom—a hint of Patrick's millenarian view of his mission.

8 Acts 10:47.

9 2 Corinthians 3:3.

10 A pagan rite of initiation. This sentence, which appears to have been misplaced, has been brought up from the end of the paragraph.

11 Joel 2:12. Patrick quotes much from such millenarian passages, reinforcing the impression that he associates his mission to the ends of the earth with the end of time: "Blow ye the trumpet in Zion, and sound an alarm in my holy mountain: let all the inhabitants of the earth tremble; for the day of the Lord cometh, for it is nigh at hand . . .".

12 See p. 108, where Patrick again uses the image of Christ as the sun—the true *Sol Invictus*.

13 An echo of his earlier quotation of Psalm 50: "Out of Zion, the perfection of beauty, God hath shined . . . . And the heavens shall declare his righteousness; for God is judge himself . . . . And call upon me in the day of trouble: I will deliver thee and thou shalt glorify me . . .". He probably had in mind his trial and vindication.

14 Further reference to his trial. Matthew 10:16–20: "Behold, I send you forth as sheep in the midst of wolves: be ye therefore wise as serpents, and harmless as doves. But beware of men: for they will deliver you up to the councils, and they will scourge you in their synagogues. And ye shall be brought before governors and kings for my sake, for a testimony against them, and the Gentiles. But when they deliver you up, take no thought how or what ye shall speak. For it is not ye that speak, but the Spirit of your Father which speaketh in you."

15 The phrasing suggests the story of Joseph, Genesis 37:21.

16 Romans: 8.26.

17 Hebrews: 9.24.

18 Patrick here refers to the prophetic passage in Zechariah 2:8—". . . After the glory hath he sent me unto the nations which spoiled you: for he that toucheth you toucheth the apple of his eye."

19 Patrick is citing 1 Timothy 1:12, where St Paul is commenting on the law: ". . . But we know that the law is good, if a man use it lawfully; knowing this, that the law is not made for a righteous man, but for the lawless and disobedient, for the ungodly and for sinners . . ."

20 John 10:29. "My sheep hear my voice, and I know them, and they follow me: And I shall give unto them eternal life; and they shall never perish, neither shall any man pluck them out of my hand. My Father, which gave them to me, is greater than them all; and no man is able to pluck them out of my Father's hand."

21 Patrick returns to his recurrent chilisatic theme: "But this is that which was spoken by the prophet Joel: And it shall come to pass in the last days, saith God, I will pour out of my spirit upon all flesh: and your sons and your daughters shall prophesy, and your young men shall see visions, and your old men shall dream dreams." (Acts 2:17.) "And this gospel of the kingdom shall be preached in all the world for a witness unto all nations; and then shall the end come." (Matthew 24:14.)

22 Jeremiah 16:19.

23 Acts 13:47.

24 Luke 13:29.

25 Mark 1:17.

26 Jeremiah 16:16.

27 Matthew 28:19, 20.

28 Mark 16:15, 16.

29 Matthew 24:14.

30 Joel 2:28.

31 Hosea 1:10.

32 Identical words occur in the Letter. See p. 111.

33 This case has been singled out for report probably because the lady, like Patrick himself, had received a direct command from God in a dream.

34 This is almost certainly a reference to the children of the numerous British slaves held in Ireland after raids on the Roman province.

35 "... Wherefore I am appointed a preacher and an apostle, and a teacher of the Gentiles ..." 2 Timothy 9:11.

36 Proverbs: 10:1.

37 Leviticus 24:16.

38 Psalm 55:22; also 1 Peter 5:7.

St Patrick's Letter against Coroticus (pp. 109–113)

1 Psalm 119:53.

2 Ecclesiasticus 34:20.

3 Job 20:15–27.

4 Habbakuk 2:6.

5 Matthew 16:26; Mark 8:36; Luke 9:25.

6 Exodus 20:17.

7 Exodus 20:13.

8 1 John 3:15.

9 1 John 3:10.

10 Matthew 13:57; Mark 6:4; John 4:44.

11 Matthew 12:30.

12 Romans 1:32.

13 Romans 12:15.

14 1 Corinthians 12:26.

15 Luke 14:28–29.

16 Revelation 22:15.

17 Revelation 21:8.

18 1 Peter 4:18.

19 John 3:18.

From the Annals of Ulster (pp. 118–122)

1 Forty-ninth bishop.

2 A misplaced entry. See J. Carney in *Studies*, 363–364.

3 440. The fiftieth bishop.

4 451.

5 461.

6 Fifty-first.

7 468.

8 Fifty-third.

9 Fifty-fourth (492–496).

10 Fifty-fifth (496–498).

11 Fifty-sixth (498–514).

12 Fifty-seventh (514–523).

13 Fifty-eighth (523–526).

14 12 July 526–22 September 530.

15 530.

16 530–532. The see was briefly occupied in 530 by the anti-pope Dioscorus.

17 This has the appearance of being a genuine copy of the salutation from a letter of Mochta.

18 533–535. There was an interval of two and a half months between Boniface and John, who assumed a Christian in place of a pagan name on his election to the see.

19 535–536.

20 536–537.

21 537–555.

22 "Justinian's Plague", which reached Alexandria from the Far East in the 540s and spread to Italy and westward.

23 The reference to a shadowy and dubious Bishop David of Armagh may arise from a misreading of a record concerning St David of Wales.

24 556–561.

From the Annals of Inisfallen (pp. 123–125)

1 The word "Patrick" occurs here by mistake. Bieler has suggested amending this to "returned." The annalist is attempting to establish that Palladius left almost immediately, while Patrick arrived.

2 Duplicated. St Augustine died in 430 and his death is recorded above under 431.

3 This is usually rendered "approval" of Patrick, since that is the commoner meaning of "*probatio*". See O'Rahilly, *Early Irish History and Mythology* (1946), 509.

4 The Emperor Leo began his reign in 457. The relic of St John was found in 453.

5 The correct date.

6 i.e. Pope Hilary, 461–468. See p. 227.

7 The missing name is certainly that of Pope Hilary, who died this year.

8 See p. 119: "bishop".

9 The calculation is self-contradictory. The Passion dating would give a date about AD 460 for St Patrick's death.

10 i.e. Ciarán of Clonmacnoise. The birth-dates of church founders in the

annals are obviously due to the calcu-
lations of historical scholars and
chronologists of later times—mainly
in the eighth century.

11 i.e. Pope Gregory I, "the Great". The
date is approximately correct.

12 Often called "Justinian's Plague".
That it is called "the first plague" here
shows that this was written after the
"second plague"—of the late seventh
century. The entry under AD 551 is
obviously a duplicate.

**From the Annals of the Four Masters
(pp. 126–134)**

1 *Recte* 431.

2 The Laws and History. This refers,
however, to the Laws—the Senchus
Már—alone, with which Patrick was
connected in later legend.

3 Legendary ancestor of the Eóganachta of Munster. According to the
traditional chronology he would have
been long dead at this time.

4 Benignus, who, according to the Lives
of the saints, would have been a small
boy at this time.

5 Said to have died in AD 530.

6 Secundinus, whose church was at
Dunshaughlin, Co. Meath.

7 Maucteus, of Louth.

8 Of Slane, Co. Meath.

9 Of Clogher, Co. Tyrone.

10 Of Kilbennan, Co. Galway.

11 Apparently of Cell Riada. There was
such a place in the diocese of Derry.
See Hogan, *Onomasticon Goedelicum*,
209.

12 Of Cell Dareis; apparently by Lough
Melvin, in Co. Leitrim or Co.
Fermanagh.

13 Of Badoney (Both-Domhnaich), near
Strabane, Co. Tyrone.

14 Of Domhnach Mescain; somewhere
by the Faughan river in Co. Derry.

15 Of Domhnach Dula, in Magh Dula,
south Co. Derry.

16 i.e. Patrick son of Calpurnius. "Mac
Calpuirn" has been corrupted to
"Mac Alprainn."

17 Of Domhnach Arnoin. Not known.

18 Of Domhnach Laebháin. In the diocese of Clonfert.

19 Of Trim, Co. Meath and Cill
Forthchern, in Co. Carlow.

20 Tasach of Raholp (Raith Choloptha),
near Saul, Co. Down. The other two
are unidentified.

21 Lupita: in late legend St Patrick's sister.

22 Ergnata—legendary daughter of the
Dáire who is said to have made the
grant of Armagh to Patrick.

23 Of Kenngobha, east of Armagh.

24 Of Disert Odrain in Uí Failge.

25 Known only in this legendary connection.

26 Said in legend to have been five sisters of Patrick.

27 Elsewhere "Gornias". Known only in
this connection.

28 St Germanus of Auxerre. See p. 40.

29 Known only in this connection.

30 Otherwise Sennan, his "brother" or
"cousin". Known only in this connection.

31 St Martin of Tours.

32 St Cádán of Tamlaghtard, Ardma-
gilligan, Co. Derry.

33 Of Kill Forclann, near Killala, Co.
Mayo.

34 Brocanus, said to have been St
Patrick's nephew.

35 Otherwise Lughna, of Inchagoill,
Lough Corrib, Co. Galway.

36 St Mochaí, of Nendrum, Co. Down.

37 The list of St Patrick's household—
here taken from a tenth-century
poem by Flann Mainistreach—is an
obviously late compendium of fabulous
and legendary material.

38 St Auxilius.

39 Killossy, or Killashee, near Naas, Co.
Kildare.

40 The plain of north Co. Kildare.

41 i.e. Benignus, of Kilbennan, Co.
Galway.

42 Of Tuam, Co. Galway.

43 Said to have given the veil to St Brigid
on Croghan Hill, Co. Offaly.

44 Of Begerin, Co. Wexford. One of
the reputed "pre-Patrician" saints.

45 Known as "Justinian's Plague".

46 Probably the same as the bishop
Iserninus.

47 A druidic fence, or magic circle. Diarmaid is associated in some legends with
the last rally of paganism in Ireland.

48 The earlier annals date Diarmaid's death to AD 565.

The "First Synod of St Patrick" (pp. 135–138)

1 The word *plebs*, which occurs several times in this text, probably refers to the *tuath*—tribe or chiefdom—rather than to a monastic or other religious community. The *tuath*, next to the extended family, was the basic unit of early Irish society. However, *plebs* here may mean the Christian community.
2 "Finally" ("*denique*") probably indicates that this regulation is copied from a list of which it is the final item. See Bieler, *Irish Penitentials*, 240.
3 The reference here is to Irish pagan customary law.

From Adomnán's Life of Columba (pp. 139–140)

1 Proverbs 22:1.

From St Columbanus's Letter to Pope Boniface IV (pp. 141–143)

1 Proverbs 10:1. Cf. St Patrick's Declaration, p. 105. But Patrick and Columbanus quote it differently: Patrick: "*Filius sapiens gloria patris est.*"; Columbanus (who modifies it to his sentence): "[*si*] *sapienter* [*locutus fuerit*] *filius, laetificabitur pater.*"
2 Apparently Bishop of Como. The letter has not survived. See Walker (1970), 41 (footnote).
3 1 Cor. 12:26.
4 Psalm 19:1: "The heavens declare the glory of God; and the firmament showeth his handiwork."
5 Roman 10:18. See also Psalm 19:4.

From Bede's Church History of the English People (pp. 144–150)

1 Archbishop of Canterbury, the successor of the first archbishop, St Augustine, who died some time in the first decade of the seventh century.
2 Not certainly identified. Probably the bishop named Dagán who is listed in the Martyrology of Tallaght under 12 March. Anne O'Sullivan,

ed., *The Book of Leinster*, 6 (Dublin 1983), 1605.
3 See p. 151.
4 625–638.
5 638– .
6 Plummer, in his edition of this text, identified the Irish recipients of the letter as far as possible: Tomíne, Bishop of Armagh (significantly placed first); Colmán, Bishop of Clonard; Crónán, Bishop of Nendrum; Dimma, Bishop of Connor; Báetán, possibly the Bishop of Bangor; Crónán Abbot of Moville; Ernéne, Abbot of Tory; Laisréne, Abbot of Leighlin; Sillán, Bishop of Devenish; Segéne, Abbot of Iona; Sarán ua Critain—northerners all.
7 Psalm 51:5.

From Cummian's Letter to Segéne and Beccán (pp. 151–153)

1 "Pope": the term *papa* was used of a primatial or metropolitan bishop. Its use here indicates that Cummian regarded Patrick as having a special status.
2 Deuteronomy 32:7.
3 Of Emly.
4 Not certainly identified: probably of Birr; possibly of Clonfert.
5 Of Mungret (Co. Limerick).
6 Otherwise Mo-lua; of Clonfert Molua (Co. Laois).

Bishop Tírechán's Account of St Patrick's Journeys (pp. 154–174)

1 This account is also found, twice, in the prologue to Muirchú's Life of St Patrick (p. 175). "Cothirtiacus" is the name Patricius rendered by a Goidelic speaker. See R. Thurneysen, *A Grammar of Old Irish*, trans. D.A. Binchy and O. Bergin (1946), 571. Tírechán is deriving it from the Irish word for "four": "cethir". "Succetus" was, as he was aware, the name of a Celtic war god, and he assumes this to be its derivation here. It may possibly, however, derive from Patrick's reputed services as a swineherd.
2 A scribe has had difficulty (in the text he was copying) in distinguishing between 2 (**ıı**) and 5 (**ıı**).

3 Compare St Patrick's figure of Christ as the sun, p. 108.

4 At this point in the Book of Armagh, a list of bishops, priests and churches intrudes into the middle of a sentence about Benignus. See p. 198. It seems that a leaf containing this aide-memoire was gathered mistakenly into a manuscript and copied as part of Tírechán's text.

5 At this point a few lines occur in the text which appear to be misplaced. They read: "Further, he founded a church at Carric Dagri [*Killineer, Drogheda?*], and he wrote an alphabet for Cerpanus . . .".

6 See the story about Succetus on Slemish, p. 174.

7 Tírechán speaks here as a descendant of Énde.

8 Dallbrónach, in some versions of St Brigid's Life, figures as her father. His rath, according to this itinerary, is placed close to Croghan Hill in Offaly [*Brí Éile*], where, according to one tradition, St Brigid received the veil.

9 See p. 173.

10 There is a hiatus here in the manuscripts.

11 This, introducing the main part of Tírechán's account, is a kind of manifesto, stating his purpose and aim. He expresses Patrick's (i.e. Armagh's) claims in terms of Irish legal custom and practice.

12 Compare the similar contest in Muirchú's account, pp. 185–187.

13 This passage appears to be misplaced. The story is told more fully later (pp. 163–165), but not in Tírechán's words. The next paragraph returns to the main narrative.

14 This episode is a quotation, or "insert". It is written in a style quite different from Tírechán's, and has been incorporated into his narrative by him or a copyist from some other source.

15 Otherworld people.

16 This, the only mention of Mathonus, suggests that he, not Patrick, may have been the original protagonist of the episode, into which Patrick's name was later introduced.

17 From the Latin "*reliquiae*"—"remains".

18 Ciarán, the founder of Clonmacnoise.

19 The birth of Ciarán is entered in the Annals of Ulster at dates corresponding to AD 512 and 517. Bury pointed out that Tírechán's mistake here arose from the use of an 84-year Paschal cycle. He was taking 461 as the year of Patrick's death and 517 as the year of Ciarán's birth. The interval is 56, to which, by using the wrong phase of the cycle, he has inadvertently added 84. *English Historical Review* (1902), 239ff. T.F. O'Rahilly, *Early Irish History and Mythology*, 236.

20 This list is not part of Tírechán's text but has been inserted here by a scribe and then copied as part of the narrative.

21 The text here reads: ". . . *in quo fiunt mulieres* . . .". I have taken this to be a mistranscription of ". . . *in quo fiunt molares* . . .".

22 This seems to be a misplaced fragment.

23 This may be suggested by the passage in St Patrick's Declaration, p. 103.

24 The text is defective here.

25 The scribe has written here: "*vestigium regale*" ("royal path"), which is probably a mistranscription for something like "*vestigium rigatum.*"

26 See pp. 173, 226.

27 The tomb described here is certainly a Neolithic chambered tomb of the Court Tomb class, of which there are still numbers in the vicinity of Ballina, some of them of the dimensions described. In modern times too, they were known as "Giants' Graves."

28 Coirpre was a legendary Leinster King of Tara, Lugaid mac Con, a legendary ancestor of the Érainn. See O'Rahilly, *Early Irish History and Mythology*, 201–202.

29 This passage is an aside, obviously suggested by the episode of the grandson of Cas son of Glas. It interrupts the narrative of Patrick's journey from the Reek to the Wood of Foclut with a story from another part of the country.

30 The word "*fatui*" has here been amended to "*fati*".

31 "*Machinensem episcopum*": Bury and Bieler both suggest that this is a corruption of "*Maginensem*".
32 Mac Tail and Iserninus are possibly the same person.
33 i.e. "Patrick's Rock".

Muirchú's Life of St Patrick (pp. 175–197)

1 This appears in the manuscripts after the opening paragraph of the account, but has been moved forward here.
2 The two passages from a Life of St Basil, probably being used here as a model of hagiographical writing, have been copied by mistake and are inserted in a garbled form into this narrative.
3 This is an imperfect version of the paragraph in Tírechán's memoir (p. 154), inserted by a copyist.
4 Bishop Áed of Slébte, successor of Bishop Fiacc.
5 There follow at this point in the MS the summary and contents table which have here been moved forward to the beginning.
6 Exodus 16:13.
7 St Patrick's Declaration. See p. 100.
8 See the discussion of Segitius and of this passage, p. 40. See also pp. 57–58, 179.
9 Celestine, AD 422–432, was the forty-first successor of St Peter.
10 See p. 40.
11 This probably refers to Amator, Germanus's predecessor as Bishop of Auxerre, who was long dead at the implied date. He could well, however, have conferred the diaconal order on Palladius earlier in the century.
12 This refers to the Roman tonsure.
13 Daniel 2:2.
14 Matthew 2:1–23.
15 Psalms 20:7.
16 Daniel 3:14–28.
17 To complete the story, the key of his fetter should have been found in a fish's belly. See *Ériu*, 30 (1979), 100.
18 See Bieler, *Patrician Texts*, 205: "*Mudebroth* (*Mudebrod* I 26.2) is an Irish corruption of British or Welsh *min Duw braut* 'by the God of judgment' . . .".

19 A corruption of something like "*Gratias agimus*": "We give thanks."
20 See note 18 above.
21 Judges 6:34–40.
22 Exodus 3:2.
23 2 Kings 20:8–11; Joshua 10:12–13.
24 Genesis 27:27. The quotation is not from "the blessings of Jacob", but from Isaac's blessing given when Jacob, pretending to be his brother Esau, deceived his father.
25 2 Kings: 6.18–20.

From the notes to Tírechán's narrative in the Book of Armagh (pp. 200–201)

1 The addition is wrong.
2 Possibly Constans "the wise", anchorite of Eó-Inis, Loch Éirne. See P. Grosjean, *Analecta Bollandiana*, 42, 62, and L. Bieler, *Patrician Texts*, 213.
3 This paragraph is in Tírechán's style, and would appear to belong to his narrative: see p. 167. See also the discussion of Sacellus.
4 This paragraph, tacked on to the preceding one, is not by Tírechán, but has been added by some later supporter of the primacy of Armagh.

From the further fragments in the Book of Armagh (pp. 203–206)

1 Probably a reference to the *faithche*, the open space before a homestead.
2 At this point, Irish replaces Latin, indicating that the following passage has been added by another narrator.
3 Another name for Iserninus.

Cogitosus's Life of St Brigid the Virgin (pp. 207–224)

1 The Uí Eachach were in the Louth-Armagh-Down area.
2 The tradition in other sources is that St Brigid's mother was a slave. In Cogitosus her parents are said to have been noble. This was to become a common device in hagiography, to confer additional prestige on the subject.
3 John 9:5; Matthew 5:14; John 15:12.
4 Since early Hallstatt times, and through into late Celtic culture, ducks

and swans seem to have had religious and cult significance. This apparently pointless anecdote may reflect an aspect of the Celtic goddess with whom Brigid is confused.

The Three Orders of Saints (pp. 225–226)

1 The conventional annalistic dates (for what they are worth) of the deaths of these kings of Tara are: Loeguire son of Niall: 461; Ailill Molt, son of Nath I: 482; Lugaid, son of Loeguire: 507; Tuathal Maelgarb, son of Cormac Cáech: 544. Muirchertach mac Ercae, who is generally listed after Lugaid (his death is noted in 536) is omitted from the text.
2 Báetán, son of Muirchertach, and Eochu, son of Domnall Ilchelgach son of Muirchertach, both of whom are said to have died in 572.
3 The intervening kings were Ainmere (d. 569) and Báetán, son of Ninnid (d. 586). Áed's death is recorded for 598.
4 Áed Sláine died in 604. Máel Cobo, King of Ulaid, died in 647. Áed Allán and Domnall, however, died in 743 and 763 respectively: the chronology is confused here.
5 The plague of the 660s.

The Life of St Ailbe (pp. 227–243)

1 Or Sanct, i.e. sanctus—a Christian.
2 A folk etymology, as Plummer points out in his edition of the text. It derives from the Irish words "*ail*" ("rock") and "*beo*" ("alive").
3 Palladius. The name is mentioned in some versions of the text.
4 It is just possible that "the sons of Goll" is a corrupt transcription of a phrase meaning "the people of Gaul."
5 The Cruthnean territory of south Antrim and north Down.
6 The Dál nAraidi were connected by the genealogists with the Dál Cairbre Arad of Munster through a mythical ancestor, Laider Ara. See O'Rahilly, *Early Irish History and Mythology*, 20–21.

7 See L. de Paor, "St Mac Creiche of Liscannor", *Ériu*, 30 (1979), 109–115.
8 Of Mungret, Co. Limerick.

The Life of St Declan of Ardmore (pp. 244–271)

1 Jeremiah 1:5.
2 Psalm 89:7: "God is greatly to be feared in the assembly of the saints."
3 Probably Youghal Bay and Dungarvan Harbour.
4 John 15:16.
5 Psalms 107:33.
6 Psalms 9:6.
7 Two major plagues are reported in the annals, "Justinian's Plague" in the 540s and 550s and a plague of 665 or 666. They seem to be confused in the later reconstructions of chronology. The yellowing, or jaundice, effect is attributed to both.
8 Mark 16:18.
9 ". . . saith the Lord." Romans 12:19.
10 Psalm 66:6.
11 This translation—"hide"—is only a guess. The word used, "*habellum*", puzzled the copyists of the text and is left in Latin, untranslated, in the Irish Life. It is possible that the word was "*flabellum*"—a ceremonial fan: *flabella* are depicted in the Book of Kells and elsewhere.

The Life of St Ciarán of Saigir (pp. 272–280)

1 Daniel 3:12–30.
2 Ailill, son of Nad Froích (and brother of Óengus), is not usually listed among the kings of Munster, although he is reckoned the ancestor of that branch of the Eóganacht dynasties known as Eóganacht Áine.
3 Illann, son of Dúnlaing, king of Leinster, whose death is recorded at 527.
4 "King of Connacht" according to the Life of Ciarán of Clonmacnoise—Plummer, *Vitae Sanctorum Hiberniae*, 1, 203 and 207. Not in the annals or genealogies.
5 Matthew 3:9; Luke 3:8.
6 Acts 13:47 (Isaiah 42:6).

The Life of St Darerca (pp. 281–294)

1 This suggests that possibly the Life incorporates a tradition that Darerca was a disciple (spiritual "daughter") of St Mochta, or Maucteus, whose church was at Louth, in Conaille. If so, the tradition has been superseded —reasonably plausibly—by the intrusion of the more prestigious saints Patrick and Ibar.

2 This may mean teaching them to read and write as well as teaching the Scriptures: the Psalms seem to have been used as a reading primer in early Ireland.

3 i.e. Eochu, son of Condlae, of the Cruthin (Dál nAraide), who is said to have died in AD 553.

Early incised graveslabs,
Assylin, Boyle, Co. Roscommon

Select Bibliography

A great deal has been published on the subjects covered in this book. There are listed here, first, the editions of texts which have been used for the translations; second, a short selection of general works dealing with the matters touched on.

TEXTS

Councils of the Gaulish Church: Charles Munier, ed., *Concilia Galliae 314–506*, Turnhout (1963)

Prosper of Aquitaine, *Against the Collator*: Prosper, *Liber contra collatorem*, J.P. Migne, *Patrilogia Latina* (1881), 51, 269–270

Prosper of Aquitaine, *Chronicle*: Prosper, *Chronicum integrum*, Migne, P.L., 51, 599

St Patrick, *Declaration*: L. Bieler, ed., *Libri Epistolarum Sancti Patricii Episcopi* (1952)

St Patrick, *Letter against the Soldiers of Coroticus*: L. Bieler, ed., *Libri Epistolarum*

The Annals of Ulster: Seán Mac Airt and G. Mac Niocaill, ed., *The Annals of Ulster* (1983)

The Annals of Inisfallen: Seán Mac Airt, *The Annals of Inisfallen* (1951)

The Annals of the Four Masters: John O'Donovan, ed., *The Annals of the Four Masters* (1848–51)

The "First Synod of St Patrick": L. Bieler, ed., *The Irish Penitentials* (1963)

Adomnán, *Life of St Columba*: A.O. and M.O. Anderson, ed., *Adomnan's Life of Columba* (1961), 182

St Columbanus, Letter to Pope Boniface IV: G.S.M. Walker, ed., *Sancti Columbani Opera* (1970)

Bede, *Church History of the English People*: B. Colgrave and R.A.B. Mynors, ed., *Bede's Ecclesiastical History of the English People* (1969)

Cummian, Letter on the Easter Question: M. Walsh and D. Ó Cróinín, ed., *Cummian's Letter De Controversia Paschali and the De Ratione Conputandi* (1988)

Tírechán, Account of St Patrick: L. Bieler and F. Kelly, *The Patrician Texts in the Book of Armagh* (1979)

Muirchú, Life of St Patrick: Bieler and Kelly, *Patrician Texts*

A misplaced list: Bieler and Kelly, *op. cit.*

From the notes to Tírechán's narrative in the Book of Armagh: Bieler and Kelly, *op. cit.*

"Sayings of St Patrick": Bieler and Kelly, *op. cit.*

From further fragments: Bieler and Kelly, *op. cit.*

Cogitosus, Life of St Brigid: J.P. Migne, *Patrilogia Latina*, 72 (1878) (a reprint of the second edition of the text first published by Canisius in 1604). Colgan, *Triadis Thaumaturgae* (1647), has also been consulted for this translation.

"The Three Orders of Saints": W.W. Heist, ed., *Vitae Sanctorum Hiberniae ex Codice olim Salmanticensi nunc Bruxellensi* (1965), 81–83

The Life of St Ailbe: C. Plummer, ed. *Vitae Sanctorum Hiberniae* 1 (1910), 46–64

The Life of St Declan: C. Plummer, *op.cit.*, 2 (1910), 32–59

The Life of St Ciarán of Saigir: W.W. Heist, *op. cit.*, 346–353

The Life of St Darerca: W.W. Heist, *op. cit.*, 83–95

SELECT READING LIST

Olwen Brogan, *Roman Gaul* (1953)
C. Thomas, *Christianity in Roman and Sub-Roman Britain to A.D. 500* (1979)
M.W. Barley and R.P.C. Hanson, ed., *Christianity in Britain 300–700* (1967)
E.A. Thompson, *St Germanus of Auxerre and the End of Roman Britain* (1984)

J.B. Bury, *The Life of St Patrick and his Place in History* (1905)

T.F. O'Rahilly, *Early Irish History and Mythology* (1946)

F.J. Byrne, *Irish Kings and High-Kings* (1973)

K. Hughes, *The Church in Early Irish Society* (1966)

M. and L. de Paor, *Early Christian Ireland* (1958)

J. Ryan, ed., *St Patrick* (1964)

L. Bieler, *The Life and Legend of St Patrick* (1949)

R.P.C. Hanson, *St Patrick—His Origins and Career* (1968)

T.F. O'Rahilly, *The Two Patricks* (1942)

J. Carney, *The Problem of St Patrick* (1961)

D. Binchy, "Patrick and his biographers: ancient and Modern", *Studia Hibernica*, 2 (1962), 7–173

E.A. Thompson, *Who was St Patrick?* (1985)

J.F. Kenney, *The Sources for the Early History of Ireland: Ecclesiastical* (1929)

C. Plummer, *Vitae Sanctorum Hiberniae*, 1 (1910), Introduction, ix–clxxxviii

Index of Place and Population Names

Abercorn, 146
Abha Mhór, river, 247
Achad Bó (Aghaboe), 120, 121
Achad Cáerach, 238
Achadh Farcha, 130
Aebbercurnig (Abercorn), 146
Achad Fobair, 168
Achadh Cinn, 133
Achilon, 195
Aegean Sea, 9
Aendruim (Nendrum), 129
Africa, 14–15, 18, 56, 74, 76–80, 82
Aghaboe, 120 (*see* "Achad Bó")
Aghade, 41, 206
Ailbhine, river, 155
Ailech Airthicc, 200
Ailech Esrachta, 200
Ailenn (Dún Ailinne), 36
Ailgi, 173
Ail Cluait (Alcluith, Aloo), 145–146, 176
Ailmag, 172
Airgialla, 32, 34, 129, 191
Airthir, 191, 197
Alamanni, 9
Alans, 15, 75
Alexandria, 14, 16, 19, 71, 75, 79,
    83–84, 87, 121, 125, 152
Alps, 14, 25, 85 (*see* "Maritime Alps")
Angers, 65
Anglo-Saxons, 18, 21 (*see* "English",
    "Saxons")
Antibes, 59, 63
Antioch, 14, 16, 20, 152
Antrim, county, 30, 95, 125, 133–134,
    154, 181–182, 234
Apt, 55, 58–59
Apulia, 55
Aquileia, 55, 73

Aquitaine (Aquitania), 16, 55, 77
Araid Cliach, 228, 242
Aralensis, 154
Aran islands, 236
Arda Huimnonn, 190
Ard Aisse, 199
Ardbraccan, 174
Ard Carna (Ardcarne), 131
Ardagh (Ard Achad) (Co. Longford),
    44, 119, 128, 159
Ardagh, Co. Meath, 185
Ard Conais, 283–284
Ardd Eólurg, 173
Ardfinnan, 268
Ardd Licce, 165, 199
Ard Macha: *see* "Armagh"
Ard Mór (Ardmore), 46, 251, 254, 256,
    264, 266, 271
Ard na gCáerach, 254
Ard Roissen, 173
Ard Senlis, 165
Ard Sratho, 173 (*see* "Ardstraw")
Ardstraw, 162, 173
Ard Uiscon, 168
Argetbor, 199
Arklow, 180
Arles, 12, 15–17, 20, 41, 53–59, 61,
    63, 76, 78, 93, 152, 154, 202
Armagh, 4, 41–46, 48–50, 64, 88, 91,
    95, 118–120, 122, 124–125, 128,
    130, 132, 155, 162, 167, 174, 176,
    191–195, 199, 201, 203–204;
    county: 36, 120, 130, 191, 244, 287
Armorica, 144
Artrige, 228
Art's Head, 159
Ashbourne, 199
Asia Minor, 9, 12, 16

Assaroe, 172
Assylinn, 167
Atecotti, 18
Athbron, 156
Áth Cinn Conn, 158
Áth Carnoi, 158
Áth dá Ioarcc, 166
Áth Dara, 237
Áth Fithboth, 41, 206
Athlone, 170
Áth Segi, 158
Áth Truim, 126, 203 (*see* "Trim")
Attica, 80
Aughenagh, 172
Aughnakilly, 133
Aurchuil, 170
Authuile strand, 172
Autun, 55
Auxerre, 19, 21, 39–40, 79, 178, 205
Avignon, 58–59, 63
Avoca, river, 180
Avrolles, 40

Babylon, 183
Ballon, 205
Ballina, 158, 170–171, 199
Ballinrobe, 168
Ballintober (Co. Mayo), 168
Ballintober (Co. Roscommon), 161, 165
Ballycowan, 159
Ballymore Eustace, 206
Ballynagore, 158
Ballynew, 170
Bandae (Bann), river, 173
Bangor, 3, 120, 122, 125, 132
Bannavem Taberniae (Banna Venta
    Burniae), 88, 96, 177
Barnesmore Gap, 173
Barrow, river, 30, 33, 236, 247, 269
Bartragh (Co. Mayo and Co. Sligo), 172
Basilica Sanctorum (Baslick), 41,
    166–167
Beacia, 56
Begerin (Becc Ériu, Beggary), 48, 206,
    282
Beniata, 56
Bennchor: *see* "Bangor"
Bertriga, 172 (*see* "Bartragh")
Bethlehem, 73
Béziers, 12
Bil, 158–159
Bile Torten, 174
Birdoswald, 88

Birr, 133, 226
Bizerte, 56
Blackwater, river (Meath), 158, 172
Blackwater, river (Munster), 247, 249,
    252, 268
Blaitiniu, 199
Bog of Allen, 48
Boidmal's Wood, 160
Bonn, 73
Bordeaux, 9, 12, 55, 73
Bordj-Bou-Djadi, 56
Bosphorus, 14
Bourges, 65
Boyle, 167
Boyne, river, 29, 44, 183, 199, 203–204
Braith, river, 172
Bray, 151
Breaghy, 44, 204
Brecmag, 44, 204
Brega, 45, 155, 180, 182, 183, 199,
    204, 218, 263
Bréne, 180
Brer Garad, 166
Brí Dam, 199
Brí Éile, 47–48
Brí Gobban (Brigown), 247
Britain (Brittania), 4–6, 9–22, 25–26,
    28–29, 33–34, 36, 38, 40, 44, 53,
    56, 71, 73, 75, 79, 88–90, 93–95,
    100, 102, 104, 123, 125, 144–146,
    148, 177–179, 187, 226, 229, 234,
    251, 289
Britons (British), 18–19, 21, 25, 35, 40,
    45, 53, 65, 79, 89–90, 119,
    144–148, 177, 179, 204, 225,
    228–229, 253, 257
Brittany, 53, 144, 233
Bríu, pool of, 281
Bruree, 238
Buanann Chelle Ruaid, river, 234
Buas (Bush), river, 173
Burgundians, 76, 80
Byzantium, 14

Cabcenne, river, 197
Caerleon-on-Usk, 10
Cagliari, 56
Caher, 265–266, 268
Cahore Point, 206
Cairech, 198
Callan, 247
Callraige, 172, 205
Calry, 172

Campania, 55, 81
Cana, 211
Canterbury, 44, 144
Capua, 55
Carbury, 158
Cardigan, 94
Carlisle, 18, 88, 90, 96
Carlow, county, 34, 205–206, 237
Carmell's Head, 158
Carn Achaid Lethdeirg, 32
Carndonagh, 173
Carnes, 158
Carn Tigernaig, 36
Carpentras, 57–59, 63
Carrick-on-Suir, 247
Carrowmagley, 172
Carthage, 53, 56, 74–75, 77, 81–82, 87
Cashel, 31, 34, 174, 235–236, 252,
    254, 256–261
Castellane, 58, 60
Castlebar, 169, 173
Castlerea, 160
Catrige, 205
Cavaillon, 59, 63
Cavan, county, 160
Cell Achaid Druimfhata (Killeigh), 122,
    132
Cell Angle, 172
Cell Bile, 158
Cell Chuilind (Cell Cuilinn), 41, 43–44,
    122, 132, 174
Cell Cobthaigh, 247
Cell Coluim Deirg, 263
Cell Cumili, 226
Cell Dara, 131 (*see* "Kildare")
Cell Dumi Glinn, 44, 204
Cell Fhine, 126
Cell Muni, 234, 253 (*see* "St Davids")
Cell Ruaid, 234
Cell Senchuae, 172
Cell Sléibe Cuilinn, 120, 130, 287 (*see*
    "Killeevy")
Cell Tóch (Cell Tóg), 170, 173
Cell Usailli, 41, 128, 174 (*see* "Killashee")
Celts, 25–26, 28, 90
Cenél gConaill, 28
Cenél Énde, 200
Cenn Losnada, 34
Cenn Sali, 240
Cenn Tíre (Kintyre), 124
Cenn Trágha, 285
Centocelli, 56
Cerne, 173, 199

Chalcedon, 61, 84–85, 119, 124, 141
Chalons-sur-Marne, 65
Cherchell, 56
Cianachta, 166
Ciarraige Airnen, 167
Ciarraige Connacht, 44, 204
Cillín Chormaic, 126
Cimiez, 59, 63
Clare, county, 122, 242
Clébach, well of, 163, 165
Cliach, 227
Cliu, 205
Clochar (Clogher), 120, 196
Clonard, 125, 132, 226
Clonduff, 237
Clones, 198, 122, 132
Clonfert, 122, 125, 131, 133, 151
Clonlyon, 204
Clonmacnoise, 3, 122, 125, 132, 152,
    163, 173
Cluain Aird Mo Becoc, 151
Cluain Auiss (Cluain Eois): *see* "Clones"
Cluain Damdaim, 237
Cluain Ferta Brénainn: *see* "Clonfert"
Cluain Iraird: *see* "Clonard"
Cluain Lagen, 204
Cluain moccu Nois: *see* "Clonmacnoise"
Clyde, river, 145–146, 176
Cobha, 291
Coindire (Connor, Condere), 120, 124,
    130–131, 173
Coirp Raithe, 158
Coithrige's Rock (at Cashel), 174
Coithrige's Rock (Meath), 159
Colchester, 12
Coleraine, 173
Collum Bovis, 191
Collumbus, 199
Collunt, 174
Cologne, 12, 14–15, 55
Comar na dTrí nUisce, 247
Commienses, tribe of, 159
Conaille, 180, 281–282, 286
Conchubar, tribe of, 154
Con Inga, 263
Conmaicne of Cúl Tolith, 168
Conmaicne Mara, 166
Connacht, 160, 165, 206, 234–235, 239
Connachta, 25–26, 31–34, 36, 45, 130,
    133, 246
Connemara, 166 (*see* "Conmaicne Mara")
Constantinople, 14–15, 61, 72–75, 78,
    80, 83–84, 120

Cooldroman, 125
Cooley, 282, 291
Corcumruad, 242
Corcu Roide, 159
Corcu Saí, 166
Corcu Temne, 169–170, 173
Cork, county, 33, 36, 167, 240, 247, 268
Corkaree, 159
Cornwall, 26
Coslas, 74
Cothirbe, 159
Críoch-in-Ernaidhe, 129
Críoch Loeghaire, 129
Croagh Patrick, 158, 168
Croch Cuile, 166
Crochan Aigli: *see* "Sliab Aigli"
Croghan Hill, 44, 48
Cruachu, 31–33, 35–36, 41, 44–45, 163, 201
Cruanakeely, 166
Cruthin, 30, 126, 181
Cualgne, 291
Cualu, 180
Cúl Corrae, 159
Cúl Dreimne, 125, 133
Cúl Irra, 130
Cúl Maige, 206
Cúl Raithne, 173
Cúl Tolith, 168
Cuircni, 44
Curlew Mountain, 161, 163, 172
Curt, grove of, 268

Daiminis (Daminis) (Co. Fermanagh), 134
Daiminis, on the Blackwater, 173
Daire Calgach: *see* "Derry"
Dalmatia, 79
Dál Messincorb, 263–264
Dál nAraide, 30, 134, 234
Dál Fiatach, 30
Dál Riata (Dalreuda), 30, 145
Danube, river, 10, 14, 21, 85
Darragh Fort, 159
Deece, 246
Delvin, river, 155
Dercan's Rock, 263
Derry, 131; county, 174
Derver, 130
Dési, 26, 34, 246–247, 249, 252–254, 256–260, 264, 267, 270
Devenish, 134, 173
Dichuil, 170

Die, 58–59
Doburbar, river, 173
Dol (Dolo Moir), 233
Dam Liacc (Duleek), 124, 128, 166
Domnach Ailmaige, 172
Domnach Arta (Donard), 126
Domnach Féicc, 206
Domnach Mór Criathar (Domnach Mór Maige Criathar), 206
Domnach Sairigi, 166
Domnach Sechnaill, 41
Domnainn, 30
Donaghmore, Co. Donegal, 173
Donaghmore, Co. Meath, 158
Donaghmore, Co. Sligo, 172
Donaghmore, Co. Wexford, 206
Donaghmoyne, 174
Donaghpatrick, Co. Galway, 162
Donaghpatrick, Co. Meath, 156
Donaseery, 166
Donegal, county, 29, 32, 162, 172–173
Donegore, 134
Doogarry, 161
Down, county, 30, 32, 48, 122, 125, 129, 132, 180–182, 190–192, 196–197, 245, 281, 291
Downpatrick, 122, 129, 131, 196
Dromahaire, 172
Dromore, 189
Drowse, river, 29, 172
Druim Buan (?), 268
Druim Daire, 199
Druim Daro, 205
Druim Derb, 120, 130
Druim Léas (Druim Lias, Drumlease), 172, 205
Druim Luchtri, 267
Druim moccu Echach, 189
Druim Sailech, 191
Drumcliff, 125
Drummae, 166
Drummut Cérrigi, 167, 200
Drumsna, 160
Drumtemple, 167
Dublin, Institute for Advanced Studies, 7; county, 124, 180, 199
Duff, river, 172
Duhallow, 167
Duleek, 124, 128, 166, 199
Dul Ocheni, 173
Dumbarton, 94, 145–146, 176
Dumech, 163
Dún Ailinne, 41 (*see* "Ailenn")

Dunamon, 167
Dunboyne, 158
Dún-dá-Lethglas (Dún Lethglaise), 196
   (*see* "Downpatrick")
Dunegore, 125
Dunseverick (Dún Sobhairce), 173
Dunshaughlin 41–42, 173
Durrow, 3, 162

Eauze, 56
Ebmoria, 40, 179
Ebredunum, 40
Eburobrica, 40
Echnach (Echenach), 158, 172
Echredd, 158
Eclanum, 81
Edenderry, 158
Egypt, 12, 14–16, 37, 182
Eilne, 173
Elphin, 161–163, 167, 200
Elvira, 53, 93
Emain Macha, 32–33, 36, 41, 244
Embrun, 40, 58, 60, 63
Emlagh, 44, 161, 204
Emly, 46, 48, 121, 125, 132, 227, 237–
   238, 243, 267
England, 18, 144
English, 148
English Channel, 251
Eóganachta, 33–34, 36, 253, 264
Ephesus, 19, 41, 61, 79, 84
Érainn, 30, 34
Érend, 265
Erne, 172
Ess Mac nErcc, 167
Ess Ruaid, 172
Ethne, river, 159
Euoe, 172
Euonia, 190
Europe, 14, 23–27, 95

Farragh, 171
Faughart (Fachart), 48, 287
Fermanagh, county, 134, 173
Fermoy, 247
Fernmag, 32
Ferta Cherpáin (Feart Cearbáin), 120,
   124, 129
Ferta Fer Féich, 130, 183–184, 199
Fertach Decláin, 256
Fertae Martar, Armagh, 191
Fertullagh, 158
Fidarte, 166

Findmag, 169–170
Findubar, 196
Fir Galian, 247, 270
Firlee, 173
Fir Maige, 247
Firth of Clyde, 146
Firth of Forth, 146
Foclut (Focloth), 95, 100, 157–158,
   169, 171, 179
Foirrgea, 171
Ford of Two Birds, 160
Ford of Two Forks, 166
Forgnide (Forgney), 44, 204
Fotharta, 47
Foyle, river, 173
Franks, 9–10, 15, 18, 79, 111, 166, 199,
   225
Fréjus, 58, 60
Fuerty, 166

Gabaon, 195
Gabran, 174
Gabur Life, 206, 214
Gaedhil, 126
Gair, 166
Galicia, 58, 72
Galilee, 8
Gallia Belgica, 16
Gallia Lugdunensis, 16
Galloway, 289
Galway, county, 125, 162, 166
Gaul, 4–5, 9–11, 13, 15–18, 20–22,
   25–26, 29, 35–36, 39–41, 43, 53,
   55, 61–62, 71, 73–76, 79–81, 85,
   89–90, 104, 154, 175, 178, 200,
   202, 227, 229, 251
Gauls, 45, 111, 155
Geneva, 57, 59
Germans, 27, 35
Germany, 16, 36, 72
Gevaudan, 55
Gibraltar, Strait of, 14
Giudi, 146
Glais Naidhen (Glasnevin), 132
Glastonbury, 9
Glen of Aherlow, 151
Glenn Rige, 32
Glentogher, 173
Gorey, 206
Goths, 13, 18, 21, 38, 72, 75–76, 78,
   80–81, 84–85, 89
Gowran, 174
Grabor, mountain, 214

Granard, 159
Gregrige, 166
Grenoble, 58, 59

Hadrianople, 21
Hellenes, 26
Hellespontus, 41
Hiberione (Ireland), 93
Hiberionaces, 93
Hibernii, 31
Hill of the Rocks, 167
Hippo, 18, 74, 80
Hirota: see "Uí Rota"
Holy island, 122
Hono's Imbliuch, 161
House of the Martyrs, 174
Humal, 168
Huns, 21, 78–83, 85

Iceland, 241
Idrone, 205
Illyricum, 16, 82
Imbliuch Ech, 44, 204
Imbliuch Iubair (Imlech Ibair, Emly),
    121, 125, 132, 238–240, 243, 267
Imgoe Már Cerrigi, 167
Inber Colptha, 183
Inber Dee, 180
Inis Becc (Beggary), 206
Inis Fáil (Beggary), 206
Inisfallen, 7, 41, 117, 227
Inishcaltra, 122, 132
Inishowen, 173
Inneoin, 257, 260
Inny, river, 159
Iona, 47, 134, 151, 162
Irish, the, 13, 15–16, 19, 21, 25, 27,
    29–30, 35, 50, 79, 90–91, 93, 100,
    103, 112, 126, 128, 144–148, 185,
    188, 202, 207, 225, 232, 254
Irlochair, 167
Italy, 10, 12, 14–16, 18, 55, 71, 75, 79,
    85, 142, 154, 202, 250, 257
Iverni, 30

Jerusalem, 8, 15–16, 18, 152

Keenagh, 166
Keilin, 206
Kellistown, 34
Kells, 156, 166
Kilbennan, 166
Kilcullen, 41, 122, 132, 174

Kildare, 44, 46–49, 120, 130–131, 156,
    174, 206, 237; county: 36, 122,
    126, 132, 199, 207, 236
Kildoney, 172
Kilglinn, 45, 204
Kilkenny, county, 174, 247
Killala, 95, 100, 171
Killanly, 172
Killeraght, 167
Killare, 158
Killeevy, 120, 130, 287, 289
Killashee (Killassy), 41, 174
Killasbugbrone, 130, 172
Killeigh, 122, 132
Kilmacnowen, 130
Kilmallock, 238
Kilmore, Co. Meath, 204
Kilmoremoy, 158, 199
Kilmore, Moyglass, 161
Kilroot, 234
Kinneil, 146
Kinsale, 240
Kintyre, 124
Knockaulin, 36
Knockmealdown, mountains, 257, 264

Lagin (Leinster), 30–31, 33–36, 39,
    43–44, 126, 174, 206, 227, 236,
    240, 244–247, 263, 277, 282
Langres, 63
Laois, county, 42, 120, 174, 186
Larah, 205
Lathrach dá Arad, 205
Lathru, tribe of, 173
Latteragh, 132
Lecale, 129, 182, 190, 192
Lee Bendraige, 173
Legis Volumni, 56
Leighlinbridge, 237
Leitrim, county, 29, 32, 159, 172, 205
Leitrioch Odhrain, 132
Le Mans, 65
León, 58
Lérins, 154, 202
Leth Cuinn, 31, 125
Leth Moga, 31
Levant, 16
Licky, river, 268
Liffe (Liphe), 43, 128, 156, 236
Liffey, river, 132, 285
Lilcach, 130
Limavady, 173
Limerick, county, 228, 242

Lincoln, 12, 18, 56
Linnan, river, 247
Lipara, 77
Lismore (Liss Mor), 249, 252, 267
Little Island, 282
Loígles, 156
Lombards, 72–73, 77
London, 10, 12, 18, 44, 56
Longford, county, 42, 44, 159, 204
Lough Carra, 168
Lough Derg (Shannon), 30, 122
Lough Erne, 173
Lough Gara, 166
Lough Hackett, 182
Louth, 131, 139; county: 48–49, 130, 166, 180, 281–282, 285, 287, 291
Luasc, river, 247
Luch, river, 268
Lugdunum, 29
Lugmag: *see* "Louth"
Luguvalium (Carlisle), 88
Lusca (Lusk), 44, 119, 124
Lyon, 9, 19, 55, 57, 73

Macha, tribe of, 167
Mag Aí, 44–45, 160–162, 201, 204
Mag Áine, 172
Mag Airthic, 167, 200
Mag Cáeri, 168
Mag Cairetho, 165
Mag Cetni, 172
Mag Cobha, 245, 281
Mag Cumi, 159
Mag Domnon, 157, 171
Magerow, 172
Mag Femin, 236, 247, 257–258, 261, 264–265
Mag Foimsen, 168
Mag Gabra, 264
Mag Glais, 161
Mag Humail, 169
Mag Inis, 129, 182–183, 190–191
Mag Itho, 173
Mag Latrain, 173
Mag Lifi (Mag Life), 174, 199, 236
Mag Léne, 151–152
Mag Line, 134
Mag Locha, 268
Mag Rathen, 168
Mag Réin, 159
Mag Scéith, 249–250, 252
Mag Sereth, 162, 172–173
Mag Tochuir, 173

Maigen, 174
Mainistir (Buite), 130
Mainz, 15
Maistiu, 156
Man, Isle of, 190
Manx, 90
Maritime Alps, 58–61 (*see* "Alps")
Marseille, 9, 55, 63, 79
Maugdornai, 174
Mauretania, 10, 56
Maynooth, 5
Mayo, county, 30, 95, 100, 167–173, 199, 200
Meath, county, 45, 124–126, 128–132, 155, 166, 172, 180, 183, 185, 199, 203–204, 218, 246, 263
Mediterranean, 14–15
Merida, 56
Middle East, 14
Mide, 31, 33, 158, 146
Miledach, estuary, 247, 269
Milan, 11, 14, 16, 53, 55, 74
Mitchelstown, 247
Moccu Conchubair, 160, 175
Moccu Chor, 155
Moccu Ercae, 170
Moesia, 16
Mogdurn Breg, 185
Monaghan, county, 122, 132
Monasterboice, 130
Mound of Grad, 161
Mound of the Uí Ailello, 163
Mountain of the Uí Ailello, 161, 163, 172
Mount Leinster, 206
Mourne, 174
Moy, river, 170
Moylurg, 167
Moyola, river, 173
Moyvore, 159
Muada, river, 170, 172
Mucno (Mucnagh), 42, 167
Muin Daim (Collum), 191, 197
Muirisc Aigli, 168
Muirisc in Tireragh, 172
Muirtheimhne, 285, 291
Mullaghmast, 156
Mullaghnoney, 257, 260
Mumu (Munster), 30–31, 33–36, 174, 227–228, 235–236, 246–247, 252–253, 256, 259–261, 263, 267, 272, 275, 277
Munster, river, 247

Murrisk, 172
Muscraige, 34

Naas, 41, 174
Nairniu, 167, 200
Nanny Water, 172
Nantes, 65
Narbonne, 16, 58–61, 63, 80
Navan, Co. Meath, 158, 199
Navan Fort, 36, 244
Nem, river, 247
Nendrum (Naendruim), 120, 124, 129
Neocaesarea, 90
Newry, river, 32
New York, 95
Nice, 16, 55
Nicaea, 12, 16, 20, 152
Nîmes, 12
Nore, river, 247
North Africa, 10, 14, 23
North Sea, 13
Nothi, race of, 200
Numidia, 56

Ocha, 33
Offaly, county, 44, 48, 122, 132–133,
    151–152, 159, 273
Ogulla, well, 163
Oingae, river, 172
Oirghialla: *see* "Airgialla"
Old Church of the Mound, 163 (*see*
    "Senchell")
Ól nÉcmacht, fifth of, 30, 32
Oran, 166
Orange, 40, 55, 57–60, 63
Oriens, 16
Orior, 191
Osraige (Ossory), 240, 246–247, 263,
    272, 275–276
Ossuna, 56
Ostia, 56
Oudna, 56
Owles, the, 168
Oxford, 117

Palestine, 8
Pannonia, 16, 79, 85
Paris, 12, 73
Pass of the Sons of Conall, 173
Patrick's Island, 155, 180
Patrick's Rock 173, 174
Patrick's Well (Ballina), 158
Patrick's Well (near Suir) 258

Peakaun, 151
Peanfahel, 146
Penneltun, 146
Peterborough, 17
Picts, 13, 18, 21, 27, 30, 90, 109, 111–
    112, 144–148
Plain of Nente, 166
Platten, 199
Pobble O'Keefe, 167
Pocofeltus, 56
Pollentia, 75
Pontus, 16, 75
Port of Rome, 56
Pretani, 30
Puteolanum (Pitgliano), 84

Quoyle, river, 191

Racoon Hill, 162, 173
Rahan, 159
Ráith Bec (Rathbeg), 125, 134
Ráith Bilech, 205
Ráith Breasail, 254, 264
Ráith Cungai, 162, 173
Ráith Decláin, 249
Ráith Dobráin, 249
Ráith Foalascich, 205
Ráith na nIrlann, 260–261
Raphoe, 173
Rathcroghan, 166
Rathvilly, 205
Ravenna, 121
Reek (Croagh Patrick), 168
Reims, 55
Rennes, 65
Reti, 30
Rhine, river, 10, 13–14, 18, 76, 79, 84
Rhone, river, 29
Riez, 58, 60, 63
Rigbairt, 172
Rimini, 12
Robeen, 169
Rochuil, 162
Roigne, 174
Roman Empire, 8–10, 13–16, 18,
    21–22, 24–25, 27–28, 35, 38–39,
    44, 53, 90, 95
Rome, 9, 14, 16, 18–21, 26, 35, 37–38,
    40, 53, 55, 72–73, 75, 77–78,
    82–83, 86–87, 89, 91, 118–123,
    126, 142–144, 146, 151–153, 179,
    200, 203, 229–233, 240, 250–251,
    253, 257, 273

Rooskey, 282
Roscommon, county, 32, 44, 131, 161, 163, 165–167, 170, 200–201, 204
Ros Dregnige, 172
Rosnatense, 289
Ross Point, 171
Rouen, 55, 65
Runtir, tribe of, 155
Ruscach, 282

Sahara, 14
Saí, tribe of, 166
Saigir, 226, 272–273, 277
St Albans, 10, 18
St Davids, 253
St Maugholds, 190
Salamanca, codex, 48
Salapia, 55
Samaria, 197
Saône, river, 29
Sardica, 20
Sardinia, 56
Saul, 181, 191, 194, 197
Saxons, 13, 18, 21, 119
Scandinavia, 72
Scire, 158
Scotch street, Armagh, 191
Scotland, 90, 124, 134
Scotti, 18, 31, 33, 90, 93–94, 104, 109, 111, 123–124
Scythia, 144
Sea of Icht, 229, 251
Seanchua Ua nOiliolla, 132
Seirkeeran, 273 (*see* "Saigir")
Selc, 166
Sele, river (Blackwater), 156, 172
Senchell Dumiche, 163
Sendomnach, 165, 199
Senes, 42, 167, 199
Seól, 162
Sescnán's Valley, 155
Síd Nento, 165
Sine, well, 169
Sirdruimm, 173
Shancoe, 132
Shankill, 163, 167, 199
Shannon, river, 25–26, 30, 32–33, 38, 44, 158, 160–161, 173, 200
Sicily, 16, 55, 81–82
Sidhe Truim, 130
Singite, 158
Skerries, 155, 180
Skerry, mountain, 182

Skreen, 199
Slán (well), 169
Slane, 120, 125, 130, 183–184, 199
Sleaty (Slébte), 42, 46, 174, 176, 185, 206
Slecht, earthwork, 159
Slemish (Sliab Miss), 95, 154, 173, 181–182
Sliab Aigle, 158, 168
Sliab gCrot, 266
Sliab gCua, 257, 264, 266
Sliab gCulind, 287
Sliab Gabuil, 214
Sliab Liacc, 162
Sliab Miss: *see* "Slemish"
Sliab Scirit (Skerry), 154, 174, 182
Slicech (Sligo), river, 172
Slieve Gullion: *see* "Sliab gCulind"
Slieve League (Sliab Liacc), 162
Slievenamon, 236
Sligo, county, 130, 132, 163, 166–167, 172, 199, 205; river: *see* "Slicech"; town, 125, 133
Snám dá én, 160
Sons of Ercc (moccu Ercc), 167
Spain (Hispania), 10–11, 13–16, 53, 56, 75–78, 82, 93, 144, 227
Stackallen, 174
Strandhill, 172
Strangford Lough, 180
Stringell, well, 168
Suck, river, 166
Sueves, 15
Suide Laigen, 206
Suir, river, 246–247, 257, 268, 270
Syracuse, 55, 121
Syria, Syrians, 37, 197

Tadcne, plain of, 158
Tailtiu, 132
Tamnach, 163, 172
Tara, 28, 31–34, 36, 41, 120, 122, 124–125, 129, 132–133, 156, 158, 176, 179, 182–185, 187, 244–245, 247, 263, 277
Tara Hill (Co. Wexford), 206
Tarragona, 56
Tawnagh, 163, 172
Teach na Romhán, 126
Teamhair (Temoria): *see* "Tara"
Tebourba, 56
Tech Cherpáin, 174
Tech Conaill, 151

Tech Dercáin, 263
Telach, plain of, 158
Teltown, 131
Temenrige, 173
Terryglass, 125
Tethba (the two Tethbas), 128, 159
Thessalonica, 16, 72
Thorame, 5
Thrace, 16, 72, 82
Thule, 241
Thorame, 59
Thule, 241
Thrace, 16, 72, 82
Tiber, river, 86
Tibrada, 266
Tibohine, 167, 200
Tigroni, 126
Tipperary, county, 121, 125, 132, 151,
    236, 247, 257–258, 260–261,
    265–268
Tirawley, 171
Tireragh, 172, 260
Tirerrill, 163, 166
Tír na Féned, 247
Tobar Makee, 167
Toicuile, 205
Toome, 174
Tortiu, 174
Toulon, 58, 60
Tours, 53, 64–66
Trier, 12, 14–16, 56, 73
Trim, 44, 126, 129, 203–204
Troyes, 20
Tuam Dindach, 239
Tubbrid, 266
Tullamore, 151–152, 159
Tullanarock, 167, 200
Tulsk, 160, 163, 166
Turin, 12
Tuscany, 75
Tyrone, county, 174, 196
Tyrrhenian Sea, 154, 202

Uí Ailello, 161, 163, 166, 168, 199
Uí Bresail, 121, 131
Uí Cairbre Áedhbha, 238

Uí Cennselig, 206
Uí Conaill Gabra, 238
Uí Doirthin, 44, 204
Uí Eachach, 48, 208
Uí Fathid, 266
Uí Liatháin, 247
Uí Maine, 166, 170
Uí Néill, 32–34, 129, 133, 160, 197
Uí Rota, 170
Uisnech (Usnagh), 31, 44, 48, 158
Uí Tuirtri, 174, 199
Ulaid (Ulster, Ulta), 25–26, 29–33,
    35–36, 48, 91–92, 94–95, 129, 180,
    182, 189, 195, 197, 245
Ulba of Grian Fothart, 206
Ullath Declain, 268
Ulster, annals of, 117, 118–122, 227
Urbs Legionum, 10
Uzes, 59–63

Vaison-la-Romaine, 40, 55, 58, 59–60, 63
Valence, 12, 60
Vandals, 15, 18, 72, 75, 79–80, 82
Vannes, 66–69
Vence, 59
Ventre, 177
Vertriga, 172
Verulamium, 10, 18
Vienne, 9, 16–17, 55, 57–61, 74

Wales, 33, 234, 253
Water Newton, 17
Waterford, county, 30, 34, 247, 249,
    251–252, 254, 257, 267
Wearmouth-Jarrow, 144
Westmeath, county, 31, 33, 158–159
Westport, 173
Wexford, 48, 206, 282–283
Whithorn, 289
Wicklow, county, 126, 151, 180, 206

York, 12, 18, 44
Youghal, 268

Zaragoza, 56

Index of Persons

Aaron, martyr, 10
Abacuc, 131
Abraham, 80, 188
Acaz, 195
Acpitetus (Epictatus, Epistitus), bishop from Cenocelli, 56
Adam, 30
Adelfius (Adelfus), bishop of Lincoln, 56
Admonius (Ammonius), priest of Cagliari, 56
Adomnán, 47, 139
Adrocht daughter of Talan, 167
Áed, abbot, 226
Áed, bishop of Slébte, 176
Áed son of Ainmire, 225
Áed son of Eochaid Tirmcharna, 133
Áed son of Fintán, 266
Áed Allán, 226
Áed Dub son of Suibne, 122, 125, 134
Áed Sláine, 226
Áedán, bishop, 226
Áedhán Ó Fiachrach, 134
Aenghus (Mac Nisse), bishop of Conor, 130 (*see also* Óengus)
Áesbuite, artificer, 127
Aeternus, bishop, 198
Aetherius, bishop, 63
Aëtius, Roman general, 78–82, 85, 86
Afer, deacon of Arles, 55
Agapitus (Agapius), exorcist of Nice, 55
Agapitus, pope, 121
Agelmund, king of Lombards, 73
Agreppa (Agrepinus, Cyprianus, Agrippa), deacon of Capua, 55
Aggripinus, 142
Agrestius, bishop of León, 58
Agricola, British Pelagian, 19–20, 79
Agrucius (Agraecius, Agricius, Agrecius), bishop of Trier, 56

Agustalis, bishop of Toulon, 58, 60
Agustun (Agathon, Agaton), deacon of Aquileia, 55
Ailbe (Albeus, Ailbeus), 41–42, 48–49, 121, 122, 125, 132, 152, 227–243, 250–252, 259, 267
Ailbe of Seanchua, 132, 161
Ailill mac Mágach, 123
Ailill son of Eochu, 32
Ailill Aulom, king of Munster, 246, 277
Ailill, bishop of Armagh, 121, 131
Ailill Molt king of Tara, 128, 225
Anastasius, pope, 120
Ainmire son of Sétna, 125, 133
Ainnedid son of Fergus, 125
Ainnidh son of Duach, 133
Aionis, Lombard leader, 72–73
Airendán, priest, 228
Aitchen, "St Patrick's cook", 127
Alaric, 75
Alban, martyr, 10
Albinus, bishop, 67
Albinus, Roman general, 82
Alprann (Calpurnius), 127
Amandinus, bishop of Chalons, 65
Amandus, bishop, 63
Amandus, priest of Autun, 55
Amatorex (Amator?), 39–40, 43, 175, 179
Ambrose, bishop of Milan, 46, 72, 74
Amirgenus, priest, 199
Amolngid, 158, 170
Amolngid son of Fergus, 171
Anastasius (Anestesius), bishop of Beniata, 56
Anastasius, pope, 120
Anaxilla, Roman general, 82
Anemius, bishop, 63
Anicius, priest, 199
Antony, monk, 121, 125

Aper, priest of Lyon, 57

Arbogast, Roman count, 73–74

Arcadius, emperor, 73–75

Arcadius, Hispano-Roman, 80, 123

Ard Corp son of Mess Corp, 247

Areobinda, general, 82

Arius, priest, 12

Armentarius, bishop, 63

Armentarius, bishop of Antibes, 59, 63

Arminius (Menius), deacon of Lincoln, 56

Art son of Conn, 31

Asacus, bishop, 198

Ascholius, bishop of Thessalonica, 72

Asclepius, bishop of Cavaillon, 59, 63

Assicus, coppersmith, 162, 173

Athanaric, king of Goths, 73

Athaulf, king of Goths, 76

Athenius, bishop of Rennes, 65, 67

Attalus, Roman general, 75–77

Attila, king of the Huns, 83–84

Audentius, bishop of Die, 58–59

Augusta, wife of Valentinian, 86

Augustine, bishop of Canterbury, 44, 144

Augustine, bishop of Hippo, 18–19, 38, 70–71, 74, 77, 79, 123–124

Augustine, disciple of Palladius, 40, 126, 179

Augustine of Inis Becc, 206

Aurelian, emperor, 10

Ausanius (Ibidanius, Avidianus, Avidanus, Avitanus), bishop of Rouen, 55

Auspicius, bishop of Vaison, 58–59

Auxilius, deacon, bishop, 23, 40–43, 57, 59, 118–119, 124, 135, 174, 179

Avienus, consul, 85

Baillin, disciple of Patrick, 269

Baithanus, bishop, 149

Banbán, nephew of Patrick, 127

Barnabus, Apostle, 8, 120

Barra, 226 (*see also* "Findbarr")

Bec mac Dé, 134

Beccán, hermit, 151–152

Bede, 10–11, 118–119, 144

Beflas (Beclus, Becles), exorcist of Vienne, 55

Benedict, disciple of Palladius, 40, 126, 179

Benen: *see* "Benignus"

Benignus, 42, 119, 124, 127–128, 155, 166, 187–188, 198, 205

Beoidh, bishop, 131

Berach, nun, 240

Berchán, 132 (*see also* "Mobhí Cláiríneach")

Bernicius, deacon, 166, 199

Bescna, priest, 127

Betheus (Bitheus), bishop, 162–163

Bieler, Ludwig, 40, 94

Binchy, Daniel, 5

Binén, scribe and anchorite, 204–205

Bitheus, bishop, 198

Bitio, deacon of Grenoble, 59

Bledas, brother of Attila, 83

Boethius, praetorian prefect, 88

Boidmal, charioteer, 160

Boniface I, pope, 70, 77

Boniface II, pope, 121

Boniface IV, pope, 141

Boniface, Roman general, 77–79

Brendan (Brénainn) of Birr, 133, 152, 226

Brendan (Brénainn) of Clonfert, son of Findlug, 122, 124, 131, 133, 226

Brendan, 226

Brendan, two holy men named, 279–280 (i.e., B. of Birr and B. of Clonfert), 279–280

Bres son of Eochu, 244

Bressialus, bishop, 198

Brian son of Eógan, 247

Brichin, saint of second order, 226

Briga, nun, 290

Brige, nun, 240

Brigid (Brigit), abbess, 44, 47, 48–49, 119–121, 124–125, 130–131, 158, 207–224, 236, 282–283, 285

Brignat, nun, 289

Brigson, priest, 199

Brión son of Eochu, 32, 166

Brocanus (Broccán), priest, 44, 199, 204

Broccaid (Brocidius), priest, 44, 166, 199, 204

Brógán, scribe, 127

Broicsech, mother of Brigid, 208

Brónach, priest, 166

Brón (Bronus), bishop, 120, 130, 161, 163, 166, 171–172, 198

Broscus (Bruscus), priest, 159, 199

Brunech, nun, 273

Buairnen, servant of Ailbe, 242

Búite son of Bronach, bishop, 120, 125, 130–131

Caecilianus, bishop of Carthage, 53, 56

Caesar, 28, 244

Caeta, man blessed by Patrick, 169

Caichán, baptized by Patrick, 205
Cainnech of Achad Bó, 120–121, 226
Cainnech, chief of Dési, 267–268
Cairbre son of Colum, 249
Cairbre (Corpre) Lifeachair, 31, 123
Cairbre (Coirpre) Nia Fer, 170
Cairbre Rigruad son of Eógan, 247
Cairniuch (Carniuch), priest, 127
Calpurnius (Calfornius, Cathbad,
    Cualfornius, Calphurn), father of
    Patrick, 96, 128, 175, 177 (see also
    Alprann)
Calvus (Máel), druid, 160, 165
Camín of Mag Scéith, 252
Campán, the daughters of, 285
Camulacus, bishop, 159, 198
Cancen, priest, 199
Capitolavium (Caplit), druid, 160, 165
Carentinus, priest of Orange, 58
Cariattonus, bishop of Valence, 60
Carney, James, 39, 41, 43
Cartenus, bishop, 198
Carthach of Lismore, 249
Carthach, disciple of Ciarán of Saigir,
    276, 278–279
Carthacus, bishop, 198
Cas son of Glas, 170
Cassanus, priest, 158, 166, 199
Cassian, John, 79
Castinus, deacon of Geneva, 59
Castorius, deacon of Tarragona, 56
Catanus, priest, 199
Cathaceus, disciple of Patrick, 156
Cathbad, bishop, 125
Cathboth, seven sons of, 205–206
Cathdub of Achad Cinn, 133
Cathlaid of Trim, 204
Cathurus, disciple of Patrick, 156
Catideus, priest, 199
Catnea, disciple of Patrick, 156
Catneus, disciple of Patrick, 156
Catus, priest, 199 (Mo-Chatocc?), 199
Cecrops, king of Attica, 80
Celestine I, pope, 5–6, 19–21, 40, 70–71,
    77–78, 89, 118, 123, 126, 128, 179,
    203, 250, 256, 275
Celestius, Pelagian, 18, 71, 76
Cellach son of Cormac, 245–246
Cennanus, bishop, 198
Ceredic of Cardigan, 94
Ceredic of Dumbarton, 94
Cerpán (Cerbán), bishop, 120, 124, 129
Cétgen, disciple of Patrick, 163

Cethiacus (Caetiacus), bishop, 158, 166,
    171, 198, 201
Cheretius, bishop of Grenoble, 58
Chrispinus, priest of Fréjus, 58
Chrysaphius, bishop, 63, 84
Cianán, disciple of Ailbe, 237
Cianán of Duleek, 119, 124, 128
Ciarán of Clonmacnoise, 120, 124, 125,
    132, 152, 166, 199, 226, 279, 280
Ciarán of Saigir, 226, 252, 257,
    272–280
Ciarán son of Eochu, 265–266
Cinnena, disciple of Patrick, 158
Cipia, mother of Bishop Betheus, 162
Citerius (Ceterius, Citirius, Colman,
    Aetherius), deacon of Ossuna, 56
Claudian, poet, 74
Claudian (Claudius), priest of Rome, 55
Claudius, bishop of Castellane?, 58, 60
Claudius, bishop of Vienne, 40, 57, 59
Claudius, deacon of Geneva, 59
Clementius (Clemens, Lementius),
    priest of Zaragoza, 56
Clothra daughter of Eochu, 244
Coemgen of Glendalough, 226
Coemhán, "chamberlain" of Patrick, 127
Cogitosus ua hÁeda, 44, 47–49, 177,
    207, 224
Coimanus, deacon, 165, 199
Coirpriticus son of Niall, 156
Colla Uais, 132
Collas, the three, 32–33
Colmán, 248–249
Colmán, abbot, 226
Colmán, bishop, 226
Colmán, brother of Declan, 252
Colmán of Mág Scéith, 252
Colmán, monk of Ailbe, 234
Colmáns, the twelve, 232
Colum son of Crimthainn (Columba,
    Colum Cille), 47, 120, 122, 125, 131,
    133–134, 139, 152, 162, 226
Colum ua Cremthainn (Colum of Inis
    Celtra, Colum of Terryglass), 122,
    125, 132
Columbanus, abbot, 16, 48, 141, 148
Columbanus, bishop, 149
Comangens, the twelve (Coemgens?),
    232
Comgall of Bangor, 120, 125, 132, 226
Comgella, nun, 166
Conán, priest, 168
Conán, disciple of Declan, 263

Conal, cattle-owner, 196
Conall Gulban son of Niall, 32, 131, 156, 158, 174
Conall son of Énde, 171
Concessa, mother of Patrick, 177
Conchubar mac Nessa, 123
Concordius, deacon of Apt, 58–59
Concraid, king of Osraige, 276–277
Conindrus, evangelist of Man, 190
Conláed (Conlaeth), bishop of Kildare, 48, 120, 125, 130, 219, 222
Conlaid, 168
Conlang, priest, 199
Conn Cétchathach, 31–34, 245, 246
Connanus, bishop, 198
Conra Cathbuadach son of Cairbre, 247
Constans, emperor, 295
Constantianus, bishop of Carpentras, 59, 63
Constantine, emperor, 11–12, 14, 53
Constantine, usurper, 75–76
Constantius bishop of Carpentras, 40, 58
Constantius, bishop of Uzes, 59, 63
Constantius, general of Honorius, 76–77
Constantius of Lyon, 19–21
Constantius Chlorus, 11
Corc, king, 127
Cormac, bishop of Armagh, 120, 124, 129
Cormac mac Airt, 31, 245–246
Coroticus (Coirthech, Corictic), 94, 109–113, 176, 188
Cothirtiacus (Contice, Cothraige), 154, 175
Cribri daughter of Gleaghrann, 127
Crimthainn son of Énde, 205–206
Crimthainn son of Lugaid Reoderg, 244
Criscens (Chrispus, Cretus, Christus), bishop of Syracuse, 55
Criscens (Cressentius, Crescens), deacon of Salapia, 55
Crónán, king of Artrige, 228
Crónán, priest, 226
Cronanus, bishop, 149
Cronanus, priest, 149
Cruimthiris, embroiderer for Patrick, 127
Cruth, druid, 155
Cuana Cambretach son of Conra, 247
Cuanu, book of, 119, 122, 167
Cúchulainn, 123
Cuinnidh son of Cathmugh (Mac Cuilinn), 44, 120
Culeneus, bishop, 198

Cumména (Cuimíne) Ailbe, abbot of Iona, 47, 151
Cuimíne Fota of Clonfert, 151
Cummian, 48, 151, 153
Cummíne, priest, 226
Cummíne son of Eochaid, 238
Curnán son of Áedh, 133
Cyril of Alexandria, 19, 71, 79, 118

Dafenus (Dafinus, Danas, Damnas), bishop of Vaison, 55
Dagan, bishop, 148
Dagda, the, 29
Daigreus, bishop, 198
Daimene, bishop, 198
Dáire, 127–128, 176, 191–192
Dallbrónach, 158
Damasus, pope, 73
Daniel, 288
Darerca (Moninna), 46, 48, 50, 120, 125, 130, 281–294
Darerca, sister of Patrick, 127
Darius, 80
David, bishop of Armagh, 122, 133
David of Wales, 226, 234, 253
Decius, emperor, 10
Declan of Ardmore, 41–42, 232, 244–271
Dedad mac Sin, 123
Delphidius, orator, 73
Dénech, neighbour of Brigid, 286
Dercán of Con Ingi, 261–263
Derclaid son of Conlaid, 168
Derlasra, abbess of Killeevy, 293–294
Dethidin, mother of Declan, 247
Deudatus, deacon of León, 58
Deuterius, deacon of Cherchell, 56
Diarmait, disciple of Fiacc, 206
Diarmait son of Cerbél, 122, 125, 131–134, 225
Dichu, convert of Patrick, 180–183, 195
Dimaus, bishop, 149
Dimma, teacher of Declan, 249–250
Dimma, petty chief, 273–274, 276
Diocletian, emperor, 10–11, 14, 16, 121
Dionysius, 118, 121
Dioscorus, bishop of Alexandria, 83–85
Dobranus foster-father of Declan, 247, 249
Doc (Doccus), bishop, 119, 226
Domangort of Kintyre, 124
Domnall, king, 125, 133, 226
Domnallus, bishop, 198

Dualach, convert of Declan, 264–265
Dubtach, bishop of Armagh, 120, 125, 130, 132
Dubtach, father of Brigid, 208
Dubtach moccu Lugir, poet, 127, 176, 185–186, 206
Dúnlaing, king of Lagin, 156, 174
Dynamius, bishop, 63

Eborius (Aeburius, Eburius, Euortius), bishop of York, 56
Eibeachta, disciple of Patrick, 127
Elijah, 287
Elisha, 197
Emeterius, deacon of Vence, 59
Enda (Énde) of Aran, 226, 236
Énde Cennselach, 205
Énde son of Amolngid, 157–158, 171
Eochaid Finn, 245
Eochu, brother of Declan, 252
Eochu Domlén, 32
Eochu Fedlach, 244
Eochu Mugmedón, 31–33
Eógan Már, 34
Eógan son of Ard Corp, 247
Eógan son of Corcran (Mac Tail), 132
Eógan son of Fiacha, 245, 247
Eógan son of Niall, 32
Eparchius, bishop, 63
Erc, chief of Dési, 247, 249
Erc, bishop of Slane, 120, 125, 127, 130, 156, 176, 184, 199
Erc son of Trén, 247
Erca, embroiderer to Patrick, 127
Erclang, priest, 199
Ernán, priest, 226
Ernascus of Mag Aí, 204
Ernianus, priest, 149
Ernicius, deacon, 199 (*see* "Hernicius")
Eserninus (Esserninus), 43, 174 (*see* "Iserninus")
Ethne daughter of Loiguire, 160, 163
Ethne Uathach, wife of Óengus son of Nad Froích, 276
Eucherius, bishop of Lyon, 57
Eucrocia, wife of Delphidius, 73
Eudoxia, wife of Arcadius, 75
Eugenius, bishop (in Gaul), 63
Eugenius, bishop (in Ireland), 199
Eugenius, deacon of Rome, 34
Eugenius, ruler of Gaul, 74
Eugenius son of Conaille, 291
Eulalius, antipope, 77

Elualius, bishop, 63
Eusebius, 9
Eusebius, bishop of Nantes, 65
Eustathius, bishop, 63
Eutropius, consul, 75
Eutyches, Monophysite, 61, 83, 85
Eutychius, Hispano-Roman, 80–81
Evagrius, monk, 74
Evodius, praetorian prefect, 73
Ezechias, 195

Fáelán, priest, 226
Falertus, bishop, 198
Faustinus, priest of Orange, 55
Faustinus, bishop of Tebourba, 56
Feardomhnach, scribe, 88
Fearghus, "antiquary", 127
Fearghus son of Muirchertach, 133
Feccus, 198 (*see* "Fiacc")
Fechín, priest, 226
Fedelm daughter of Loiguire, 160, 163
Fedelmid, disciple of Fiacc, 206
Fedelmid Rechtaid, 245, 247
Fedelmid (Fedhlim) son of Loiguire, 126, 203–204
Felartus (Fallart), bishop, 162, 166, 168
Felix, exorcist of Trier, 56
Felix, pope, 119, 121
Felix, Roman general, 78–79
Felomasius (Flomatius, Flem13atius, Filomatius), deacon of Autun, 55
Feradach Finn Fechtnach, 244
Feradach son of Hercaith, 200
Ferchertne, druidic prophet, 183
Fergal son of Cormac, chief of Dési, 258, 260
Fergus son of Eochu, 32, 173
Fiacha Suigde, 245
Fiachna son of Fintán, 266
Fiachra son of Eochu, 32
Fiachu Findfholadh, 244
Fiachu son of Niall, 159
Fiachu Sraibtine, 31–32
Findbarr moccu Bardeni (Barra), 118, 294
Findlug of Mag Scéith, 252
Finnio moccu Telduib (Finnian, Finnén), 122, 125, 226, 132–133
Fintán, 266
Fintán, king of Dál nAraide, 234–235
Fintans, the twelve, 232
Firtranus, bishop, 198
Fith, bishop, 205–206
Flacilla daughter of Arcadius, 74

Flavian, bishop of Constantinople, 61, 83–84
Flavius (Faustus, Flavus), deacon of Bordeaux, 55
Florentius (Frominianus, Frondinus, Frontinus), deacon of Merida, 56
Florus, bishop, 63
Florus (Florentius), deacon of Syracuse, 55
Fontedius, priest of Vaison, 58–59, 63
Fontedius, deacon (later lector) of Avignon, 58–59
Fortchern of Trim, 126–127, 203–204
Fortunatus, bishop of Cherchell, 56
Fothad, king, 173
Fraechan son of Teniusan, 133
Fraternus, bishop, 63
Furbaide, king, 279

Galatheus, archdeacon of Valence, 60
Galbio, Roman general, 78
Galerius Augustus, 11
Gamaliel, 178
Geiseric, king of Vandals, 80–82, 86
Genget, monk, 199
Genialis (Geniales), deacon of Gevaudan, 55
Gerald of Wales, 28
Germanus (German), bishop of Auxerre, 19–21, 39–40, 43, 79, 90, 127, 175, 178–179, 205
Germanus, bishop of Rouen, 65
Germanus, disciple of Ciarán of Saigir, 278–279
Germanus, Roman general, 82
Gerontius, bishop, 63
Gerontius Cormes, 76
Getnesius (Termatius, Termasius, Germasius), priest of Ecija, 56
Gideon, 194
Gildas, 11, 21, 144, 236
Gobbán, servant, 240
Goll, sons of, 233
Gollit, Briton, 204
Gosachtus (Gosacht) son of Miliuc, 159, 173, 198
Gratian, emperor, 72–73
Gregory, bishop of Port of Rome, 56
Gregory of Nanzianus, 73
Gregory, pope, 44, 125
Grunnitus, deacon, 79
Gundicar, king of Burgundians, 80

Helladius, bishop, 63
Heraclianus, consul, 76

Heraclius, eunuch, 86
Herbus (Herbeus), bishop, 285, 291, 293
Hercaith, convert of Patrick, 200
Hernicius, sub-deacon, 166, 199
Herod, king, 184
Heros, bishop of Arles, 76
Hess, H., 92
Hesychius, letter to, 38
Hilarus, bishop, 63
Hilarus, archpriest of Rome, 149
Hilary, bishop, 230–231, 250
Hilary, bishop of Arles, 16, 57, 59, 227
Hilary, deacon of Rome, 84
Hilary, pope, 119, 124, 227
Hinu (Ineus), 173
Homer, 26
Hono, druid, 161
Honoratus, bishop, 63
Honorius, emperor, 73–78
Honorius, pope, 149, 151
Honorius son of Placidia, 77
Hormisdas, pope, 120

Iarlath mac Tréne, bishop, 119, 124, 128
Iarnascus, abbot, 167
Ibar (Ibor, Iborus, Ibur), bishop, 44, 48–50, 120, 124, 129, 198, 236, 252, 257, 282–284
Iboreas, Lombard leader, 72
Illann, king of North Leinster, 277
Inaepius, Frankish disciple of Patrick, 199
Inbetausius (Imbetausius, Inbitausius), bishop of Reims, 55
Ineus (Hinu), convert of Patrick, 173
Ingenuus, bishop of Embrun, 58, 60, 63
Innocent I, pope, 70, 75, 77
Innocentius, deacon of Nice, 55
Iocondus, deacon of Genoble, 58–59
Ippis, disciple of Patrick, 127
Isaiah, 80
Iserninus (Esserninus) 40–41, 43–44, 118–119, 124, 135, 179, 205–206
Isidore of Seville, 118
Ithacius, bishop, 73
Iucundinus, priest, 65
Iulianus, bishop, 63
Iulianus, deacon of Vaison, 58
Iulius, bishop of Apt, 58–59
Iustianus mac Hii, bishop, 198
Iustus, bishop of Orange, 58, 60, 63
Iustus, deacon, 166, 199

Jerome, 18, 38, 46, 49, 73, 77, 94
John the Baptist, 74, 124, 178, 287

John, bishop of Constantinople, 75
John, counsellor of the Apostolic See, 149
John, deacon of Rome, 149
John, monk, 74
John I, pope, 120–121
John IV, pope, 44, 149
Jonah, 139, 177
Jovinus, usurper, 76
Julian, bishop of Eclanum, 70, 76, 79–81
Julius, bishop of Puteolanum, 84
Julius, martyr, 10
Justanus, priest, 174
Justinian, emperor, 141
Justus, bishop, 148

Kannanus, bishop, 199

Lachlan of Mag Scéith, 252
Laebhann, smith of Patrick, 127
Laisranus (Laisrén), priest, 149, 226, 263
Laithphri, son of, 199
Laloca of Ard Senlis, 166
Lamissus, king of Lombards, 78
Lampadius, bishop of Oudna, 56
Lasra daughter of Gleaghrann, 127
Lassar daughter of Anflomith, 205
Latronianus, Priscillianist, 73
Laurence, archbishop of Canterbury, 44, 148
Lawrence, relics of, 201
Ledbán, chief of Dési, 258
Leo I, pope, 16, 41, 61, 63, 81–87, 90, 92, 118–119, 124, 227
Leontinus, deacon of Arles, 59
Leontius (Leoncius), deacon of Eauze, 56
Leontius, priest from Ostia, 56
Leontius, sub-deacon of Riez, 60
Lethlanu, druid, 155
Liamhain, disciple of Patrick, 127
Liberalis, bishop, 67
Liberius, bishop of Merida, 56
Licinius, emperor, 11
Lidán, mother of Ciarán of Saigir, 272–273, 278
Littorius, count, 80–81
Loarn, bishop?, 204
Loch (Lochletheus), druid, 155
Lochan son of Lugir, 228
Locharnach son of Iarnascus, 167
Logha, priest, 127

Loiguire (Loegare, Laeghaire) son of Niall, 123, 126–128, 154–156, 158, 160, 163, 174, 176, 179, 183, 185, 187, 225
Lommanus (Lommán) of Trim, 44, 126, 166, 199, 203–204
Lommán, bishop, 226
Lommanus Turrescus, 168
Lothar son of Eochu, 244
Losca, exorcist, 199
Lothrach (Lochru), druid, 179, 184
Lucet Máel, druid,179, 184, 186
Luchte son of Conlaid, 168
Lug, 29
Lugaid Reoderg, 244
Lugaid son of Brian, 247
Lugaid son of Loeguire, 128–130, 225
Lugaith son of Netu, 204
Lugid, abbot, 226
Lugid, holy man, 240
Lugar, chief of Hirota, 170
Luger fosterson of Darerca, 282
Lugne, father of Ciarán of Saigir
Lugaid moccu Ochae, 122
Luguidam, a very strong man, 216
Lugaid, bishop of Connor, 131, 152
Lunanus, "son of the king of Rome", 250–251, 253
Lupaid, embroiderer to Patrick, 127
Lupicinus, priest of Carpentras, 59
Lupus, bishop of Troyes, 20
Lycorius, priest of Carpentras, 58

Mac Airt, Seán, 117
Mac Caille, bishop, 44, 48, 119, 124, 128, 158, 209
Mac Cairtin, bishop, 120, 127, 205
Mac Chire (Mac Creiche), hermit, 238
Mac Dara of Áth Dara, 236
Macécht, smith to Patrick, 127
MacCraith the wise, disciple of Patrick, 127
MacCuilinn (Cuinnidh), bishop of Lusk, 44, 119, 124
MacCuill moccu Greccae, 176, 189–190
Macedonius, 72
Macet, disciple of Patrick, 163
Mac Ercc son of Macc Dregin, bishop, 171–173
Machiu, fosterson of Patrick, 128
Mac Liag, fosterson of Declan, 269–270
MacNisse, bishop, 120, 124, 130
Macrinus (Magrinus), deacon of Cologne, 55

MacTail (Mactaleus), bishop, 41, 43, 122, 132, 174, 198
Maculeus, bishop, 198
Máel (Calvus), druid, 165
Máel Cobo, sons of, 226
Máel Odur, 125
Mag Laim, killed at Cúl Dreimhne, 134
Magnentius, priest of Riez, 58
Magnus Maximus, 13, 73
Magonus (Mauonius), one of Patrick's names, 154, 175
Mamertinus (Mamartinus), bishop of Eauze, 56
Manach, priest, 127
Manchán, 206
Manchín, disciple of Declan, 255
Maneus, convert of Patrick, 161
Mansuetus, bishop of the Britons, 53, 65
Marcellinus, chronicler, 118
Marcian, emperor, 84, 87
Marcus Aurelius, emperor, 9
Marcus Cassianus Latinius Postumus, usurping emperor, 10
Marinus, bishop of Arles, 55
Marius, deacon of Geneva, 57
Martin, bishop of Tours, 46, 64, 73, 76, 127
Maternus, bishop of Cologne, 55
Mathona, sister of Benignus, 163, 168
Mathonus, 165
Maucteus (Mochta), priest, 49, 119, 121, 127, 131, 139
Mavortius, Roman general, 78
Maximinus, bishop, 63
Maximus, 86
Maximus, bishop, 63
Maximus, bishop of Riez, 58, 60, 63
Maximus, Spanish general, 80, 376
Medb (Medbu), priest, 167, 204
Medb Lethderg, 28, 32
Mel (Melus), bishop, 44, 48, 119, 128, 159, 198
Mellitus, bishop, 148
Menathus, bishop, 198
Mercurius (John), pope, 121
Mercurius (Mamertinus), priest from Ostia, 56
Mercury, 29
Merobaudis, Roman general, 73
Meroclis (Merocles), bishop of Milan, 55
Mescan, priest, 127
Mess Fore son of Cuanu, 247

Miliúc moccu Bóin, 154, 173, 175–176, 180–181
Miserneus, bishop, 198
Mo-Bhí Cláirínech, 122, 125, 132, 226
Mobhí of Mag Scéith, 252
Mo-Chatócc of Inis Fáil, 206
Mochellóc of Mag Scéith, 252
Mochoba, disciple of Declan, 263
Mo-Choí (Mochoe, Mochaoi), 120, 124, 129
Mochonnóc, disciple of Patrick, 127
Mogenóc of Cell Cuimili, 226
Mocteus, father of Darerca, 48, 281
Modan of Tuam Dindach, 239
Molaise of Devenish, 134
Moneisen (Monesan), Saxon girl, 176, 187
Moninna (Darerca), 120, 130, 281
Moscegrai son of Mess Fore, 247
Moses, 80, 177, 184, 200, 255
Mess Corp son of Moscegrai, 247
Mucneus of Kilmoremoy, 158, 171
Mugenóc of Cell Dumi Gluinn, 44, 204
Mug Nuadat, 31
Muirchertach mac Ercae, 130–131
Muirchú moccu Mactheni, 39–40, 43, 47, 49–50, 57, 175–176
Muiredach king of Tara, 225
Muiredach Tírech, 31–32
Muirethach (Muirethacus), bishop, 172, 198
Munis of Forgnide, 44, 204

Nabuchadonosor, 183
Nachtan, bishop, 43
Naindid, disciple of Fiacc, 206
Namatius, deacon of Vienne, 59
Nar son of Eochu, 244
Natalis (Natales), priest of Ossuna, 56
Nathí son of Garchú, 126
Nazareus (Nazoreus), reader of Marseille, 55
Nazarius, bishop, 198
Nazarus, bishop, 198
Neasan the leper, 132
Nectarius, bishop of Avignon, 58–59, 63
Nero, emperor, 244
Nessán, deacon of Mungret, 152, 241
Nestorius, bishop of Constantinople, 19, 78–79
Niall Noígiallach, 32–33, 156
Niath son of Brian, 247

Nicasius (Nicacius, Niasius), deacon of Arles, 55
Nie Froích (Nad Froích), 174
Nieth Brain, 159
Nicetius (Nicecius), deacon of Rouen, 55
Nichtan, the leper, 125
Ninis, 80
Ninnid Lamderc, 226
Nitria, Frankish nun, 166
Nonnechlus, bishop, 67
Novatus, bishop, 80
Nos, swineherd, 125

Ó Cróinín, Dáibhí, 151
Odhrán, charioteer, 127, 132
O'Donovan, John, vi, 117, 126
Óengus son of Fiacha, 245–247
Óengus son of Nad Froích, 34, 235–236, 241, 252, 256–261, 275–277
Óengus son of Senachus, 168
Oilioll Molt: *see* "Ailill Molt"
Olcanus, bishop, 171, 173, 198–199
Olcnais, father of Ailbe, 227–228
O'Rahilly, T.F., 7, 32–33, 39–40, 89
Ordius, bishop, 198
Oresius (Horosius, Heresius), bishop of Marseille, 55
Orientalis (Orientales), bishop of Bordeaux, 55
Orosius, 74, 118

Padusia, wife of Felix, 79
Palladius, bishop, 63
Palladius, bishop of Hellespontus, 41
Palladius, bishop of the Irish, 6–7, 19, 21–22, 39–41, 43–44, 61, 71, 79, 89–91, 118, 123, 126, 141, 175, 179, 203, 228
Pandus (Pardus), bishop of Salapia, 55
Paschasius, a pious Spaniard, 80–81
Paternus, bishop of Vannes, 66–67
Patricius, 154
Patrick, vi, 4–7, 13–14, 23–25, 37–50, 57, 88–113, 117–124, 126–130, 135, 139, 141, 144, 152, 154–206, 225–227, 235, 250–253, 256–259, 268–269, 275, 281, 285
Patrick (Old), 119, 128
Patroclus, bishop of Arles, 76, 78
Paul, 8–9, 126, 142–143, 173, 178, 201, 232, 244, 291, 293
Paulillus, pious Spanish boy, 81

Pelagius, 18–19, 38, 70, 76
Pelagius, pope, 122
Perpetuus, bishop of Tours, 65–67
Pertran, bishop, 226
Peter, 9, 70, 119–122, 141–143, 152, 173, 179, 184, 201, 203, 232, 244, 291, 293
Peter, deacon of Arles, 55
Petronius, bishop of Bonn, 73
Petronius, bishop of Digne, 63
Petronius, deacon of Arles, 57, 59
Petulinus (Pytolinus, Pilatinus, Pitulinus, Bitulinus), exorcist of Lyon, 55
Philip, 8
Pinus (Agrepinus, Tutus), deacon of Capua, 55
Placidia Augusta, 76–78, 84
Pool, disciple of Fiacc, 206
Posidonius, deacon, 19
Posidonius, ethnographer, 25
Possidus, bishop, 80
Potitus (Potaide), priest, 95, 128, 177
Primigenius (Primogenius, Progenius, Nicetius), deacon of Reims, 55
Principius, deacon of Uzes, 59
Priscillian, 72–73
Probatius, priest of Tarragona, 56
Probus, Hispano-Roman, 8
Proculeianus, bishop, 63
Prosper of Aquitaine, 6, 19, 20, 39, 61, 70, 72, 89
Proterius (Protinus, Protenus), bishop of Capua, 55

Quintasius, bishop of Cagliari, 56
Quiriacus (Chyriacus, Cyricus), deacon of Rome, 55

Ravennius, bishop of Arles, 41, 57, 61, 63
Recradus, druid, 170
Rees, Alwyn and Brinley, 31
Restitutus, bishop of London, 56
Reuda, 145
Rhadagaisus, leader of Goths, 75
Riadain of Mag Scéith, 252
Riticius (Reticius, Retius, Ruticius, Reticus), bishop of Autun, 55
Ródán (Rodanus), priest, 127, 163, 166, 199
Ronanus, priest of Apt, 55
Rónal, druid, 179
Ross, historian, 127

Ross son of Fiacha, 245, 247
Rufinus, exorcist of Zaragoza, 56
Ruadán of Lorrha, 226
Rumilus of Man, 190
Rusticus, bishop of Narbonne, 63

Sabinus, bishop, 63
Sabinus (Savinus), priest of Beacia, 56
Sacerdus, priest of Lincoln, 56
Sacellus (Sachellus), bishop, 41, 166,
    167, 198, 201, 204
Sadb daughter of Conn, 246
Sailchin, disciple of Ailbe, 240
Salamas (Salmas, Silimas), priest of Arles,
    55
Salonius (Salunius), bishop of Geneva, 57,
    59
Salvian, 15
Samson of Dol, 233
Sanclit, mother of Ailbe, 228
Sannuch, monk of Patrick, 199
Saranus, teacher, 149
Saturninus, deacon of Vaison, 59
Saturninus, lector of Avignon, 59
Scanlán, king, 240
Scellanus, priest, 149
Scietha, daughter of Mechar, 238, 239
Scoth Noe, 204
Sebastian, usurper, 76, 82
Secundinus (Seachnall mac an Bhaird),
    bishop, 23, 41–43, 118, 124, 127,
    167, 198, 206, 259
Segéne (Segenus) of Iona, 149, 151
Segetius (Segitius), priest, 40, 57–58, 179
Seman, priest, 199
Semiramis, 80
Sempronius, scholar, 72
Senach (Senachus), bishop, 168, 198, 226
Sencatius, bishop, 198
Senmeda daughter of Énde, 168
Sesceneus, bishop, 155, 168, 198
Sescnán, father of Sesceneus, 155
Severianus, bishop in Africa, 80
Severianus, bishop in Britain, 79
Severianus, bishop of Thorame, 59
Severinus, pope, 149
Severus, bishop of Vence, 59
Severus, deacon of Milan, 55
Severus, deacon of Vienne, 57
Severus, Roman general, 147
Siggeus, bishop, 198
Sigisvult, count, 78
Silverius, pope, 121
Silvester, disciple of Palladius, 126

Simon, 184
Simplicius, pope, 119
Sinchell son of Cennanan, 122, 132, 237
Sinell, disciple of Patrick, 127
Sinell son of Maenach, 226
Sinoces, Roman general, 78
Siricius, pope, 16, 73, 90
Sjoestedt, Marie-Louise, 29
Solinus, disciple of Palladius, 126
Solomon, 80, 135
Sperantius, deacon of Carthage, 56
Sproule, David, 32, 34
Stephen, 188, 201
Stilicho, Roman general, 75
Succetus (Sucestus, Sochet), name of
    Patrick, 154, 174–175, 177
Sucio, deacon of Cimiez, 59
Sulpicius Severus, 64
Superventur, priest of Castellane, 58, 60;
    (bishop), 63
Surgentius, bishop(?) of Pocofeltus, 56
Sylvester, pope, 54
Symmachus, pope, 120

Tairill, disciple of Patrick, 127
Tasach (Tassach), bishop, 127, 129, 193,
    195
Taunat, nun, 293
Tecan, of Fiacc's community, 206
Testa, son of, 253
Tetricus, usurper, 10
Thalasius, bishop of Angers, 65, 67
Theodora, empress, 141
Theodoric, king of Goths, 85, 120
Theodorus (Theudorus, Teudosus),
    bishop of Aquileia, 55
Theodosius the Great, emperor, 21,
    72–74, 76
Theodosius II, emperor, 75, 78, 80,
    82–84, 118, 123, 203
Theophilus, bishop of Alexandria, 75
Theudorus, bishop of Fréjus, 58, 60
Thitus (Betus, Verus, Citus, Bitus),
    priest of Rome, 55
Thomas, Charles, 88, 94
Thompson, E.A., 91, 94
Thorismodus son of Theodoric, 85
Tiberius, emperor, 80
Tibraide Tírech, 245
Tigernach of Clones, 122, 132
Tigernach Tétbannach, king, 123
Tigris, disciple of Patrick, 127
Tírechán, bishop, 7, 42–44, 49–50,
    154, 160, 200, 203

Titus, deacon of Rome, 78 (*see* "Thitus")
Tomianus, bishop, 149
Totus Calvus (Totmael), charioteer of
    Patrick, 168
Trén son of Lugaid, 247
Trianus, bishop, 199
Trigetius, Roman general, 80, 85
Tuathal Maelgarb, 131, 225
Tuathal Techtmhar, 244–245
Tuathan son of Dimman, 133

Ulphulas, Roman general, 76
Ultan, bishop of Ardbraccan, 154, 160,
    174, 226
Ultan son of Erc, 263, 268
Urbeia, disciple of Priscillian, 73
Ursacius, bishop, 73
Ursinus, deacon of Arles, 55
Ursus, bishop, 63
Usaille (Auxilius), 41, 43, 128

Valens, emperor, 21, 72
Valentinian II, emperor, 72–74
Valentinian III, emperor, 72, 77–78, 80,
    82, 86
Valerian (Valerianus), bishop of Cimiez,
    59, 63
Valerian, emperor, 10
Valerius, bishop, 63
Venerandus, bishop, 65
Venerius, bishop of Marseille, 63
Veranus, deacon of Lyon, 57

Verus, bishop, 63
Verus, bishop of Vienne, 55
Victor (Victoricus), angel, 40, 100, 123,
    154, 177–178, 181, 194–195, 203
Victor, bishop of Bizerta, 56
Victor, bishop of Legis Volumni, 56
Victor, Caesar, 73
Victor, exorcist of Apt, 55
Victor, exorcist of Vaison, 55
Victor, lector of Ecija, 56
Victoricus, angel: *see* "Victor"
Victoricus, bishop of Donaghmoyne,
    174, 198
Victorius, astronomer, 119, 124
Victorius, bishop of Le Mans, 65, 67
Victricius, general, 81
Victurus, bishop, 63
Vigilius, pope, 121, 141
Vincent, historian, 119
Vitalis, bishop of Bordj-Bou-Djadi, 56
Vosius (Voceius, Vocitus, Voccius,
    Votius), bishop of Lyon, 55

Wallia, king of Goths, 76–77
Walsh, Maura, 151

Xistus, pope, 11, 79, 81–82, 118, 123

Ydatius, bishop, 63
Ynantius, bishop, 63

Zozimus, pope, 16, 20, 70, 77